NBER
Macroeconomics
Annual 1998

Editors
Ben S. Bernanke and
Julio J. Rotemberg

THE MIT PRESS
Cambridge, Massachusetts
London, England

Send orders and business information to:
The MIT Press
Five Cambridge Center
Cambridge, MA 02142

In the United Kingdom, continental Europe, and the Middle East and Africa, send orders and business correspondence to:
The MIT Press, Ltd.
Fitzroy House, 11 Chenies Street
London WC1E 7ET England

ISSN: 0889-3365
ISBN: hardcover 0-262-02455-1
       paperback 0-262-52256-X

Contents

Editorial, NBER Macroeconomics Annual 1998   1

Abstracts   7

WHY IS THE U.S. UNEMPLOYMENT RATE SO MUCH LOWER?   11
Robert Shimer
COMMENTS: Richard Rogerson   61
           Robert Topel   67
DISCUSSION   72

SUBSTITUTION OVER TIME: ANOTHER LOOK AT LIFE-CYCLE
LABOR SUPPLY   75
Casey B. Mulligan
COMMENTS: Robert E. Hall   134
           Jörn-Steffen Pischke   138
DISCUSSION   151

EXCHANGE RATES AND JOBS: WHAT DO WE LEARN FROM
JOB FLOWS?   153
Pierre-Olivier Gourinchas
COMMENTS: David Backus   208
           Russell Cooper   212
DISCUSSION   221

INVESTMENT: FUNDAMENTALS AND FINANCE   223
Simon Gilchrist and Charles Himmelberg

COMMENTS: David B. Gross   262
             Kenneth D. West   266
DISCUSSION   272

WHAT DO TECHNOLOGY SHOCKS DO?   275
John Shea
COMMENTS: Jordi Galí   310
             Adam B. Jaffe   317
DISCUSSION   320

A FRICTIONLESS VIEW OF U.S. INFLATION   323
John H. Cochrane
COMMENTS: Henning Bohn   384
             Michael Woodford   390
DISCUSSION   418

Editorial, NBER Macroeconomics Annual 1998

Like past volumes, the 1998 edition of the *NBER Macroeconomics Annual* includes papers studying a variety of aspects of the macroeconomy and macroeconomic policy. Three papers address issues related to the labor market: In the opening paper of the volume, Robert Shimer tackles the question of why U.S. unemployment rates have trended downward since about 1980, concluding that changes in the age composition of the U.S. population are the primary cause. Age is an important determinant of labor-market outcomes not only in the unemployment sphere but also in terms of what people earn: In his paper, Casey Mulligan uses the link between age and wages to try to infer the degree to which people are willing to substitute work effort over time in response to changes in the expected discounted value of future wages relative to current wages. He finds that people's willingness to vary labor supply over time is relatively high, a result with important implications for a variety of policy questions. In the third paper bearing on the labor market, Pierre-Olivier Gourinchas analyzes the impacts of exchange-rate changes on job creation and destruction in sectors sensitive to foreign competition; he finds the puzzling result that exchange-rate appreciations not only increase rates of job destruction in those sectors, as expected, but they also increase rates of job creation as well.

Two papers in the volume focus on firms' behavior, in particular their responses to technical change and changes in opportunities for capital investment. John Shea studies the effects of inventive activity, as measured by R&D expenditures and patents, on outputs and the use of inputs in individual manufacturing sectors. His provocative conclusion is that inventive activity does not seem to be strongly related to sectoral total factor productivity, as usually measured. Simon Gilchrist and Charles Himmelberg study the effects of changes in firms' cash flows on their rates of capital investment, addressing an ongoing debate of what underlies the correlation between cash flows and investment.

The paper by John Cochrane is perhaps the one that is most directly addressed to policy analysis. Applying the so-called fiscal theory of the price level to the postwar United States, Cochrane asks to what degree the history of U.S. inflation can be explained by fiscal factors alone, and how fiscal policy could have been conducted to achieve a more stable rate of inflation.

Unemployment in the United States exhibited an upward trend through the 1970s and into the recessions of the early 1980s. Since that time, however, the unemployment rate has declined, recently reaching low levels not seen for decades. What accounts for these trends? Demographic change is a leading potential explanation: Because various groups in the population differ in their average unemployment rates, it makes intuitive sense that the economy's overall unemployment rate is affected by changes in the composition of the population. In his paper, Shimer analyzes the relationship of demography and noncyclical unemployment. Empirically, Shimer finds that the age structure of the population is a key determinant of the aggregate unemployment rate; in particular, the aging of the workforce (and the declining share of young workers) can account for much of the decline in U.S. unemployment of the past two decades. By contrast, another important demographic trend, the increasing share of the population with advanced educational attainment, is found not to be a major determinant of unemployment patterns. To help rationalize these findings, Shimer provides a model of the labor market in which noncyclical unemployment reflects the process of searching for an appropriate job match. The model predicts that the aggregate unemployment rate depends on the fraction of young people in the labor force, because young people have the strongest incentive to devote their time to searching for a good match. The educational attainment of the population does not affect unemployment in this model, however, so long as education is simply a signal of employee quality rather than a direct determinant of employee productivity. More generally, Shimer argues that, consistent with the data, there are good theoretical reasons to expect a change in the average level of education to have a smaller effect than changes in the age structure on the level of aggregate unemployment.

Mulligan investigates a different aspect of the labor market, the extent to which people are willing to substitute current work for future work in response to a change in the present value of future wages relative to current wages (that is, when the relative price for work done at different times changes). As Mulligan argues, chronological age is the source of most predictable changes in individual wages. Wages are expected to rise when individuals are young, they remain roughly constant from 35 to 45 years of age, and they fall thereafter, particularly after age 55. Mulligan uses this fact to measure the extent to which people respond to expected wage increases by postponing work. Consistent with the idea that intertemporal substitution of work is important, hours worked do increase over time when workers are young, they are roughly constant in middle age, and they decline as people approach retirement age. Mulligan argues that a given percentage increase in wages is associated with a larger increase in hours (so that the measured degree of intertemporal substitution is greater) once one makes some corrections to previous studies. Taking account of the greater share of work time devoted to on-the-job training by young people, for example, leads to a higher estimate of the growth rate of hours over the life cycle and a lower estimate of the growth rate of compensation per hour of work, leading to a higher estimate of the intertemporal elasticity of substitution. After making this and other corrections, Mulligan concludes that intertemporal substitution is more important than is generally acknowledged. He provides additional evidence for this conclusion by studying the work behavior of AFDC recipients, whose transfer income predictably declines when the youngest child in the family turns eighteen.

In theoretical analyses of macroeconomics, fluctuations in aggregate economic activity are often attributed to stochastic technical progress. Despite this common practice, we have little concrete knowledge about how technical change actually affects output, employment, and productivity in individual sectors of the economy. Shea addresses this issue by using R&D activity and rates of patenting as proxies for technical change within a sample of industries. Using VAR analysis and his proxies for technical change, Shea is able to trace out the effects of technical progress on industry output and inputs. He shows that, typically, technical change leads to increases in both inputs and outputs, but that the link between the proxies for technical change and measured changes in total factor productivity is weak (except when technical progress takes place in process-intensive industries). This finding casts doubt on approaches which equate changes in measured TFP (i.e., the Solow residual) with technological change, as opposed to such factors as variation in the utilization of inputs.

While changes in exchange rates appear to have only modest effects on the economy as a whole, Gourinchas shows in his paper that they can have important effects on export-oriented and import-competing sectors. Not surprisingly, an appreciation of the U.S. dollar increases job destruction and reduces employment in both types of sectors. What is much more surprising is that job creation increases as well when the dollar appreciates, so that the labor market in these sectors becomes more "turbulent." Similarly, a depreciation depresses both job creation and job destruction in sectors vulnerable to foreign competition, creating a job-market "chill." As Gourinchas shows in a formal model of the labor market, these results pose a puzzle for existing theories of job creation and destruction. In particular, existing models are designed to rationalize the observation that declines in economic activity resulting from aggregate shocks are associated with increases in job destruction and *reductions* in job creation. But why should job creation fall when the economy as a whole produces less, while job creation rises when the reduction in output is confined to sectors that are negatively affected by an exchange-rate appreciation?

Gilchrist and Himmelberg revisit the question of whether the observed correlation between firm cash flows and rates of capital investment is the result of imperfections in capital markets, or instead reflects a tendency of cash flow to act as a signal of future profitability. Using a novel approach for measuring a firm's opportunity to invest profitably (which is based on the deviation of the firm's sales-to-capital ratio from that of the industry as a whole), Gilchrist and Himmelberg conclude that cash flow matters primarily because capital markets do not work perfectly. An implication is that much of the correlation of investment and GDP is the result of these imperfections, rather than being due to changes in the marginal profitability of investment.

Cochrane's paper attempts to apply the "fiscal theory of the price level" in the postwar U.S. context. An interesting and important claim of the paper is that it is impossible to know for certain whether fiscal policy or monetary policy has played the central role in determining the U.S. price level. Thus, rather than attempting to test the fiscal theory, the paper focuses instead on providing a "fiscal reading" of U.S. inflation history, including a discussion of ways in which the fiscal authority might have stabilized the price level to a greater degree than occurred. That it is possible to interpret U.S. inflation as being the result of fiscal policies is perhaps surprising, given that the real surplus of the government has historically been positively associated with inflation. (For example, the Reagan deficits were associated with inflation that was much lower than in the 1970s.) One might expect instead that a fiscal-centered story would imply that inflation must rise when there are large *deficits*. In fact, what the theory requires is that prices adjust to ensure that the real value of the debt equals the expected present value of future surpluses. Cochrane shows that a fiscal interpretation of U.S. inflation history thus becomes possible once one recognizes that high current real surpluses have historically been associated with large expected future deficits. Following an unexpected increase in the surplus, prices must therefore rise to reduce the value of the government debt and satisfy the government's intertemporal budget constraint. Interestingly, this reading suggests that postwar U.S. fiscal policy would have had to change very little to stabilize the price level.

We want to thank once again the National Bureau of Economic Research, and especially its highly efficient conference department, for making the conference and this resulting volume possible. Our gratitude also goes to the National Science Foundation for its continued financial support. Finally, we would like to extend special thanks to Cedric Tille for his meticulous editorial assistance.

Ben S. Bernanke and Julio J. Rotemberg

Abstracts

Why Is the U.S. Unemployment Rate So Much Lower?

ROBERT SHIMER

The U.S. unemployment rate is so much lower because the population is so much older. This paper argues that in the absence of the baby boom, the unemployment rate would neither have increased from 1957 to 1979, nor have fallen in the subsequent two decades. The paper also considers other demographic changes: The most quantitatively significant is the increased educational attainment of the labor force. Since more-educated workers have lower unemployment rates, it might appear that this should have (counterfactually) caused a secular decline in unemployment. However, there are theoretical reasons to believe that an increase in education will not translate into a reduction in unemployment, and independent empirical evidence tends to support this view.

Substitution over Time: Another Look at Life-Cycle Labor Supply

CASEY B. MULLIGAN

Most studies of the intertemporal substitution of work use life-cycle data, and from those studies many have concluded that intertemporal labor substitution is unimportant for macroeconomics. This paper takes another look at life-cycle data and argues that a consideration of measurement errors, taxes, on-the-job training, older workers, hours reporting bias, and all of the "margins" composing aggregate labor supply over the life cycle suggests that substitution over time may be very important for macro fluctuations. The life-cycle data used include fairly standard male cross-section and panel-data samples as well as a sample of women experiencing the termination of AFDC benefits as their youngest child turns 18 years old.

Exchange Rates and Jobs: What Do We Learn from Job Flows?

PIERRE-OLIVIER GOURINCHAS

Currency fluctuations provide a substantial source of movements in relative prices that is largely exogenous to the firm. This paper evaluates empirically and theoretically the importance of exchange-rate movements on job reallocation across and within sectors. The objective is (1) to provide accurate estimates of the impact of exchange-rate fluctuations and (2) to further our understanding of how reallocative shocks propagate through the economy. The empirical results indicate that exchange rates have a significant effect on gross and net job flows in the traded goods sector. Moreover, the paper finds that job creation and destruction comove positively, following a real-exchange-rate shock. Appreciations are associated with additional turbulence, and depreciations with a "chill." The paper then argues that existing nonrepresentative agent reallocation models have a hard time replicating the salient features of the data. The results indicate a strong tension between the positive comovements of gross flows in response to reallocative disturbances and the negative comovement in response to aggregate shocks.

Investment: Fundamentals and Finance

SIMON GILCHRIST AND CHARLES HIMMELBERG

Financial variables such as cash flow and cash stocks are robust and quantitatively important explanatory variables for investment at the firm level. A large body of recent empirical work attributes these findings to capital-market imperfections. This interpretation is controversial, however, because even in the absence of capital-market imperfections, such financial variables may appear as an explanatory variable for investment if they contain information about the expected marginal value of capital. In this paper, we show how structural models of investment with costly external finance can be used to identify and quantify the *fundamental* vs. the *financial* determinants of investment. Our empirical results show that investment responds significantly to both fundamental and financial factors. Point estimates from our structural model imply that, for the average firm in our sample, financial factors raise the overall response of investment to an expansionary shock by 25%, relative to a baseline case where financial frictions are zero. Consistent with theory, small firms and firms without bond ratings show the strongest response to financial factors, while bond-rated firms show little if any response, once we control for investment fundamentals.

What Do Technology Shocks Do?

JOHN SHEA

The real-business-cycle literature has largely ignored the empirical question of what role technology shocks actually play in business cycles. The observed procyclicality of total factor productivity (TFP) does not prove that technology shocks are important to business cycles, since demand shocks could generate procyclical TFP due to increasing returns or other reasons. I address the role of technology by investigating the dynamic interactions of inputs, TFP and two observable indicators of technology shocks: R&D spending and patent applica-

tions. Using annual panel data on 19 U.S. manufacturing industries from 1959 to 1991, I find that favorable R&D or patent shocks tend to increase inputs, especially labor, in the short run, but to decrease inputs in the long run, while tilting the mix of inputs towards capital and nonproduction labor. Favorable technology shocks do not significantly increase measured TFP at any horizon, except for a subset of industries dominated by process innovations, suggesting that available price data do not capture productivity improvements due to product innovations. Technology shocks explain only a small fraction of input and TFP volatility at business-cycle horizons.

A Frictionless View of U.S. Inflation

JOHN H. COCHRANE

Financial innovation challenges the foundations of monetary theory, and standard monetary theory has not been very successful at describing the history of U.S. inflation. Motivated by these observations, I ask: Can we understand the history of U.S. inflation using a framework that ignores monetary frictions? The fiscal theory of the price level allows us to think about price-level determination with no monetary frictions. According to this approach, the price level adjusts to equilibrate the real value of nominal government debt with the present value of surpluses. I describe the theory, and I argue that it is a return to pre-quantity-theoretic ideas in which money is valued via a commodity standard or because the government accepts it to pay taxes. Both sources of value are immune to financial innovation and the presence or absence of monetary frictions. I then interpret the history of U.S. inflation with a fiscal-theory, frictionless view. I show how the fiscal theory can accommodate the stylized fact that deficits and inflation seem to be negatively, not positively, correlated. I verify its prediction that open-market operations do not affect inflation. I show how debt policy has already smoothed inflation a great deal.

Robert Shimer

PRINCETON UNIVERSITY

Why Is the U.S. Unemployment Rate So Much Lower?

In a well-known paper in one of the inaugural issues of the Brookings Papers, *Robert Hall posed the question, "Why is the Unemployment Rate So High at Full Employment?" (Hall, 1970). Hall, writing in the context of the 3.5% unemployment rate that prevailed in 1969, answered his question by explaining that the full-employment rate was so high because of the normal turnover that is inevitable in a dynamic economy. . . . Today [in 1986], four years into an economic recovery, the unemployment rate hovers around 7%. Over the past decade, it has averaged 7.6% and never fallen below 5.8%. . . . While some of the difference between recent and past levels of unemployment has resulted from cyclical developments, it is clear that a substantial increase in the normal or natural rate of unemployment has taken place. (Summers, 1986)*

1. Introduction

In November 1997, the U.S. unemployment rate fell to 4.6%, the lowest level since 1973. This monthly report was not a fluke; the aggregate unemployment has remained below 4.7% for six months, for the first

The title is intended to recall Hall (1970) ("Why is the Unemployment Rate So High at Full Employment?") and Summers (1986) ("Why is the Unemployment Rate So Very High Near Full Employment?"). The wording of this title reflects the recent decline in the unemployment rate in the United States. Explaining the cross-sectional behavior of unemployment, e.g. why the U.S. unemployment rate is so much lower than Europe's, is beyond the scope of this paper.

I have benefited from discussions with and comments and suggestions by Daron Acemoglu, Ben Bernanke, Alan Krueger, Greg Mankiw, Richard Rogerson, Julio Rotemberg, Martin Gonzalez Rozada, Robert Topel, Paul Willen, Mike Woodford, and seminar participants at Chicago, MIT, NYU, and the NBER Macroeconomics Annual 1998 Conference. Thanks also to Steve Haugen for help with some of the data, and to Mark Watson for providing me with Staiger, Stock, and Watson's (1997) series for the NAIRU. Financial support from the National Science Foundation Grant SBR-9709881 is gratefully acknowledged.

Figure 1 THE AGGREGATE UNEMPLOYMENT RATE IS AT THE LOWEST
SUSTAINED LEVEL SINCE 1970, PART OF A DOWNWARD TREND
SINCE THE EARLY 1980S

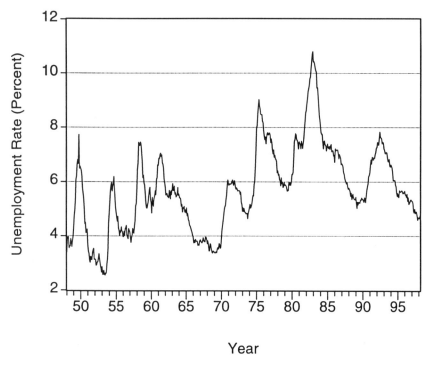

Year

Computed from seasonally adjusted labor-force series based on the Current Population Survey.

time since 1970. Figure 1 documents the decrease in unemployment
during the past 19 years, following decades of secular increases. The
unemployment rate fell by 63 basis points (hundredths of a percentage
point), from 5.66% just before the second oil shock in 1979 to 5.03% at
the end of the long expansion in 1989. It has fallen by an additional 43
basis points since then. This prompted Federal Reserve Chairman Alan
Greenspan to ask in his semiannual testimony to Congress whether
there has been a structural change in the U.S. economy:

*We do not know, nor do I suspect can anyone know, whether current develop-
ments are part of a once or twice in a century phenomenon that will carry
productivity trends nationally and globally to a new higher track, or whether we
are merely observing some unusual variations within the context of an otherwise
generally conventional business cycle expansion. (Greenspan, 1997)*

This paper argues that "current developments are part of a once or twice in a century phenomenon," albeit one far more mundane than Greenspan suggests in his testimony.

The U.S. labor force has changed significantly during the past two decades, primarily due to the aging of the baby-boom generation. Because the teenage unemployment rate is several times higher than the aggregate unemployment rate, historical changes in the percentage of teenagers in the population have had a significant effect on the aggregate unemployment rate. I calculate that the entry of the baby boom into the labor market in the 1960s and 1970s raised the aggregate unemployment rate by about 2 percentage points. The subsequent aging of the baby boom has reduced it by about $1\frac{1}{2}$ percentage points. This is the bulk of the low-frequency fluctuation in unemployment since World War II.

This demographic story fits with other characteristics of the current expansion. For example, Greenspan (1997) notes that although consumers "indicate greater optimism about the economy," many do not perceive an unusually attractive labor market: "Persisting insecurity would help explain why measured personal savings rates have not declined as would have been expected . . . ." An explanation for these apparently contradictory opinions is that the probability of being unemployed conditional on demographic characteristics is higher now than during most other recent business-cycle peaks, particularly for men. A 42-year-old man sees that 3.7% of his peers are unemployed today, but remembers that when his father was about his age in 1973, only 2.0% of his father's peers were unemployed. He looks at his 18-year-old son, who is unemployed with 17.2% probability. He recalls that in 1973, only 13.9% of his peers were unemployed.

1.1 A PRELIMINARY CALCULATION

A simple way of establishing the magnitude of the covariance between the unemployment and the baby boom is through a linear regression of the aggregate unemployment rate at time t, U_t, on a constant and on the fraction of the working-age population (age 16–64) in its youth (age 16–24), YouthShare$_t$[1]:

$$U_t = \underset{(0.0049)}{0.0211} + \underset{(0.0255)}{0.1895} \text{ YouthShare}_t + \epsilon_t, \qquad R^2 = 0.08.$$

(Standard errors in parentheses.) The youth share of the working-age population peaked at 23% in 1976, and has since declined to 16%. Thus

---

1. Thanks to Greg Mankiw for suggesting this calculation.

the declining youth population is correlated with a 130-basis-point reduction [0.1895 × (23% − 16%) ≈ 1.3%] in the unemployment rate. If we include a time trend in the regression, the coefficient on youth population falls to 0.1589 (standard error 0.0224), and so the point estimate of the impact of the declining youth population is 110 basis points.

There are two problems with these calculations. First, they demonstrate that there is a correlation between the youth population and the aggregate unemployment rate, but do not establish any causal mechanism. Second, the result is sensitive to the precise specification. For example, if we define the youth share to be the fraction of the working-age population between the ages of 16 and 34, the coefficient on youth share rises considerably. The same back-of-the-envelope calculation implies that the aging of the baby boom reduced the aggregate unemployment rate by about 270 basis points! Thus one should be hesitant in interpreting these regressions structurally.

1.2 PROJECT OUTLINE

The remainder of this paper gives a structural interpretation to the relationship between demographics and aggregate unemployment. Summers (1986) asserts, "There is no reason why the logic of adjusting for changes in labor force composition should be applied only to changes in" the age structure. The first goal of this paper (Section 2) is to document the disaggregated unemployment rate of different groups of workers. Using data based on the Current Population Survey, the source of official U.S. unemployment statistics, I calculate the unemployment rate of workers grouped by their observable characteristics—age, sex, race, and education.

Next I follow Perry (1970) and Gordon (1982) in calculating how much of the recent decline in unemployment is attributable to these demographic factors and how much of the decline would have happened if all demographic variables had remained constant. To perform this counterfactual exercise, I maintain the hypothesis that the unemployment rate of each group of workers is unaffected by demographics. Any change in unemployment for a group of workers would therefore have happened in the absence of demographic changes; it is a *genuine* change in unemployment. Any remaining changes in unemployment are *demographic*. I find that the changing age structure of the population reduced the unemployment rate by more than 75 basis points since the business-cycle peak in 1979. The increased participation of women has had virtually no effect on unemployment in the last two decades, while the increase in the nonwhite population raised unemployment moderately, by about 13 basis points. Finally, under the maintained hypothesis, the increase in education has been much more important: it has reduced the unemployment rate by another 99 basis points.

In summary, the aggregate unemployment rate fell by about 106 basis points since 1979. Under the maintained hypothesis, if labor-force demographics had remained unchanged, the aggregate unemployment rate would have *increased* by about 55 basis points during that 19-year period. I should not be asking why the aggregate unemployment rate is so low, but rather why the genuine unemployment rate is still so very high.

If this is a puzzle during the 1980s and 1990s, it is more so during the 1960s and 1970s, a time of rising aggregate unemployment. Summers (1986) calculates that increased education during the 1960s and 1970s should have reduced the unemployment rate by about one full percentage point, enough to outweigh all other demographic effects. He writes, "taking into account the changing composition of the labor force does not reduce and may even increase the size of the rise in unemployment [in the 1960s and 1970s] that must be explained." More generally, increases in education should have caused a sharp secular decline in unemployment in the United States and throughout the world over long time horizons. This has of course not happened, leading Summers to dismiss the relevance of demographic explanations of changes in unemployment.

A more rigorous method of dismissing demographic adjustments would be to invalidate the maintained hypothesis that the unemployment rate of different groups of workers is unaffected by demographics. The second goal of this paper is then to provide a framework for evaluating the hypothesis. I argue that there are good theoretical reasons to believe it is adequate with respect to changes in the age structure, but that it might be violated when there are changes in educational attainment.

Section 3 develops a simple model of youth unemployment with the key feature that the source is not that young workers have trouble finding jobs, but that new jobs are easily destroyed. Young workers are learning about their comparative advantage by experimenting, and so necessarily endure many brief unemployment spells. In contrast, many older workers are in extremely stable jobs. Now consider the effect of the baby boom. There are more young workers, and so more unemployment. If this gives rise to a proportional incentive to create jobs, it has no effect on the rate that young workers find jobs. The age-specific unemployment rate is unaffected by population dynamics, and it makes sense to demographically adjust the unemployment rate for age.

Section 4 points out that education may be quite different. First, employers may care about relative education more than the absolute level of education. Thus an increase in the fraction of college graduates may simply lead employers to increase the educational requirement of jobs.

This says that a shift in the education distribution may have no real effects. Second, educational choice is endogenous and correlated with (unobserved) ability. Abler workers are likely to have a lower unemployment rate for a given level of education, and an increase in education reduces the ability of the average worker with a given level of education. Therefore an increase in education will tend to raise the unemployment rate conditional on education, even if it has little or no effect on aggregate unemployment. A demographic adjustment for education would be unwarranted and potentially misleading.

Ultimately, the appropriateness of a demographic adjustment is an empirical issue, and so in Section 5 I return to the data. I first test whether changes in a group's size are correlated with changes in the group's relative unemployment rate. The reduction in the population of high-school dropouts is highly correlated with a relative increase in their unemployment rate. That is a prediction of the theory in Section 4, and implies that demographic adjustments for educational attainment are inappropriate.

Next I look at age. I find that when an age group gets larger, its unemployment rate increases relative to the aggregate unemployment rate. In particular, when the baby-boom generation was young, the youth unemployment rate increased. It correspondingly fell as the baby boom aged. In terms of the model of youth unemployment, job creation did not keep pace with the increase in young workers. The maintained hypothesis *understates* the effect of the baby boom on aggregate unemployment.

In light of this evidence, I construct a series for the effect of the baby boom on unemployment. My new hypothesis, supported by the model in Section 3 and the data in Section 5, is that the unemployment rate of prime-age workers was unaffected by the baby boom. Any movement in the aggregate unemployment rate that cannot be explained by movements in the prime-age unemployment rate is due to demographics. This includes both the direct effect under the original hypothesis of having more young workers, and the indirect effect that the baby boom apparently had on the youth unemployment rate. Figures 19 and 20 display the genuine and demographic fluctuations in unemployment. The baby boom explains a 190-basis-point increase in unemployment from 1954 to 1980 and a 150-basis-point decrease in unemployment from 1980 to 1993, which was moderated by about 30 basis points in the last five years. This is the bulk of the low-frequency fluctuations in unemployment since World War II.

1.3 RELATED LITERATURE

An older literature looks at whether changes in the age and sex composition of the labor force could explain the increase in unemployment in the

1960s and 1970s. Prominent papers include Perry (1970) and Gordon (1982). They found, as I confirm, that these variables have explanatory power. There are two significant differences between their papers and mine. First, they use a different method to calculate the demographic unemployment rate, as I explain in footnote 8. My demographic adjustment is suggested by the theory I develop in later sections of the paper, and requires less data than Perry's.

Second, these earlier papers focus on changes in the *nonaccelerating inflation rate of unemployment* (NAIRU), while I look at changes in the actual unemployment rate. I do this primarily for expository simplicity. If one has a model connecting equilibrium unemployment and inflation in mind, these two objectives are likely to be almost equivalent. If the actual unemployment rate requires a demographic adjustment, then so surely must the unemployment rate associated with no wage-push inflation. Conversely, if demographics have no effect on unemployment, then they should have no effect on the NAIRU, in the absence of some other channel connecting demographics and inflation. In support of this idea, I show at the end of this paper (Figure 21) that my demographic adjustment of the unemployment rate is remarkably similar to Staiger, Stock, and Watson's (1997) nonstructurally estimated series for the NAIRU.

Demographic adjustments to the unemployment rate have attracted less attention in recent years.[2] There are two apparent reasons. First, the aging of the baby boom should have led to a decline in the unemployment rate starting in 1980, but 1980–1986 marked a period of very high unemployment. In response, early proponents of demographic adjustments stopped making them. For example, Gordon (1997) writes, ". . . when I tested in the late 1980s to see whether the demographic changes of the 1980s . . . had reduced the NAIRU accordingly, I found that it had not. Without any justification other than its empirical performance, I arbitrarily set the textbook NAIRU equal to 6.0 percent for the entire period after 1978." This paper argues that Gordon was too quick to abandon his model. High unemployment in the early 1980s was a temporary phenomenon.

2. An exception is Council of Economic Advisors (1997). In a discussion of the NAIRU, the report notes, ". . . about 0.5 percentage point of the decline in the NAIRU since the early 1980s can be attributed to demographic changes. The single most important demographic change is the aging of the baby-boom generation: the United States now has a more mature labor force, with smaller representation of age groups that traditionally have higher unemployment rates." It is not clear what other demographic changes are considered, although education must surely not have been, since I show in Section 2.4 that college enrollment is more important than the aging baby boom. The reason the demographic adjustment is smaller in the Council's report than in this paper appears to be that they are focusing on a shorter time interval and ignoring the impact that the baby boom had on the youth unemployment rate.

Second, and more to the point of this paper, the validity of demographic adjustments came under attack by Summers (1986), who argued that if one is going to adjust the unemployment rate for changes in the age and sex composition of the labor force, one logically must adjust it for changes in education. He shows that the effect of a demographic adjustment for education in the 1970s is larger in magnitude and opposite in sign to the effects emphasized by Gordon (1982). He concludes that demographics increase the unexplained change in unemployment. An important goal of this paper is then to examine his premise, that education and age adjustments are equally sensible. Moreover, to the extent that the reader does not believe my conclusion that demographic adjustments for education are unwarranted, we must ask why the aggregate unemployment rate has not fallen steadily during the twentieth century.

Finally, many other papers seek to explain why the U.S. unemployment rate has fallen so much, or alternatively why it in fact is not low by historical standards. Making a complete list of proposed explanations is beyond the scope of this paper. I mention only one, chosen because it may be as large in magnitude and as fundamental as demographics. Juhn, Murphy, and Topel (1991) note that the labor-market participation of men has declined sharply over the last thirty years. For example, the participation of men aged 35–44 declined from 97% in 1968 to 93% today. Part of the reason for this has to do with how we measure unemployment. There has been an increase in the number of *discouraged* workers, who are without a job and available for work, but who view job search as hopeless. They are not counted as unemployed, although this omission may seem somewhat arbitrary. The implications of this can be added to the implications of the demographic adjustment, leading us to conclude that by historical standards, the U.S. *nonemployment* rate is quite high.

2. Disaggregating Unemployment

The U.S. Bureau of Labor Statistics (BLS) publishes its monthly unemployment report using data gathered in the Current Population Survey (CPS), a representative sample of about 50,000 households. These data can therefore also be used to calculate the unemployment rate of a group of workers sharing certain characteristics.[3] The BLS in fact publishes monthly official statistics on unemployment as a function of age, sex, and race.[4] Also, the BLS maintains annual observations of unemployment as a func-

3. Throughout this paper, I use statistics for the unemployment rate of the civilian labor force.
4. The data in this paper are available from the BLS Web site, **http://stats.bls.gov**, except where noted otherwise. The specific series used are available upon request.

tion of education. This section uses those data to characterize the unemployment experience of different groups of workers. I then reaggregate the data to construct series for the demographic and genuine components of unemployment.

2.1 AGE

After years of depression and war, the birth rate in the United States reached unprecedented levels from 1946 to 1964, the baby boom (Ventura, Martin, Mathews, and Clarke, 1996). In 1940, 8% of women aged 15–44 gave birth. At the peak of the baby boom, the birth rate rose to over 12%, but by 1975, it had fallen to less than 7%, where it has remained.

One effect of the baby boom was a large increase in the fraction of young workers in the labor force in the late 1960s and 1970s, as Figure 2 documents. Because of the low birth rate during the Great Depression

Figure 2 DURING THE LATE 1960S AND 1970S, THE SHARE OF YOUNG WORKERS IN THE LABOR FORCE INCREASED DRAMATICALLY, AS THE PEAK OF THE BABY BOOM PASSED THROUGH ITS TEENS AND EARLY TWENTIES

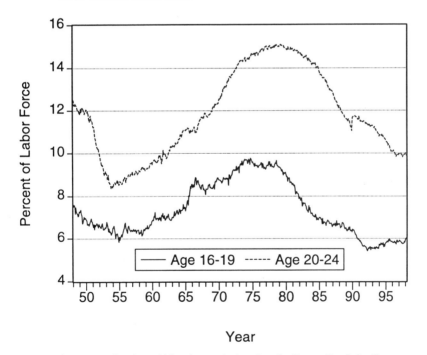

Computed from seasonally adjusted labor-force series based on the Current Population Survey.

Figure 3 THE UNEMPLOYMENT RATE OF TEENAGERS IS TYPICALLY AT
LEAST 3 TIMES THE UNEMPLOYMENT RATE OF WORKERS OVER
35; THAT OF YOUNG ADULTS IS TYPICALLY ABOUT TWICE AS
HIGH

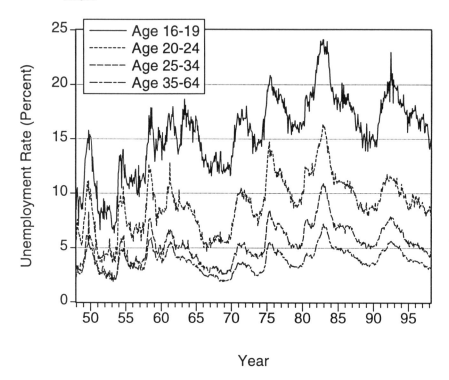

Computed from seasonally adjusted labor-force series based on the Current Population Survey.

and World War II, only 6.1% of the labor force were in their teens in 1958. This increased steadily during the next sixteen years, until by 1974, nearly 10% of the labor force was 16 to 19 years old. The teenage share then declined even more sharply, bottoming out at 5.4% in 1992, before climbing slightly in the last half decade. The share of young adults followed a similar pattern, with a natural small lag.

These demographic changes are important for aggregate unemployment, because the unemployment rate of young workers is much higher than the unemployment rate of adult workers. Figure 3 provides a graphical depiction of this fact. To be more rigorous, the unemployment rate of workers in age group i, $u_t(i)$, is described well by an ARMA(2,2) process:

Table 1   ARMA COEFFICIENTS FROM EQUATION (1), FROM OCTOBER
1957 TO NOVEMBER 1997

Age	$\bar{u}(i)$	$\alpha_1(i)$	$\alpha_2(i)$	$\theta_1(i)$	$\theta_2(i)$	$\sigma(i)$
16–19	0.169	1.620	−0.632	−1.061	0.341	0.008
	(0.009)	(0.070)	(0.068)	(0.062)	(0.044)	
20–24	0.095	1.828	−0.835	−1.048	0.264	0.005
	(0.007)	(0.064)	(0.063)	(0.061)	(0.035)	
25–34	0.056	1.824	−0.831	−0.888	0.212	0.002
	(0.005)	(0.078)	(0.076)	(0.083)	(0.049)	
35+	0.039	1.816	−0.824	−0.861	0.220	0.001
	(0.003)	(0.073)	(0.071)	(0.072)	(0.045)	

Newey–West standard errors in parentheses.

$$u_t(i) = \bar{u}(i) + \alpha_1(i)[u_{t-1}(i) - \bar{u}(i)] + \alpha_2(i)[u_{t-2}(i) - \bar{u}(i)] + \eta_t(i), \qquad (1)$$
$$\eta_t(i) = \epsilon_t(i) + \theta_1(i)\epsilon_{t-1}(i) + \theta_2(i)\epsilon_{t-2}(i),$$

where $\bar{u}(i)$ is the unconditional expectation of the unemployment rate of group i, and $\epsilon_t(i)$ is white noise with variance $\sigma_t^2(i)$, allowing for heteroscedasticity. Table 1 shows the ARMA coefficients for four different groups of workers during the last forty years.[5] The coefficients have been stable and are remarkably consistent across groups. The unconditional unemployment rate of teenage workers is more than four times the unemployment rate of prime-age workers, while the unemployment rate of workers in their early twenties is nearly three times as high.

To quantify the importance of the changing age structure of the labor force, I divide the labor force into seven age groups: $I = \{16–19, 20–24, 25–34, 35–44, 45–54, 55–64, 65+\}$. Define $\omega_t(i)$ to be the fraction of workers who are in group i at time t, so $\sum_{i \in I}\omega_t(i) = 1$ for all t. Let $u_t(i)$ denote the unemployment rate of age group i at time t. Then the aggregate unemployment rate at time t is

$$U_t \equiv \sum_{i \in I}\omega_t(i)u_t(i). \qquad (2)$$

There are two ways that aggregate unemployment might fall. First, the unemployment rate of different groups of workers, $u_t(i)$, might fall. Second, the population might shift towards groups with lower unemployment rates, so $\omega_t(i)$ increases for i with small $u_t(i)$ and decreases for i with large $u_t(i)$.

5. The years from 1948 to 1957 were characterized by higher-frequency cyclical fluctuations and the Korean War, so these results are sensitive to a choice of initial year before 1957. However, they are not sensitive to a choice of a later initial year.

I want to understand how much of that change would have happened if demographics had remained the same. I will refer to this as the *genuine* change in unemployment. A useful hypothesis is that if demographics had remained unchanged at some initial shares $\omega_{t_0}(\cdot)$, the disaggregate unemployment rates $u_t(\cdot)$ would have followed the same path that we observed from t_0 to t_1. This implies that the unemployment rate at time t_1 would have been

$$U^G_{t_1,t_0} \equiv \sum_{i \in I} \omega_{t_0}(i) u_{t_1}(i) \tag{3}$$

if demographics had remained the same from t_0 to t_1. The calculation of $U^G_{t_1,t_0}$ naturally depends on the choice of the base year t_0. An interesting candidate is August 1978 (78:08), as this is the demographically "worst" point in recent U.S. history. That is, $U^G_{t_1,78:08} \geq U_{t_1}$ for all t_1 since World War II, as shown in Figure 4.

$U^G_{t_1,78:08}$ rose by 208 basis points from the peak of the expansion in 1969 to the peak in 1979, a period during which the aggregate unemployment rate U_t rose by 229 basis points. Thus genuine unemployment changes

Figure 4 $U^G_{t_1,78:08}$ AND U_{t_1} FOR SEVEN AGE GROUPS

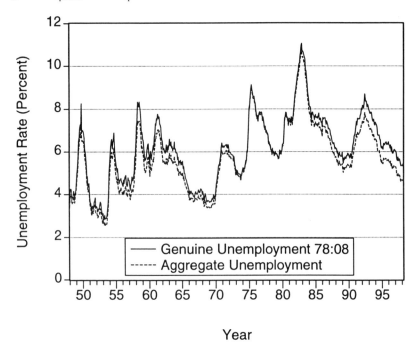

Less than 40% of the decline in aggregate unemployment during the last two decades is genuine.

Figure 5 DEMOGRAPHIC ADJUSTMENT FOR SEVEN AGE GROUPS

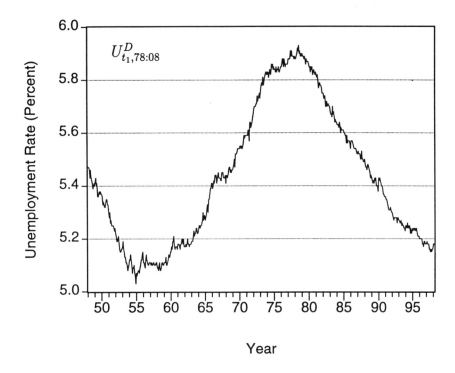

Year

account for most of the action in the 1970s. In contrast, $U^G_{t_1,78:08}$ only declined by 25 basis points from 1979 to 1989 and by 12 basis points from 1989 to the present, about 40% of the total decline in aggregate unemployment in the first interval, and less than 30% in the second interval.[6]

The obvious alternative is to ask how much the unemployment rate changed because of demographics. Maintain our hypothesis that demographics do not affect disaggregate unemployment rates. Then if the only changes in the economy from t_0 to t_1 were demographic, the unemployment rate at t_1 would be

$$U^D_{t_1,t_0} \equiv \sum_{i \in I} \omega_{t_1}(i) u_{t_0}(i). \qquad (4)$$

Changes in U^D are *demographic* unemployment changes. Figure 5 plots this series, again using a base of August 1978. $U^D_{t_1,78:08}$ rose by 90 basis

6. Using a different base year gives similar results. For example, $U^G_{t_1,54:12}$ (using the demographically "best" point as the base year) rose by 179 basis points in the 1970s and declined by 38 basis points in the last 19 years. $U^G_{t_1,97:11}$ rose by 185 basis points and then declined by 38.

points from its lowest level in 1954 to its peak in 1978, and has since declined by 78 basis points. About 65% of the decline in unemployment from the peak in 1979 to the peak in 1997 is picked up by $U^D_{t_1;78:08}$.[7]

One problem with these measures of demographic change is that they depend on a choice of base year. To avoid this issue, I introduce a *chain-weighted* measure of the change in unemployment attributable to demographics. Given an initial time period t_0, define for $t_1 > t_0$

$$\Delta_{t_1,t_0} = \sum_{t=t_0}^{t_1-1} \sum_{i \in I} [\omega_{t+1}(i) - \omega_t(i)] \frac{u_{t+1}(i) + u_t(i)}{2}. \tag{5}$$

$\Delta_{t+1,t_0} - \Delta_{t,t_0}$ reflects the change in demographics from t to $t + 1$. Thus Δ_{t_1,t_0} reflects the cumulative effect of changing demographics since period t_0. This series rose by 84 basis points from 1954 to its high point in August 1978, and has since fallen by 81 basis points (Figure 6). Since the 1979

Figure 6 DEMOGRAPHIC ADJUSTMENT FOR SEVEN AGE GROUPS

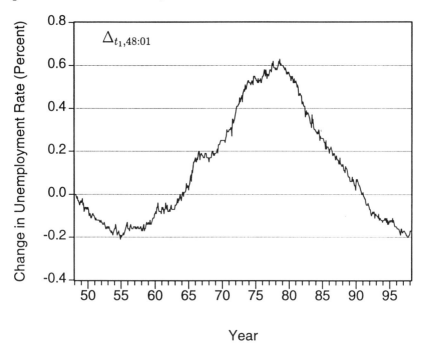

7. Different base years give similar results. We can also let $u_{t_0}(i)$ equal the unconditional expectation of group i's unemployment rate, as estimated by an ARMA(2,2) like equation (1). This implies a 91-basis-point increase in unemployment due to demographics from 1954 to 1978 and a subsequent 80-basis-point decline.

business cycle peak, $\Delta_{t_1,48:01}$ declined by 76 basis points, 68% of the total decline in unemployment.

Δ is not a perfect measure of demographics either,[8] since it may be affected by the cyclicality of labor market participation. For example, youth participation varies more with the business cycle, since prime-age workers do not move in and out of the labor market very easily.[9] During the 1960s and 1970s, when the youth population was increasing, this should have reduced the change in the weights $\omega(i)$ during recessions, since the secular increase in the share of youth was offset by their cyclical decrease in participation. It should have increased the change in the weights during expansions, since the two effects moved in the same direction. In calculating Δ, we multiply these weights by the current unemployment rate, which is higher during recessions. This would tend to moderate the change in Δ. This argument can be reversed to suggest that changes in Δ during the 1980s and 1990s are exaggerated. This may help explain why the simple demographically adjusted unemployment series U^D changed by more than the chain-weighted series Δ in the 1960s and 1970s, and by less in the 1980s and 1990s. Still, Figure 2 demonstrates that the secular shifts in labor-market shares swamp any cyclical variations, so this issue in unlikely to be quantitatively important.

Data problems may bias both demographic adjustments to zero. Suppose we divide the population into only two age groups, 16–24 and 25+. We find that Δ rose by 74 basis points from 1954 to 1978, and then declined by 73 basis points from 1978 to 1997. Any other division into two groups gives smaller changes. For example, with age groups 16–19 and 20+, we only observe half of the change in Δ during both time intervals. It is not surprising that aggregation reduces the measured demographic changes, since it is precisely the differences in disaggre-

---

8. Both of my measures of the demographic unemployment rate differ from the measure suggested by Perry (1970) and used by him and by Gordon (1982). Perry and Gordon weight different groups by their members' total annual earnings, and construct an alternative measure of unemployment using these weights. The demographic adjustment is then the difference between the actual unemployment rate and this series. I show in Section 3 that a simple model justifies the use of U^G to represent genuine changes in unemployment, and U^D or Δ to represent demographic changes. My theory does not suggest Perry's demographic adjustment.

9. One way to quantify this is to look at the covariance between real GDP growth and labor-market participation growth for different age groups. If a group moves out of the labor market during recessions, this should be positive. From 1948 to 1979, the covariance for teenage workers was 8 times the covariance for workers aged 45–54 and 10 times the covariance for workers aged 55–64. For the remaining four groups of workers, the covariance was actually negative. Since 1980, the covariance between these two series has become positive for all groups. Still, the covariance is 3 times as large for teenagers as for workers 20–24, and at least 8 times larger than for the remaining five groups.

Figure 7 THE FRACTION OF THE LABOR FORCE THAT IS FEMALE HAS
STEADILY INCREASED SINCE WORLD WAR II

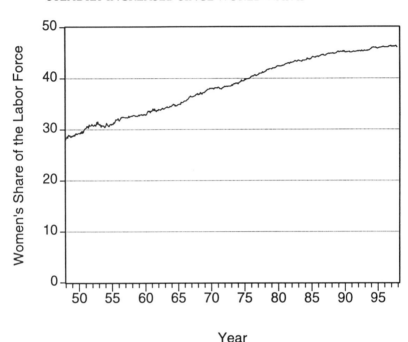

Year

Computed from seasonally adjusted labor-force series based on the Current Population Survey.

gate unemployment rates and the changes in labor-market shares that
result in demographic adjustments. If we could divide the population
into more age groups, logic and evidence suggest that we would attribute more of the decline in unemployment to the changing age structure
of the labor force.

In light of these caveats, under the maintained hypothesis, the aging
of the baby boom explains at least 70% of the decline in unemployment
since 1979, leaving about 30 or 40 basis points unexplained. The entry of
the baby boom into the labor market had the opposite effect, but explains a smaller percentage of the larger increase in unemployment during the sixties and seventies.

2.2 SEX

Another dramatic trend has been the increasing participation of women
in the U.S. labor market (Figure 7). This would have the potential to
explain a change in the aggregate unemployment rate if women had a

different unemployment rate than men. Historically this was the case, although the gap has disappeared during the last fifteen years (Figure 8). More precisely, both series are described by statistically identical ARMA(2,2) processes.

As this suggests, female participation cannot explain much of the change in unemployment. For example, divide workers up by sex and construct the chain-weighted series Δ as in equation (5). This explains a 19-basis-point rise in the unemployment rate from 1950 to 1979, and then virtually no change in the unemployment rate from 1979 to 1997 (Figure 9).

The behavior of U^D defined in equation (4) depends strongly on the choice of base year. If we choose a year when women's unemployment is lower (higher) than men's, then U^D monotonically declines (increases). This highlights the disadvantage of U^D when the relationship between disaggregate unemployment rates is unstable. For this reason I use Δ as my primary measure of demographic unemployment.

One might be tempted to add the demographic changes reported here

Figure 8 DURING THE 1960S AND 1970S, THE UNEMPLOYMENT RATE OF MEN WAS ABOUT 2 PERCENTAGE POINTS BELOW THAT OF WOMEN, BUT THAT GAP DISAPPEARED IN 1980

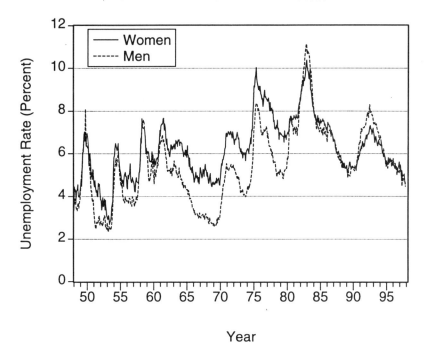

Computed from seasonally adjusted labor-force series based on the Current Population Survey.

Figure 9 DEMOGRAPHIC ADJUSTMENT FOR INCREASED FEMALE
PARTICIPATION

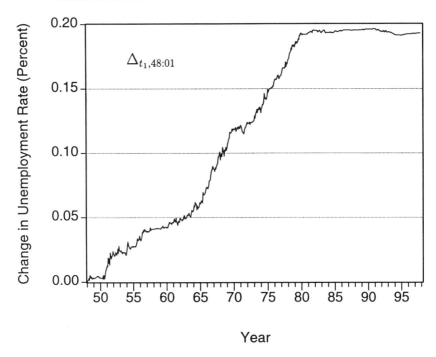

and in the first part of this section, in order to obtain the effects of the changes in the age and sex composition of the labor force—a 103-basis-point increase in unemployment from 1954 to 1978, followed by an 81-basis-point decline in unemployment from 1978 to 1997. That calculation is incorrect if there are any *mix effects* between age and sex. For example, the increase in participation has been most dramatic for prime-age women, who have a much lower unemployment rate than teenage women. Thus the increase in female participation may be double-counted as a relative decrease in teenage participation. Constructing Δ with fourteen age and sex groups, we find that age and sex jointly account for a 96-basis-point increase in the unemployment rate from 1954 to 1978, followed by an 80-basis-point decline in the unemployment rate from 1978 to 1997. Mix effects are quantitatively unimportant.

2.3 RACE

The fraction of the labor force that is white was nearly constant from 1948 to 1971. Since then, it has declined from 89% to 84%. Figure 10

Figure 10 THE FRACTION OF BLACKS HAS INCREASED BY LESS THAN 2%, WHILE THE FRACTION OF WHITES HAS DECLINED BY ABOUT 5%

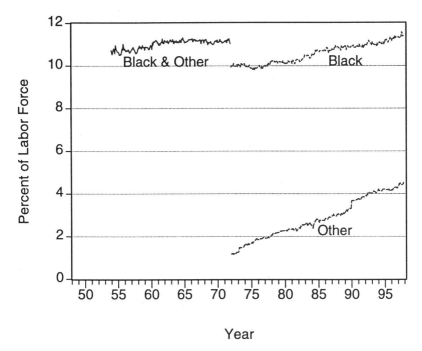

Year

Computed from seasonally adjusted labor-force series based on the Current Population Survey. Data limitations only allow me to divide the labor force into two groups, white and other, before 1972.

shows that most of the increase in labor-force share has been for people who are neither white nor black. The white unemployment rate is only slightly lower than the unemployment rate for this group (Figure 11). The big gap between black and white unemployment rates should have had little effect on demographics, since the black labor-force share has been stable.

Dividing the labor force into three race categories, black, white, and other,[10] I find that Δ was constant from 1960 to 1977, and has since increased by 16 basis points (Figure 12). The changing racial composition has slightly mitigated the decline in unemployment in the last two decades.

10. Data limitations only allow me to divide the labor force into two groups, white and other, before 1972. Since whites and blacks account for 98.8% of the labor force in 1972, this is unlikely to be a problem. After 1972, separating out blacks and other nonwhites is quantitatively important.

Figure 11 THE BLACK UNEMPLOYMENT RATE IS MUCH HIGHER THAN THE WHITE UNEMPLOYMENT RATE

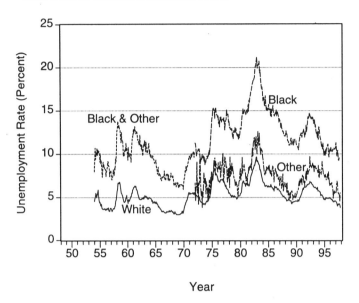

Computed from seasonally adjusted labor-force series based on the Current Population Survey. Data limitations only allow me to divide the labor force into two groups, white and other, before 1972.

Figure 12 DEMOGRAPHIC ADJUSTMENT FOR INCREASED NONWHITE PARTICIPATION

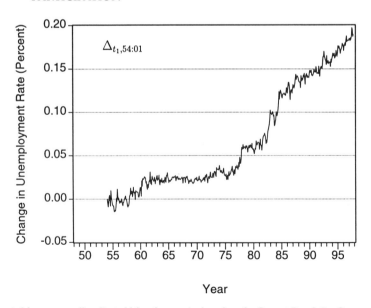

Computed from seasonally adjusted labor-force series based on the Current Population Survey.

I do not expect that it is race *per se* that leads nonwhites to have a high unemployment rate.[11] Instead, it is variables such as poor schooling and poverty. A demographic adjustment for the changing race composition would be misleading, if the relationship between race, quality of school, and wealth is changing over time. Since the magnitude of the race adjustment is not very large, this distinction is economically not very important. In practice, I do not adjust the unemployment rate for the racial composition of the labor force.

2.4 EDUCATION

The final trend that I examine is the increased education of the U.S. labor force (Figure 13). Since 1970, the percentage of workers[12] with at least some college education has increased from 26% to 56%. The percentage with only a high-school diploma increased from 38% in 1970 to 40% in the early 1980s, and has since fallen to 33%. The percentage with less than a high-school diploma fell steadily from 36% to 11% during this time period.

Also, less educated workers have a much higher unemployment rate (Figure 14). The unemployment rate of workers with less than a high-school diploma has been three to five times as high as the unemployment rate of workers with a college degree throughout this time period. The unemployment rate of those with a high-school diploma has been two to three times as high. These differences have increased over time.

I can again construct the variable Δ as in equation (5), using the four education categories (Figure 15). I find that Δ has fallen by 99 basis points since 1979.[13] This is larger than the decline that can be explained by the changing age structure, so changes in education appear to be a promising explanation for the recent decline in aggregate unemployment. In fact, the sum of an age and an education adjustment is a 175-basis-point decline in unemployment during the 1980s and 1990s, while the actual unemployment rate only fell by 106 basis points.

I will argue in the remainder of this paper that this education adjustment is misguided. As indirect evidence for this claim, one can perform

11. Employer preference for hiring whites rather than blacks would give one direct link between race and unemployment. One implication of the model in Section 4.1 is that if unemployment differences are due to discriminatory hiring, demographic adjustments to the unemployment rate are inappropriate.
12. Throughout this section, I look at workers between the ages of 25 and 64. A 16-year-old who works while in high school is probably quite different than an adult who dropped out of high school many years before. Since most workers have completed their education by age 25, I avoid complex aggregation issues by focusing on these workers.
13. The annual change of about six basis points remains the same if we omit 1993 and 1994, the years that were affected by the redesign of the CPS.

Figure 13 THE FRACTION OF WORKERS WITH AT LEAST SOME COLLEGE
EDUCATION HAS INCREASED STEADILY SINCE 1970, AT THE
EXPENSE OF WORKERS WITH LESS THAN A HIGH-SCHOOL
DIPLOMA

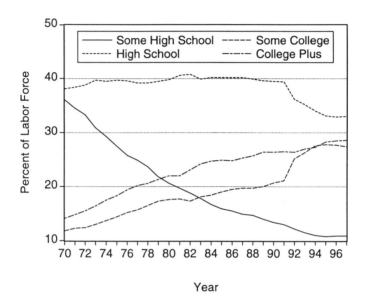

Year

Data are for March of each year. Since 1992, data on educational attainment have been based on the
highest diploma or degree received, rather than the number of years of school completed. Data from 1994
forward are not directly comparable with data for earlier years, due to the Current Population Survey
redesign. I am grateful to Steve Haugen at the Bureau of Labor Statistics for providing me with these data.

the same exercise in previous decades. My data show a decline in Δ of
almost 60 basis points during the 1970s. Similarly, Summers (1986) calculates that the increase in education in the 1960s reduced the aggregate
unemployment rate at a similar rate, about 50 basis points during the
decade.[14] As Summers pointed out, if education explains the unemployment decline during the last two decades, then it increases the mystery
of why the unemployment rate was so very high in 1979.

There are two possible solutions to this issue. First, the problem could
be ameliorated by the mix effects between age and education. Unemployment among college graduates may have been rising in the 1950s and
1960s because most college graduates were young. This solution does
not appear promising, because in looking at education, I have restricted

14. Summers effectively calculates the change in the gap between the actual unemployment
rate and the genuine unemployment rate $U^G_{t_1, t_0}$, where the base year t_0 is 1965.

Figure 14 THE UNEMPLOYMENT RATE OF LESS-EDUCATED WORKERS IS
MUCH HIGHER THAN THE UNEMPLOYMENT RATE OF MORE-
EDUCATED WORKERS; THE GAP HAS BEEN GROWING RECENTLY

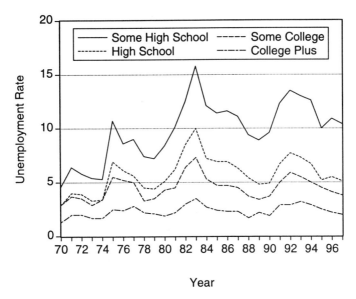

Data are for March of each year. Since 1992, data on educational attainment have been based on the highest diploma or degree received, rather than the number of years of school completed. Data from 1994 forward are not directly comparable with data for earlier years due to the Current Population Survey redesign. I am grateful to Steve Haugen at the Bureau of Labor Statistics for providing me with these data.

Figure 15 DEMOGRAPHIC ADJUSTMENT FOR INCREASED EDUCATION

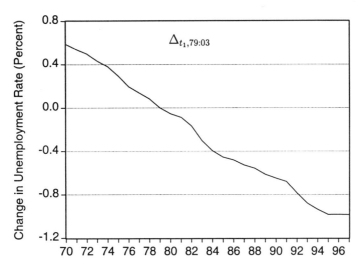

attention to workers aged 25–64. Empirically, the relationship between age and unemployment is weak for these workers, and so there is unlikely to be much overlap between the two demographic adjustments. Second, the maintained hypothesis, that changes in education do not affect unemployment conditional on education, may be false. The next two sections address the theoretical foundations of the maintained hypothesis, and the final section evaluates it empirically.

3. Youth Unemployment

Empirically, changes in the age and education composition of the labor force account for large changes in aggregate unemployment under the maintained hypothesis. Other demographic changes do not have as much potential explanatory power. Thus the remainder of this paper focuses exclusively on age and education.

This section develops a benchmark model of youth unemployment, in order to explore whether changes in the age structure of the population affect unemployment rates conditional on age. The model illustrates conditions under which the maintained hypothesis is satisfied, while simultaneously helping us to understand the bias that would be introduced by plausible violations of the hypothesis.

The premise of the model is that young workers do not have a particularly hard time finding jobs, but instead they have trouble keeping jobs. This is motivated by the fact that the mean and median unemployment durations in the United States are increasing functions of age. For example, the median unemployment duration of unemployed teenage workers during 1997 averaged 5.6 weeks, and the mean was 10.3 weeks. For workers between 55 and 64 years old, the median unemployment duration was 10.3 weeks and the mean was 21.9. This monotonic order surprisingly holds for the six working age groups (16–19, 20–24, 25–34, 35–44, 45–54, and 55–64) and for every year since 1976, when the Bureau of Labor Statistics began reporting unemployment duration data.[15] Since more young workers are unemployed, but those who lose their jobs stay unemployed for shorter times, it follows that young workers are much more likely to lose their jobs.[16]

---

15. The fact that older workers stay unemployed for longer may be due to their superior access to unemployment insurance. This possibility goes beyond the model here.
16. There is some controversy about this conclusion. Clark and Summers (1982) argue that youth unemployment duration is reduced by unemployed workers leaving and re-entering the labor force, and that the source of youth unemployment is a core group of young workers who cannot find jobs.

I assume that young people lose their jobs more frequently not because they are young, but because they are inexperienced. More precisely, the hazard rate of job loss is decreasing in the length of time since the worker was last unemployed or out of the labor force, her *job tenure*. Thus, when an older worker loses her job, she is thrust back into the same situation as a younger worker. There are a number of theoretical justifications for this assumption. A new employee may be unsuitable for her job, but this can only be learned by trial and error. After surviving an apprenticeship, her job security increases. Moreover, as she stays on the job for a long period of time, she acquires specific human capital, making firing costly. Even if she quits her job to take a new one, she will tend to do so only if she expects it will enhance her job security. There is also an empirical justification for the assumption: it matches U.S. data.

3.1 MODELING JOB LOSS

I do not take a stand on why the hazard rate of job loss is decreasing, but instead set up a simple model with that property. A representative worker is "born" unemployed. She looks for a job, and is hired with flow probability M. That is, during any interval of length t, an unemployed worker is hired with probability $1 - e^{-Mt}$. When she is hired, her marginal product is initially equal to some constant s. Thereafter, productivity follows a random walk in continuous time: the productivity after t periods is $x(t) = s + \sigma Z(t)$, where $Z(t)$ is a standard Brownian motion. Thus after $\tau < t$ periods, $x(t)$ is a normally distributed random variable with mean $x(\tau)$ and variance $\sigma^2(t - \tau)$. I assume that the job is destroyed when productivity falls below some threshold $\underline{x} < s$.[17] Following a separation, she looks for a new job, finding one with flow probability M. The productivity in the new job is again initially equal to s, and again follows a random walk. This repeats forever. The unemployment rate of workers at age t is equal to the probability that this representative worker is unemployed at age t. Later in this section, I endogenize the separation threshold $\underline{x}$ and the hiring rate M. However, it is simpler at this stage to treat these two variables as exogenous.

Under these assumptions, a match ends within t periods with probability

$$F(t) = 2\Phi\left(-\frac{s - \underline{x}}{\sigma\sqrt{t}}\right),\tag{6}$$

---

17. If $\underline{x} \geq s$, all matches are destroyed immediately upon creation, an uninteresting case.

where Φ is the cumulative distribution of a standard normal random variable. Figure 16 depicts the match survival probability for one particular value of $(s - \underline{x})/\sigma$.

The intuition for this result is the *reflection principle* (Karatzas and Shreve, 1991). Momentarily ignore the fact that matches are terminated when productivity reaches the threshold $\underline{x}$. Consider a sample path that first reaches $\underline{x}$ after t' periods. Given this, productivity at some time $t > t'$ is distributed normally with mean $\underline{x}$. Thus among sample paths that first reach the separation threshold after t' periods, only half of them have productivity less than $\underline{x}$ after $t > t'$ periods. Since t' was chosen arbitrarily, this is true for any $t' \in [0,t]$. Thus for sample paths that reached the separation threshold within t periods, exactly half of them have productivity less than the separation threshold after t periods. The fraction of sample paths that are below the separation threshold after t periods is

$$\Phi\left(-\frac{s-\underline{x}}{\sigma\sqrt{t}}\right).$$

Figure 16 THE PROBABILITY OF A MATCH SURVIVING FOR t PERIODS

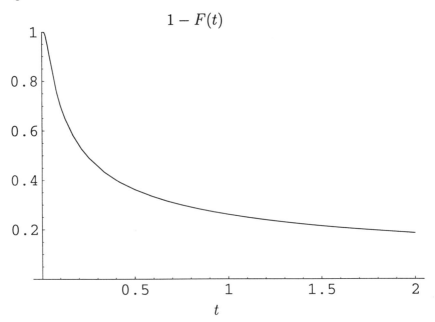

$$1 - F(t)$$

Drawn for $(s - \underline{x})/\sigma = \frac{1}{3}$.

Figure 17 THE HAZARD RATE FOR MATCH SEPARATIONS AFTER *t*
PERIODS

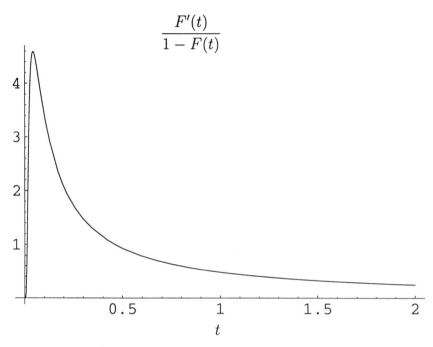

Drawn for $(s - \underline{x})/\sigma = \frac{1}{3}$.

This must be half of the fraction of sample paths that reach the separation threshold within *t* periods, and hence half the fraction of matches
that are terminated within *t* periods, $F(t)/2$.

The hazard rate of separation in a *t*-period-old match is $F'(t)/[1 - F(t)]$,
depicted in Figure 17. This is increasing for small values of *t*, since a
sample path is unlikely to fall from *s* to $\underline{x}$ in a very short period of time. It
is decreasing for large values of *t*, since, conditional on a match having
survived for a long period of time, the productivity is likely to be much
larger than the separation threshold.

3.2 THE RELATIONSHIP BETWEEN UNEMPLOYMENT AND AGE

Let $u(t)$ denote the probability that the representative worker is unemployed at age *t*. This must satisfy a backward-looking differential equation

$$\dot{u}(t) = -Mu(t) + M\int_0^t u(\tau)F'(t - \tau)\, d\tau \qquad (7)$$

with initial condition $u(0) = 1$. Unemployment decreases due to match creation and increases due to match separations. The flow probability that a worker is hired at age t is the flow probability that an unemployed worker is hired M times the probability that she is actually unemployed at t. The flow of separations depends on earlier hiring probabilities. She was hired at age $\tau \in [0,t]$ with flow probability $Mu(\tau)$. The flow probability that this job ends at t is $F'(t - \tau)$, where F is the probability that a match does not survive, given in equation (6).

One can show that $u(t)$ converges to zero over time, because everyone winds up in very good matches eventually. Also, simulations show that $u(t)$ is monotonically decreasing (Figure 18), although, since the separation hazard rate is nonmonotonic, I cannot prove this analytically.

A simpler model in which the flow probability of a separation is a constant $\delta > 0$ (e.g. Mortensen and Pissarides, 1994) would deliver the same qualitative predictions as this model. However, quantitatively the models are extremely different. In the Mortensen–Pissarides model, the unemployment rate moves exponentially towards its steady-state value; half the gap between the actual and steady-state unemployment

Figure 18 THE UNEMPLOYMENT RATE OF A WORKER AS A FUNCTION
OF HER LABOR-MARKET EXPERIENCE

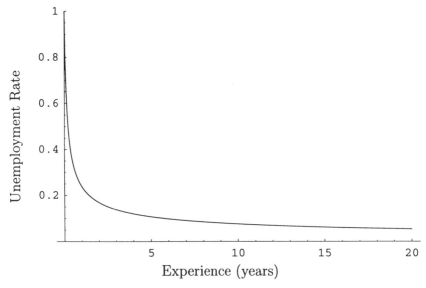

Drawn for $(s - \underline{x})/\sigma = \frac{1}{3}$ and $M = 5$.

rate is closed in $(\log 2)/(\delta + M)$ periods. For plausible parameters, this implies the unemployment rate of workers with one year of labor-force experience will be indistinguishable from the unemployment rate of prime-age workers. This would be an inadequate explanation for youth unemployment.

The (mostly) declining hazard rate of job loss in this model implies a much slower decline in unemployment as a function of age. In the example depicted in Figure 18, the unemployment rate of workers with 1 year's labor-market experience is 24%. It declines to 12% after 4 years and 6% after 16 years. The eventual steady-state unemployment rate is zero. Thus there is a quantitatively strong and persistent relationship between age and unemployment in this model which is absent from the simpler model. This is why a declining hazard rate of job loss is a necessary ingredient in a model that explains youth unemployment through differential rates of job destruction. The interesting point is that it appears to be a sufficient ingredient as well.

3.3 DEMOGRAPHIC ADJUSTMENT

I am now in a position to ask whether the demographic adjustments U^D and Δ and the genuine unemployment rate U^G appropriately reflect the impact of changes in the age structure of the population. Let $N(t)$ denote the population measure of infinite-lived workers at time t. Each worker's life proceeds as described above. To avoid introducing aggregate uncertainty, assume that all the stochastic processes in the economy are independent. That is, the hiring probabilities of different workers are independent, and the stochastic process for the productivity of worker i in job j, $Z_{ij}(t)$, is independently distributed.

The sole source of aggregate fluctuations is variations in the population growth rate, $\dot{N}(t)/N(t)$. Applying equation (2) and the law of large numbers, the aggregate unemployment rate must equal

$$U_t = \int_0^\infty u_t(\tau) \frac{\dot{N}(t-\tau)}{N(t)} d\tau,$$

where $u_t(\tau)$ is the unemployment rate of τ-year-old workers in period t, as given by the solution to differential equation (7), $\dot{N}(t-\tau)$ workers were born τ periods ago, and the current population is $N(t)$. Thus the labor-market share of τ-period-old workers is $\omega_t(\tau) = \dot{N}(t-\tau)/N(t)$.

Since the only shocks in this model are demographic, all fluctuations in unemployment should be attributed to demographics. It is easy to verify conditions under which our constructions from Section 2 behave correctly. Use (3), (4), and the continuous time limit of (5):

$$U^G_{t_1,t_0} = \int_0^\infty u_{t_1}(\tau) \frac{\dot{N}(t_0 - \tau)}{N(t_0)} \, d\tau,$$

$$U^D_{t_1,t_0} = \int_0^\infty u_{t_0}(\tau) \frac{\dot{N}(t_1 - \tau)}{N(t_1)} \, d\tau,$$

$$\Delta_{t_1,t_0} = \int_{t_0}^{t_1} \int_0^\infty u_t(\tau) \frac{d}{dt} \left(\frac{\dot{N}(t - \tau)}{N(t)} \right) d\tau \, dt.$$

Now suppose the unemployment rate of workers conditional on their age does not vary over time: $u_t(\tau) = u_{t_0}(\tau)$ for all t, t_0, and τ. Simplifying the equations above yields three conclusions:

1. The genuine unemployment rate is constant over time t_1 for fixed initial time t_0: $U^G_{t_1,t_0} \equiv U_{t_0}$, so none of the changes in unemployment are genuine.
2. The demographic unemployment rate tracks the actual unemployment rate, $U^D_{t_1,t_0} \equiv U_{t_1}$, so all of the changes in unemployment are demographic.
3. The chain-weighted unemployment rate tracks the change in the unemployment rate, $\Delta_{t_1,t_0} \equiv U_{t_1} - U_{t_0}$, again stating that all of the changes in unemployment are demographic.

All three constructions recognize that the change in aggregate unemployment is demographic. On the other hand, if the age-specific unemployment rates depend on the age distribution, and so vary over time, demographic adjustments are misleading.

In summary, the question of whether these constructions capture demographic changes well is equivalent to the question of whether the disaggregate unemployment rates $u(\tau)$ are independent of the age distribution.[18] By equations (6) and (7), this requires that the age distribution not affect the hiring rate M and the threshold $\underline{x}$.[19]

---

18. This is certainly not the only model that ensures that disaggregate unemployment rates satisfy this property. For example, if heterogeneous workers choose to segregate themselves into separate labor markets, as in Acemoglu and Shimer (1997), a change in the distribution of workers changes the size of each labor market, but has no effect on unemployment rates. I do not use this segregation model to study youth unemployment, since it focuses attention on job creation. As discussed before, the primary cause of youth unemployment is the high rate of job destruction.
19. I assume that the technological parameters s and σ are unaffected by demographics.

3.4 CLOSING THE MODEL

To see whether this is a reasonable assumption, I endogenize these two variables, following the general methodology of Pissarides (1985). I have already discussed workers' lifetime in some detail, and here I briefly outline the environment faced by firms. I assume firms use a constant-returns-to-scale technology, and so without loss of generality I impose that a firm can employ at most one worker. It can either have a vacancy (and be looking for a worker) or have a filled job (and be producing). When a firm has a filled job, its productivity follows a random walk, as described before. The first issue is the determination of the separation threshold $\underline{x}$. My solution assumes that the economy is in steady state, but these results can all be generalized to nonstationary environments.

The Separation Threshold. An employment relationship is terminated when it is in the mutual interest of the worker and her employer.[20] Let $\mathcal{W}(x)$ denote the expected present value of the firm's profits plus the worker's wages, discounted at the interest rate $r > 0$, as a function of current productivity x. Let $\mathcal{U}$ denote the worker's value following a separation, the expected present value of her future wages while she is unemployed; and $\mathcal{V}$ denote the firm's value, the expected present value of its future profits while it has a vacancy. These values do not depend on x, as this represents an idiosyncratic or match-specific shock. Then the match ends if $\mathcal{W}(x) \leq \mathcal{U} + \mathcal{V}$. Otherwise, the productivity process implies $\mathcal{W}(x)$ satisfies a second-order differential equation:

$$r\mathcal{W}(x) = x + \tfrac{1}{2}\sigma^2 \mathcal{W}''(x).$$

The flow value of a match comes from its current productivity x plus the capital gain from changes in x. Although there is no drift in the stochastic process for productivity, variability of x raises the value if $\mathcal{W}$ is a convex function. The expected value of $\mathcal{W}$ next period is larger than $\mathcal{W}$ evaluated at the expected productivity, an application of Jensen's inequality.

The general solution to this differential equation is

$$r\mathcal{W}(x) = x + k_1 e^{-(\sqrt{2r}/\sigma)x} + k_2 e^{(\sqrt{2r}/\sigma)x}$$

20. A generous interpretation of this model would recognize that it allows for job-to-job movement. Suppose an employed worker takes a new job when it is in the mutual interest of her current and future employers and herself. This may be ensured by the structure of her contract, which can include breach-of-contract penalties, such as vested pension plans (Diamond and Maskin, 1979, 1981). Then $x(t)$ should be interpreted as the productivity after t periods, assuming the worker follows an optimal sequence of job-to-job moves.

for constants k_1 and k_2. We require two terminal conditions. First, if x is very large, the threat of a separation is remote. An additional unit of productivity must raise the value of a match by $1/r$. We have $\lim_{x \to \infty} W'(x) = 1/r$, so $k_2 = 0$.

Next, observe that W is weakly increasing.[21] This verifies the optimality of a threshold rule. Now if productivity x is close to the threshold $\underline{x}$, it will fall below $\underline{x}$ in a short interval of time with probability close to 1. This property of Brownian motions implies that a small change in productivity near the threshold $\underline{x}$ will have almost no effect on the present value, $W'(\underline{x}) = 0$. Thus

$$k_1 = \frac{\sigma}{\sqrt{2r}}\, e^{(\sqrt{2r/\sigma})\underline{x}},$$

so

$$rW(x) = x + \frac{\sigma}{\sqrt{2r}}\, e^{-(\sqrt{2r/\sigma})(x-\underline{x})}. \tag{8}$$

Finally, the value of the match at the threshold must equal the sum of the values after a separation, $W(\underline{x}) = \mathcal{U} + \mathcal{V}$:

$$\underline{x} = r(\mathcal{U} + \mathcal{V}) - \frac{\sigma}{\sqrt{2r}}. \tag{9}$$

Matches survive even after productivity passes below the myopic threshold $x = r(\mathcal{U} + \mathcal{V})$. The reason is that a separation destroys the option to take advantage of future productivity increases. The option is worth more when agents are patient (r is small) and when the variability of output is large (σ is large), since productivity is more likely to increase substantially in the near future.

Job Search and the Hiring Rate. I next turn to the job search process. This will allow me to determine the continuation values $\mathcal{U}$ and $\mathcal{V}$ and the hiring rate M.

An important question is how wages are determined in this environment. There is generally surplus when a new match is created, since the worker and firm are jointly better off matching instead of waiting for

---

21. To prove this formally, use the fact that the optimal stopping rule for one value of x can also be used for a higher value x'. This must yield at least as high a value. Using an optimal termination rule must yield a still-higher value.

new partners. There are a number of ways that the surplus can be divided.[22] At this point choosing how is not very important. However, later in the paper it is convenient to use a multilateral bargaining rule (Shimer, 1997), and so I introduce it now.

Multilateral bargaining focuses on the mechanics of the matching process. Every unemployed worker targets her job search towards one vacancy, selected at random. With exogenous flow probability π, the vacancy closes. However, that does not guarantee the worker a job. Other unemployed workers may also be applying for the job opening, giving the firm an opportunity to hire one of the competing applicants. The multilateral bargaining rule is that the firm sells the job to the highest bidder. This can equivalently be thought of as Bertrand competition or a second-price auction between job applicants.[23] As a result, a worker's wage depends on the circumstances under which she was hired.

Since all workers are equally likely to apply for all job openings, the number of applicants for a given vacancy is a Poisson random variable with expectation q, equal to the ratio of the measure of unemployed workers to the measure of firms with vacancies. That is, the probability that $n \in \{0, 1, 2, \ldots\}$ other applicants compete for a particular job is $q^n e^{-q}/n!$. In particular, when a worker's desired job vacancy closes, there are no other applicants with probability e^{-q}. In this event, she is hired and is able to extract all the surplus from the match. Her value jumps by $\mathcal{W}(s) - \mathcal{V} - \mathcal{U}$ upon being hired, where $\mathcal{W}(s)$ is the value of a new match. She may still be hired if there are other job applicants; however, if this happens, the firm is able to extract all the surplus. The firm's value jumps by $\mathcal{W}(s) - \mathcal{V} - \mathcal{U}$, while all the applicants' values are constant whether or not they are hired.

Putting this together, the value of an unemployed worker satisfies

$$r\mathcal{U} = y + \pi e^{-q}[\mathcal{W}(s) - \mathcal{V} - \mathcal{U}]. \tag{10}$$

22. For example, Pissarides (1985) sparked a literature that assumes wages are set by *Nash bargaining*. A worker and firm divide the difference between the value of a match and the sum of their outside options. Let $\beta \in [0,1]$ denote the worker's bargaining power. Her value increases by $\beta[\mathcal{W}(s) - \mathcal{V} - \mathcal{U}]$ when she gets a job. The value of a firm jumps by $(1 - \beta)[\mathcal{W}(s) - \mathcal{V} - \mathcal{U}]$. The conclusions in this section would be unchanged by this bargaining rule.

23. This wage-setting procedure is equivalent to other job auctions (Shimer, 1997). For example, workers may not know the number of competing applicants. They bid for jobs by committing to a wage if they are hired, and the firm accepts the worker who demands the lowest wage. Although the analysis is more complex, since one must solve for the equilibrium (mixed) bidding strategy, the conclusions are unchanged. In particular, $\mathcal{U}$ and $\mathcal{V}$ are the same as with this wage-setting rule. This is essentially an application of the revenue equivalence theorem (Riley and Samuelson, 1981).

Here y represents a worker's exogenous unemployment benefit or value of leisure. With flow probability e^{-q} the worker is the only applicant for a vacancy when it closes, and so enjoys a capital gain. Similarly, the value of a vacant firm satisfies

$$r\mathcal{V} = -c + \pi[1 - e^{-q}(1 + q)][\mathcal{W}(s) - \mathcal{V} - \mathcal{U}] \tag{11}$$

where c is the cost of maintaining an open vacancy. When the vacancy closes, there is a probability e^{-q} of there being no applicants. The firm must reopen the vacancy. With probability qe^{-q}, the firm receives one application, and so hires the applicant; but she keeps the whole surplus. Otherwise the firm enjoys a capital gain. Equations (8), (9), (10), and (11) can be solved for the endogenous variables $\underline{x}$, $\mathcal{U}$, $\mathcal{V}$, and $\mathcal{W}$ as functions of the various parameters and the unemployment–vacancy ratio q.

Finally, since conditional on a vacancy closing with n other applicants, a worker is hired with probability $1/(n + 1)$, the flow rate at which she is hired is

$$M = \pi \sum_{n=0}^{\infty} \frac{q^n e^{-q}}{(n + 1)!} = \pi \frac{1 - e^{-q}}{q}. \tag{12}$$

Thus M is a simple function of the unemployment–vacancy ratio q as well. If q does not depend on the age distribution of the population, the disaggregate unemployment rates do not depend on the age distribution, and a demographic adjustment for the baby boom is justified.

3.5 CONCLUSION

What does it mean for q to be independent of the age distribution? The most sensible interpretation is that job creation and labor demand are perfectly elastic. If free entry drives the value of a vacant job, $\mathcal{V}$, to zero, one can solve for the equilibrium values of q and $\mathcal{U}$ with no reference to the age distribution. Essentially, changes in labor supply are accommodated by changes in labor demand, leaving the hiring rate M and separation threshold $\underline{x}$ unchanged.

The evidence on the elasticity of labor demand is mixed. More populous countries do not have higher unemployment rates, so the cross-sectional evidence is that labor demand is elastic. But it is less clear whether this is true within countries over medium time horizons. Katz and Murphy (1992) argue that from 1965 to 1980, wages tended to decrease for a group of workers when the size of that group increased, evidence for relatively stable labor demand curves. During the 1980s, wages tended to increase, suggesting that labor demand might have *overreacted* to labor-supply shifts. Also, Krueger and Pischke (1997) argue that the U.S. "employment miracle" is due to the ability of the labor market to absorb large changes in supply. They cite the wage *decreases* for young workers at the time that the baby bust entered the labor force as supporting evidence. Another famous example is the large migration of Cubans to Miami, which had little effect on wages in Miami (Card, 1990). Thus the benchmark model offers a simple, plausible condition under which the baby boom should have had no effect on disaggregate unemployment rates, and the demographic adjustment performed in Section 2 is justified.

4. Low Skilled Unemployment

I now turn to the source of low skilled unemployment. Skilled workers have a lower unemployment rate because their skills are most useful while they are employed. The gap between their productivity while employed and while unemployed is large, and so the cost of searching for a job is small compared to the potential reward. Similarly, firms will spend much more effort recruiting skilled workers. There is even an industry ("headhunters") that attempts to match skilled workers with jobs. Reinforcing this effect, the large gap between skilled workers' productivity s and reservation wage $\underline{x}$ implies that they are much less likely to be fired during downturns. In short, skilled workers are rarely fired, and have a relatively easy time finding a job when they are.

Since more-educated workers tend to be more skilled, increases in education raise the fraction of the population in low unemployment categories. This suggests a demographic adjustment is merited. There are at least two objections to this reasoning. First, the absolute level of education may be less important than relative education attainment. An increase in the percentage of job seekers with a college degree not only increases the competition for jobs among college graduates, but puts workers with only a high-school diploma at a further disadvantage. Thus the unemployment rate of all education levels may increase when all workers get more education, even if the aggregate unemployment rate is unchanged. A demographic adjustment would incorrectly interpret this as a demographic reduction in unemployment and an offsetting genuine increase, and so is misleading.

Second, the fact that more-educated workers tend to be more skilled does not imply that increases in education raise the skill level of the labor force. This point is crystallized by Spence's (1973) job-market signaling model. If education is more costly for low-ability workers, it may be used to indicate ability to future employers, and hence may be undertaken even if it conveys no direct benefit. Changes in the cost of education or the return to ability may then alter workers' education decision, but this has no effect on the skill distribution. More generally, if education is positively correlated with ability, the average college graduate today is less able than the average college graduate was twenty years ago. Again, a demographic adjustment for education overstates the true effect of a change in education.

4.1 A MODEL OF RELATIVE EDUCATIONAL ATTAINMENT

I begin by showing that if employers only care about workers' relative educational attainment, demographic adjustments are extremely misleading.[24] I extend the model in Section 3 by assuming that when workers are born, they are randomly and independently assigned an educational attainment or schooling level $s \in S \subset \mathbb{R}_+$. Let $g : S \mapsto \mathbb{R}_+$ represent the atomless density of educational attainment.

I make two simplifications to the basic model. First, the population growth rate is a constant $\dot{N}(t)/N(t) \equiv \gamma > 0$. Second, when a type-$s$ worker gets a job, her productivity is equal to s and is constant thereafter. In the language of Section 3, $\sigma = 0$. As a result, jobs last forever, and I can ignore job destruction. With this assumption, it is obviously not true that more-educated workers lose their jobs less frequently. However, it simplifies the analysis considerably: equation (8) implies that the value of a type-s job is $\mathcal{W}^*(s) \equiv s/r$. This helps elucidate the main point, which is about relative rates of job creation. The analysis here could be extended to allow $\sigma > 0$ without qualitatively changing the results.

Balanced-Growth Path. I look for a balanced growth path. On this path, the type-dependent flow matching probabilities $M(s)$ are constant over time, so the unemployment rate of type-s workers at age t is $e^{-M(s)t}$. Using the fact that age-t workers constitute a density $\gamma e^{-\gamma t}$ of the labor force at any point in time, the unemployment rate of the average type-s worker, aggregating across age cohorts, is

$$\tilde{u}(s) = \frac{\gamma}{\gamma + M(s)}. \tag{13}$$

---

24. This is related to the point made by Blanchard and Diamond (1994) that if firms prefer to hire workers who have been unemployed for less time, a worker's relative, not absolute, unemployment duration affects her probability of finding a job. The model here is an extension of Blanchard and Diamond (1995) and Shimer (1997).

This is decreasing in the flow matching probability for obvious reasons. It is increasing in the population growth rate, since fast population growth increases the relative proportion of young workers.

It is also convenient to define the fraction of unemployed workers with schooling less than s:

$$\theta(s) = \frac{\int_0^s \bar{u}(s')g(s')\,ds'}{U}, \tag{14}$$

where $U \equiv \int_s \bar{u}(s)g(s)\,ds$ is the aggregate unemployment rate.

Matching Probabilities. The job search process is a generalization of the process described in Section 3.3. In this stylized model, there is only one type of job, so college graduates and high-school dropouts compete directly against each other for jobs. This represents a more realistic world of *interlinked competition*, in which college graduates compete against workers with some college education, and workers with some college education apply for other jobs, in which they compete against high-school graduates, who apply for still other jobs in which they compete against dropouts.

Job vacancies close with flow probability π. The number of other applicants is a Poisson random variable with expectation q. I assume that the most educated applicant always gets the job, and verify in the next paragraph that this ranking rule is an equilibrium.[25] Thus s is hired with flow probability

$$M(s) = \pi e^{-q[1-\theta(s)]}. \tag{15}$$

Since $\theta(s)$ is monotonically increasing, less-educated workers are hired less frequently, and so have a higher unemployment rate.

Now return to the assumption that the most educated applicant is always hired. To verify this, I must generalize the multilateral bargaining game to this environment. If there is only one applicant s for a job, she retains the entire match surplus $\mathcal{W}^*(s) - \mathcal{U}(s) - \mathcal{V}$. If there are multiple applicants, the firm cannot extract the most educated applicant's entire

25. One can also prove that the equilibrium is unique. See Shimer (1997), which also argues that for a wide range of wage determination procedures, more-productive workers will always be hired in preference to less-productive ones. This contrasts with Blanchard and Diamond (1995), which shows that with the Nash bargaining rule described in footnote 24, lower-quality workers may be ranked ahead of higher-quality ones. The important distinction is whether the presence of workers who are not hired affects the wage of workers who are hired.

value, but it instead extracts the value that it would get if it hired the second most educated applicant and retained the entire surplus. If the second highest applicant's type is s', then s enjoys a gain $[W^{*}(s) - \mathcal{U}(s)]$ $- [W^{*}(s') - \mathcal{U}(s')]$. For s to be willing to outbid s', this must be positive.

Using this bargaining rule, one can prove that

$$r\mathcal{U}'(s) = M(s)[W^{*\prime}(s) - \mathcal{U}'(s)]. \tag{16}$$

Intuitively, the gain to a small increase in schooling ds is that with probability $M(s + ds)$, a type $s + ds$ worker is hired, and in that event she keeps an extra bit of surplus $[W^{*\prime}(s) - \mathcal{U}'(s)]\,ds$. The fact that she is hired more often, $M(s + ds) - M(s) \approx M'(s)\,ds > 0$, is a second-order effect. To the extent that $s + ds$ is hired more often than s, this happens only if she is hired in preference to some s' between s and $s + ds$. The value of the job to s' is nearly the same as the value to $s + ds$, so multilateral bargaining holds $s + ds$ nearly to her reservation value.

The return to education, $\mathcal{U}'(s)$, is strictly positive but less than the productivity increase $W^{*\prime}(s) \equiv 1/r$. This implies that the match surplus $W^{*}(s) - \mathcal{U}(s) - V$ is increasing in s, so more-educated workers will always outbid less-educated ones. The ranking rule described here is in fact an equilibrium, and so the probability that a type-s worker is hired is given by (15).

Effect of Demographics. Now I can address the effect of an increase in education on unemployment. I begin by showing that the aggregate unemployment rate does not depend on demographics g. Rewriting the education-specific unemployment rate (13) as $\tilde{u}(s) = 1 - M(s)\tilde{u}(s)/\gamma(s)$, the aggregate unemployment rate satisfies

$$U = \int_{s}\left(1 - \frac{M(s)\tilde{u}(s)}{\gamma}\right)g(s)\,ds.$$

Expanding $M(s)$ and then using the fact that $\theta'(s) = \tilde{u}(s)g(s)/U$ yields

$$U = 1 - \frac{\pi}{\gamma}\int_{s}e^{-q[1-\theta(s)]}\tilde{u}(s)g(s)\,ds = 1 - \frac{\pi}{\gamma}\frac{e^{-q}}{q}U.$$

This is easily solved for U with no reference to the schooling distribution g. Since changes in schooling have no effect on unemployment, any demographic adjustment is completely spurious.

Despite this, under the maintained hypothesis, demographic changes would lead us to make significant demographic adjustments. This is because demographic changes affect disaggregate unemployment rates, a violation of the maintained hypothesis. Consider the effect of a first-order stochastic dominating "improvement" in the schooling density from g_1 to g_2.[26] That is, for all $s \in \tilde{S} \subseteq S$,

$$\int_0^s g_1(s') \, ds' > \int_0^s g_2(s') \, ds' \tag{17}$$

with a weak inequality for $s \in S \setminus \tilde{S}$. I will prove that this raises all the type-contingent unemployment rates:

$$\tilde{u}_1(s) < \tilde{u}_2(s) \qquad \text{for all} \quad s \in \tilde{S}. \tag{18}$$

I omit the similar proof that the unemployment rates are equal for other $s \in S \setminus \tilde{S}$.

According to (13), my claim is equivalent to $M_1(s) > M_2(s)$ for all s; by (15), that is equivalent to $\theta_1(s) > \theta_2(s)$ for all s. So in order to find a contradiction, assume that $\theta_1(s) \leq \theta_2(s)$ for some s. By (14) and the fact that aggregate unemployment U is unchanged,

$$\int_0^s \tilde{u}_1(s') g_1(s') \, ds' \leq \int_0^s \tilde{u}_2(s') g_2(s') \, ds'.$$

Subtract this from (17), multiply both sides by γ, and then again apply the relationship $\gamma[1 - \tilde{u}_i(s')] = M_i(s')\tilde{u}_i(s')$:

$$\int_0^s M_1(s')\tilde{u}_1(s')g_1(s') \, ds' > \int_0^s M_2(s')\tilde{u}_2(s')g_2(s') \, ds'.$$

Now replace $M_i(s')$ using (15), and evaluate the resulting integrals to find $e^{-q[1 - \theta_1(s)]} > e^{-q[1 - \theta_2(s)]}$ or $\theta_1(s) > \theta_2(s)$, contradicting our hypothesis and establishing (18).

Now suppose one naïvely calculated the change in the "genuine unemployment rate" as in Section 2:

$$U_{2,1}^G - U_{1,1}^G = \int_s g_1(s)[\tilde{u}_2(s) - \tilde{u}_1(s)] \, ds = \int_{\tilde{s}} g_1(s)[\tilde{u}_2(s) - \tilde{u}_1(s)] \, ds > 0,$$

where the inequality is an application of (18). One would mistakenly interpret the increase in type-specific unemployment rates as a genuine increase in unemployment. Conversely, one would find that the "demographic" decline in unemployment exactly offsets the "genuine" in-

---

26. I perform a comparative statics exercise here, though recent decades are probably better characterized by a transition to a new steady state. These results also hold along the transition path.

crease: $U_{2,1}^D - U_{1,1}^D = -(U_{2,1}^G - U_{1,1}^G) < 0$. But we just proved that the aggregate unemployment rate is unaffected by demographics! Thus this model illustrates a case in which demographic adjustments are theoretical nonsense and extremely misleading.

The Difference between Age and Education. An important question is why this model describes the effect of changes in the schooling distribution, but cannot be altered to describe the effect of changes in the age distribution. That is, another potential explanation for youth unemployment is that firms hire older workers in preference to younger ones. The problem with this explanation is that it has the counterfactual prediction that older workers have a shorter unemployment duration. As I discussed at the start of Section 3, youth unemployment is a consequence of the short duration of jobs, not the length of unemployment spells. Thus an argument that "relative age not absolute age" matters appears incorrect. Section 5 also provides empirical evidence that changes in schooling have very different effects than changes in the age distribution.

4.2 ENDOGENOUS EDUCATION

My analysis has glossed over one important issue: an increase in skills raises the value of a vacancy in the ranking model. In treating q as exogenous, I have implicitly assumed that labor demand is perfectly inelastic in the long run. The analytical proof of this is an algebraic mess, but the intuition is clear. The value of a firm is increasing in the skill of the second best applicant, since surplus is increasing in skill by equation (16). The expected skill level of this applicant is higher when the labor force is more skilled.

Making q endogenous and $\mathcal{V}$ exogenous through an elastic job creation condition clouds the analysis considerably. With elastic labor demand, the increase in the value of a vacancy will cause entry, which will reduce aggregate unemployment. Some of the disaggregate unemployment rates will decrease, although many will continue to increase. A demographic adjustment is still misleading, since one would conclude that there had been a sharp demographic decline in unemployment, partially offset by a genuine increase. However, it would be less misleading than the analysis in the text suggests.

Ability Bias. Fortunately, this issue is probably not very relevant, because a change in education is unlikely to have as large an effect on unemployment as Figure 14 suggests. The key reason for this, and another important difference between age and education, is that educational choice is endogenous. A number of theories predict that more-able workers will opt for more education, so some of the unemployment rate differential attributed to education is in fact due to ability differences. Since we cannot observe workers' ability in the Current Population Survey (CPS), this problem is not easily corrected.

The basic issue is illustrated with another small extension to the model. When workers are born, they are endowed exogenously with an ability a drawn from a known density $\tilde{g}$. They are then given an option to invest in a unit of education (go to college) at unit cost. If they go to college, they are left with skill $s = a + b$. If they do not make the investment (drop out of high school), $s = a$. The decision is irreversible. The rest of the model is unchanged. In particular, a worker's productivity is equal to her skill.

A college degree is worth more to a more able worker. The reason is that she will be employed more frequently, and therefore she makes better use of her educational investment. More formally, (16) implies that $\mathcal{U}'$ is increasing, since M is increasing. Convexity of $\mathcal{U}$ implies that the slope of the secant, $[\mathcal{U}(a + b) - \mathcal{U}(a)]/b$, is increasing in ability a. There is a threshold $\bar{a}$ such that workers with higher ability go to college, while those with lower ability drop out.

Since workers who go to college are more able and better educated, they are more skilled. Following the logic of the first part of this section, they are always hired in preference to dropouts, and so have a lower unemployment rate. However, this is not because they went to college. In this simple model, any college graduate is more able than all the dropouts, and so would have been hired in preference to them even if she had not gone to college. Likewise, if a high-school dropout went to college, she would still be ranked below college graduates, and so would be unemployed more frequently. More to the point, despite the fact that the returns to education are positive and that college graduates have a lower unemployment rate than dropouts, the unemployment rate of college graduates would be the same if none of them went to college; and the unemployment rate of high-school dropouts would be the same if all of them went to college.

To see why this matters, suppose there is a decrease in the cost of education or an increase in the returns to education. The threshold for attending college will fall. Since the marginal college graduate is of lower ability than the rest of the college graduates, this reduces the quality of the average college graduate. Since she is of higher ability than all the dropouts, it also reduces the quality of the average dropout. If we could observe workers' ability, we would realize that neither relative rankings nor unemployment rates conditional on ability have changed. We would conclude that there had been no change in unemployment, demographic or genuine. But since we observe education, not ability, we would see that unemployment has increased for both groups. A demographic adjustment would mistake this for a genuine increase in unemployment offset by a demographic decline. The fact that ability is unobservable leads to a further bias in the demographically adjusted unemployment rate.

Education as a Signal. Spence's (1973) signaling model affords an extreme case where education has no effect on skills, and so a change in the education distribution has no effect on the value of a vacancy.[27] People pay the high cost of a college degree and forgo years of labor income, because if they did not use this costly signal, they would be unable to obtain a high wage.

Suppose firms cannot observe applicants' skill but can observe how much they have invested in education, now a continuous choice variable $b \geq 0$. Applicants make wage demands, and the firm hires the applicant who it expects will yield the most profit, retaining the expected profit from the second most attractive applicant. To do this, the firm must form beliefs about each applicant's skill based on its knowledge of her education and the relationship between skill and education. The most interesting case is a separating equilibrium, in which more-skilled workers choose more education: $b = B(s)$ for some strictly increasing function B. This implies that upon observing education b, the firm can simply invert the education schedule B to calculate the implied skill. The firm believes that it has complete information, and so we can apply the analysis of the case with exogenous skill (Section 4.1). Firms always hire the most educated applicant, so the hiring rate as a function of education must satisfy an analogue of equation (15):

$$\tilde{M}(b) = \pi e^{-q[1 - \theta(B^{-1}(b))]},$$

where $B^{-1}(b)$ is the skill of a worker who chooses b units of education in equilibrium.

What keeps an unskilled worker from getting a lot of education and claiming that she is skilled? If she did so, she would be hired more rapidly, and more importantly, would be able to demand higher wages. The marginal value of an additional unit of education for an unemployed worker is the analogue of equation (16):

27. Recent papers by Farber and Gibbons (1996) and especially Altonji and Pierret (1997) provide empirical support for the notion that firms discriminate statistically on the basis of education, so education indeed serves as a costly signal. However, they conclude that education raises productivity as well.

$$\tilde{u}'(b) = \frac{\tilde{M}(b)}{r + \tilde{M}(b)} \mathcal{W}'(B^{-1}(b)).$$

This does not depend on a worker's skill.[28] Thus to sustain a separating equilibrium, we require that the cost of education depend on a worker's skill $C(b,s)$. More precisely, we need a single-crossing property that the marginal cost of education is lower for abler workers. Given this restriction, a simple revealed-preference argument implies that high-skilled workers will opt for more education,[29] and strictly so if C is a continuously differentiable function (Edlin and Shannon, 1996).

Consider the effect of an increase in the returns to skill (skill-biased technical change), modeled as an increase in $\mathcal{W}'(s)$. To restore a separating equilibrium, all workers must endure more of the costly signal. Otherwise, it would pay unskilled workers to imitate the education choice of skilled workers. It is clear that this change in education can have no real effect on the economy, since it is simply a change in the expenditure on the costly signal. In particular, it gives firms neither more nor less of an incentive to create jobs. Despite this, because we cannot observe the decline in skill conditional on education, we would measure it as an increase in unemployment conditional on education. This is then misinterpreted as a genuine increase in unemployment, offset by the increase in expenditures on education, the costly signal.

5. How Much do Demographics Explain?

I have shown that there are theoretical reasons why demographic adjustments to the unemployment rate may or may not be appropriate, but ultimately this is an empirical question. If changes in a group's labor-market share $\omega(i)$ do not affect any disaggregate unemployment rate $u(j)$, then $U^G_{t_1,t_0}$ is an accurate measure of what the unemployment rate would be at time t_1 if the demographics looked as they did in period t_0. The difference $U_{t_1} - U^G_{t_1,t_0}$ measures how much the unemployment rate increased due to demographics. Similarly, $U^P_{t_1,t_0}$ is an accurate measure of what the unemployment rate would be if the only changes had been demographic, so $U^P_{t_1,t_0} - U_{t_0}$ is another measure of how much the unem-

---

28. I am implicitly assuming that firms cannot punish workers who "lie" about their skill by choosing the "wrong" amount of education, $b \neq B(s)$. Firms must learn a worker's skill when they observe her productivity, and so I am imposing that contracts are incomplete.

29. Proof: Take $s > s'$ who choose education b and b' respectively. Revealed preference implies $\tilde{U}(b) - C(b, s) \geq \tilde{U}(b') - C(b', s)$ and $\tilde{U}(b') - C(b', s') \geq \tilde{U}(b) - C(b, s')$. Add these inequalities, and use the single-crossing property to prove $b \geq b'$.

ployment rate increased due to demographics. To the extent that U_{t_1} − $U_{t_1,t_0}^G \neq U_{t_1,t_0}^D - U_{t_0}$, the quantities U^G and U^D are poor measures of genuine and demographic unemployment.

With a little algebraic manipulation, one finds that

$$(U_{t_1} - U_{t_1,t_0}^G) - (U_{t_1,t_0}^D - U_{t_0}) = \sum_{i \in I} [\omega_{t_1}(i) - \omega_{t_0}(i)][u_{t_1}(i) - u_{t_0}(i)]$$

$$= \sum_{i \in I} [\omega_{t_1}(i) - \omega_{t_0}(i)]\{[u_{t_1}(i) - U_{t_1}] - [u_{t_0}(i) - U_{t_0}]\}.$$

If this number is positive, groups that increase their labor-market share tend to have *relative* increases in unemployment.[30] The problem with using this as a measure of the quality of demographic adjustments is that if demographic changes or relative unemployment-rate changes are small, this inner product (covariance) will be small. Therefore I construct a measure that normalizes by the size of these changes, analogous to a correlation:

$$\rho = \frac{(\vec{\omega}_{t_1} - \vec{\omega}_{t_0}) \cdot (\vec{u}_{t_1} - \vec{u}_{t_0})}{|\vec{\omega}_{t_1} - \vec{\omega}_{t_0}| \, |\vec{u}_{t_1} - \vec{u}_{t_0}|} \in [+1,1],$$

where $\vec{\omega}$ and $\vec{u}$ are the vectors of labor-market shares and disaggregate unemployment rates, and the vertical bars indicate the Euclidean length of the indicated vectors. If ρ is positive, then there is a relatively large increase in unemployment for groups that grow relatively larger. If ρ is negative, then groups that grow larger had a relative decline in unemployment. Only if $\rho = 0$ do U^G and U^D have the desired interpretations.

Table 2 shows the value of ρ obtained by dividing the population according to age and education. These estimates are fairly robust to changes in the time period. For example, changing the initial or terminal time by one year does not change the sign of any of the entries.

Education. I discuss the negative results for education, before moving on to the positive results for age. The second column of Table 2 shows that when an education category gets smaller, its members' unemployment rate increases relatively more. This reflects the disproportionate increase in unemployment for high-school dropouts (Figure 13). This is inconsistent with a model in which the reduced supply of high-school dropouts has made them a scarce resource.

However, it is consistent with the models suggested in Section 4. First,

---

30. This is similar to the method used by Katz and Murphy (1992) to test for relative demand shifts.

Table 2 MEASURES OF THE
CORRELATION BETWEEN A
GROUP'S GROWTH IN
LABOR-MARKET SHARE
AND ITS RELATIVE
GROWTH IN
UNEMPLOYMENT

| | Correlation | |
Year	Age	Education
1957–69	0.35	—
1969–79	0.29	−0.48
1979–89	0.44	−0.77
1989–97	−0.09	−0.24

*Comparisons are March to March for the indicated years.
Data availability precludes calculating this for education
from 1957 to 1970; the first entry is for 1970–1979.*

the ranking model tells us that the increase in a skill group's unemployment rate for a decrease in the relative ranking is larger in magnitude for groups that are unemployed more frequently (low-skilled workers). To see this, differentiate equations (13) and (15):

$$\frac{\partial \tilde{u}(s)}{\partial \theta(s)} = -q\tilde{u}(s)[1 - \tilde{u}(s)].$$

Since $\tilde{u}(s)$ is decreasing in skill, the magnitude of this partial derivative is decreasing in s as long as the skill group's unemployment rate is less than 50%. Intuitively, the most-skilled workers find jobs almost instantly, and so if they fall slightly down the ladder, they will suffer only a slight increase in unemployment (but a larger percentage increase).

A second explanation for the negative correlation is that when high-school dropouts constituted almost 40% of the labor force in 1970, lack of a high-school degree did not signal anything special. In contrast, now all but the very least-skilled, lowest-ability workers stay in high school, so that there is a precipitous drop in the quality of high-school graduates. In summary, the maintained hypothesis that changes in education have no effect on unemployment rates conditional on education is false, making a demographic adjustment for changes in education severely overestimate the actual impact of changes in education. I conclude that the logic of adjusting for changes in labor-force composition does not apply to changes in education, contrary to Summers (1986).

Age. The first column of Table 2 shows that from 1957 to 1989, age groups that increased in size had a correspondingly larger increase in unemployment. Looking back at Figure 2, this is saying that the youth unemployment rate increased disproportionately from 1957 to 1978, and then decreased disproportionately from 1978 to 1989. Since 1989, there has been a negative correlation between changes in labor-market share and changes in unemployment. However, the magnitude is much smaller, and is exactly zero for the interval 1988–1997.

The maintained hypothesis, that changes in age structure do not affect disaggregate unemployment rates, appears to be false. The baby boom caused an increase in youth unemployment, and so estimates like Δ and U^D *understate* the size of the demographic unemployment increase. The question is, by how much?

The theory in Section 3 provides some guidance. Suppose labor demand is not perfectly elastic, even in the long run. When the baby boom entered the labor market, there was a sharp increase in the number of unemployed workers, without a correspondingly large increase in the number of vacancies. From equation (12), the increase in the equilibrium unemployment–vacancy ratio q reduced the hiring rate M. However, it had an ambiguous effect on the separation threshold $\underline{x}$. To see why, recall that by (9), the separation threshold is increasing in $\mathcal{U} + \mathcal{V}$. Adding (10) and (11) implies[31]

$$r(\mathcal{U} + \mathcal{V}) = y - c + \pi(1 - qe^{-q})[\mathcal{W}(s) - \mathcal{U} - \mathcal{V}].$$

Thus if qe^{-q} is increasing in q, as is the case for $q < 1$, an increase in the relative number of unemployed workers reduces $\mathcal{U} + \mathcal{V}$ and $\underline{x}$. If $q > 1$, then qe^{-q} is decreasing in q, and so the separation threshold is increasing in q.

As the baby boom was gradually absorbed into the employed population, the unemployment–vacancy ratio slowly returned to its previous levels, restoring the old hiring rate and separation threshold. In short, the entry of the baby boom led to a temporary reduction in hiring rates, and perhaps a small change in separations. For prime-age workers entrenched in stable jobs, this had little effect. However, it led to two decades of high youth unemployment.

A reasonable alternative hypothesis is that the unemployment rate of prime-age workers, say the unemployment rate of workers aged 35–64,

---

31. Interpreting this expression is complicated by the fact that $\mathcal{W}(s)$ depends on $\mathcal{U} + \mathcal{V}$ through (8) and (9). Still, the joint gain from creating a new job, $\mathcal{W}(s) - \mathcal{U} - \mathcal{V}$, is decreasing in $\mathcal{U} + \mathcal{V}$.

Figure 19 GENUINE UNEMPLOYMENT, DEFINED AS THE PART OF
UNEMPLOYMENT THAT CAN BE PREDICTED FROM PRIME-AGE
UNEMPLOYMENT

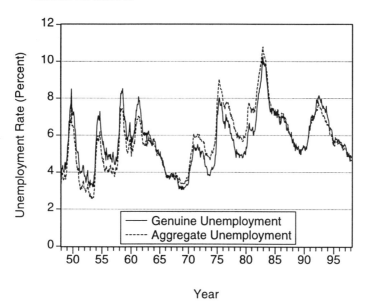

Year

Prime-age workers are aged 35–65.

was unaffected by the baby boom.[32] The part of aggregate unemployment that can be predicted by this series is genuine. The orthogonal residual is demographic. That is, I regress aggregate unemployment on a constant and the prime-age unemployment rate, yielding

$$U_t = 0.0051 + 1.3531\ u_t(\text{prime}) + \epsilon_t, \qquad R^2 = 0.834$$
$$\quad (0.0010) \quad (0.0246)$$

(standard errors in parentheses). Genuine unemployment is $0.0051 + 1.3531u_t$(prime) (Figure 19). Notably, this is approximately the same in 1957, 1979, 1989, and 1998, as the prime-age unemployment rate has not changed over long time horizons. The demographic unemployment rate

32. If q is much smaller than 1, the prime-age unemployment rate may have dropped, because the decrease in job destruction from the reduced threshold outweighed the decrease in job creation from the reduced hiring rate. Under these conditions, the alternative hypothesis overstates the effect of the baby boom on unemployment. However, for $q \geq 1$, the unemployment rate of prime-age workers unambiguously increased because of the baby boom. Job destruction increased and job creation fell. Then the analysis here understates the effect of the baby boom on unemployment.

at time *t* is the residual $\hat{\epsilon}_t$ (Figure 20). The shape of the series looks very much like the age-adjusted series in Figures 5 and 6, but the magnitude of the adjustment is much larger. A Hodrick–Prescott (HP) filter of the residuals removes the high-frequency fluctuations and shows that the baby boom explains about a 180-basis-point increase in demographic unemployment from 1959 to 1980, and more than a 145-basis-point decline in demographic unemployment from 1980 to 1993, offset by a slight increase in the last five years.

Despite the crudeness of this measure of demographic unemployment, the result is robust. I illustrate this in three ways. First, the definition of prime age is not very important. Using the unemployment rate of workers aged 35–54 or 35+ as our measure of prime-age unemployment has no discernable effect on the demographic unemployment rate. Including younger workers aged 25–34 in our measure reduces the magnitude of the residuals by about half, as would be expected if these workers still have some characteristics of youth.

Second, omitting extreme cyclical fluctuations in unemployment does not affect the result. I regressed an HP-filtered series for aggregate unem-

Figure 20 CHANGES IN DEMOGRAPHIC UNEMPLOYMENT, DEFINED AS THE UNPREDICTABLE RESIDUAL, TOGETHER WITH A HODRICK–PRESCOTT FILTER OF THE RESIDUALS

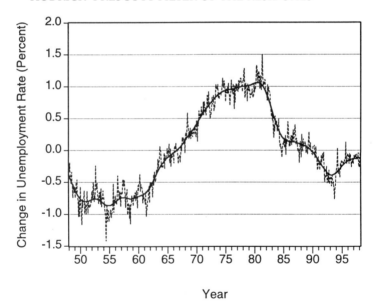

Prime-age workers are aged 35–65.

Figure 21 A SMOOTHED SERIES OF DEMOGRAPHIC UNEMPLOYMENT
FITS EASILY WITHIN STAIGER, STOCK, AND WATSON'S 95%
CONFIDENCE INTERVAL FOR THE NAIRU

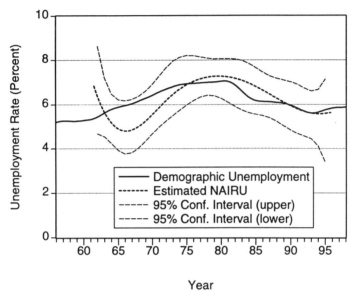

Year

Thanks to Mark Watson for providing me with the calculation of the NAIRU.

ployment on an HP-filtered series for prime-age unemployment.[33] The
residuals are nearly identical to the HP-filtered residuals in the basic
regression.

Third, since female participation has increased enormously during
these decades, I regressed aggregate unemployment on the unemployment rate of men aged 35–64. The peak of the HP-filtered residual
increased by about 50 basis points compared to the basic regression,
without any other substantial effect. According to this calculation, the
demographic portion of unemployment rose by 250 basis points from
1953 to 1976, and has subsequently fallen by 200 basis points.

Any variant of these numbers is large. For example, compare my series
for the demographic component of unemployment with Staiger, Stock,
and Watson's (1997) nonstructurally estimated series for the NAIRU,
which presumably represents some sort of equilibrium rate of unemployment. Figure 21 reproduces Staiger, Stock, and Watson's (1997) point
estimate for the NAIRU and their 95% confidence interval. I then juxta-

33. Thanks to Richard Rogerson for suggesting this calculation.

pose the HP-filtered residuals from Figure 20, renormalizing the mean of the residuals to 6%, which represents long-run average unemployment. My series for the demographic component of unemployment fits easily within the confidence interval, and actually reproduces their point estimate of the NAIRU quite well, except during the Vietnam War.

I conclude that changes in the age composition of the labor force explain the bulk of the rise in unemployment during the fifties and sixties, and the subsequent decline in the eighties and nineties. However, the simplest demographic story, that a group's unemployment rate is unaffected by the size of that group, is inadequate. The entry of the baby boom into the labor force led to an increase in youth unemployment, multiplying the size of the demographic shock from a direct effect of about 80 basis points (the estimate of the change in Δ from Section 2) to nearly 200 basis points. The subsequent effect of the aging of the baby boom has been almost as important, again multiplying the size of the demographic shock from about 80 basis points to at least 120. The answer to why the U.S. unemployment rate is so much lower is that the population is so much older.

REFERENCES

Acemoglu, D., and R. Shimer. (1997). Efficient unemployment insurance. Mimeo.
Altonji, J., and C. Pierret. (1997). Employer learning and statistical discrimination. Northwestern University. Mimeo.
Blanchard, O., and P. Diamond. (1994). Ranking, unemployment duration, and wages. *Review of Economic Studies* 61(3):417–434.
———, and ———. (1995). Ranking, unemployment duration, and training costs. M.I.T. Mimeo.
Card, D. (1990). The impact of the Mariel boatlift on the Miami labor market. *Industrial and Labor Relations Review* 43(2):245–247.
Clark, K., and L. Summers. (1982). The dynamics of youth unemployment. In *The Youth Labor Market Problem: Its Nature, Causes, and Consequences*, R. Freeman and D. Wise (eds.). Chicago: University of Chicago Press, pp. 199–235.
Council of Economic Advisors. (1997). *Economic Report of the President*. Washington: U.S. Government Printing Office.
Diamond, P., and E. Maskin. (1979). An equilibrium analysis of search and breach of contract, I: Steady states. *Bell Journal of Economics* 10:282–316.
———, and ———. (1981). An equilibrium analysis of search and breach of contract, II: A non-steady state example. *Journal of Economic Theory* 25:165–195.
Edlin, A., and C. Shannon. (1996). Strict monotonicity in comparative statics. University of California, Berkeley. Mimeo.
Farber, H., and R. Gibbons. (1996). Learning and wage dynamics. *Quart. Journal of Economics,* 111(4):1007–1047.
Gordon, R. (1982). Inflation, flexible exchange rates, and the natural rate of unemployment. In *Workers, Jobs and Inflation,* M. Baily (ed.). Washington: Brookings Institute, pp. 89–152.

———. (1997). The time-varying NAIRU and its implications for economic policy. *Journal of Economic Perspectives*, 11(1):11–32.

Greenspan, A. (1997). Monetary policy testimony and report to the congress. Humphrey–Hawkins Testimony, July 22.

Hall, R. (1970). Why is the unemployment rate so high at full employment. *Brookings Papers on Economic Activity,* 33:369–402.

Juhn, C., K. M. Murphy, and R. Topel. (1991). Why has the natural rate of unemployment increased over time. *Brookings Papers on Economic Activity,* 22:75–142.

Karatzas, I., and S. Shreve. (1991). *Brownian Motion and Stochastic Calculus,* 2nd ed. Graduate Texts in Mathematics. New York: Springer-Verlag.

Katz, L., and K. Murphy. (1992). Changes in relative wages, 1963–1987: Supply and demand factors. *Quarterly Journal of Economics,* 107(1):35–78.

Krueger, A., and J.-S. Pischke. (1997). Observations and conjectures on the U.S. employment miracle. Princeton University. Mimeo.

Mortensen, D., and C. Pissarides. (1994). Job creation and job destruction in the theory of unemployment. *Review of Economic Studies* 61:397–415.

Perry, G. (1970). Changing labor markets and inflation. *Brookings Papers on Economic Activity* 33:411–441.

Pissarides, C. (1985). Short-run equilibrium dynamics of unemployment, vacancies, and real wages. *American Economic Review* 75:676–690.

Riley, J., and W. Samuelson. (1981). Optimal auctions. *American Economic Review,* 71(3):381–392.

Shimer, R. (1997). Do good guys come in first? How wage determination affects the ranking of job applicants. Mimeo.

Spence, M. (1973). Job market signaling. *Quarterly Journal of Economics* 87(3):355–374.

Staiger, D., J. Stock, and M. Watson. (1997). The NAIRU, unemployment, and monetary policy. *Journal of Economic Perspectives,* 11(1):33–49.

Summers, L. (1986). Why is the unemployment rate so very high near full employment? *Brookings Papers on Economic Activity* 22:339–383.

Ventura, S., J. Martin, T. Mathews, and S. Clarke. (1996). Advance report of final natality statistics, 1994. *Monthly Vital Statistics Report* 44(11 Supplement):1–87.

Comment

RICHARD ROGERSON
University of Pennsylvania

The recent decrease in the U.S. unemployment rate to levels not seen in almost three decades has attracted much attention from policymakers and media analysts. Following nearly two decades of secular increases in the unemployment rate, many are inclined to view this recent development as evidence of some fundamental improvement in the state of the U.S. economy, due either to improvements in productivity, good policymaking, or both. Shimer deflates this view by arguing that much of the secular

Table 1   AGGREGATE AND DISAGGREGATED U.S. UNEMPLOYMENT

| | Unemployment Rate (%) | | | |
Year	Total	Male 16–19	Male 35–44	Male 55–64
1952	3.0	8.9	1.9	2.4
1957	4.3	12.4	2.8	3.5
1960	5.5	15.3	3.8	4.6
1969	3.5	11.4	1.5	1.8
1974	5.6	15.6	2.6	2.6
1979	5.8	15.9	2.9	2.7
1989	5.3	15.9	3.7	3.5
1997	4.9	16.9	3.6	3.1

change in unemployment over the last three decades can be attributed to the simple process of the aging of the baby-boom generation.

I am largely persuaded by the author's main point. I will begin my comments by offering a slightly different presentation of the facts. This serves two purposes: first, it provides direct support for the important role that compositional effects have had on the aggregate unemployment rate, and second, it highlights another important secular trend in the labor market that recent discussions seem to gloss over.

Consider Table 1. The years for this table were chosen to correspond to similar points of the business cycle, with the exception of 1997, which is simply the most recent (complete) year in the current expansion. The first column, which displays the aggregate unemployment rate, presents the following picture. After World War II there was a secular increase in unemployment, followed by a substantial drop during the 1960s. This was followed by another period of secular increase, which continued into the 1980s. In the most recent period the unemployment rate has declined significantly. It is natural to ask what lies behind these low-frequency waves in the aggregate unemployment rate. This paper is specifically concerned with what has given rise to the most recent wave.

Consider first, however, the data in the next three columns of Table 1, which show unemployment rates for males of three different age groups. It is quite remarkable that while there is some evidence of a decrease in unemployment for some of these groups in the 1990s, each of them shows a substantial increase relative to 1979—despite the fact that the aggregate unemployment rate has increased by almost a full percentage point. In particular, the first wave seems quite different from the second wave in that the 1960s witnessed not only a decrease in aggregate unemployment but also a decrease in the unemployment rate for each of the age groups displayed.

Table 2 pursues this issue a bit further by showing some additional information for males aged 35–44, which is traditionally the group with the strongest attachment to the labor force and hence of particular interest.

It is remarkable that if one looks at the employment-to-population ratio for this group, there is no secular decline in the post-1969 period. The basic message one gets from this table is that there is no puzzle about declining "unemployment"—rather, the puzzle suggested by these data is how to account for the uninterrupted secular decrease in *employment* among prime-aged males since 1969. Though there has been a slight decrease in the unemployment rate for this group since 1989, it has been accompanied by a substantial drop in both the participation rate and the employment-to-population ratio. Again, the second wave appears very different from the first wave, as the 1960s brought a substantial increase in the employment-to-population ratio of prime-aged males. An important question that I do not have space to go into here concerns the interpretation of the decreased participation rate. I think an argument can be made that the nonparticipating individuals are largely those with poor labor-market opportunities who have stopped searching, and hence are best viewed as discouraged workers.

Finally, Table 3 provides some information on international comparisons using data from the OECD. It is interesting that, in contrast to the picture painted by the aggregate unemployment rate numbers, the U.S. and Europe are basically experiencing a similar phenomenon in terms of employment ratios, though it is clearly more intense in Europe.

Table 2   U.S. LABOR-MARKET DATA FOR MALES AGED 35–44

Year	Unemployment Rate (%)	Participation Rate (%)	Employment/ Population (%)
1952	1.9	97.8	96.0
1957	2.8	97.9	95.1
1960	3.8	97.7	94.0
1969	1.5	96.9	95.5
1974	2.6	96.0	93.5
1979	2.9	95.8	93.0
1989	3.7	95.3	92.2
1997	3.6	92.6	88.9

The data surveyed above lead one to ask three questions:

1. Why has there been a secular decline in employment-to-population ratios for prime-age males in the post-1969 period?
2. Why has this decrease been so much larger in some countries than others?
3. Why does the aggregate unemployment rate behave so differently after 1969 than do the age-specific unemployment rates?

I think it is fair to say that although much work has addressed the first two questions, there is presently no clear consensus on their answers. The present paper is effectively focused on the third question, and having seen the various facts displayed above, it is not surprising that the entry of the baby boom into the labor force and its subsequent aging figure prominently in the answer. The main contribution of this paper, then, is to quantify the effect of the baby boom on the evolution of the unemployment rate over the last three decades.

Young people have much higher unemployment rates than do old people. In trying to assess the dynamic impact of a large cohort on aggregate unemployment, there are two channels to consider. The first is a direct effect—even if the presence of a large cohort has no effect on the labor-market history of any individual, there will be a direct effect on aggregate unemployment due to the change in the age composition of the labor force. The second channel involves potential general equilibrium effects, whereby the presence of a large cohort may affect the labor-market history of each individual, in particular their unemployment experiences. For example, a large group of young workers entering the labor force may plausibly be expected to lead to higher unemployment rates among younger workers as they compete with more people for

Table 3   INTERNATIONAL COMPARISONS FOR MALES 25–54

Year	Unemployment Rate (%)		
	United States	Germany	France
1979	3.4	2.0	3.2
1995	4.4	6.3	8.8
	Employment/Population(%)		
1979	91.2	93.0	93.3
1995	87.6	87.3	86.6

entry-level positions. For other age groups the effects may be more difficult to assess, even at a qualitative level. Intuitively, it would seem to depend on the extent to which older and younger workers are substitutes or complements.

How large is the direct effect? The basic idea is that there is an age-specific unemployment rate for each age, and that these can be used in combination with the age distribution of the labor force to determine the magnitude of the direct effect as the baby-boom cohort enters the labor force and ages. One issue however, is how to determine these age-specific unemployment rates. A quick look at the time-series data reveals that the gap between unemployment of young and old workers is not constant and in fact is subject to a substantial amount of variation. To deal with this issue Shimer carries out a couple of different exercises, one using the unemployment rates from some arbitrary benchmark year, and another using a chain-weighted series. The point estimate that he produces is roughly 0.8%, i.e., the direct effect of the baby boom was to cause an increase of the unemployment rate by 0.8% prior to 1979, and then an 0.8% decrease subsequently.

Another approach is to assess the range of magnitudes for the direct effect, rather than trying to produce a single point estimate. For example, over the period 1950–1980, which includes the period in which the baby-boom cohort enters the labor force, the minimum difference between the unemployment rates of those 16–19 and those 20 and older was 5 percentage points, which obtained in 1953, and the maximum difference was 12.5 percentage points, which obtained in 1976. The increase in the share of 16–19-year-olds in the labor force was approximately 8%. It follows that the minimum direct effect is about 0.4%, while the maximum was about 1%. Shimer's preferred point estimate of 0.8% is not that far from the midpoint of this interval. Redoing this calculation with three age groups (16–19, 20–24, and 25 and older) would also increase the effect somewhat. Using the years 1953 and 1976 as above, and allowing for an increase of 4% in the labor-force share of 20–24-year-olds, the range of estimates for the direct effect is between 0.5% and 1.4%.

At this point I think Shimer has effectively made his main point—basically that the changing age distribution between 1960 and the present may have led to a secular increase and subsequent decrease on the order of 1 percentage point. From Table 1, it is clear that this is a quantitatively significant development.

Shimer goes on to ask how significant the indirect effect may be, in an attempt to give a more definitive estimate for the effect of the baby boom on aggregate unemployment. Here, however, I do not find the analysis very persuasive. The basic objective is to ascertain to what extent the entry of the baby boom into the labor force may have had an additional effect on total unemployment by increasing the unemployment rate of young workers. The main difficulty here is the typical one for this type of exercise: the baby boom entering the labor force is only one of many changes that have potentially affected the unemployment experiences of various labor-market groups, and it is very difficult to sort out the contributions of various shocks by running a single regression.

Shimer's methodology is to assume that the prime-age unemployment rate was unaffected by the baby boom and that the effect of any factors other than the baby boom on aggregate unemployment can be captured by their effect on prime-age male unemployment. It follows that any part of unemployment that is not "explained" in a regression sense by prime-age unemployment can be attributed to the baby boom.

Unfortunately, this methodology seems inadequate. First, as indicated by Table 2, since the unemployment rate for prime-aged males is not necessarily a good indicator of secular patterns in the labor-market experience of these individuals, it is not clear exactly what this unemployment rate is proxying for in terms of secular developments. Second, without naming the other factors that are being considered, how can we judge the reasonableness of the assumption that the baby boom can be assumed to account for the entire residual in the regression equation? Changes in length of schooling, fertility, and marriage rates would all presumably affect the relationship between prime-age unemployment and total unemployment, but these effects should not be attributed to the size of the baby-boom cohort. Additionally, the literature on wage inequality has documented that there were substantial changes in the return to experience since 1970, which may also affect the relative employment prospects of young and prime-aged individuals.

The paper also raises some additional issues of interest, though I will comment on only one of them. It concerns whether the distribution of educational attainment should be viewed analogously to the age distribution from the perspective of accounting for changes in unemployment. Shimer argues not, for the reason that changes in the distribution of education have direct effects that may be largely offsetting to the indirect effects induced by compositional changes. While I don't disagree with the conclusion that he draws, I feel that the analysis ignores a key difference between changes in the age distribution and changes in the educational-attainment distribution: Whereas it seems appropriate to view the baby boom as an exogenous event, this does not seem to be appropriate for thinking about changes in educational attainment. Rather, changes in educational attainment are themselves a response to changes in the economy which affect the incentive for individuals to acquire education. It seems less interesting to ask what would have happened to aggregate unemployment if educational attainment had changed but there had been no change in the factors which affect the choice of educational attainment.

In summary, I think that Shimer has argued persuasively that the changing age composition of the U.S. labor force associated with the baby-boom cohort has had a significant impact on the evolution of the U.S. aggregate unemployment rate. In particular, much of the apparent decline since 1979 may be attributed to this factor. However, while much attention is currently focused on the recent decreases in aggregate unemployment, it is at the expense of attention that should be focused on accounting for what appears to be an underlying secular increase in "true" unemployment since 1969.

Comment

ROBERT TOPEL
University of Chicago and NBER

Robert Shimer has written an intriguing paper on an important topic. While I don't agree with all that he does, I think the bottom line of his paper is largely correct. I also think that the problem he studies has broader importance than he attributes to it.

Unemployment rates are interesting to economists and the general public because they are a sort of summary statistic for the current state of the labor market, and even for the success or failure of economic policies. Given that they are used in these ways, it would be nice if they were comparable over time. Then policymakers who congratulate themselves for being in office when unemployment reached "its lowest level since 19-whatever" would at least be saying something. Part of Shimer's point is that unemployment rates are not comparable over time. The basis of his conclusion is that demographics change, so that unemployment rises and falls as high-unemployment groups become more or less prominent in the labor force. In the 1990s, he points out, high-unemployment youths are a smaller portion of the labor force than in the 1970s. This means that aggregate unemployment will be lower, so that aggregate unemployment does not measure the same thing today as it did 20 years ago. Indeed, Shimer provides strong evidence that changes in labor-force shares of young workers—driven by the baby boom and subsequent baby bust—explain most of the low-frequency changes in measured unemployment from the 1960s to today. On this point, which is his main conclusion, I think he is right.

As an empirical matter Shimer also argues—again I think correctly—that other changes in demographic characteristics of the labor force do not have the same impact as age. Specifically, he points out that secular increases in the average educational attainment of the workforce do not reduce unemployment, as one might expect from the negative cross-sectional relationship between education and unemployment.

Should we be surprised by these findings? Suppose that in 1979 we had asked an economist the following two questions. (Question 1 is easy.)

1. With the aging of the baby-boom generation, the proportion of youths in the labor force will fall over the next two decades. Youths are known to have higher unemployment. Other things being equal, will this demographic change cause aggregate unemployment to be lower in 1998 than it is today?
2. Due to increased educational attainment in successive cohorts, the workforce in 1998 will be more educated than it is today. More-educated workers are known to have lower unemployment rates. Will this demographic change cause aggregate unemployment to be lower in 1998 than it is today?

I think that the right answers, in 1979 and today, are "yes" to question 1 and "probably not" to question 2. Those are the answers provided by Shimer as well, though we differ over the reasons why.

Why "yes" to the first question? In addition to being less skilled, young workers are known to have weaker labor-force attachments and high turnover rates, the latter because of the matching process that characterizes early careers. These features of young workers imply higher unemployment rates for them, as the sampled jobs of early careers are less likely to survive. Most importantly, these facts about youth won't change much simply because there are more or fewer youths at a particular point in time. So the cross-sectional relationship between age and unemployment is likely to hold in time series too. More youths as a proportion of the labor force means higher aggregate unemployment.

Why "probably not" to the second question? An initial reaction might be that educated workers have lower unemployment, so an increase in average education should cause aggregate unemployment to fall. There is some merit to that response, at least in the short run. But reflection on the past would give an empirically minded economist pause. Surely the labor force in 1979 is much more educated than it was in, say, 1879. Yet there is no evidence of a century-long decline in unemployment. Looking across countries, average unemployment rates bear no obvious relationship to schooling levels. There is clearly something different about education, as a demographic indicator of unemployment, as compared to age.

In Shimer's analysis, this difference follows from a search technology in which employers care about relative schooling levels of workers. When multiple workers apply for the same job, the one with more schooling gets it, after engaging in a multilateral bargaining game that determines the division of surplus. Giving everyone more schooling won't change relative rankings, so equilibrium unemployment isn't affected. To me, the real reason seems much simpler than that. Indeed, I think the broad facts about unemployment documented here would be true in an economy of independent farmers who bargain with no one. These facts have vastly more to do with labor-supply behavior than with search and bargaining games.

Why is education different than age? I don't believe it's because employers care about relative educational attainments, nor do I think that signaling models of education have much credibility in this context, especially over long periods of time. Indeed, I believe it's because rising education—as a measure of human capital investment—*is* an indicator of long-term productivity growth. In most models that fit broad macroeconomic facts, productivity growth will have no effect on the natural rate of unemployment, because wages and reservation wages rise together.

A touch of formalism helps. Let the utility of consumption and leisure be from the class in which income and substitution effects are offsetting, for example Cobb–Douglas. Then long-run desired labor supply is independent of the wage, and the reservation wage is

$$\ln W_R = a + \ln C - \ln L, \tag{1}$$

where C is consumption and L is nonworking time. With L constant, the reservation wage is proportional to consumption. Over long periods of rising productivity, the elasticity of consumption with respect to the wage is unity, so the wage and value of nonworking time move in unison. All aspects of labor supply, including unemployment, are constant over time. If education is human capital, and human capital is productive, then a rightward shift in the distribution of education should have no impact on the natural rate.

This is only part of the story, however. One of the most prominent facts about unemployment is that *at any point in time* unemployment is higher among the least productive. Another way of putting this is that while the long-run relationship between productivity and the natural rate is zero, the cross-sectional relationship is always negative. How do we reconcile these seemingly contradictory facts?

Figure 1 OLF, UNEMPLOYMENT, AND NONEMPLOYMENT RATES: 1967–1994

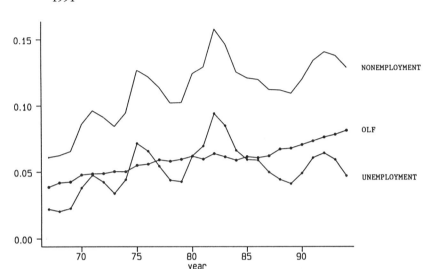

In the context of labor supply and desired consumption in equation (1), it must be the case that the cross-sectional elasticity of consumption with respect to the wage is smaller than 1.0, though the aggregate time-series elasticity is 1.0. This will be satisfied in the cross section so long as assets and other forms of nonwage income (including family and other sources of support) do not vary proportionally with wages. For example, suppose that high-school graduates earn 50% less than college graduates. If the gap in nonwage incomes is smaller than 50%, the condition is satisfied. Then in any cross section, college graduates will have lower unemployment (higher labor supply), but growth that raises wage and nonwage incomes by proportional amounts will leave the labor supply of each group unchanged.

I strongly suspect that this condition is satisfied. Juhn, Murphy, and Topel (1991) provide some evidence related to this point. They find that during the 1970s and 1980s, while real wages and employment of low-skill workers were falling, the household incomes of those workers were nearly constant. In other words, low-skill workers had sources of non-wage income that did not fall in proportion to wages, so their desired labor supply declined. This underlies our contention that declining labor-market opportunities for less-skilled workers—reflected in declining wages—explained rising unemployment and nonparticipation after 1970.

I agree with Shimer's conclusion that today's low measured unemployment rate is not directly comparable to unemployment rates of the past, and that labor-market conditions are not as strong as such comparisons might suggest. Shimer rests much of his conclusion on simple demographics—the aging of the baby-boom generation reduced unemployment—but I think the conclusion is broader and stronger. In my view, an oddity of Shimer's analysis is that it focuses so narrowly on unemployment. Labor-force participation and changes in labor demand conditions are conspicuous by their absence. For prime-aged men, the fact is that while unemployment rates have been falling, their labor-force participation rates have continued to decline, *especially among the least skilled.*

Murphy and Topel (1997) argue that long-term changes in labor demands have changed the returns to work, most notably among the least skilled. We argue that this decline in labor-market opportunities drove declining employment rates among the least skilled, which raised both unemployment and the rate of labor-force withdrawal. Since unemployment data alone exclude workers who have withdrawn from the labor force for market-driven reasons, they miss a key part of the story.

How big are these effects? Figures 1 and 2 show the data. Among workers with 1–30 years of potential experience, the nonparticipation

Figure 2 OLF RATE BY INTERVALS OF THE WAGE DISTRIBUTION

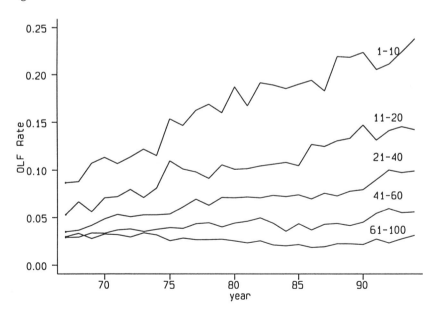

rate rose by over 2 percentage points between 1979 (Shimer's benchmark year) and 1994 (the last year for which I did the calculations). This increase was fairly steady over time. Among workers in the bottom decile of the wage distribution the increase was much more dramatic, from about 16% in 1979 to 24% in 1994 (see Figure 2).

Why is this important? As I noted above, many economists and almost all of the general public think of the unemployment rate as a summary measure of labor-market conditions, and of even the success or failure of economic policy. If these labor-force withdrawals are driven by long-term changes in labor demand, as the evidence strongly suggests, then measured *unemployment* misses a large part of the market-driven reason for declining *employment*. As Robert Shimer argues from his analysis, this means that unemployment rates of the 1990s are different animals than the rates of earlier decades. But the reasons go well beyond simple demographics. I think the evidence is strong that unemployment rates have become poorer measures of the joblessness that is caused by labor demand conditions. How much poorer? To compare current conditions with 1979, I think a useful rule of thumb might be to add two percentage points to the current unemployment rate, at least for men.

This leads to a final point. If labor-force withdrawals mean that "true" unemployment is higher than measured unemployment, concerns about accelerating inflation at today's "low" unemployment rates may be misplaced. While I'm no fan of the Phillips curve, and I've never come close to estimating a NAIRU, the distinction I've made here may be useful to those who are, and do.

REFERENCES

Juhn, C., K. M. Murphy, and R. Topel. (1991). Why has the natural rate of unemployment increased over time? *Brookings Papers on Economic Activity*, 2:75–142.
Murphy, K. M., and R. Topel. (1997). Unemployment and nonemployment. *American Economic Review* 87:295–300.

Discussion

There was considerable interest in whether Shimer's results for the United States might generalize to other countries: Pierre-Olivier Gourinchas wondered how European unemployment might look if corrected for baby-boom effects in those countries. Ben Bernanke suggested that a systematic comparison across industrialized countries of age effects on aggregate unemployment would be a useful extension of this research; he noted that Japan, with its dramatic demographic changes in the postwar period, is a particularly interesting case. Shimer expressed skepticism about the potential of demographic effects to explain much of the European experience in particular, noting the importance there of labor-market regulation and other structural factors.

John Shea thought that it would be interesting to analyze some conventional empirical relationships, such as the Beveridge curve and the Phillips curve, using demographically adjusted unemployment rates. For example, how do vacancy rates covary with the adjusted unemployment rates? In a Phillips-curve context, are changes in unemployment arising from demographic factors related to inflation in a way different from other changes in unemployment? On a related point, Herschel Grossman noted that the cyclical peaks considered in the paper may not correspond to peaks of the inflation cycle; it would be interesting to compare values of group-specific unemployment rates at inflation peaks.

Gregory Mankiw suggested that Shimer's use of the prime-age unemployment rate in his attempt to assess the importance of indirect demographic effects (such as the effects of generational crowding) may not be appropriate. He suggested that, instead, age-group-specific unemployment rates be regressed on a variable such as the share of young people in the population, with the fitted values being used to estimate the trends arising from demographic factors. Mankiw also expressed surprise that such a straightforward explanation of the decline in U.S. unemployment had not appeared previously in the literature. Shimer credited the *Economic Report of the President* with having noted earlier the possible link between demographic changes and the unemployment decline.

There was general agreement with Robert Topel's point, made in his formal comment, that it is as important to explain changes in employment and participation rates as changes in unemployment rates. Shimer responded that simultaneous modeling of employment, participation, and unemployment was beyond the scope of the current paper, but indicated that demographic changes, including possibly changes in educational attainment, might well be useful in explaining the trends both in employment and in participation as well as in unemployment.

Casey B. Mulligan
UNIVERSITY OF CHICAGO

Substitution over Time: Another Look at Life-Cycle Labor Supply

1. Introduction

Today macroeconomics relies almost exclusively on intertemporal models, models which are also quite common in other areas of economic inquiry. One important question that must be answered in the building of a dynamic model is "What are the possibilities for substitution over time?" This paper is about one potential margin of substitution, the substitution of work over time.

An analysis of the substitution of work over time dates at least back to Hicks (1939, Chapters XVI, XVII), and since Lucas and Rapping (1969) this margin of substitution has been included in a substantial number of macro models. The presence of this margin affects predictions for labor-market and output fluctuations in response to aggregate productivity shocks (Hall, 1980; Hansen, 1985), to changes in the timing of taxes (Judd, 1987), to changes in the timing of government spending (Aiyagari, Christiano, and Eichenbaum, 1992; Barro, 1981, 1987; Baxter and King, 1993), and to monetary shocks (Lucas, 1972), as well as many other questions of substantial interest. But since a series of studies by Altonji (1986), MaCurdy (1981), and Abowd and Card (1989) and analy-

Casey B. Mulligan is an assistant professor of economics at the University of Chicago, a Faculty Research Fellow of the NBER, and a John M. Olin Faculty Fellow. Mulligan gratefully acknowledges the careful research assistance of Song Han and comments by Gary Becker, Ben Bernanke, John Cawley, Bob Hall, Dan Hamermesh, Jim Heckman, Steve Levitt, Bob Lucas, Costas Meghir, Jacob Mincer, Derek Neal, Steve Pischke, Julio Rotemberg, Xavier Sala-i-Martin, University of Chicago Economics 203 and 337 students, and seminar participants at the University of Chicago, CEPR, MIT, NBER, Northwestern, the University of Rochester, and Vanderbilt. Jim Heckman and Lance Lochner generously provided their life-cycle estimates of worker-financed training time. The University of Chicago Center on Aging grant P20 AG12857 from the National Institute on Aging provided financial support.

ses of tax experiments [some of which are surveyed by Hausman (1985) and Pencavel (1986)], it has been widely believed that the substitution of work over time is a quantitatively unimportant margin. This belief and its origins can be seen in Pencavel's (1986) and Card's (1994) surveys, in the comments by Ashenfelter (1984), Mankiw (1989), and Plosser (1989), and in the calibration of macro models by Auerbach and Kotlikoff (1987, p. 50), Judd (1987), and many others exploring the consequences of some interesting and important policy changes.

This paper revisits the *life-cycle* evidence—evidence on low-frequency changes in wages and time worked with age. My goal here is not to reconcile the variety of life-cycle and non-life-cycle studies that are available [I do attempt this in another paper, Mulligan (1995)]. Nor is my goal to argue that the substitution of work over time is the single missing piece for every macroeconomic puzzle. Instead, I revisit life-cycle evidence to show that it is consistent with quantitatively important substitution of labor over time. Although I do not think that life-cycle evidence is necessarily the best evidence for getting at this issue, it is true that the widely cited studies based on the PSID and other micro data sets are basically life-cycle studies. I then show that the usual cohort data might be reasonably modified in several ways, including the aggregation of micro measures of labor supply, taking account of time spent training on the job, using different techniques for measuring work time, measuring marginal tax rates, and including older workers.

Although the usual cohort data are consistent with a lot of substitution over time, there are some problems with their construction. There is no obvious way to infer the wages of those who are not working at various points in the life cycle. Nor is it particularly plausible that tastes, health, and other relevant variables are independent of age or even uncorrelated with wages. Nor is it particularly obvious exactly what procedure should be used to obtain the "right" estimate from the usual cohort samples. These problems are enough to make one eagerly search elsewhere for anticipated wage changes and associated changes in work. My search led me to another life-cycle event that has not yet been studied: the termination of aid to families with dependent children (AFDC) at the 18th birthday of a family's youngest child.[1] Section 4 explains how this study can alleviate some of the apparent problems with a synthetic-cohort sample, that it is consistent with substantial substitution over time, and—perhaps surprisingly—that its estimates are similar to the synthetic-cohort estimates.

---

1. I have also been led to look at the anticipated wage changes associated with non-life-cycle events, including seasons, wars, and agricultural shocks (Mulligan, 1995).

2. A Life-Cycle Model of Labor Supply

2.1 AN OVERVIEW OF THE INTERTEMPORAL SUBSTITUTION HYPOTHESIS

The intertemporal substitution hypothesis (ISH) can be simply stated: workers intertemporally reallocate their work in response to changes in the relevant relative price. A statistical model that captures this idea is

$$E_t\left[\ln\frac{n_{t+1}^i}{n_t^i}\right] = -\sigma r_t + \sigma E_t\left[\ln\frac{w_{t+1}^i}{w_t^i}\right] + \epsilon_t^i \tag{1}$$

where n_t^i is the labor supply of worker i at date t, w_t^i is worker i's date-t after-tax market value of time, and r_t is the real rate of return to savings between periods t and $t+1$. The term ϵ_t includes preference parameters and, in some models, a precautionary motive for working. $\sigma > 0$ is the intertemporal elasticity of substitution (IES). In many environments, labor-supply decisions are made sequentially in time rather than at the "beginning of time," so the law of demand more appropriately applies to *plans* for labor supply as a function of anticipated wages. E_t denotes date-t expectations of future variables and is therefore included in equation (1).

Notice that the model does not necessarily predict that workers will work the hardest when the conventionally measured "real wage" is the highest. There are two relevant forces at work. First, the relative price of leisure in any two periods depends not only on the ratio of the wages but also on an interest rate. Second, through the taste term ϵ_t, the model allows for impatience, prudence, or other reasons that workers may have different preferences for current and future leisure. Consider, for example, a perfectly flat time profile for wages. A worker will choose more leisure in the later periods if the interest rate is high enough, or more leisure in the earlier periods if he is impatient enough. Without data on the interest rate and preferences, it is necessary to estimate the trend component of the intertemporal labor allocation together with the responsiveness of work effort to incentives.

Beneath any notational complexities, the econometrics of estimating the elasticity σ is also quite straightforward: identify situations with different anticipated rates of wage growth, and measure the associated differences in anticipated labor-supply growth. The implementation of this can be quite challenging (e.g., how is anticipated wage growth measured?), but the thought experiment is simple enough. I (and many others in the empirical literature) do not intend to say or do anything more complicated than this, but a more complicated model is needed to be clear about the measurement of the variables of interest and interpretation of the parameter σ. My life-cycle model includes several complications necessary for understanding the data: (1) uncertainty about future wages, (2) various measurement errors in hours and wages, (3) discrete choices about labor-force participation at various points in time, (4) time aggregation in the measurement of labor supply, and (5) potentially nonlinear labor income tax schedules.

2.2 INDIVISIBLE LABOR

A person's lifetime includes many potential *work sessions*, equally spaced in time. For our purposes, it may be useful to think of a potential work session as a day or week, although a month is in some ways a more convenient definition for the AFDC application in Section 4.3. If work is to occur during a potential session, it must occur for exactly $\bar{n}$ units of time. This indivisibility of labor might be interpreted as the optimal bunching of labor in continuous time in the presence of fixed commuting costs and high-frequency fatigue effects (see Mulligan, 1998), in which case $\bar{n}$ is a function of the magnitude of the fixed cost and of the form of the fatigue effects, but not the other variables in the model such as wages, taxes, or tastes for leisure. w denotes the average product of labor for the session, so that $w\bar{n}$ is the total amount produced by a worker who chooses to work the session. w and $\bar{n}$ may vary over time and across states of nature.

2.3 HUMAN-CAPITAL ACCUMULATION

Two things can happen during a work session: goods production or the production of one's own human capital. When goods production occurs, the worker is paid $w\bar{n}$. When human-capital accumulation occurs, the worker may or may not be paid, depending on whether the firm is financing the training or not. If the firm does not finance the training, the worker does not have any earnings for that session but still values the training for the future earnings it produces. In this case, I let $w\bar{n}$ denote that valuation.[2]

In Section 3, I use two measures of time spent producing human capital. The first is time spent searching for a job. The second is time at work spent learning new things.

2.4 TIME AGGREGATION

It will be assumed that the econometrician observes only time-aggregated measures of the relevant variables, so it is convenient to use

---

2. Human-capital accumulation can be valued more than $w\bar{n}$ without changing the interpretation of my results, although see my discussion of time aggregation.

two indices t and k to identify a potential work session. t indexes the time-aggregated periods, or *time intervals*, and varies for 0 to T during a consumer's lifetime. k indexes the potential *sessions* within any particular time interval and varies from 1 to K for each t. Thus there are a total of $K(T+1)$ potential sessions in a consumer's lifetime.

2.5 TAX AND BENEFIT SYSTEM

During any potential session, a consumer receives government transfer payments in the amount $b_{t,k}$ (the consumer is a net taxpayer in the case $b < 0$). Benefits are determined according to the formula

$$b_{t,k} = \max\left\{ \underline{b}_{t,k},\, \overline{b}_{t,k} - R_{t,k}\max\left[w_{t,k}n_{t,k}I_{t,k} - d_{t,k},\, 0 \right]\right\}, \tag{2}$$

where $w_{t,k}$ is the average product of time during the kth session of time interval t (time which may be spent either in goods or human-capital production), $n_{t,k}$ is time worked, $I_{t,k}$ is an indicator variable for goods production or firm-financed human-capital production, $I_{t,k}w_{t,k}n_{t,k}$ is labor earnings, $d_{t,k}$ are deductions from earnings and *earnings disregards*, $R_{t,k}$ is the *benefit reduction rate* or *marginal labor income tax rate*, $\overline{b}_{t,k}$ is the maximum benefit available (and in some applications may be a function of family composition, asset holdings, and other variables), and $\underline{b}_{t,k}$ is the minimum benefit available. Benefits are reduced $R_{t,k}$ dollars for every dollar of net earnings, where net earnings are computed as gross earnings net of deductions.

Notice that earnings and deductions are not aggregated across sessions for the purposes of computing taxes and benefits. I note in the text where this assumption may be unrealistic and of some consequence for the results.

2.6 UNCERTAINTY, BUDGET CONSTRAINTS, AND UTILITY FUNCTIONS

I index a realization of a consumer's life history by ω. For each possible realization $\omega \in \Omega$, consumer choices of stochastic processes for consumption $c_{t,k}(\omega)$, work $n_{t,k}(\omega)$, and tax deductions $d_{t,k}(\omega)$ must satisfy a present-value budget constraint:

$$\sum_{t=0}^{T}\sum_{k=1}^{K} e^{-\rho(tK+k)}Q_{t,k}(\omega)\,[c_{t,k}(\omega) - w_{t,k}(\omega)n_{t,k}(\omega) - b_{t,k}(\omega)$$
$$+f_{t,k}(d_{t,k}(\omega),\omega) + H_{t,k}(\omega)w_{t,k}(\omega)\bar{n}_{t,k}(\omega)] = A_0, \tag{3}$$
$$\ln Q_{t,k}(\omega) \equiv -\sum_{s=0}^{t-1}\sum_{l=1}^{K}[r_{s,l}(\omega) - \rho] - \sum_{l=1}^{k}[r_{t,l}(\omega) - \rho],$$

where $r_{t,k}$ is the *ex post* real return on a one-period bond purchased at date $t,k-1$, and $H_{t,k}$ is an indicator variable for purchases of self-financed human capital. In addition to (3), we have the constraints (2) and $n_{t,k}(\omega)$ $\in \{0,\bar{n}_{t,k}(\omega)\}$ for all $t=0, \ldots ,T$, $k=1, \ldots ,K$, and $\omega \in \Omega$.

Deductions are costly. Deductions in the amount d cost $f_{t,k}(d,\omega)$. For each t,k,ω, the deduction cost function is nondecreasing and nonconcave in the amount deducted. There is no cost if no deductions are taken.

The revelation of information over time is modeled with the filtered probability space $(\Omega,\mathcal{F},F,\pi)$. Each state of nature ω has unconditional probability $\pi(\omega)$. The filtration $F=\{\mathcal{F}_{0,1}, \mathcal{F}_{0,2}, \ldots ,\mathcal{F}_{T,K}\}$ on Ω is assumed to be increasing, and the stochastic processes $w_{t,k}$, $\bar{n}_{t,k}$, $\gamma_{t,k}$, $r_{t,k}$, $\bar{b}_{t,k}$, $R_{t,k}$, and $\underline{b}_{t,k}$, are adapted to it.[3]

Consumption and work are assumed to evolve as if workers chose functions $c_{t,k}(\omega)$, $n_{t,k}(\omega)$, and $d_{t,k}(\omega)$ adapted to the filtration F with the objective of maximizing the expected value of an intertemporally and intratemporally separable utility function (4) subject to the constraints (2), (3), and $n_{t,k}(\omega) \in \{0,\bar{n}_{t,k}(\omega)\}$:

$$\sum_{\omega\in\Omega} \pi(\omega)\sum_{t=0}^{T}\sum_{k=1}^{K}e^{-\rho(tK+k)}\left[u\left(c_{t,k}(\omega)\right) - \gamma_{t,k}(\omega)v\left(n_{t,k}(\omega)\right) \right],$$
$$\rho > 0, \quad v(0) \equiv 0, \quad v_{t,k}(\omega) \equiv v\left(\bar{n}_{t,k}(\omega)\right) > 0. \tag{4}$$

Notice that I do not treat $H_{t,k}$ and $I_{t,k}$ as choice variables and do not say exactly how sessions devoted to human-capital production translate into higher future wages, but the first-order conditions of the problem described above are among those of the larger problem that include optimal human-capital accumulation over the life cycle.[4]

2.7 WHEN TO WORK

When describing the decision to work, it is useful to define $\tau_{t,k}(\omega)$ as the implicit tax rate on work in session k of time interval t:

$$\tau_{t,k}(\omega) \equiv \min\left\{ \frac{\bar{b}_{t,k}(\omega)-\underline{b}_{t,k}(\omega)}{w_{t,k}(\omega)\bar{n}_{t,k}(\omega)} , R_{t,k}(\omega) - \frac{R_{t,k}(\omega)d_{t,k}^{*}(\omega)-f_{t,k}\left(d_{t,k}^{*}(\omega),\omega\right)}{w_{t,k}(\omega)\bar{n}_{t,k}(\omega)} \right\} \leq R_{t,k}(\omega),$$
$$\tag{5}$$

$$d_{t,k}^{*}(\omega) \equiv \underset{d\in[0,w_{t,k}(\omega)\bar{n}_{t,k}(\omega)]}{\arg\min} \left\{ f_{t,k}(d,\omega) - R_{t,k}(\omega)d \right\}.$$

3. The random function $f_{t,k}$ should be measurable with respect to $\mathcal{F}_{t,k}$.
4. See Ghez and Becker (1975). The larger problem with $H_{t,k}$ and $I_{t,k}$ as choice variables has the constraint $H_{t,k}n_{t,k} = I_{t,k}n_{t,k}$ for all t,k,ω.

If $\bar{b}_{t,k}$ is large enough (in what follows, I suppress the index ω), the implicit tax rate is related to the *benefit reduction rate* $R_{t,k}$. However, when positive deductions are optimal and the deduction cost function is strictly concave, the indivisibility of labor means that the implicit tax rate is strictly less than the benefit reduction rate. If $\bar{b}_{t,k}$ is small enough, $\tau_{t,k}$ is unrelated to $R_{t,k}$.

The first-order condition determining where $n_{t,k}$ equals 0 or $\bar{n}_{t,k}$ is

$$\gamma_{t,k}\, v_{t,k} \gtreqless Q_{t,k}\, w_{t,k}\, \bar{n}_{t,k}\, (1 - \tau_{t,k})\, E_{t,k}\lambda_{t,k}, \tag{6}$$

where $E_{t,k}$ denotes date-t,k expectations and $\lambda_{t,k}$ is the lifetime "marginal" utility of wealth.[5] The expression (6) simply says that people work during those periods when the benefit exceeds the cost. The benefit of working is the discounted after-tax earnings (or the value of self-financed human-capital production) for session k of interval t, given by $Q_{t,k}w_{t,k}\bar{n}_{t,k}(1-\tau_{t,k})$, times the expected marginal utility of wealth, $E_{t,k}\lambda_{t,k}$. The cost is the disutility of work, $\gamma_{t,k}v_{t,k}$. Comparative static changes in $Q_{t,k}w_{t,k}(1-\tau_{t,k})$ can be interpreted as generating a substitution effect, while changes in $E_{t,k}\lambda_{t,k}$ can be interpreted as generating a wealth effect.

2.8 CONSUMPTION INSURANCE?

The problem described above presumes that insurance against surprises to wages, taxes, and interest rates is unavailable.[6] It is straightforward to allow for perfect consumption insurance by collapsing the series of budget constraints (3) into a single budget constraint that equates the expected present value of expenditures to the expected present value of resources. In this case, the lifetime marginal utility of wealth, $\lambda_{t,k}$, is no longer a random variable with respect to $\mathcal{F}_{t,k}$ (that is, $E_{t,k}\lambda_{t,k} = \lambda_{t,k}$). Otherwise the conditions for working session k of interval t is the same as (6).

2.9 INFORMATION LOST FROM TIME AGGREGATION

Given time-aggregated lifetime data on all of the exogenous variables of the model, we cannot make sharp predictions about time-aggregated labor supply without answering three questions:

5. Because of its discreteness, the labor-supply decision at any date and state has a discrete effect on expected remaining lifetime discounted utility of consumption, and $\lambda_{t,k}$ is the size of this effect per dollar of date-t,k after-tax earnings $w_{t,k}\bar{n}_{t,k}(1-\tau_{t,k})$. The value of $\lambda_{t,k}$ approaches the "marginal" utility as $w_{t,k}\bar{n}_{t,k}(1-\tau_{t,k})$ goes to zero. Mulligan (1998) also shows that $\lambda_{t,k}$ is literally a marginal utility when particular lotteries and "taste insurance" contracts are introduced as choice variables.

6. Although one of Mulligan's (1998) interpretations of equation (6) presumes that "taste insurance" or some other mechanism is available to compensate those who are unlucky enough to especially dislike work when wages are high.

1. How is information about future wages and interest rates revealed during a time interval?
2. What is a worker's market value of time at each potential session, including those sessions he did not work?
3. What is a worker's nonmarket value of time at each potential session?

I make three assumptions about this:

(A1) No information is revealed within time intervals: $\mathscr{F}_{t,k} = \mathscr{F}_{t,1}$ for all $k = 1, \ldots , K$.

(A2) The market value of time and the indivisibility of labor do not vary within time intervals: $Q_{t,k}w_{t,k}\bar{n}_{t,k}(1-\tau_{t,k}) = Q_{t,1}w_{t,1}\bar{n}_{t,1}(1-\tau_{t,1})$ and $\bar{n}_{t,k} = \bar{n}_{t,1}$ for all $k = 1, \ldots , K$

(A3) $\gamma_{t,k} = \gamma_t g_{t,k}$, where $\sigma \ln g_{t,k}$, $k = 1, \ldots , K$, are drawn according to the distribution function G with unbounded support. $\sigma > 0$ is a constant. $E[\sigma \ln g_{t,k}] = 0$ and $E[(\sigma \ln g_{t,k})^2] = 1$. Without loss of generality, the K draws are assumed to be independent.

Assumptions (A1) and (A2), although often only implicit, are extremely common in the labor-supply literature. (A3) produces increasing marginal disutility of work within a time interval, an assumption which appears in one form or another in the literature. To see mechanically how (A3) produces increasing marginal disutility, notice that, given (A1) and (A2), workers that work at all during a time interval will work during the low disutility sessions. Since sessions differ in their marginal disutility, workers require a higher wage to work a larger fraction of the time interval.[7] I use (A1)–(A3) to derive some empirical specifications, but comment further on their relevance as I discuss the empirical results.

In accordance with assumption (A2), I suppress the subscript k except where necessary for clarity.

2.10 CONSUMER HETEROGENEITY AND THE INDIVIDUAL LABOR-SUPPLY EQUATION

Consumers may differ in their realizations of the exogenous variables $w_{t,k}$ and $\gamma_{t,k}$. They are the same regarding the stochastic processes generating these realizations, the utility functions $u(c)$ and $v(n)$, the parameter σ, and the way in which information arrives (including the function G defined above).

Consider a group of consumers who are identical in terms of the two

---

7. Lucas (1970, p. 25) has exactly the specification (A3), except that he has a continuum of potential work sessions per time interval (as compared to my K).

random variables $\gamma_t v_t$ and $Q_t w_t \bar{n}_t (1-\tau_t) E_t \lambda_t$. We compute the group average N_t of each individual's time worked during the time interval t, including those who did not work at all during the interval:

$$G^{-1}\left(\frac{N_t}{K\bar{n}_t}\right) = \sigma \ln w_t(1 - \tau_t) + \sigma \ln \bar{n}_t + \sigma \ln \frac{Q_t E_t \lambda_t}{\gamma_t v_t}. \tag{7}$$

This is a nonlinear version of MaCurdy's (1981) "λ-constant labor supply function," which may be surprising given MaCurdy's apparently different description of the labor-supply problem. In fact, the only difference is in the measurement of labor supply.

For a group of consumers who, for some integer $s > 0$, have the four random variables $\gamma_t v_t$, $Q_t w_t \bar{n}_t (1-\tau_t) E_t \lambda_t$, $E_t[\gamma_{t+s} v_{t+s}]$, $E_t[Q_{t+s} w_t \bar{n}_{t+s}(1-\tau_{t+s}) \lambda_{t+s}]$ in common, we have a version of equation (1):

$$
\begin{aligned}
E_t &\left[G^{-1}\left(\frac{N_{t+s}}{K\bar{n}_{t+s}}\right) - G^{-1}\left(\frac{N_t}{K\bar{n}_t}\right) \right] \\
&= \sigma K \sum_{s'=1}^{s} (E_t r_{t+s'} - \rho) + \sigma E_t \ln \frac{w_{t+s}(1 - \tau_{t+s})}{w_t(1 - \tau_t)} + \sigma E_t \ln \frac{\bar{n}_{t+s} \gamma_t v_t}{\bar{n}_t \gamma_{t+s} v_{t+s}} \\
&\quad + \sigma(E_t \ln E_{t+s}\lambda_{t+s} - \ln E_t E_{t+s}\lambda_{t+s}).
\end{aligned} \tag{8}
$$

The only difference between an individual's labor supply plans and those of the group is the sampling error due to the fact that a single individual only samples K times from the distribution G during a time interval. The probability that a particular individual does not work at all during a particular time interval is

$$\left[1 - G\left(\sigma \ln \frac{w_t \bar{n}_t Q_t (1 - \tau_t) E_t \lambda_t}{\gamma_t v_t} \right) \right]^K.$$

Thus extended intervals of participation and nonparticipation during a person's lifetime are evidence of either (a) large and persistent changes in tastes or the value of time or (b) a large willingness to substitute over time, σ.

The responsiveness of labor supply to wages depends on the level of labor supply in the model (8). Typically there will be little response of N when N is near 0 or $K\bar{n}$. This is even true in the special case that $g_{t,k}^q$ is distributed uniformly on $[0,e]$ and the equation (1) obtains—a special case which gets a lot of attention in the literature—once the possibilities of corner solutions for N_t and N_{t+s} are taken into account.[8] The bulk of my analysis follows Altonji (1986), Ghez and Becker (1975), MaCurdy (1981), and others by focusing on this special case and ignoring possible corner solutions. My Section 4 returns to the more general model (8) and includes some analysis of how the responsiveness of labor supply might vary with its level.

The derivation of equation (8) reveals several points that are quite relevant for the empirical applications in this paper:

1. The market value of time, w_t, for the time interval t can, for those who have some earnings during the interval, be measured as $y_t/[N_t(1-h_t)]$, where h_t is the fraction of sessions worked that were devoted to self-financed human-capital production, and y_t is the total pretax labor earnings for the time interval.
2. σ measures the responsiveness of *anticipated* labor-supply changes to anticipated wage changes, not *ex post* labor changes to *ex post* wage changes.
3. The implicit tax on work has the *benefit reduction rate* or *marginal labor income tax rate* $R_{t,k}$ as its upper bound.
4. The derivation shows how time aggregation is related to the measurement of labor supply, wages, tax rates, and other variables.
5. The derivation shows how measured employment and hours are related.
6. Those who are not working during any particular work session are not a random sample of the population, but are those for whom work yields a greater disutility.
7. The derivation shows the effect of consumption insurance on comovements of wages and labor supply.

2.11 MACRO "EXPERIMENTS" TO BE CALIBRATED
FROM LIFE-CYCLE DATA

Before reviewing empirical studies and proposing ways to improve them, something must be said about why life-cycle substitution is of interest for macroeconomics. One item of substantial interest is the response of *aggregate* labor supply to aggregate temporary shocks to the market value of time. Candidate shocks to the market value of time include productivity shocks such as those in Kydland and Prescott (1982), monetary shocks such as those in Lucas (1972), temporary government spending shocks such as those modeled by Hall (1980), Barro

8. See Smith (1977, p. 249) for a discussion, and Rogerson and Rupert (1991) for estimates of a labor-supply model with corners at year-round work.

(1981), and Baxter and King (1993), an income-tax cut that is phased in over time, or a tax or subsidy on savings. Computing the response to these shocks probably requires a general equilibrium model of which my model (8) would be one piece, but the parameter σ in my model is the most crucial ingredient. When we, for example, compare two equilibria (which differ, say, according to the processes generating policy or productivity shocks) which have different anticipated rates of growth of the after-tax discounted market value of time, σ will—up to an aggregation bias term—measure the cross-equilibria difference in anticipated rates of aggregate labor-supply growth. This paper uses various life-cycle data to estimate σ. Whether the world actually exhibits the temporary wage fluctuations predicted by these models is an interesting empirical question, but one beyond the scope of this paper.

Although very high-frequency nonseparabilities can be used to motivate my indivisible-labor model (see Mulligan, 1998), labor supply should be separable over time at low frequencies in order for the degree of intertemporal substitution found in life-cycle data to be the same as that applicable to higher-frequency temporary wage movements. If, for example, nonmarket capital were accumulated while a person was not working and that capital increased the marginal utility of leisure, then people would be more willing to substitute time over long periods than over short periods. Or if, as modeled by Kydland and Prescott (1982), extended nonmarket time lowered the marginal utility of leisure, then people would be more willing to substitute time over short periods than over long periods.

The model also has strong predictions for consumption which have been the subject of extensive testing in the literature (e.g., Friedman, 1957; Hall 1978, 1988; Shea, 1995). One area of testing relates to the responsiveness of consumption growth to interest rates and is intimately related to my analysis of labor-supply growth. However, variations in *ex ante* real interest rates that are uncorrelated with tastes and other relevant variables are even tougher to find than are variations in anticipated wage growth. Furthermore, my model is perfectly consistent with lots of substitution of work over time but little substitution of consumption (just set σ large and make u'' highly negative).

A second area of consumption testing relates to the predictions of the permanent income hypothesis for the effect of income shocks on consumption. But, because the consumption side of the model could easily be modified to include intertemporal consumption nonseparabilities (e.g., Becker and Murphy, 1988; Becker and Mulligan, 1997) or even consumption–leisure nonseparabilities (Heckman, 1974; Ghez and Becker, 1975), a variety of observed responses of consumption to income shocks are consistent with the hypothesis that labor supply is correlated with anticipated wage growth.

If workers in my data were literally unable to transfer resources across periods by borrowing, saving, or consuming assets, then the static model of labor supply would apply period by period (whatever "period" means). The sign and magnitude of the synthetic cohort correlation between work and wages would depend on offsetting "income" and "substitution" effects, and, assuming the income effect is positive, the regression (10) would underestimate σ in my synthetic cohort data.[9] As discussed below, σ would be overestimated in my AFDC samples, because the income and substitution effects are in the same direction.

3. Synthetic-Cohort Samples

3.1 INDIVIDUAL-PANEL AND COHORT CROSS-SECTION APPROACHES COMPARED

There are two approaches that have commonly been used to estimate σ (with pretty similar results), and each has its advantages. The first focuses on equation (1) and uses individual panel data. Anticipated labor-supply growth is measured as actual annual hours growth for those working at t and $t+1$ (as reported in the survey), and anticipated wage growth is estimated in a first-stage regression of the growth in actual average hourly earnings on a variety of variables presumed to be in the date-t information set. However, it is important to note that, among those variables that have been used to predict wage growth, functions of age are the best predictors. To see this, consider Altonji's (1986) prediction of average-hourly-earnings growth in a sample of 10,036 continuously married prime-aged man-years from the 1968–1981 waves of the PSID. With two socioeconomic indicators for parents, years of schooling of father and mother, age, a schooling quadratic, age interacted with a schooling quadratic, and year dummies as explanatory variables, his prediction equation has an R^2 of 0.0054 and a standard error of 0.254. In other words, the standard deviation of his predicted wage growth is 0.0187, which can be compared with the standard deviation of average-hourly-earnings growth of 0.037 in my CPS synthetic-cohort data for cohorts aged 25–60, and 0.087 for cohorts aged 25–79.[10] Hence, among

---

9. An exhaustive list of tests of "liquidity constraints" is beyond the scope of this paper, but I point out that an inability to transfer resources across periods would also imply extraordinary rates of return to schooling and OJT (on-the-job training), a prediction which is at odds with the empirical findings of Mincer (1974) and others.

10. It is interesting to note that, if the intertemporal substitution elasticity of hours were as large as one and the intertemporal model fitted Altonji's data perfectly, the standard

the variables that have been used in the literature to predict wage growth, age dummies have the vast majority of the explanatory power. This, of course, does not rule out the possibility that someday someone will use the PSID or other individual-panel data to identify quantitatively important anticipated wage changes that are not associated with age.

The second approach studies cross-sectional cohort ("synthetic cohort") specifications motivated by equation (7). First, we make the decomposition (9) and assume that the cross-sectional covariance is zero:

$$\sigma \ln \frac{Q_t^i \, (E_t \lambda_t^i)}{\gamma_t^i v_t^i} = \alpha_t a_t^i + \epsilon_t^i, \qquad \mathrm{cov}_t\!\left(\epsilon_t^i, w_t^i(1 - \tau_t^i) \right) = 0, \tag{9}$$

where i indexes individuals and a denotes a person's age. Second, assume that $g_{t,k}^a$ is distributed uniformly on $[0,e]$ (or, equivalently, integrate equation (1) over time], and obtain (10) by averaging (7) across consumers of the same age:

$$\ln N_t^a = \sigma \ln \tilde{w}_t^a + (1 + \sigma) \ln \tilde{n}_t + \ln K + \alpha_t a_t + \epsilon_t^a + A_t^a, \tag{10}$$

where N_t^a is the cohort *arithmetic*-average annual hours worked, $\tilde{w}_t^a$ is the cohort *geometric*-average after-tax market value of time, and A_t^a is a within-cohort aggregation bias depending on the second and higher moments of the within-cohort distributions of ϵ_t and $\ln \tilde{w}_t$.[11] A very similar expression can be derived relating arithmetic averages of work hours to arithmetic averages of after-tax market values of time, but I use the geometric average $\tilde{w}_t^a$ because it can be decomposed in a straightforward way into geometric averages of tax factors, measured pretax wages, and proportional measurement errors.[12]

Treating $\tilde{n}$ and K as constants in the cross section and assuming that the aggregation bias is uncorrelated with $\tilde{w}_t^a$ across cohorts, equation (10) is then estimated by least squares in the cross section of workers aggregated by cohort. Notice that age is included in the regression because—

---

deviation of log hours growth would be 0.0187. This is the difference between no wage growth and the growth of annual hours from 2000 to 2038.

11. $A_t^a = \ln \{1 + \sum_{i=2}^{\infty} [\mu_i^a(\epsilon) + \sigma^i \mu_i^a(\ln w)]/i!\}$, where $\mu_i^a(\epsilon)$ is the ith moment of the within-cohort distribution of ϵ, and $\mu_i^a(\ln \tilde{w})$ is the ith moment of the within-cohort distribution of $\ln \tilde{w}$.

12. Similar regression estimates of σ are obtained when arithmetic averages are used. Even if the aggregation bias term were correlated with $\tilde{w}_t^a$, an estimate of σ inclusive of that correlation may be the more relevant for macroeconomic forecasting because macro data are by definition aggregated.

as mentioned in the above discussion of equation (1)—the ISH has nothing to say about the rate of growth of labor supply that would occur in the absence of growth of the after-tax value of time. Age is also included in the regression (10) because cohorts may differ in their time-t tastes or their expected lifetime marginal utility of wealth, $E_t\lambda_t$.

The slope parameter σ in equation (10) is a well-defined structural parameter in my life-cycle model. Indeed, contrary to the claims of Smith (1977, p. 249), σ is a parameter of an individual's preferences—it describes the amount of intertemporal heterogeneity in his marginal disutility of work (see also Lucas, 1970). σ also dictates the response of *aggregate* labor supply—including all its components (the fraction working sometime during the year, weeks worked conditional on working, weekly hours, etc.)—to temporary wage fluctuations, as well as the welfare implications of those fluctuations. Most important, the value of σ is the major determinant of the response of macro variables to temporary monetary, fiscal, technological, and other shocks.

Assumption (9) is crucial, so it deserves some interpretation. It says that those tastes for work and interest rates which cannot be explained by a linear term in age are uncorrelated with after-tax market values of time. Part of this is effectively a recursivity assumption—that, given wage growth, workers of all ages trade off working this period or next in the same way. But (9) is also an assumption about *cohort effects*.[13] Assumption (9) is violated, for example, when health affects tastes for work and health deteriorates at an increasing rate with age (i.e., recursivity is violated) or the detrended expected lifetime marginal utility of wealth, $E_t\lambda^a$, varies with date of birth in a way that is correlated with detrended $\tilde{w}_t^a$ (i.e., cohort effects do not follow a trend). A weaker assumption than (9) can be used when proxies for tastes or interest rates are included in the regression (10). The presence of cohort effects can also be tested by obtaining cohort cross-section estimates at different points in time. Mulligan (1995) does so and finds similar regression estimates of σ for 1979, 1980, and 1985 (which are in turn similar to the 1976 estimates reported here).

The cross-section approach has three important advantages. First, cross-section studies offer a number of interesting and highly relevant variables—such as measures of health, training, and alternative measures of time use—that are unavailable in panel studies. Second, cross-section samples are typically much larger than panel samples, so older workers may be more reliably studied and a much richer relationship

---

13. Depending on the interpretation of λ_t, (9) may also limit the length of a time period or the degree to which λ_t diminishes with lifetime wealth. See Mulligan (1998).

between age and wages can be accurately estimated in cross sections. Third, some of the disadvantages of cross-section data can be overcome by complementing the cross sections with some information from panel studies.

Another difference between individual-panel and cross-sectional cohort analyses is that the latter is subject to a *composition bias* due to the death of cohort members and (because in practice the market value of time can only be observed for those who work sometime during the year) the variation across age groups in the fraction and types of individuals who are employed during the year. However, I argue in Section 3.6 that cross-section cohort data can be supplemented with individual-panel data to correct for the composition bias.

Both individual-panel and cross-sectional cohort studies must make inferences about the market value of time when a man is not working. When someone is not working at instant t, it is typically assumed that the market value of time can be inferred from earnings during some other nearby period or from the earnings of a similar person who is working, or some combination of these. But it might be the case that a person's market value of time when not working is low compared to the time he does work or compared with the market value of time of apparently similar people who are working. I see no solution to this form of "selection bias" for the individual-panel and cohort studies in the literature or for my own cross-section cohort study, but point out that another advantage of my panel study of welfare mothers in Section 4 is that we can be confident that changes in the tax rules dominate any unobserved changes in the market value of time.

I begin by revisiting the cross-section cohort (synthetic cohort) samples, sticking with the same basic specification (10) but emphasizing the measurement of the key variables of interest. First, I include the employment margin in my measures of labor supply as suggested by my model. Second, I include income and social security taxes in the calculations of the value of time. Third, I assume that average hourly earnings misestimates the value of time in a way that is related to the amount of time training on the job. Fourth, I consider the possibility that hours worked as reported by employees to standard demographic surveys are systematically biased. Because many of the data needed to address these issues are only available in micro cross sections, I am necessarily constrained to construct cross-section cohort samples instead of individual-panel samples. But, fifth, I do use panel data to supplement the cross-section data and address a measurement problem that is peculiar to the latter— *composition bias*. I return also to an individual-panel sample later in the paper.

Figure 1 MALE HOURS WORKED BY AGE GROUP

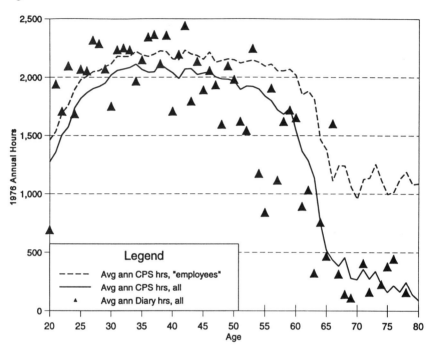

Formally, I decompose cohort a's geometric-average after-tax market value of time, $\tilde{w}_t^a$, into five components:

$$\tilde{w}_t^a = \hat{w}_t^a(1 - \tau_t^a)\frac{1}{1 - h_t^a}\,\nu_t^a B_t^a,$$

$$\nu^a \equiv \frac{\hat{N}_t^a}{N_t^a},$$

(11)

where

$$
\begin{aligned}
\hat{w}_t^a &= \text{pretax CPS average hourly earnings,}\\
1 - \tau_t^a &= \text{tax factor,}\\
1/(1 - h_t^a) &= \text{correction for those reported hours that are self-financed OJT,}\\
\nu_t^a &= \text{correction for CPS hours reporting error,}\\
B_t^a &= \text{composition bias.}
\end{aligned}
$$

Below I show how $\hat{w}_t^a$, $1 - \tau_t^a$, and B_t^a are computed as cohort geometric averages from micro-level data, and h_t^a is computed as an arithmetic average from micro-level data. N_t^a and $\hat{N}_t^a$ are computed as cohort arithmetic averages from separate micro data sets, and then their ratio is used to compute ν_t^a.

3.2 TOTAL LABOR SUPPLY IN A CROSS-SECTION OF COHORTS

Figure 1 displays hours worked for male cohorts aged 20–80 in 1976.[14] The solid line displays CPS average annual hours for all men in each of 61 age brackets. Because annual hours worked are zero for some men, this solid line lies below the dashed line, which displays average annual hours for only those men who worked positive hours in 1976.

The CPS cohort geometric mean of average hourly earnings (which are measured only for those working positive hours in 1976) are displayed as a solid line in Figure 2. Judging from the cross-sectional data dis-

Figure 2 MALE PRETAX MARKET VALUE OF TIME BY AGE GROUP

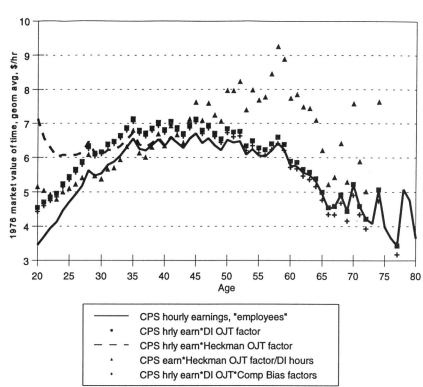

14. The cross section is the March 1977 CPS (ICPSR study 7784). Hours are measured as "usual weekly hours last year" times "weeks worked last year." Average annual earnings is measured as "earnings last year" divided by annual hours.

played in that figure, wages almost double between ages 20 and 40. CPS annual hours worked by "employees" shown in Figure 1 increase, but more modestly. The increase in average hours by all between ages 20 and 40 is more substantial, almost doubling. The data in Figures 1 and 2 suggest that both hours and wages fall dramatically between ages 55 and 80.

Using the 1960 Census 1/1000 Public Use Micro Sample (PUMS), Ghez and Becker (1975) study the hourly earnings of *employed* white men aged 22 to 65. They compute the average annual hours and average hourly earnings by age for the men in their sample. In a regression of each age group's log average hours on its age and its log average pretax average hourly earnings, they obtain a wage coefficient of 0.39.[15] When the log of *leisure* (5096 minus annual hours worked) is used as the dependent variable, they find a coefficient of 0.25. Because they study samples of employed men, measure annual hours and earnings, and isolate the wage variation that occurs with age, Ghez and Becker's specification is essentially the same as those of Altonji (1986) and MaCurdy (1981) (subject to the caveats mentioned in Section 3.1 above).

My cohort analysis begins with 1976 annual hours and earnings as reported in the 1977 CPS. In a regression of each age group's log average hours of employees on its age and its average log pretax average hourly earnings of employees, I report a wage coefficient of 0.37 in the first cell of Table 1 for a sample of men aged 25–55. Like Ghez and Becker's, my estimate of 0.37 is from a sample of only those employed sometime during the year.[16]

However, hours of employees are difficult to interpret in my life-cycle model and may be of limited interest for making predictions for the aggregate labor supply N_t^a. For example, the hours of employees are constant over time and equal to $\bar{n}$ in the special case of $K=1$, while the aggregate labor supply might be quite sensitive to temporary wage changes. When aggregate labor supply is measured as in the model—annual hours averaged across all men, including those who did not work during the year—I obtain a σ-estimate of 0.57.

Heckman (1993, pp. 116, 119) suggests that changes in labor supply

---

15. They smooth their data by taking three-year moving averages. Their more widely cited estimate of 0.45 is obtained when income and family size regressors are included. See their Table 3.5.

16. Our samples sizes are quite similar: they have 33,591 men and I have 34,654 men. I include all men regardless of race and do not smooth my cohort data by computing moving averages. Estimates of σ obtained with 3-year moving averages (not reported in this paper) are typically 20% larger than the corresponding estimates reported here. Ghez and Becker (1975) also include workers aged 56–65, but, since retirement ages have fallen over time and the importance of social security has grown over time (Costa, 1998, Chapter 2), my aged 25–55 sample is probably the better comparison.

Table 1   ESTIMATES OF σ, WITH OJT AND TAX FACTORS

		IES estimates			
		Ages 25–55		*Ages 24–64*	
OJT source	Tax factor	Employees only	All men	Employees only	All men
None	None	0.370	0.569	0.650	1.406
	Marginal A (MA)	0.388	0.588	0.665	1.462
	Marginal B (MB)	0.406	0.613	0.693	1.525
	Average A (AA)	0.366	0.555	0.661	1.407
	Average B (AB)	0.376	0.571	0.673	1.440
SRC	None	0.397	0.614	0.710	1.551
	Marginal A (MA)	0.424	0.646	0.786	1.695
	Marginal B (MB)	0.442	0.671	0.818	1.778
	Average A (AA)	0.425	0.635	0.764	1.590
	Average B (AB)	0.435	0.651	0.783	1.641
Heckman	None	0.463	0.761	1.184	2.770
et al.	Marginal A (MA)	0.500	0.784	1.348	3.163
	Marginal B (MB)	0.487	0.755	1.363	3.223
	Average A (AA)	0.512	0.767	1.265	2.829
	Average B (AB)	0.501	0.756	1.335	3.029

1. IES estimates are coefficients from regressions of log age-group hours on age and age-group workers' average log after-tax average hourly earnings. Earnings and hours (inclusive of OJT) from the 1977 CPS.
2. Marginal tax factor A is one minus the 1976 Federal individual income tax (IIT), and social security old age, survivors, disability, and hospital insurance (OASDI & HI) tax on an additional dollar of gross earnings minus—for those aged 62–71 and receiving social security—the implicit marginal tax of social security benefits.
3. Marginal tax factor B is marginal tax factor A plus the accumulation of social security wealth (SSW) asociated with an additional dollar of gross earnings.
4. Average tax factor A is the increment to 1976 IIT, OASDI & HI, and the implicit tax on social security benefits that would result from not working at all during 1976, as a fraction of 1976 gross earnings, plus one.
5. Average tax factor B is an age-weighted average of average tax factor A and marginal tax factor B.
6. The log of each tax factor is averaged across workers within each cohort to obtain a cohort tax factor. See Appendix A for more details of the computation of the four tax factors.
7. Employees are those men reporting positive work hours and average hourly earnings between $1 and $100 for calendar year 1976.
8. SRC OJT is cohort average self-financed on-the-job training, computing from the 1976 Time Use Study as indicated in the text.
9. Heckman *et al.* OJT is on-the-job training inferred from earnings panel data for young men. See Heckman, Lochner, and Taber (1998).

over the life cycle consist of changes at both the *intensive* and the *extensive* margin. This is not true in my model, in which *all* changes are at the extensive margin. However, my model, Heckman's discussion, and Coleman's [1984] and Alogoskoufos's (1987a,b) studies of business-cycle fluctuations agree that annual hours worked by those working positive hours is not the same as aggregate labor supply and that the difference between the two—the fraction of workers who work positive hours during a year—may also respond to wage fluctuations. And the larger elasticity estimates in my Table 1 for "all" as compared to "employees only" confirm Heckman's (1993) life-cycle conjecture.[17]

CPS estimates of σ are sensitive to the number of older age groups included. Table 1 reports estimates about twice as large for samples aged 24–64.[18] After introducing data on taxes and health, I return in Section 3.8 to some of the differences between young and older workers.

3.3 TAXES AND INCENTIVES TO WORK OVER THE LIFE CYCLE

One difference between CPS average hourly earnings and the after-tax market value of time, $w_t(1-\tau_t)$, is the labor-income-tax factor $1-\tau_t$. This factor can vary with age because of the progressivity of the federal individual-income-tax system and its dependence on marital status, because of the regressivity of social security payroll taxes, and because of the effect of age on the rate of accumulation of social security wealth. Four components of federal tax and benefit rules are included in my calculations of the tax factor:

1. Individual income taxes
2. Social security OAS, DI, and HI payroll taxes (employee component only)[19]
3. Implicit taxation by social security benefit formulae from earnings limits (applies only to men aged 62–71 who receive a social security benefit) and inadequate delayed retirement credits (applies only to men age 65–71)
4. The accumulation of social security wealth (applies to men under age 72)

The fourth component is the least straightforward, both because the rules are complicated and cohort-specific and because computation of the tax factor requires information about workers' expectations of future benefit formulae. I therefore report calculations with and without this fourth component.

17. Given the maximum feasible work during a time interval $(K\bar{n})$, the parameter K dictates in my model how aggregate labor-supply responses are partitioned between employment and employee hours. For $K=1$, employment is the entire response. For, say, $K=2$, employment is half of the response at the margin for a group with an 89% employment rate.

18. Depending on the specification, including the four age groups 20–23 or excluding some of the younger age groups affects estimates of σ, although not systematically in one direction or another. These results are available from the author.

19. It is assumed that the earnings data measured by the CPS are net of employer social security contributions.

The accounting period for individual income and social security taxes is a calendar year. If potential work sessions coincide with the tax accounting period (as they do in my model), then incorporating taxes into the estimation of σ is fairly straightforward [see equation (5)], although the CPS does not provide much information about the deductions that families might be taking from their individual income tax or the costs they bear in the acquisition of those deductions. I therefore assume that all families take the standard deduction and, according to equation (5), compare the taxes paid with taxes that would be paid if the man's earnings were set to zero. This produces an average-tax-rate measure of the tax factor.

Another implication of a long work session is that the decision to work before age 62 typically has a negligible effect on the accumulation of social security wealth. 1976 earnings affects social security benefit formulae by affecting the lifetime average of one's top index earnings years (AIME). If someone plans to work most of his prime-age years, then not working a long session in a particular year can only affect the AIME by dropping that year from the calculation and adding another year to the calculation.[20] I therefore exclude SSW from any calculations of the average tax rate.

If the tax accounting period includes multiple potential work sessions, incorporating taxes into the estimation of σ is significantly more complicated. In one extreme (and counterfactual) case, however, the appropriate tax factor is one minus the marginal tax rate on an additional dollar of earnings.[21] Shorter work sessions also imply that a work decision might have an important effect on social security wealth, so I include one computation of the marginal tax rate that includes the effect of work on SSW. Three of the four measures of the tax factor used in my analysis are:

MA. Marginal tax rate, PIA fixed (IIT, OASDI and HI payroll, phaseout of OA benefits)

MB. Marginal tax rate with accumulation of SSW (IIT, OASDI and HI payroll, phaseout of OA benefits, and accumulation of SSW)

AA. Average tax rate (IIT, OASDI and HI payroll, phaseout of OA benefits, and effect of retirement decision on OA benefits)

20. In the extreme case that a worker's earnings during the years he works grows at the same rate as the national index, this substitution of one year for another has zero effect on AIME and therefore zero effect on SSW.

21. This special case requires that the marginal tax rate be a continuous function of earnings [otherwise one has to allow for the "kinky" behavior described by Hausman (1985)] and that each tax accounting period include very many potential work sessions.

My model supposes that K and $\bar{n}$ are the same for all age groups, but another interesting model might allow $\bar{n}$ to increase with age (while holding $K\bar{n}$ constant). The growth of $\bar{n}$ with age would, for example, explain why the employment rate appears to be (at least in CPS data) a relatively more important margin for the old than for the young, even before the "old" reach age 62. I therefore consider a fourth measure of the tax rate that averages the tax rates MB and AA with the weights depending on age:

AB. Age-weighted average of MB and AA

The four tax rates for each cohort (one minus the within-cohort geometric average of their corresponding tax factor) are displayed in Figure 3. With the exception of men aged 65–71, average rates (AA) are lower than marginal rates (MA and MB). But what is more relevant for estima-

Figure 3 LABOR INCOME TAX RATES BY AGE GROUP

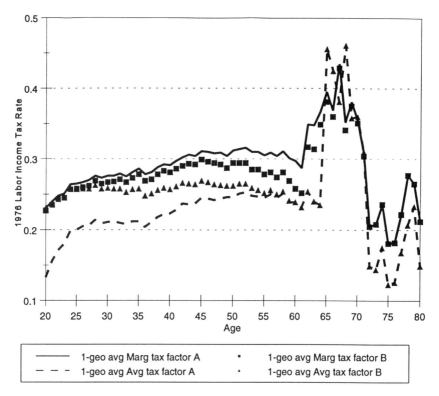

tion of σ is the change in the tax rate with age, and we see that average rates (AA) rise more rapidly for prime-aged men, a difference which can be attributed to the fact that marginal rates are well above average rates for young men and taxable income is rising with age and, for the tax measure MB, the increased rate of accumulation of SSW with age.[22]

Rates of change of the four tax series differ most at ages 62–65. Here average tax rates remain relatively low because most men have not yet retired by age 61 and retirement at age 62 is not particularly encouraged or discouraged by social security benefit formulae. For ages 65–71, however, the social security disincentive for work in the following year is pretty large—over 90% of a year's benefits are lost by delaying retirement one year (Appendix A). Thus Figure 3 displays low cohort-average tax rates except for ages 65–71. Marginal tax rates increase a bit at age 62 because some of the men who do begin to take social security still earn above the earnings limit and are subject to an additional 50% marginal tax. As men age, more are in this situation, so cohort-average marginal tax rates continue to rise in Figure 3.

It is important to note that none of the series in Figure 3 fully capture the work disincentives of social security. One consequence of the social security benefit formulae is that some men aged 62–71 switch to part-time jobs to keep their earnings at or below the earnings limit. The part-time jobs have lower hourly pretax wages, so a man's acceptance of a part-time job—which shows up in Figure 2 as a lower pretax wage—is itself a tax even if he does not pay a dime of the 50% tax implicit in the social security benefit formulae. Thus there are a variety of ways one might partition the after-tax market value of time, $\tilde{w}_t^a$, into a pretax component and a tax factor; my Figures 2 and 3 are only one such way.

Estimates of σ derived from the various tax factors are shown in Tables 1 and 3. The sign and magnitude of the effect of including the tax factor depends on the method of its calculation. To the extent that detrended tastes for work do vary with age (even in a way that is uncorrelated with pretax wages), the tax accounting period differs from the period of labor indivisibility, and the tax system is progressive, $1 - \tau_t$ is negatively correlated with ϵ_t and estimates of σ derived from the various tax factors are biased downwards.

3.4 ON-THE-JOB TRAINING OVER THE LIFE CYCLE

My empirical analysis so far treats a worker's productivity growth as exogenous. It is quite plausible that the increase in productivity of young

---

22. See Appendix A for some details of my calculations, and Feldstein and Samwick (1992) for a study of the accumulation of SSW.

men is due to the accumulation of skills over time and that the decrease (or slower growth) in old age is due to depreciation and low levels of skill accumulation. If time is an important component of skill accumulation and skill accumulation occurs on the job, then the correlation of skill accumulation with age leads to a problem with the interpretation of life-cycle wage estimates such as those as the solid line in Figure 2. The problem is that worker productivity is estimated as the ratio of earnings to hours spent at work but some of the hours at work are not spent producing and are not compensated by the employer. Younger men are presumably engaged in the most skill accumulation, so that their productivity is underestimated the most. As men age, the underestimation is mitigated as skill accumulation time falls. For this reason, the growth of the market value of time of young men is overstated.[23]

Few data are available on time spent training on the job, and even less on the question of who finances that training. A 1976 study of time use by the Survey Research Center (SRC) asked study participants two relevant questions[24]:

(i) "Do you feel you are learning skills on your job that could lead to a better job or to a promotion?" (IF YES) "Sometimes people learn these skills as part of their regular work, while others use time at work to learn skills that are *not* part of their regular job. About how many hours *per week* do you usually spend learning new things as *part* of your regular work?"
(ii) "And how many hours *per week* do you spend learning new things that are *not* part of your regular work?" (Stafford and Duncan, 1985, p. 284).

Under the assumption that 100% of the hours reported as a response to (ii) and 50% of the hours reported as a response to (i) are not compensated by employers, I display as a solid line in Figure 4 the total hours of worker-financed training time for each of 61 male age groups.

23. Jacob Mincer has made this point in several studies (including Mincer, 1974, 1977), distinguishing between average hourly earnings ("wages") and the market value of time ("capacity wages") and deriving implications for the life cycle pattern of hours and earnings. Ghez and Becker (1975, pp. 94, 100) and Heckman (1975, p. 228) also make this point in their studies of labor supply, but Heckman treats training time as unobservable, while Ghez and Becker correct for the bias only by including age squared in equation (10).
24. The 2406 respondents are the same 2406 respondents who filled out the time diaries that are the object of my study in Section 3.5 below, although the two OJT questions were part of the questionnaire and not part of the diary section of the study (my sample sizes are also smaller because I use only men and require that the necessary variables have valid codes).

Figure 4 ESTIMATES OF THE LIFE-CYCLE PATTERN OF WORKER-
FINANCED ON-THE-JOB TRAINING

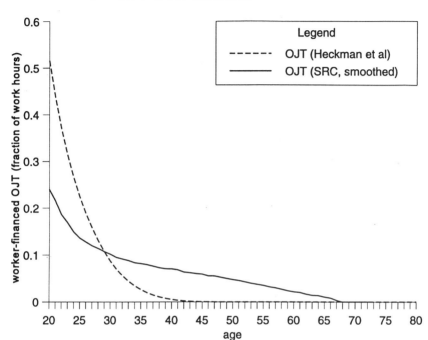

Rather than attempting to measure time spent training on the job, Heckman, Lochner, and Taber (1998) infer OJT time from the earnings growth they observe in a panel study of young men. Figure 4 displays their estimates as a dashed line. Because their method of measuring training time is so different from the SRC survey method, it is a nice complement to the SRC measure, although it should be noted that the Heckman–Lochner–Taber measure is derived from a model with exogenous labor supply.[25]

The 1976 SRC OJT data are first smoothed by regressing OJT on a quadratic in experience, and then the two OJT estimates are used to adjust the CPS estimates of the after-tax market value of time according to equation (11) and displayed in Figure 4. Both measures result in a substantially reduced rate of growth in the after-tax market value of

25. Heckman (1975, p. 255) reports estimates of training time derived from a model with endogenous labor supply that are very similar to the numbers in Heckman, Lochner, and Taber (1998). Heckman (1975, p. 251) also reports another set of estimates which are very much like the SRC numbers before age 30 and like the estimates in Heckman, Lochner, and Taber (1998) after age 30.

time, and the data of Heckman, Lochner, and Taber actually imply a decline in that value of time between the ages of 20 and 23. Not surprisingly, larger estimates of σ are reported in Table 1 when OJT time is used to adjust CPS average hourly earnings. The OJT numbers of Heckman, Lochner, and Taber typically make the biggest difference.[26]

Consistent with the models of Ben-Porath (1967) and Mincer (1974), my measurement of OJT implicitly assumes that human capital is accumulated through training time that cannot be used to produce current output. But an upward adjustment of the value of time that declines with age and hence flattens the profile of the life-cycle value of time can be derived from a number of other accumulation models, including those with learning by doing, signaling, or firm financing of some general training [see Rosen (1972) or Gibbons and Murphy (1992)].

3.5 HOURS-REPORTING BIAS

It has been argued by Juster and Stafford (1991, p. 496), Stafford and Duncan (1985), and others that life-cycle studies of labor supply are sensitive to the method of measuring labor supply. In particular, they claim that larger life-cycle changes in hours are found in time-diary data than in CPS-type survey data.

There are a variety of reasons one expects the time-diary estimates to be more accurate than measures based on CPS-type surveys. First, CPS respondents merely answer the questions "How many weeks did you work last year?" and "In the weeks you worked, how many hours did you usually work?"[27] whereas time-diary respondents are obligated to account for all of their time in a particular day or days. The stereotypical response of "40 hours" might be expected for the CPS respondent, but such a response by a time-diary respondent would create inconsistencies in his diary unless he actually worked 40 hours [although Pencavel (1986, p. 14) suggests that common reports of 40 are real and the result of legal restrictions]. Suppose, for example, that a time-diary respondent works more than 40 hours in a week. A response of "40 hours" would leave a hole in his schedule, which he would have to fill by fabricating a

---

26. Notice that log CPS hours are still used as the independent variable, as suggested by my model, where OJT yields disutility just like other work.

27. CPS respondents are also asked about hours worked in the week prior to the interview, but there is no corresponding earnings question (for example, there are many CPS men who did not work in the week prior to the interview but had substantial earnings in the prior calendar year). One might use log CPS cohort hours last week as the LHS variable in equation (10) and CPS average log hourly earnings last year as the RHS variable. Slightly higher IES estimates are found, but closer to those reported in the first two columns in Table 1 than to those in the last two columns [results available upon request; see also Mulligan (1995)].

story for what he was doing when he was actually working. Casual "40 hours" responses by CPS respondents would generate the appearance that hours do not fluctuate over the life cycle. A second reason to prefer the time diary is that an attempt is made to measure travel time, coffee breaks, lunches at work, and other activities done "at work" while not actually working. A third advantage of the diary data is that it measures time devoted to finding a job. According to my model, time spent searching for a job is work even though it is not compensated. A fourth reason that CPS annual hours are misreported is that they include time spent on paid vacation or sick leave. Fifth, there is some evidence that—aside from the distinction between weeks worked and weeks paid—workers make systematic errors in their responses to retrospective questions about weeks worked (Horvath, 1982).

I suggest four separate corrections for hours-reporting bias. The first and preferred method discards CPS hours all together and computes age-group hours from a study of time use. Figure 1 compares the reports of 1977 CPS respondents with results from a 1975–1976 SRC time-diary study by age group. 624 male respondents completed time diaries for three or four days between October 1975 and September 1976. Total minutes of "normal work," "work on a second job," and "unemployment activities" were summed over the diary days, weighted in such a way as to represent a seven-day synthetic week.[28,29] The sum does not include minutes spent on coffee breaks at work, eating lunch at work, or commuting. There is more idiosyncratic variability in the diary data, which is certainly due to (1) the smaller sample sizes used to compute age-group means and (2) the greater micro-level variation in diary hours. But it seems clear that, as compared to the CPS survey, somewhat more hours are measured for younger men by the diaries and substantially fewer hours for men nearing retirement age (1976 hours for men aged 50–64 are 1448 in the diary, and 1685 in the CPS). This second discrepancy with the CPS is consistent with Ruhm's (1990) study of *bridge jobs* (switches away from career occupation or industry) and, for those aged 62–64, his study of *partial retirement* (periods of employment separated by spells of retirement).

28. My sample is larger than that of Stafford and Duncan (1985) because, apparently, they restrict attention to people aged 64 or less with "regular work schedules," exclude "supplemental respondents," and use only one of the four waves of the 1975–1976 time study.

29. I assume that each respondent's three or four diary days are randomly chosen from the year (actually they're chosen from October, November, February, May, June, and September), so that the SRC's calculation of minutes per synthetic week is a calculation of minutes per representative week. I multiply minutes per synthetic week by 52/60 to get annual hours. Mechanically, the scaling up is done first by the SRC, who computes minutes per representative week, and then I multiply by 52 and divide by 60 to get hours per year.

Table 2   ESTIMATES OF σ CORRECTED FOR HOURS REPORTING ERRORS

Method	Age group	Only hours corrected	Hours and wages corrected[a]	Addendum: no correction[b]
Compute age-group hours	25–55	1.357	6.417	0.569
from time diary	24–64	1.991	4.797	1.406
Compression model, $\theta = 0.7$	25–55	0.729	0.815	0.569
	24–64	1.685	2.088	1.406
Liars model, $\theta = 0.3$	25–55	0.729	1.140	0.569
	24–64	1.685	6.412	1.406
Drop CPS men reporting	25–55	1.000	0.809	0.569
exactly 40 hr/wk	24–64	2.261	1.942	1.406

1. IES estimates are coefficients from regressions of log age-group hours on age and age-group workers' average log market value of time. "All" sample (workers and nonworkers) is used.
2. No tax or OJT factors are used.
[a]When diary hours are used to compute the wage (first two rows), log CPS wage instruments for the corrected wage.
[b]From Table 1.

Table 2 shows that the elasticity of hours (workers and nonworkers) with respect to the CPS hourly wage is about 1.4 for the 25–55-year-old sample and larger for samples that include older men. Elasticities of 2 are typical when the CPS hourly wage is corrected using the SRC OJT hours (see Table 3), and even larger when Heckman, Lochman, and Taber's (1998) numbers are used (not reported).[30]

Like those based on CPS hours, estimates of σ based on diary hours are sensitive to the number of older age groups included, and this sensitivity can be seen in Tables 2 and 3. The diary estimates are even more sensitive to the truncation of older workers in the 50–64 age range, because this is the largest discrepancy between CPS and diary hours.

If it is true that the life-cycle hours profile is misestimated with CPS data, then average hourly earnings are also likely to be misestimated. Ideally, one would like to discard the CPS hours data from the computation of average hourly earnings and replace them with diary data, but, due to the relatively small sample size, Figure 1 shows that the age-grouped diary data are fairly idiosyncratic. This means that average hourly earnings computed with diary data would be idiosyncratic and *in a way that is correlated with idiosyncratic errors in measured hours*. One ap-

30. As is obvious from Figure 1, there is substantially more sampling error when time-diary cohorts are used to estimate cohort hours. Not surprisingly, OLS standard errors for σ are larger, typically between 0.2 and 0.6, as compared to a typical range of 0.02 to 0.25 when CPS hours are used. Of course, serial correlation and a number of first-stage estimation errors mean that OLS standard errors overstate the precision of my estimates.

proach is to instrument for log (CPS earnings/diary hours) with log (CPS earnings/CPS hours) in the regression of diary hours on average hourly earnings. We see in the first two rows of Table 2 that doing so substantially increases point estimates of σ. However, because of the poor fit of the first-stage regression, the magnitude of the increase is quite sensitive to the tax factor, OJT factor, and sample used.

Diary age-group sample sizes are fairly small, with as few as 5 men and 18 days sampled in any single group aged 24–55.[31] The typical age group samples 12 men and 47 days. Hence, my second and third corrections for hours-reporting bias are of some interest, because they do not rely on grouping the diary study by age. Both methods assume a model of hours-reporting bias, calibrate the model by comparing histograms of reported hours for 365 diary men and 23,899 CPS men aged 25–55 report-

Table 3 ESTIMATES OF σ INCLUDING OLDER MEN, WITH TAX, OJT, HEALTH, AND COMPOSITION-BIAS CORRECTIONS

		IES Estimates[a]					
		1977 CPS: Health regressors?[c]			1975–1976 time-diary hours, CPS average hourly earnings: Health regressors?[c]		
Age group	Tax factor[b]	No	Yes	Yes, AA[d]	No	Yes	woPC[e]
24–64	None	1.488	1.238	0.984	2.088	1.167	1.897
	MA	1.538	1.270	1.147	2.132	1.262	1.898
	MB	1.604	1.317	1.225	2.181	1.251	1.888
	AA	1.509	1.135	0.944	2.128	1.058	1.749
	AB	1.542	1.191	1.052	2.173	1.117	1.829
24–79	None	2.953	2.799	1.027	2.923	1.139	1.766
	MA	2.672	2.685	1.168	2.438	1.186	1.695
	MB	2.668	2.597	1.363	2.413	1.110	1.583
	AA	2.193	1.991	1.366	1.916	0.780	1.167
	AB	2.198	1.982	1.425	1.924	0.777	1.159

1. OJT is cohort-average self-financed on-the-job training, computing from the 1976 Time Use Study as indicated in the text.
2. See text for details of computation of composition-bias correction of wages.
[a]Coefficients from regressions of log age-group hours on age and age-group workers' average log after-tax market value of time. "All" sample (workers and nonworkers) is used.
[b]See Notes to Table 1 and Appendix A for explanation.
[c]Health regressors are age-group averages of hours spent on personal care and four indicators of physical condition.
[d]Uses arithmetic-average rather than geometric-average CPS wage.
[e]Personal-care hours omitted.

31. Among groups aged 56–69, only the aged-63 group samples fewer days, 8.

ing positive hours, and infer the true hours elasticity from estimated CPS hours elasticities. The first model is a *compression model*, assuming that reported hours $\hat{n}$ is closer to some stereotypical number $\tilde{n}$ than is true hours n for those whose true hours are positive: $\ln \hat{n} - \ln \tilde{n} = \theta (\ln n - \ln \tilde{n})$. The second, the *liars model*, assumes that a fraction θ of those working positive hours report the stereotypical number $\tilde{n}$ while the rest report the truth. When conservatively calibrated to the cross-section of 365 diary men, both models imply substantially larger elasticities (see the middle four rows of Table 2). Details of these calculations can be found in Appendix B.

A critical review of the literature on time measurement is beyond the scope of this paper [see Juster (1986) for a favorable evaluation of diary studies, and Juster and Stafford (1991) for a literature review], but there may be other reasons to distrust time diaries, so my fourth method is based on the CPS data only. It discards those men reporting *exactly* 40 weekly hours (roughly half of the sample) before computing cohort averages and estimating cross-cohort regressions. The method implicitly assumes that all reporting 40 are liars and that the propensity to lie is unrelated to determinants of labor supply other than the wage. Estimates of 0.8 and 1.0 are found with this method for the 25–55 age group. Correcting wages in addition to hours increases estimates in the first six rows of the table, but this is not true with the fourth method.

3.6 OLDER WORKERS I: SOURCES OF WAGE VARIATION

It appears from the pretax wage series in Figure 2 and is obvious from the tax measures shown in Figure 3 that there is more age-related variation in the after-tax market value of time when older workers are included in the sample. All else the same, more variation in the after-tax market value of time might be expected to minimize underestimation of σ due to measurement and other errors. Because labor supply may not be as linear as suggested by my equation (10), it may also be desirable— from the point of view of making predictions for aggregate labor supply—to have an older sample with mean hours worked closer to the population mean.[32]

However, including older workers may increase the difficulty of inferring an age group's average market value of time, because relatively few work some time during the year (although see my discussion in the next subsection). Panel data complement the cross-section data in my Section 3.7 to make some progress on this problem.

32. The average annual hours worked for those aged 24 and over in the 1975–1976 Diary Study (including women) is 1165, which can be compared with 2047 for men aged 25–55 and 1677 for men aged 24–79.

Another problem is that older workers are more likely to hold part-time jobs for "noneconomic" reasons, and thus part-time jobs may pay less than full-time jobs (author's calculations from the March 1977 CPS). If the old-age movement to part-time jobs is in response to the declining labor productivity growth that occurs with age, my measures of wages overstate the declining rate of growth and may understate σ. However, an old-age movement to part-time employment may be in response to an exogenous change in preferences for work, so that the decline in wages is a response to a decline in labor supply (not the other way around) and σ is overestimated. One adjustment for this is to estimate the age-group average pretax market value of time from a sample of full-time workers only. Doing so produces estimates of σ which are very similar to those displayed in Tables 1–3, suggesting that these two biases are nearly offsetting.[33] It should be noted, however, that even the average hourly earnings of full-time workers in their sixties are as low as or lower than those of full-time workers aged 30.

3.7 COMPOSITION BIAS OVER THE LIFE CYCLE

Because employment rates vary with age, the average hourly earnings of a cohort's workers is an average over a sample that varies with age. In contrast, the implications of the theory have been derived for a sample which (ignoring mortality) is constant over time—the entire cohort. To the extent that the market value of time differs for employees and nonemployees, the average log hourly earnings of cohort a's workers, X^{*a}_t, is a biased estimate of the average log market value of time of the entire cohort, X^a_t. I refer to this bias as a *composition bias* and denote it by B^a_t:

$$\text{composition bias}^a_t = \ln B^a_t = (1 - \Pi^a_t)(X^{*a}_t - \tilde{X}^a_t),$$

where $\tilde{X}^a_t$ is the average log market value of time of those aged a who don't work at t. The composition-bias corrections are done separately for young and old men (age$\leq$55 and age$>$55). For young men, PSID waves 1976–1978 (referring to hours and earnings for 1975–1977) are used to correct for the composition bias arising when the average hourly earnings of workers in 1976 are used to estimate the value of time of all

---

33. Full-time wage results—including those that make OJT, tax, composition bias, and hours reporting bias corrections and include workers as old as 79—are available upon request. Of course, these calculations do not rule out the possibility that the decline in the taste for work mainly reduces wages of full-time workers rather than increasing the propensity to take low-wage part-time jobs. It is also possible that full-time wage estimates understate σ because the movement to part-time employment is part of the implicit social security tax.

cohort members. Both PSID–SRC and SEO samples are used, but, by weighting each man with his 1976 family weight, SEO members are effectively downweighted for the purpose of computing various sample average log wages.

At the annual level of time aggregation, transitions to and from employment are often associated with changes in household status. For example, a young man is likely to form his own household when he goes from a full year of no employment to a year of some employment. I therefore utilize the individual files from the PSID (in addition to the family files), because the individual files include information about hours and incomes of men who are not heads of households. The individual files report an individual's taxable income and indicate whether that income includes any nonlabor income, but not how much. This is the only measure of labor income available for PSID men who are not heads of households, but, not surprisingly, taxable income includes asset income only for 2% of these men.[34] I therefore exclude those nonheads with asset income from my calculations of average log hourly earnings.

In order to estimate the average value of time of nonworkers, some assumptions are required. I assume that, conditional on age, the annual growth rate of a person's market value of time is uncorrelated with changes in his employment status. This assumption is true under the null hypothesis of a zero labor-supply elasticity and can be true with a nonzero elasticity, but is false under other conditions. If those who change employment status have a different growth rate of their market value of time, then my estimates of the composition bias are subject to a selection bias. There is no magic correction for selection bias, so I only note that it may be a problem and also point out that nearly every other study of labor supply—including those individual-panel studies of the hours margin in isolation from the employment margin [see my discussion of assumption (A2) in Section 2.9]—has this kind of selection bias. The selection bias arises in so many studies of labor supply because there is no person who works continuously—even the hardest-working man has some time when he is not working (e.g., evenings, weekends, sick days, holidays, vacations)—and the econometrician is typically unable to directly measure the market value of time during those nonwork periods.

34. Based on comparisons of individual taxable income, individual transfer income, and household-head labor income for men who are heads of households and report no asset income, it is clear that "taxable income" excludes transfer income even though some forms of transfer income are taxable by the IRS.

3.7.1 Young Men   Over a three-year period, enough young men (95%) are employed at some time that we can obtain a reasonable estimate of the market value of time of those not employed in any particular year by looking at the earnings of those men in adjacent years. First, I compute the $(t-1,t)$ and $(t,t+1)$ average log hourly earnings growth for those employed at least 200 hours in each of the two relevant years. For those not employed at t but employed in an adjacent year, I estimate their market value of time at t by adding (or subtracting) the relevant growth rate to (or from) their average log hourly earnings when they were working at $t-1$ or $t+1$.[35]

Since employment rates are much greater than 50% for all young age groups, one might expect that the relative market value of time of those not employed is decreasing in the employment rate because those not employed are a more select sample in the high-employment age groups. In fact, the data—together with the estimation method outlined above—support this.

It is too much to use the relatively few available PSID observations to estimate the market value of time of those not employed as a *function* of age, so I compute instead the mean percentage difference between a nonworker's market value of time and the average value of time of workers his age—a 20% (in log points) difference in my sample.[36] Bils (1985) obtains a similar estimate of 20% for young men from the NLSY. Assuming that the 20% gap is independent of age, the percentage composition bias of my CPS value of time estimates is

$$\ln B_t^a = (1 - \Pi_t^a)\,0.20, \tag{12}$$

where Π_t^a is the fraction of cohort a employed at some time during year t.

If instead the relative market value of time of those not employed is decreasing in age (as the PSID data suggest), then my calculation (12) overstates the correlation between composition bias and employment rates, and I overstate the growth of the market value of time with age among young men. This error tends to reduce estimates of the labor-supply elasticity.

3.7.2 Old Men   The annual employment status is much more persistent for old men, because it is typical for a man to retire and never return to employment again. One therefore might compute the composition bias for old men by accumulating the composition bias. However, this accu-

---

35. For those working in both adjacent years, I average the results of the two methods.
36. The median difference is 11%.

mulation requires many years of a panel data set large enough to estimate age-specific employment rates and retirement hazards for each cohort. Assuming that $B^a_{t-1} = B^{a-1}_t$, the composition bias can be computed according to

$$B^a_t = (X^{*a}_t - g^a_t) - X^{*a}_{t-1} + B^{a-1}_t \qquad \text{age} > 55$$

The first term is the (log of) date-$(t-1)$ hourly earnings averaged across those working at t, which is decomposed in the parentheses into the date-t hourly earnings minus the growth rate between $t-1$ and t. The second term is estimated (log of) date-$(t-1)$ hourly earnings for those working at $t-1$. The third term is an estimate of the lagged bias, which differs from the actual lagged bias to the extent that retirement rates were different for the a and $a-1$ cohorts. Hence, the first two terms are the *increment to the composition bias*.

Another relevant complication for old men is that some of them change from full-time to part-time work and the part-time work tends to have lower hourly earnings. As discussed above, an important part of the difference between part-time and full-time wages by the elderly is the form in which they pay the implicit social security tax, so I do not want to count the retirement of a full-time worker as the exit of a relatively high-wage person unless his wage is higher than that of other high-wage workers. Yet another complication is that workers may receive a bonus, accumulated sick pay, or other extra earnings upon retirement that cannot be attributed to the work they did during the year prior to retirement. This would also make it appear that high-wage men are more likely to retire. Using the 1980 5% Census PUMS, I therefore compute the increment to the composition bias by imputing wages for sample men aged 55 and over according to the median average hourly earnings for full-time male workers aged 50–54 in the same schooling and two-digit occupation category, and then, cohort by cohort, comparing the log imputed wage for those retiring and those remaining in the labor force.[37] Those who continue to work typically earn 8% per hour more than those retiring in cohorts and 55–59, 4% more than those retiring in cohorts aged 60–69, and 6% more than those retiring in cohorts aged 70–79. In other words, low-wage men are more likely to retire, especially before age 60. This finding is consistent with the fact that social security rules encourage retirement most for low-earnings people and with the patterns of retirement by occupation and schooling documented by Costa (1998) and others.

---

37. The 1980 PUMS is used so as to have enough observations in each age–labor-force status cell and in each schooling–occupation cell.

Although the wage gap between workers and recent retirees is largest for cohorts aged 55–60, the increment to the composition bias is larger for cohorts aged 60 and over because the retirement hazard is so much larger. Figure 2 displays as crosses the age–wage profile corrected for OJT and composition biases. We see that correcting for composition bias lowers the estimated cohort market value of time (compare the crosses with the squares), especially for young and old men. Table 3 reports corresponding estimates of σ and, when compared with Tables 1 and 2, shows that correcting for composition bias in the aged-24–64 sample typically lowers estimates of σ, although the effect is quite small relative to the other adjustments I've made. Although not reported in the tables, the same is true for my estimates for the aged-25–55 and aged-24–79 samples.

3.8 OLDER WORKERS II: HEALTH AS AN INDEPENDENT DETERMINANT OF LABOR SUPPLY

Aging is associated with changes in physical capabilities, especially at older ages. Some of these changes affect labor productivity and, presuming my various measures of the market value of time are related to labor productivity, are useful sources of life-cycle wage variation. But aging may also affect the marginal disutility of work. Without a proxy for the marginal disutility of work, my basic labor-supply specifications attribute all of the age-related labor-supply changes (apart from a trend) to age-related wage changes.

I introduce several proxies for the marginal disutility of work in the specifications that include older men. One proxy is annual hours spent on *personal care:* dressing, bathing, toilet, trips to the doctor, helping another adult with personal care, sleeping, and napping. There are two reasons why one might expect this to be a good proxy for the marginal disutility of work. First, a sick and frail person who must spent extra time on these activities effectively has a shorter day to divide between work and leisure. Second, one might expect age-related changes in personal-care time to be correlated with other factors shifting the marginal disutility of work.

Men spend a substantial amount of time on personal care: 8 minutes per week on medical appointments, 268 minutes per week washing and dressing, 59 minutes per week on medical care for oneself or another adult, 2 minutes per week on other personal care, and 3455 minutes per week sleeping or napping.[38] The sum of these personal-care minutes is correlated with age, although the only subcategories with some positive correla-

---

38. These are averages for men aged 24–79.

tion are medical appointments, night sleep, and resting or napping (medical care for other adults is slightly negatively correlated with age).

I use four measures of physical capabilities from wave I of the Health and Retirement Survey (HRS) and the survey of Assets and Health Dynamics of the Oldest Old (AHEAD) to proxy for health status, although it is unfortunate that these health surveys occurred 15 years after my CPS and diary surveys were conducted.[39] Physical incapacities are likely to be associated with pain experienced during work activities and would thus be a reason why an older person might not work even if he were as productive as when young. Physical incapacity measures are also expected to be correlated with other determinants of the marginal disutility of work.

The first measure of physical (in)capabilities is the fraction of cohort affirmative answers to three questions:[40]

Is it very difficult or impossible for you to . . .
(i) . . . walk several blocks?
(ii) . . . climb a flight of stairs without resting?
(iii) . . . lift or carry weights over 10 pounds, like a heavy bag of groceries?

My second measure is the fraction of the cohort often troubled with pain that makes normal work difficult.[41] The third measure is the fraction of the cohort that had been an overnight patient in a hospital during the year prior to the interview.[42] The fourth is the *body mass index* [BMI = (weight in kilograms)/(height in meters)^2], which has been shown to be closely related to mortality, health, and labor-force participation [see Costa (1998, Chapter 4) for a review of the relevant literature]. Age-group average BMI and age-group average squared BMI are included in the cross-age-group regressions.

It is perhaps unsurprising that the inclusion of health measures does not substantially affect elasticity estimates, especially in the 24–64 age group. After all, health deteriorated relatively rapidly with age in the early part of the twentieth century, while gainful employment rates did

39. Neither HRS nor AHEAD surveyed many men aged 50 or less, so I assign all cohorts aged 24–50 the values of the health variables for the 51–52-year-old cohort.
40. Those respondents who say they cannot answer the question because they do not do the activity are assumed to be unable to do it.
41. AHEAD asks a slightly different question—whether pain "kept you from doing things you wanted to do" during the last 12 months. For the age groups that appear in both HRS and AHEAD, affirmative response rates to the AHEAD question are twice as high, so I cut AHEAD responses in half to make them comparable with HRS.
42. The HRS also includes measures of cognitive ability such as memory skills. I exclude these measures under the assumption that they are related to labor productivity but not to the marginal disutility of work.

not (Costa, 1998, Chapters 2, 4). For example, Costa (1998, Figure 2.3) reports gainful-employment rates of over 80% for white men aged 65 and over in 1880, 1900, 1910, and 1920 (as compared with 20 or 25% for the 1970s). At the same time she reports sizable majorities of veterans aged 65 and over in 1910 suffering from chronic musculoskeletal (67.7%), chronic digestive (84.0%), and chronic circulatory (90.1%) conditions and compares them with much lower rates for World War II veterans aged 65 and over in 1983 (47.2% with chronic musculoskeletal, 48.9% with chronic digestive, and 39.9% with chronic circulatory conditions). Costa also displays data from 1930 and 1992 showing a much steeper 1930 age gradient for risks of heart disease, arteriosclerosis, hypertension, and other chronic conditions. With an age–health gradient that is so small by historical standards, health probably should not explain much of the modern age–employment pattern. Furthermore, my measures of physical incapacity are not very high (e.g., only 13% of those aged 65 report that pain prevents them from working) and follow a pretty linear trend with age.

The only case in which the health variables make a substantial difference for the 24–64 group is when cohort hours are measured with the time diary. But this may be spurious, because diaries constrain that all uses of time—including the LHS variable (work hours) and one of the RHS variables (personal-care hours)—sum to 24 hours per day. So the final column of Table 3 reports wage elasticities from regressions including measures of physical incapacity but not personal-care hours.

While modern changes in health with age may not produce dramatic changes in the marginal disutility of work, this is not to say that health does not explain a lot of life-cycle labor supply through its effect on the wage. Pretax wages grow much less rapidly and even fall with age, which partly reflects some declining physical capacity with age and partly reflects human-capital investment decisions made in response to that declining physical capacity. Bartel and Taubman's (1979) study of four health conditions finds that, among those working during the year, adverse health reduces pretax wages twice as much as it reduces hours, and presumably some of this reduction in hours is a response to the wage. The U.S. House Ways and Means Committee (1996, Section 1, p. 5), Diamond and Mirlees (1978), and others suggest that even the implicit tax disincentives of the social security system are a response to the age–health relationship.

3.9 WITHIN-COHORT AGGREGATION BIAS

I estimate equation (10) by regressing log cohort average hours on age and average log after-tax market value of time. A within-cohort aggregation bias A_t^a, a function of the second and higher moments of the within-cohort distribution of ϵ_t and $\ln \tilde{w}_t$, is an omitted variable in this regression. One check for the presence of an omitted-variable bias is to use log average after-tax market value of time as an independent variable. Doing so has little effect on estimates of σ (results available upon request) with the exception of the aged 24–79 CPS sample and, to a much lesser degree, the aged 24–64 CPS sample (see the third column of Table 3). An aggregation bias term is still an omitted variable, but may be weakly or even negatively correlated with A_t^a, so the similarity of results with average log wage and with log average wage suggests that aggregation bias is not serious.

Nor is it clear that purging aggregation bias from estimates of σ is especially interesting for macroeconomic forecasting. Shocks affecting the market value of time may also affect the distribution of ϵ_t and $\ln \tilde{w}_t$ and do so in a way that is correlated with $\tilde{w}_t$ in much the same way it is in life-cycle data.

3.10 OVERVIEW OF RESULTS FROM SYNTHETIC-COHORT SAMPLES

Life-cycle data are consistent with a substantial willingness to substitute leisure over time. Hours worked by a cohort grow almost twice as fast relative to trend as that cohort's average after-tax market value of time. An important—but not the only—component of the cohort's labor-supply response is due to changes in its annual employment rate, while many previous studies of similar life-cycle data focus only on employee hours. Moreover, time-diary data suggest that the life-cycle changes in aggregate work hours are understated by CPS-type surveys. Training data suggest that life-cycle changes in the market value of time are overstated by CPS average hourly earnings. Another departure from previous studies is my consideration of behavior after age 60 or 65. Tables 1–3 review the six modifications I have made to life-cycle-based calculations of the IES. Using a sample of prime-aged working CPS males, I arrive at an estimate of 0.37 that is similar to that of Ghez and Becker (1975). Expanding the sample to include all prime-aged men increases the estimate to 0.57. Modifying this estimate by introducing older workers delivers estimates of 1.5 or higher. Instead, an elasticity of 1.36 is the result when aggregate labor supply is considered with time-diary data. If the time diaries are correct, young men slightly underreport and retirement-aged men substantially overreport annual hours in CPS-type surveys. Larger elasticity estimates are found even with CPS data when either a correction for self-financed on-the-job training or a correction for life-cycle changes in the marginal tax rate is made. Slightly smaller estimates are obtained after a correction for composition bias and an introduction of health regressors. The result of making all seven modifications—considering aggregate cohort labor supply, adding older workers, correcting for life-cycle changes in the marginal tax rate and training time, using diary data, and correcting for composition bias—produces elasticity estimates of 1 or 2. Even if one is dubious about some of my departures from previous studies of life-cycle data, it seems difficult to argue that the life-cycle data offer a powerful rejection of the ISH.

4. A Life Event: The Termination of AFDC Benefits

4.1 OVERVIEW AND COMPARISON WITH SYNTHETIC-COHORT SAMPLES

Clearly the value of time grows at different rates at different points of the life cycle. It is also clear that labor supply grows at different rates over the life cycle. But the discussion and analysis above shows that it is difficult to quantitatively determine how anticipated wage growth changes with age and to what degree labor supply responds to these changes as well as changes in the willingness to work. As an attempt to get better measures of anticipated changes in the value of time and corresponding changes in labor supply—changes which cannot be attributed to changes in the willingness to work or other unobservables—I look at a special life-cycle event, the termination of AFDC benefits at the 18th birthday of the youngest child.

4.2 TERMINATION OF AFDC AS A LIFE-CYCLE EVENT

For three reasons, the termination of AFDC benefits on the 18th birthday of the youngest child is an interesting life-cycle event. First, it is *fully anticipated.* Children can only get older or die, either of which eventually terminates AFDC benefits. Furthermore, since policy for the period 1970–1995 had been rather stable over time regarding the age at which benefits are terminated,[43] it is only reasonable for most of this period for families with youngest child aged 17 to anticipate termination of benefits. Since benefits are reduced to zero on the 18th birthday of the youngest child, the magnitude of the benefit reduction that a family with youngest child aged 17 might expect is easy for them to calculate: a reduction from current benefit levels to zero.

---

43. It can be argued that the 1996 "welfare reform" introduced substantial uncertainty about a particular family's future welfare eligibility. During the prior 25 years, the most important legislative changes were in 1981, changes which affected to some degree the magnitude of the AFDC tax on work (U.S. House Ways and Means Committee 1996, pp. 517–518).

Second, because AFDC benefits act as an implicit tax on the earnings of AFDC household heads, the event produces a quantitatively important change in the value of time. To a good approximation, AFDC and food-stamp benefits b_t for an *eligible* family at date t can be computed according to equation (2) with $\underline{b}_t = 0$, and b_t a function of calendar time, family size, state of residence, and other demographic variables. In the language of the House Ways and Means Committee, d_t are "expenses reasonably attributable to the earning of income" (including child-care costs, transportation costs, and payroll taxes) and "earnings disregards" and other deductions.[44] R_t is the "benefit reduction rate," approximately equal to 0.5 for the years 1970–1995. The benefit formula (2) thereby acts as a significant tax on work for pay, and represents a change in the value of time that is an order of magnitude larger than those teased out of synthetic cohort samples.[45]

If a work session were very short relative to the AFDC accounting period (one month) and the constraint $d_t \leqq w_t n_t$ did not bind, then labor supply might be viewed as perfectly divisible and the tax rate on an additional hour of work for otherwise eligible families would be $R_t(t)$ [see Barro and Sahasakul (1983) for a proof]. However, if participation in the labor force during an AFDC accounting period requires a discrete increase in hours, then the implicit tax rate $\tau_{t,k}$ on participation is less than $R_{t,k}$ and—to the extent that the length of a work session is similar to the AFDC accounting period—can be computed according to (5) for otherwise eligible families.[46]

While the change in the market value of time is large and anticipated, one disadvantage of a study of AFDC is that the magnitude of the change is difficult to compute exactly. An exact calculation requires information about earnings disregards, the costs of obtaining those disregards, the degree to which work is indivisible, tastes, the pretax market value of time, and other determinants of family eligibility. However, equation (5) shows that the benefit reduction rate is an upper bound on this implicit tax rate. Zero is a lower bound and applies to families whose family structure, asset holdings, or other characteristic makes them ineligible. The implicit tax rate is close to zero for a family with a high pretax market value of time.

44. U.S. House Ways and Means Committee (1996, Section 8, p. 390). This section also provides a discussion of the rules concerning deductions and how they changed over time.
45. Computing the implicit tax on work may be a difficult task (for an economist or for a welfare participant), but, since the families in my sample have youngest child aged 17, it is reasonable to expect that their experience with the welfare system will cause them to act as if they had pretty accurate estimates of the tax.
46. This formula ignores the effect of AFDC labor supply on asset holdings, which in turn affects $\bar{b}$. Mulligan (1997) shows that the effect is small.

Many studies of labor supply face the problem of estimating a person's market value of time when he or she is not working. A third advantage of studying the termination of AFDC is that we can plausibly argue that the change in the value of time associated with the termination of benefits dominates other changes over the relatively short section of the life cycle being studied. I argue that, while government policy produces an important change in the value of time, the 18th birthday of the youngest child is not associated with large and rapid changes in tastes, health, productivity, and other variables. However, it turns out that one disadvantage of this episode is that changes over time in the implicit tax rate cannot be calculated precisely.

Another disadvantage of my AFDC study is that I do not have OJT or diary hours measures. Indeed, hours reporting bias may be especially systematic before the termination of AFDC, since AFDC beneficiaries have an incentive to underreport their earnings (and hence their hours) to government agencies—although they may not have the same incentive to misreport to the PSID. If such PSID misreporting does occur, then I am likely to underestimate hours before age 18 and overestimate σ.

4.3 DATA DESCRIPTION AND TABULATION

Using the 1970–1990 waves of the PSID and including both the PSID–SRC and SEO samples, I extract all households with youngest child aged 17 and a wife or female head present. I add to these records information on the employment and family situation as well as some consumption expenditures of the wife or female household head two years earlier (when the child was 15) and two years later (when the child was 19). This main sample can be divided into two:

AFDC sample. AFDC income > 0 in calendar year of the interview when the youngest child was aged 17.
Non-AFDC sample. AFDC income $= 0$ in calendar year of the interview when the youngest child was aged 17.

If the 18th birthday of the youngest child is not associated with large and rapid changes in tastes, health, productivity, and other variables, then we expect little change in the employment of non-AFDC women whose youngest child turns 18. Column (1) of Table 4 verifies this conjecture, showing a slight decrease in the fraction of women employed sometime during the year as their youngest child ages from 15 to 19. Perhaps this decrease is to be expected given that the women in the sample are typically in their forties and fifties and labor-force participation rates of women are declining slightly in this range [Sweet (1973,

Table 4   WOMEN'S MARKET WORK AS A FUNCTION OF AGE OF
YOUNGEST CHILD[a]

	(1)	(2)	(3)	(4)	(5)
Fract. hours >0 at age 15	0.69	0.30	0.28	0.32	0.35
Fract. hours >0 at age 19	0.67	0.33	0.34	0.38	0.43
Annual hours, 15	1051	348	314	382	387
Annual hours, 19	1090	422	406	486	560
Log diff. annual hours	0.04	0.19	0.26	0.24	0.37
Annual h of workers, 15	1533	1146	1135	1192	1112
Annual h of workers, 19	1630	1283	1200	1288	1289
Log diff. ann. h of workers	0.06	0.11	0.06	0.08	0.15
Ann. h of continuous, 15[b]	1594	1264	1243	1363	1363
Ann. h of continuous, 19[b]	1679	1391	1374	1517	1517
Log. diff. ann. h of continuous	0.05	0.10	0.10	0.11	0.11
Sample	Non-AFDC	AFDC	AFDC	AFDC	AFDC
Subsample	All	All	Female head	Fem. hd., (AFDC 19) =0	Fem. hd., (AFDC 19) =0, hd. age<62
Sample size	1622	79	65	53	46

Source: Author's calculation using the PSID.
[a]Annual measures of mother's market work according to the age of the youngest child.
[b]Hours of mothers employed sometime during both of the years when the youngest was aged 15 or 19.

Table 1–4) and the author's own calculations using the 1981–1991 CPS outgoing rotation groups]. Conditional on working, annual hours worked for non-AFDC increase slightly.

Column (2) of Table 4 reports the fraction of women in the AFDC sample who were employed when the youngest child was 15 and the fraction of the same women who were employed four years later when the youngest child was 19. We see that the fraction working positive hours increases from 0.30 to 0.33. Considering that many of the families were not eligible for AFDC when the child was aged 15, the percentage change in the annual hours worked by this group is a substantial 0.19 log points. If we exclude the 14 male-headed AFDC households, the fraction increases from 0.28 to 0.34 and annual hours increase by 26%.

A few of the 65 age-17 female-headed AFDC households—12 to be exact—still receive AFDC payments after the youngest child turns 18. For all of these 12, a younger child entered the household and may be the reason for continued AFDC eligibility. If we exclude those households who do not appear to have eligibility terminated, the fraction working increases from 0.32 to 0.38 and annual hours increase by 24%.

Seven of the female household heads are old enough to be eligible for social security, although it is not clear that all of them would have had long enough work histories to be eligible. For those who do collect social security after their youngest child turns 18, the change in the incentives to work is different from those who do not. One way to separate the effect of social security is to delete all households with heads aged 62 or more when the child was 19. For those in this sample who have their AFDC eligibility terminated, annual hours increase 37%.

"Annual hours" reported in the third and fourth rows is an average across the same sample of women at two points in time, with women who do not work at all (who are 60–70% of the AFDC sample) counted as zeros. What about hours among those who do some work during the year? This is equal to annual hours of all divided by the fraction with positive hours and is reported in the sixth and seventh rows of Table 4. "Hours of workers" increase substantially in the AFDC sample, about as much as the fractions working some hours. Notice from the first two rows of the table that "hours of workers" is an average over two different samples at the two points in time, because the fraction of those working positive hours is different. Another interesting statistic is hours worked by those working in both years (annual hours of continuous workers), a statistic which is necessarily computed over the same sample at both points in time. We see even larger increases here, and it can be inferred from the table that those entering the labor force between ages 15 and 19 (i.e., those who have zero hours at 15 and positive hours at 19) work fewer hours than those who were already in the labor force and remain there.

Notice that, after the termination of benefits, the annual hours of continuous workers are quite similar to those of women in the non-AFDC sample. However, the annual hours and the fractions with positive annual hours in the AFDC and non-AFDC groups are still fairly different. Thus, although the termination of benefits has a substantial effect on work, it is clear that AFDC eligibility cannot explain all of the difference between the employment of the AFDC and non-AFDC samples.

4.4 TAX RATE AND ELASTICITY ESTIMATES

What do we learn about willingness to substitute work over time from this life-cycle event? An estimated intertemporal elasticity of substitution of work is one summary of the data which is comparable with other intertemporal studies of wage and work changes. This first requires an estimate of the change in the sample average implicit tax rate on work. I consider three estimates of the sample average τ before age 18: 0.2, 0.3, and 0.4.

At the micro level, the implicit tax rate τ is zero for families who are ineligible regardless of mother's earnings and can be bounded above by the benefit reduction rate (including the food-stamp program, 0.47 before 1981 and somewhat larger after) for otherwise eligible families. Even conditional on nonearnings determinants of eligibility, it is difficult to compute the implicit tax rate, because the tax on earnings is nonlinear, is determined by both AFDC and food-stamp rules, depends on earnings-related deductions and how they interact with other determinants of eligibility, depends on the costs of obtaining various deductions and earnings disregards, depends on the pretax market value of time and the degree to which work is indivisible, and changes with calendar time. Fraker, Moffitt, and Wolf (1985) compute average tax rates of 0.25 in 1971, 0.32 in 1979, and 0.70 in 1982, and even these are too high, because they ignore the costs of obtaining various deductions [shown as f in equation (5)]. Thus I view 0.5 as a conservative upper bound on the implicit tax rate τ for families satisfying eligibility requirements other than mother's earnings.

In order to compute a sample-average τ, we must compute the fraction of families satisfying eligibility requirements other than mother's earnings. We know that a family in my AFDC sample is eligible (or at least appears eligible to the welfare agency) when the youngest child is aged 17, because they receive AFDC income in that year. We also know that the 53 families in columns (4) and (5) of Table 4 are ineligible when the child is aged 19. What we do not know is exactly how many families are eligible when the child is aged 15. However, studies of AFDC mobility surveyed by the U.S. House Ways and Means Committee (1995, pp. 500–510) suggest that an important fraction—perhaps as much as one-half[47]—of those receiving AFDC at child age 17 would not be eligible at child age 15 because of changes in eligibility other than high earnings at that age. If so, then the sample-average age-15 implicit tax rate could eaisly be as small as 0.2. Thus I view 0.4 as a conservative upper bound on the sample-average τ.

Second, as shown in my model, we need to say something about the shape of the distribution of unobserved determinants of participation in

47. 80% of the sample of 46 families in column (5) receive AFDC sometime during the calendar year the youngest child was 15.

order to say something about how a, say, 50% wage change would affect participation rates in a group with a participation rate of 25% vs. a group with a rate of 75%. We make two assumptions in this regard—normal and uniform distributions. Then the estimated elasticity of participation is the percentage change in G^{-1} (Π_t) (where Π_t is the participation at child's age t) divided by the percentage change in the value of time (ln 0.6, ln 0.7, or ln 0.8). Table 5 reports elasticity estimates for a variety of work and tax rate estimates. An elasticity of 1 is fairly typical.

It is well known that AFDC participation involves movement into and out of the labor force [see the studies surveyed by the U.S. House Ways and Means Committee (1996)], and this fact alone strongly suggests that at least some people are willing to substitute work over time. It may even be the case that people select into the AFDC program on the basis of their willingness to substitute over time (σ) as well as income, tastes, and other variables. If so, then the elasticity estimates reported in Table 5 are not indicative of a typical person's willingness to substitute leisure over time, with the deviation determined by the importance of σ relative to income, tastes, and other variables.

AFDC is most relevant for women workers, and women may have a different willingness to substitute leisure over time [Mulligan (1995), for example, estimates larger σ's using synthetic cohorts of women]. One potential reason for a difference between women and men is that the woman is often the "secondary" and the man the "primary" household worker in a two-worker household. The bearing of children may

Table 5 INTERTEMPORAL ELASTICITY ESTIMATES

	(1)	(2)	(3)	(4)	(5)
Fract. of full-year work at age 15[a]	0.17	0.17	0.19	0.19	0.19
Fract. of full-year work at age 19[a]	0.20	0.20	0.27	0.27	0.27
Implicit tax rate[b]	0.2	0.4	0.2	0.3	0.4
ΔG^{-1}, std lognormal	0.13	0.13	0.28	0.28	0.28
σ	0.60	0.26	1.25	0.78	0.55
ΔG^{-1}, std uniform	0.19	0.19	0.37	0.37	0.37
σ	0.86	0.38	1.66	1.04	0.73
Subsample	All			Female heads, (welf 19)=0, (hd age)<62	

[a]AFDC sample average annual hours divided by 2080.
[b]See text for computation.

be another source of differences. But neither of these differences is especially relevant for our AFDC sample, because 65 of the 79 AFDC households are headed by women and the youngest child for these women is 17.

Even if the AFDC sample were special with respect to willingness to substitute over time, this select sample might be especially interesting for business-cycle and other applications where the workers whose labor supply is changing over time may also be a select sample with respect to σ.

4.5 SAMPLE SELECTION BIAS

AFDC eligibility depends on employment status, so my AFDC sample is a select sample in two ways. First, as can be seen from the age-19 employment variables for the AFDC and non-AFDC samples, the AFDC sample selects adults whose lifetime propensity to work is low. Second, to the extent that the propensity to work varies over time in ways unrelated to the AFDC benefit formulae, my AFDC sample selects parents who happened to have a low propensity to work in the year their youngest child was 17 years old. For this reason alone, employment and earnings in the AFDC sample would tend to be higher during years the child was not 17.

However, the selection bias with respect to willingness and ability to work when the child was aged 17 is not particularly relevant to my calculations unless it introduces a differential selection bias with respect to ability and willingness to work at child ages 15 and 19. In an intertemporally separable model, it seems that the selection biases should be similar for aged-15 and aged-19 work measures.

This may not be the case if there is some willingness to substitute over time *and* labor supply is not intertemporally separable. To the extent that work (leisure) capital is accumulated by working (not working), the sample of adults not working much in the year prior to an anticipated increase in the market value of time (i.e., when the child is aged 17) is a sample of adults who, for one reason or another, do not anticipate working much following the increase. If instead, work (leisure) capital is accumulated by not working (working) as in Kydland and Prescott (1982), the sample of adults not working much in the year prior to an anticipated increase in the market value of time is a sample of adults who are "resting" in anticipation of an above-average amount of work in the following year or two. Thus intertemporal nonseparabilities introduce a differential selection bias on the aged-15 and aged-19 work variables, but without saying more about the form of the nonseparabilities, the direction of the differential bias cannot be determined.

While the tastes or nonmarket value of time of a typical woman might not change substantially at the 18th birthday of her youngest child, my AFDC sample might—because of AFDC rules regarding marital status—be one where tastes do change. Marriage decreases the likelihood of AFDC eligibility (Rosenzweig, 1995), so my AFDC sample may select women who, because of program incentives or for other reasons, are more likely to get married after their youngest child's 18th birthday. If marriage increases a woman's nonmarket value of time, then this is a force *discouraging* work after age 18, which would bias my estimates downward.[48]

4.6 INCOME EFFECTS

Since the termination of AFDC benefits at date t^* is fully anticipated, it cannot be a wealth or income effect in a model in which different periods' budget are somehow tied together. In such a model, the only determinant of the *relative* labor supply before and after t^* is the relative value of time (including, if appropriate, time discounting) and the rate at which resources can be transferred across periods.

If budgets for different periods were not tied together in any way—perhaps because borrowing and lending involve a substantial fixed cost or because individuals do not realize that such transactions are possible and advantageous—then, despite its anticipation, the termination of benefits would have an income effect as well as the usual substitution effect. Both effects would tend to promote work after AFDC. One way to test for this possibility is to see whether consumption falls at t^*. Using Skinner's (1987) proxy for nondurable consumption (a weighted average of food purchased at home, food purchased away from home, and rent or housing value), real family consumption decreases 8% ($250 a year, in 1967 dollars) from age 15 to 18 in the sample from column (5) of Table 4 with valid consumption indicators. Annual family food consumption (including food stamps) falls $100. Given that AFDC–ADC annual income falls by an average of $1121, this decrease is economically insignificant. But it is a decrease, and it should be noted that a decline in consumption together with an increase in work is not found in other life-cycle studies (Ghez and Becker, 1975; Heckman, 1974).

There are two reasons why even a large reduction in consumption at t^* might be consistent with the dynamic labor-supply view. First, consumption and leisure may not be separable. Second, consumption as I measure it is excessively sensitive to household size, since it measures rent

---

48. Note that there is not an income effect of marriage in the life-cycle model unless the expectations of marriage by women in my sample deviate from the fraction of them who actually get married.

and food expenditures. If, for example, part of the effect of AFDC were to keep teenagers living at home until their benefits terminated, at which time the teenager moved out, then household rent and food expenditures would fall even though each individual's standard of living might be unchanged. Unfortunatly, there are not enough households in my AFDC sample with stable composition to test this second hypothesis.

5. Conclusions

Following Mulligan (1998), I build a model of labor-force participation and time aggregation which, in reduced form, looks very much like the empirical models used by Lucas and Rapping (1969), MaCurdy (1981), and Altonji (1986). The model predicts that labor supply is substituted over time in response to *anticipated* wage changes, although the magnitude of the response depends on the parameter σ, which in theory can vary from 0 to ∞. The model is quite explicit about the measurement of wages and hours, including the treatment of on-the-job training, time spent searching for work, nonlinear tax rules, and the aggregation of various components of labor supply.

It might be argued that people cannot substitute over time because they are unable to choose their hours or because they cannot borrow or lend as freely as the model implies. Although my model does include the idea that people are less than free to choose their hours—labor is indivisible—it is true that the present-value budget constraints (3) are crucial for deriving the main empirical specifications. While the validity of the assumptions of the theory is open to debate, I have shown that a reasonable analysis of various age-related changes in wages and labor supply confirms one main prediction of the theory—labor-supply growth is positively correlated with anticipated wage growth.

In a broad sample of men, I find that age groups of men with 1% more age-related growth in their after-tax market value of time have 1–2% more age-related growth in group hours worked. This response is an order of magnitude greater than those found in other life-cycle studies of men. Equation (11) summarizes what I believe to be my essential departures from that literature: "labor supply" is defined to include the employment and all other margins, the market value of time is adjusted for taxes, average hourly earnings are adjusted for self-financed OJT, and CPS hours are adjusted for systematic reporting bias.

Because my inferences from the life-cycle data are so different from those made in previous studies, I expose my empirical analysis through a few simple graphs, difference estimators, and regressions. More efficient estimators are certainly available, but I want it to be clear that my point of departure from previous studies is not in the econometric details but in the very basic economic and statistical issues which are arguably of primary relevance to the problem.

Studies of individual-panel or synthetic-cohort data—mine included—cannot do much about the fact that the market value of time when not working is not observed. Someone who is not working at an instant in time may have a market value of time that is low compared with his average hourly earnings at some other point in time or with the average hourly earnings of an otherwise similar person who is working at that instant. My study of the termination of AFDC benefits upon the 18th birthday of the youngest child is an attempt to mitigate this bias, since I believe that the observable change in the after-tax market value of time dominates any unobserved changes. IES estimates from this study are quite similar to those found with the synthetic-cohort data.

Social security rules create another life-cycle event that, like the termination of AFDC benefits, is a quantitatively important anticipated change in the after-tax market value of time. This event has been included in my analysis of synthetic cohorts, although, for students of intertemporal substitution, retirement is worthy of its own study. And there have been a number of studies of the effects of social security rules on retirement decisions, with a variety of results. Cross-country studies (e.g., Gruber and Wise, 1997; Modigliani and Sterling, 1983) have typically enjoyed large and fairly obvious differences in benefit rules and have found large differences in retirement. Some time-series studies (e.g., Burtless, 1986; Hausman and Wise, 1985; Krueger and Pischke, 1992) have enjoyed less variation in benefit rules and found even smaller labor-supply responses.[49] However, there are two disadvantages of social security rules as a source of an exogenous change in the anticipated rate of wage growth. First, it is not at all clear that workers are fully aware of all the subtleties of social security rules and their changes over time, including those changes that are exploited by some of the time-series studies. Second, it can be argued that social security rules and their changes are less likely than other policies to be exogenous with respect to the situation of the people affected by the policy. The American Association of Retired Persons (AARP) is America's most powerful lobby (Birnbaum, 1997), and its preferences are certainly reflected in social security legislation. The endogeneity of social security policy might also explain the relatively large cross-country correlation between labor supply and social security rules. Nevertheless, I eagerly await a

---

49. Several time-series studies also utilize unanticipated policy changes, which are less relevant for the ISH.

study of retirement designed to measure the magnitude and importance of intertemporal substitution and perhaps even to overcome some of the disadvantages I've mentioned.

Another avenue for future life-cycle research may be to exploit some of the differences in wage growth across occupation and schooling categories. However, doing so is a difficult exercise if the issues I emphasize in this paper are important. It seems that the level and life-cycle rate of change of OJT varies across occupation and schooling categories [although no such variation can be detected in my fairly small data set—see Stafford and Duncan (1985)], so that the more rapid average hourly earnings growth in some categories cannot be fully attributed to more rapid growth in the market value of time. Also, the currently available time-diary data sets seem too small to correct for hours reporting biases separately by occupation and schooling categories.

I study synthetic cohorts of men mainly because there is a greater consensus in the previous literature about the lack of response of male labor supply to temporary wage fluctuations. But macro data are an aggregate of men and women, so a differential response by gender would be one reason why my synthetic-cohort estimates might not directly apply to macro modeling. I do study women in Section 4 and obtain similar estimates of σ, but it is unclear whether the AFDC women are more like the representative man or the representative woman. Like men, the AFDC women are typically heads of household and might for that reason have a lower σ than the representative woman. On the other hand, AFDC women are women. AFDC women might even have a higher σ than other women because a higher σ makes AFDC participation more attractive.

There is another reason that caution should be exercised in the application of my estimates to macro modeling. The OJT, reporting, composition, and other biases which are important in the life-cycle data may also be present in the macro data. There is no easy solution to this, since the biases may be of different magnitudes or even different signs in the two sources, but one can try to similarly correct macro data or rely mainly on earnings data (rather than hours and wage data) where we suspect some of the biases to be less important.

Although the life-cycle data suggest that the temporal pattern of work responds to the temporal pattern of the market value of time, the data do not necessarily support the hypothesis that all or even most of the variation in work across workers or over time for a given worker can be explained as a response to temporary wage fluctuations. In fact, my model allows for a number of other potential determinants of work through the indivisibility of labor as well as cross-sectional and intertemporal variation in the taste parameter γ. I only suggest that, if and when temporary fluctuations in the after-tax market value of time occur, aggregate labor supply will respond and respond in a quantitatively important way. And, regardless of the number and importance of other determinants of labor supply, my claim has important implications for macroeconomics.

Appendix A: Notes on Social Security Benefits and Work Incentives

Because social security benefits are a function of a worker's life history of earnings and labor-force participation, they can affect incentives to work at all ages. These incentives can be parsed into two categories: (1) the effect of work on earnings and the *primary insurance amount* (PIA) that will be used to compute benefits when retirement occurs, and (2) the effect of participation and earnings at age 62 and older on the fraction of the PIA to be received as a social security benefit. This appendix draws heavily on the U.S. House Ways and Means Committee (1996, Section 1) and Myers (1993, Chapter 2, 3).

A.1 WORK BEFORE AGE 62 AND THE PIA

A person's PIA is a concave function of his lifetime average earnings where each year's earnings is indexed to reflect nationwide wage growth (with the exception of earnings after age 60, which are unindexed), the average caps each year's earnings according to the payroll tax cap, and the average drops the lowest-indexed-earnings years. The second provision means that no additional benefits accrue for men earning above the cap. If the number of potential work sessions in a year (K) is small, the last provision is particularly relevant for workers who participate most of their lives, because the marginal participation decision has no affect on PIA. To see this, notice that, unless the labor-supply trend term is very different in magnitude from the rate of nationwide wage growth, the marginal participation decision occurs in a year with low indexed earnings conditional on working.[50] I refer to this as the *PIA fixed* case.

If K is large, the marginal work session will typically affect computation of the PIA, and this is the case analyzed by Feldstein and Samwick

---

50. Even if the marginal participation decision did not occur in a low-indexed-earnings year (conditional on working), nonparticipation would produce zero earnings, remove the year from the average, and add another year to the average, so the effect of the decision on the lifetime average would be limited to the difference between what might have been earned in the year in question and what was earned in the best year not included in the average.

(1992). For single men and for married men whose wives earn enough to have substantial social security benefits, they use the following formula to compute the effect of an additional dollar of earnings at age a on discounted expected social security benefits:

$$\frac{1}{35}\, e^{0.01 \, \max\{a_R - a - 5, 0\}} \, \frac{PIA}{AIME} \left(1 - \frac{\tau^{IIT}}{2} \right) S(a_R, a, r).$$

The first factor reflects the use of 35 years to compute lifetime-average indexed earnings (AIME). The second factor reflects the indexing, where a_R is the normal retirement age and a is age (Feldstein and Samwick assume individual and national earnings growth of 1%/yr). PIA/AIME depends on AIME; Feldstein and Samwick assume the median ratio of 0.32. τ^{IIT} is the marginal individual income tax rate to be paid in the retirement years, and S is the factor used to compute the discounted expected value of an annuity that begins paying at age a_R. Feldstein and Samwick do their calculations for 1992 under the assumption that benefit rules (a_R, PIA/AIME, τ^{IIT}) will never change from the values dictated by current law. In fact, rules did change between 1976 and 1992 and probably will change again. Rather than making guesses about what each age group in 1976 knew or expected about the policy and mortality parameters, I use Feldstein and Samwick's parameters. I use their highest discount rate of 6%/yr to reflect (1) expectations of the benefit cuts in one form or another that so many experts and laymen have been forecasting and (2) the associated political risk premium.

Feldstein and Samwick also perform calculations for married men whose wives do not have substantial lifetime earnings. I do not review their calculations here, but assume that roughly half of all men earning below the cap expect to be in this category when they retire and therefore take a simple average of the formula above and the increment to discounted expected benefits enjoyed by this second category of men.

In summary, my "PIA endogenous" calculations for men earning less than the social security cap average the increment to discounted expected benefits implied by Feldstein and Samwick's (1992) columns 2 and 4 of their Table 1. This increment is subtracted from the 1976 payroll tax rate.[51]

A.2 WORKERS AGED 62–71

The same PIA effects act as a subsidy to work for those 62 and over who have not elected to begin receiving their social security benefits. I extend

---

51. Feldstein and Samwick (1992) report the increment in 5-year intervals, which I interpolate geometrically.

Feldstein and Samwick's calculations by adjusting their annuity factor $S(a_R, a, r)$ for 6% interest as age nears 65 and, after age 65, for mortality as indicated below. Those working after age 61 are also still liable for payroll taxes.

In addition to the payroll taxes, two major provisions of social security have discouraged work for pay by the elderly: earnings limits and delayed retirement credits. The earnings limit is the maximum earnings an elderly worker can earn without losing some of his old-age benefits. The limit does not apply to those aged 70 or higher. For earnings above this amount ($2760 per year in 1976 for those aged 62–71), old-age benefits are reduced (employment status does not and did not affect Medicare eligibility, although since 1980 employment status can affect the health insurance premiums paid by an elderly person (U.S. House Ways and Means Committee, 1996, Section 3, p. 223)). The rate of reduction during the 1970s was $1 for each $2 over the limit.

For those *workers* aged 62–71 who are receiving social security, I compute the additional tax on work as 0 if he earns below the limit and 0.5 if he earns at or above it. It is important to note that these men are typically part-time workers earning a lower *hourly* pretax wage than they would have earned if they had worked full time, so the use of their pretax wage in my calculations in Section 3.2 already includes some of the disincentive effects of social security.

For workers aged 72+, no additional tax or PIA subsidy is computed, although the low hourly earnings of these men is to some degree a consequence of social security's encouraging them to work fewer hours in their sixties.

If a worker elects not to receive any old-age (or disability) benefits, he is credited with some additional old-age benefits when he later retires. These credits, called *delayed retirement credits* (DRC), are however small enough (1%) that most people aged 65–71 were effectively penalized for delaying retirement.[52] A person aged 65–71 of average health planning to retire in 1976 lost over 90% of a year's benefits by delaying retirement an additional year. However, only if K is small is this provision a *marginal* tax on work.

For someone who first retired in 1976, it is straightforward to compute the amount of these benefits, the implicit tax on nonretirement for that

---

52. Hurd and Boskin (1984) and others argue that the decision to retire at age 65 is not distorted, because the delayed retirement credits are "actuarially fair." This may have been true at the time of writing their paper for a person of average mortality risk, but not before 1979 when the DRC was only 1% and before 1975 when there was no DRC (U.S. House Ways and Means Committee, 1996, Section 1). The DRC for those aged 62–64 was 8.4%, which I treat as actuarially fair.

year and (assuming K is small) the implicit marginal tax on work. However, too little is known about the earnings histories of CPS men who have not yet retired to compute exactly the benefits they would enjoy if they had retired in 1976. If these potential benefits were known, the implicit tax on work (in addition to the IIT, payroll taxes, and the accumulation of SS wealth considered previously) could be computed as

$$[0.92 + (a - 62)0.005] \frac{b_i}{e_i}$$

where b_i/e_i is person i's ratio of potential benefits to actual earnings. The factor in brackets is greater than zero and a function of age, because the delayed retirement credits were actuarially unfair.[53] I estimate the ratio b_i/e_i as 0.4 for single men, which is a fairly typical replacement rate reported by the U.S. House Ways and Means Committee (1996, Table 1–14) for cohorts retired by 1976. The value 0.6 is used for married men over 65, under the assumption that their retirement also entitles their spouses to benefits equal to half of the amount of their own benefits.

Appendix B. Two Models of Reporting Errors

Two of my four corrections for CPS hours reporting bias rely on a model of reporting errors. The first is a *compression model* (B-1) where each worker reports hours that are closer to a stereotypical number $\tilde{n}$ than are his actual hours; the second is a *liars model* (B-2) where some apparently random workers choose to report the stereotypical number $\tilde{n}$:

$$\ln \hat{n} - \ln \tilde{n} = \theta (\ln n - \ln \tilde{n}), \qquad n > 0, \tag{B-1}$$

$$\hat{n} = \begin{cases} n & \text{w.p. } 1 - \theta, \\ \tilde{n} & \text{w.p. } \theta, \end{cases} \tag{B-2}$$

where n is true hours and $\hat{n}$ is reported hours.

Remember that, by definition, aggregate labor supply is the product of average hours conditional on positive hours and the fraction working positive hours. In order to derive the effect on aggregate labor supply of reporting bias among those reporting positive hours during some time interval, we need to model both aggregate labor supply and the fraction working positive hours (the *employment rate*). My life-cycle model pro-

---

53. Details of my derivation of the factor in brackets—which equals $1 - 0.01S(a_R, a, r)$—are available upon request.

vides a quite tractable model of aggregate labor, but, unless K is known, not a model of the employment rate. Even if K were known, my model of the employment rate is not particularly tractable. So, as an approximation, I assume a log-linear model for true age-group hours averaged across those with positive hours:

$$\ln n_t^a = \eta \ln \tilde{w}_t^a + u_{t}^a, \qquad n_t^a > 0, \tag{B-3}$$

with n_t^a the arithmetic mean of true hours among those with positive hours, and $\tilde{w}_t^a$ the age-group *geometric*-average after-tax market value of time. n_t^a is assumed to be uncorrelated across age groups with $\tilde{w}_t^a$ and with the error term in equation (10). Total age-group hours N_t^a are still determined according to equation (10). It is assumed that measured average age-group hourly earnings $\hat{w}_t^a$ differ from true average age-group hourly earnings $\tilde{w}_t^a$ according to

$$\hat{w}_t^a = \tilde{w}_t^a n_t^a / \hat{n}_t^a. \tag{B-4}$$

Up to an aggregation bias term, the compression model implies equation (B-1) for average reported age-group hours conditional on positive hours $(\tilde{n}_t^a)$ as a function of average true age-group hours conditional on positive hours (n_t^a). Given the compression factor θ, the reported hours elasticity with respect to the measured wage $\hat{\eta}$, and the R^2 of the reported-hours equation, we can infer the true hours elasticity η from equations (10), (B-1), (B-3), and (B-4):[54]

$$\eta = \left(\frac{\theta}{\hat{\eta}} \frac{\theta - (1 - \theta)\hat{\eta}}{\theta - (1 - \theta)\hat{\eta} \, (1/R^2)} - (1 - \theta) \right)^{-1},$$

while the elasticity of true hours with respect to the reported wage is $\hat{\eta}/\theta$.

Given also the reported total-hours elasticity with respect to the measured wage $\hat{\sigma}$, we can infer the true total-hours elasticity σ:

$$\sigma = \eta + (\hat{\sigma} - \hat{\eta}) \frac{\eta\theta}{[1 + (1 - \theta)\eta]\hat{\eta} \dfrac{\theta - (1 - \theta)\hat{\eta} \, (1/R^2)}{\theta - (1 - \theta)\hat{\eta}} - (1 - \theta)\eta\hat{\eta}}$$

54. All of the estimated parameters are to be understood as probability limits.

The elasticity of true total hours with respect to the measured wage is $\hat{\sigma}$ $- \hat{\eta} + \hat{\eta}/\theta$. Similar calculations (not shown here) can be made for the liars model.

Both the compression and the liars model have a parameter θ which can be calibrated by comparing reported hours in the CPS and the time diaries. For example, the micro-level standard deviation of log hours is twice as large in the diaries as in the CPS and (appropriately correcting for the different sample sizes) the standard deviation across groups aged 25–55 is almost three times as large in the diaries. This suggests a compression parameter of $\theta = 0.4$ or $\theta = 0.5$. I use a conservative $\theta = 0.7$ for the compression-model calculations reported in the text.

It is beyond the scope of this paper to build and formally test various models of reporting errors, but I do comment on their "realism." Four facts come out of an elementary comparison of the distribution of positive "hours last week" (or "usual hours last year") reported by men aged 25–55 from the March 1977 CPS with positive hours worked in the synthetic week reported by men aged 25–55 from the 1975–76 time diaries. First, close to 50% of CPS respondents report exactly 40 hours, and 75% report working exactly 52 weeks in 1976, as compared to 19% of time-diary synthetic weeks between 38.0 and 42.0 hours. When either CPS measure of weekly hours is multiplied by weeks worked in 1976, about 40% report exactly 40 hours as 1976 average weekly hours. Second, the standard deviation of log reported weekly hours is twice as large in the time diary as in the CPS. Third, the fraction of CPS workers reporting exactly 40 hours is very slightly increasing in age until age 63, after which it is about half of what it is for younger workers, although the age-group variance of log reported weekly hours increases steadily with age in both the CPS and diary studies. Fourth, the central tendency of the distribution of weekly diary hours is roughly 40 hours, with a majority of synthetic weeks between 30 and 50 hours.

The first fact is more consistent with the liars model, since the compression model does not literally predict that many would report exactly 40 hours, although the compression model might be amended to account for the first fact by introducing some rounding to the nearest integer. Both models are consistent with the second fact. The third fact suggests that the liars model is more appropriate up to age 63 and the compression model after age 63, since the compression model predicts that a widening of the distribution of true hours would decrease the fraction of CPS respondents reporting hours within a given distance of 40. However, the fourth fact is more easily derived from the compression model, since, in contrast to the liars model, the stereotype is related to the distribution of misreported hours even for those not reporting the stereotype.

Notice that the liars model also justifies the procedure used to produce results in the last two rows of Table 2 if we assume in addition that all of those reporting 40 are liars. Actually, the procedure is justified even if liars are not random with respect to their wage, as long as they are random with respect to other determinants of hours.

REFERENCES

Abowd, J. M., and D. Card. (1989). On the covariance structure of earnings and hours changes. *Econometrica* 57(2, March):411–445.
Aiyagari, S. R., L. J. Christiano, M. Eichenbaum. (1992). The output, employment, and interest rate effects of government consumption. *Journal of Monetary Economics* 30(1, October):73–86.
Alogoskoufis, G. S. (1987a). Aggregate employment and intertemporal substitution in the U.K. *Economic Journal* 97(June):403–415.
———. (1987b). On intertemporal substitution and aggregate labor supply. *Journal of Political Economy* 95(5, October):938–960.
Altonji, J. G. (1986). Intertemporal substitution in labor supply: Evidence from micro data. *Journal of Political Economy* 94(3, Part 2, June):S176–S215.
Ashenfelter, O. (1984). Macroeconomic analyses and microeconomic analyses of labor supply. In *Carnegie-Rochester Conference Series on Public Policy*, K. Brunner and A. H. Meltzer (eds.). Vol. 21, Autumn, pp. 117–156.
Auerbach, A. J., and L. J. Kotlikoff. (1987). *Dynamic Fiscal Policy*. Cambridge, U.K.: Cambridge University Press.
Barro, R. J. (1981). Output effects of government purchases. *Journal of Political Economy* 89(6, December):1086–1121.
———. (1987). *Macroeconomics*. New York: John Wiley and Sons, 1987.
———, and C. Sahasakul. (1983). Measuring the average marginal tax rate from the individual income tax. *Journal of Business* 56(October):419–452.
Bartel, A., and P. Taubman. (1979). Health and labor market success: The role of various diseases. *Review of Economics and Statistics* 61(1, February):1–8.
Baxter, M., and R. G. King. (1993). Fiscal policy in general equilibrium. *American Economic Review* 83(3, June):315–334.
Becker, G. S., and C. B. Mulligan. (1997). The endogenous determination of time preference. *Quaterly Journal of Economics*, 112(3, August):729–758.
———, and K. M. Murphy. (1988). A theory of rational addiction. *Journal of Political Economy* 96(4, August):675–700.
Ben-Porath, Y., (1967). The production of human capital and the life cycle of earnings. *Journal of Political Economy* 75(4, August):352–365.
Bils, M. J. (1985). Real wages over the business cycle: Evidence from panel data. *Journal of Political Economy* 93(August):666–689.
Birnbaum, J. (1997). Washington's Power 25. *Fortune* 136(11, December):8.
Burtless, G. (1986). Social security, unanticipated benefit increases, and the timing of retirement. *Review of Economic Studies* 53(5, October):781–805.
Card, D. (1994). Intertemporal labor supply: An assessment. In *Advances in Econometrics: Sixth World Congress*, Volume II, C. A. Sims (ed.). Econometric Society Monograph No. 24. Cambridge: Cambridge University Press, pp. 49–80.
Coleman, T. S. (1984). Essays on aggregate labor market business cycle fluctuations. University of Chicago. PhD Dissertation. December.

Costa, D. L. (1998). *The Evolution of Retirement.* Chicago: Univeristy of Chicago Press.

Diamond, P. A., and J. A. Mirlees. (1978). A model of social insurance with variable retirement. *Journal of Public Economics* 10(3, December):295–336.

Feldstein, M., and A. Samwick. (1992). Social security rules and marginal tax rates. *National Tax Journal* 45(1, March):1–22.

Fraker, T., R. Moffitt, and D. Wolf. (1985). Effective tax rates and guarantees in the AFDC program, 1967–82. *Journal of Human Resources* 20(Spring):251–263.

Friedman, M. (1957). *A Theory of the Consumption Function.* Princeton, NJ: Princeton University Press.

Ghez, G. R., and G. S. Becker. (1975). *The Allocation of Time and Goods over the Life Cycle.* New York: Columbia University Press for NBER.

Gibbons, R., and K. J. Murphy. (1992). Optimal incentive contracts in the presence of career concerns: Theory and evidence. *Journal of Political Economy* 100(3, June):468–505.

Gruber, J., and D. Wise. (1997). Social security programs and retirement around the world. Cambridge, MA: National Bureau of Economic Research. NBER Working Paper 6134. August.

Hall, R. E. (1978). Stochastic implications of the life cycle–permanent income hypothesis: Theory and evidence. *Journal of Political Economy* 86(6, December):971–987.

———. (1980). Labor supply and aggregate fluctuations. *Journal of Monetary Economics* 12(6, Supplement, Spring):7–33.

———. (1988). Intertemporal substitution in consumption. *Journal of Political Economy* 96(2, April):339–357.

Hansen, G. D. (1985). Indivisible labor and the business cycle. *Journal of Monetary Economics* 16(3, November):309–327.

Hausman, J. A. (1985). Taxes and labor supply. In *Handbook of Public Economics,* A. J. Auerbach and M. Feldstein (eds.). Amsterdam: North-Holland.

———, and D. A. Wise. (1985). Social security, health status, and retirement. In *Pensions, Labor, and Individual Choice,* D. A. Wise (ed.). Chicago: University of Chicago Press, pp. 159–181.

Heckman, J. J. (1974). Life cycle consumption and labor supply: An explanation of the relationship between income and consumption over the life cycle. *American Economic Review* 64(1, March):188–194.

———. (1975). Estimates of a human capital production function embedded in a life cycle model of labor supply. In *Household Production and Consumption,* N. E. Terleckyj, (ed.). New York: Columbia University Press, pp. 227–258.

———. (1993). What has been learned about labor supply in the past twenty years? *American Economic Review* 83(2, May):116–121.

———, L. Lochner, and C. Taber. (1998). Explaining rising wage inequality: Explorations with a dynamic general equilibrium model of labor earnings with heterogeneous agents. *Review of Economic Dynamics* 1(1).

Hicks, J. R., (1939). *Value and Capital.* Oxford: Clarendon Press.

Horvath, F. W. (1982). Forgotten unemployment: Recall bias in retrospective data. *Monthly Labor Review* 105(March):40–43.

Hurd, M. D., and M. J. Boskin. (1984). The effect of social security on retirement in the early 1970s. *Quaterly Journal of Economics* 99(4, November):767–790.

Judd, K. L. (1987). The welfare cost of factor taxation in a perfect-foresight model. *Journal of Political Economy* 95(4, August):675–709.

Juster, F. T. (1986). Response errors in the measurement of time use. *Journal of the American Statistical Association* 81(394, June):390–402.

———, and F. P. Stafford. (1991). The allocation of time: Empirical findings, behavioral models, and problems of measurement. *Journal of Economic Literature* 29(June):471–522.

Krueger, A. B., and J. S. Pischke. (1992). The effect of social security on labor supply: A cohort analysis of the notch generation. *Journal of Labor Economics* 10(4, October):412–437.

Kydland, F., and E. C. Prescott. (1982). Time to build and aggregate fluctuations. *Econometrica* 50(6, November):1345–1370.

Lucas, R. E., Jr. (1970). Capacity, overtime, and empirical production functions. *American Economic Review* 60(2, May):23–27.

———. (1972). Expectations and the neutrality of money. *Journal of Economic Theory* 4(2, April):103–124.

———, and L. A. Rapping. (1969). Real wages, employment, and inflation. *Journal of Political Economy* 77 (5, September).

MaCurdy, T. E. (1981). An empirical model of labor supply in a life cycle setting. *Journal of Political Economy* 88(6, December):1059–1085.

Mankiw, N. G. (1989). Real business cycles: A new Keynesian perspective. *Journal of Economic Literature* 3(3, Summer):79–90.

Mincer, J. (1974). *Schooling, Experience, and Earnings.* New York: Columbia University Press.

———. (1997). The production of human capital and the life cycle of earnings: Variations on a theme. *Journal of Labor Economics* 15(1, Part 2, January):S26–S47.

Modigliani, F., and A. Sterling. (1983). Determinants of private saving with special reference to the role of social security—cross-country tests. In *The Determinants of National Saving and Wealth,* F. Modigliani and R. Hemming (eds.). London: MacMillan, pp. 24–55.

Mulligan, C. B. (1995). The intertemporal substitution of work—what does the evidence say? University of Chicago, Population Research Center. Discussion Paper 95-11. June.

———. (1997). Employment after AFDC. University of Chicago. Working Paper. November.

———. (1998). Microfoundations and macro implications of indivisible labor. Federal Reserve Bank of Minneapolis Discussion Paper 126, July.

Myers, R. J. (1993). *Social Security,* 4th ed. Philadelphia: University of Pennsylvania Press.

Pencavel, J. (1986). Labor supply of men: A survey. In *Handbook of Labor Economics,* O. Ashenfelter and R. Layard (eds.). Amsterdam: North Holland.

Plosser, C. I. (1989). Understanding real business cycles. *Journal of Economic Literature* 3(3, Summer):51–77.

Rogerson, R., and P. Rupert. (1991). New estimates of intertemporal substitution: The effect of corner solutions for year-round workers. *Journal of Monetary Economics* 27(2, April):255–269.

Rosen, S. (1972). Learning and experience in the labor market. *Journal of Human Resources* 7(3, Summer):326–342.

Rosenzweig, M. R. (1995). Welfare, marital prospects and nonmarital childbearing. Paper presented at a Symposium on the Economic Analysis of Social Behavior. Fraser Institute, Chicago. December 1.

Ruhm, C. J. (1990). Bridge Jobs and Partial Retirement. *Journal of Labor Economics* 8(4, October):482–501.

Shea, J. (1995). Myopia, liquidity constraints, and aggregate consumption: A simple test. *Journal of Money, Credit, and Banking* 27(3, August):798–805.

Skinner, J. (1987). A superior measure of consumption from the panel study of income dynamics. *Economics Letters* 23(2):213–216.

Smith, J. (1977). Family labor supply over the life cycle. *Explorations in Economic Research* 4(2, Spring):205–276.

Stafford, F. P., and G. J. Duncan. (1985). The use of time and technology by households in the United States. In *Time, Goods, & Well-Being*, F. T. Juster and F. P. Stafford (eds.). Ann Arbor, MI: Survey Research Center Institute for Social Research, University of Michigan.

Sweet, J. A. (1973). *Women in the Labor Force*. London: Seminar Press.

United States Congress, House Committee on Ways and Means. (1996). *Overview of Entitlement Programs, 1996 Green Book*. Washington, DC: U.S. Government Printing Office.

Comment

ROBERT E. HALL
Hoover Institution and Department of Economics, Stanford University; and NBER

When I first read this paper, I wavered a bit from my historical position that the intertemporal elasticity of substitution is fairly low. But my wavering did not last long. The paper has not moved me much in the direction of elasticities over, say, 0.4. Still, I admire the brave attempt.

Figure 1 shows the Mulligan staircase—the dramatic increase achieved by correcting what seem to be flaws in the earlier literature deriving from Ghez and Becker's first insight that age differences reveal pure substitution effects. But the paper fails to come to grips with the basic weakness of the Ghez–Becker approach—its reliance on a strong and implausible identifying condition. That condition is that all age effects are linear in labor supply. Estimates of the intertemporal elasticity of substitution are found from comparing the departures from linear growth in hours with departures from linear growth in wage rates. Under the assumption that preferences can be related in a flexible way to age, the elasticity is not identified.

To see this, consider a general specification of the disamenity of working $L(\tau)$ hours at time τ:

$$\min \int z(\tau) \frac{L(\tau)^{1+1/\sigma}}{1 + 1/\sigma} d\tau$$

Figure 1

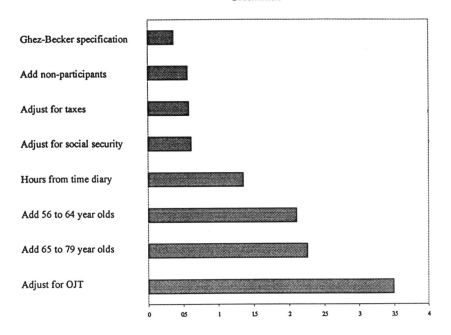

Intertemporal Elasticity of Substitution

subject to

$$\int e^{-r\tau} w(\tau) L(\tau)\, d\tau = \text{present value of consumption less wealth.}$$

Here $z(\tau)$ is a weight applied to work in time τ, σ is the intertemporal elasticity of substitution, r is the interest rate, and $w(\tau)$ is the hourly wage rate. Labor supply satisfies the first-order condition

$$L(\tau) = \left(\frac{\lambda e^{-r\tau} w(\tau)}{z(\tau)} \right)^{\sigma},$$

where λ is the Lagrange multiplier associated with the wealth constraint. In logs,

$$\log L(\tau) = \sigma[\log \lambda - r\tau + \log w(\tau) - \log z(\tau)].$$

In general, if σ and $z(\tau)$ are unknown parameters, they are not identified. Ghez and Becker made the strong identifying assumption

$$\log z(\tau) = \alpha + \beta\tau.$$

It is hard to see why this is compelling. In particular, it seems likely that the disamenity of work rises sharply after age 60. Not only does this violate the identifying assumption of linearity, but it coincides with the most important variation in the data that pins down σ. A plausible view of retirement—in direct conflict with the identifying assumption—is that the disamenity of work rises in the years after age 60.

The other big problem—one Mulligan flags repeatedly—is the lack of identification resulting from sample selection issues. This is not an arcane econometric issue, and the people who raise it should not be dismissed as perfectionists who stand in the way of practical research.

Sample selection becomes particularly acute when older people are included in the sample. Ghez and Becker's restriction to preretirement age groups can be defended as an attempt to limit the sample selection problem.

Consider the following model: With probability $\pi(\tau)$, a worker suffers a major decline in productivity because of a disabling medical condition such as stroke or heart disease. The worker's wage drops below his reservation level, and he withdraws from the labor force. Over the same range, the wages earned by those workers who do not suffer the disability decline slowly with age. Consider the example illustrated by Figure 2. Mulligan's procedure will attribute the substantial declines in labor supply caused by the disability process to the small changes in wages of participants. In the example, Mulligan's regression is

$$\log N_\tau = -107 + 44.6\log w_\tau + 0.0$$

So the estimated value of the elasticity is ridiculously high, 44.6. Large biases can result from sample selection.

These two issues of identification are much more important in Mulligan's work than in earlier work because of his extension into low-participation, high-disability groups.

I like the work with AFDC recipients much better. There is no serious identification problem either from general age-related preferences or from sample selection. But there is little surprise value in the AFDC results. The values of the intertemporal elasticity of substitution in Mulligan's Table 5 are in line with earlier work on female labor supply and are well below the surprising values of over 3 that Mulligan gets for men.

Figure 2

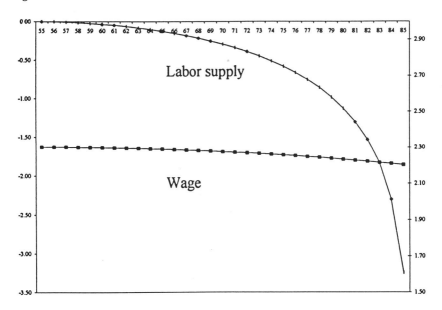

The stated motivation for the research is macro interest in intertemporal substitution in labor supply, and, in any case, this is the *Macro Annual.*

I've taken a pretty close look at the macro evidence in the light of Mulligan's equation (1) and get reasonably sharp estimates of around 0.3, driven both by predictable variation in the real interest rate and in wages. So, if Mulligan is right about micro cohort data, there is a problem reconciling his findings with macro behavior. There are enough reasons to question the accuracy of the macro findings so that the reconciliation could wind up favoring the micro view. But I'm far from convinced after reading this paper, or the ingenious companion coming out in the *Journal of Political Economy.*

Is the value of the intertemporal elasticity of substitution important for macro? John Campbell's careful work suggests that no value of σ delivers a reasonable story about employment fluctuations. One of the reasons may be that the standard dynamic stochastic general equilibrium (DSGE) model has so much intertemporal substitution in produced goods—through the timing of investment—that it makes little use of intertemporal substitution in labor supply. People don't work harder when goods are needed, because goods can be obtained by deferring investment.

In any case, Mulligan is pursuing an old issue at this point. The current crop of DSGE models delivers employment fluctuations in a new and more satisfactory way than intertemporal substitution in labor supply. These models consider a third use of time—job serach—and treat recessions as periods when there are an unusually large number of people searching. This seems more promising than the intertemporal substitution model, where recessions are times when people are substituting toward more leisure.

Comment

Jörn-Steffen Pischke
Massachusetts Institute of Technology

1. Introduction

Since the active research on intertemporal labor supply during the 1970s and 1980s, things have been mostly quiet in this area. Various reviewers have concluded that the intertemporal elasticity of substitution for hours is small for men, probably in the range from zero to one, and likely below 0.5. Many of us have come to think that this assessment is unlikely to change dramatically. When a central question has been laid to rest, it is certainly useful when someone comes along every now and then and stirs up some dust. Casey Mulligan does a remarkable job of stirring in this paper, reporting elasticities as high as 6.5. This is particularly noteworthy in that he focuses on variation in hours and wages over the life cycle, an area where large elasticities have been especially hard to find. Once the dust has settled, however, I suspect we will be back much closer to the previous range. I will organize my comments around the two empirical exercises in the paper: the estimates with synthetic-cohort data and the termination of AFDC benefits.

2. Synthetic-Cohort Data

The intertemporal substitution hypothesis says that expected hours should respond to expected, or evolutionary, changes in wages. One reason for wages to move systematically, and clearly well known among workers, is the tendency for wages to rise with age. This low-frequency variation in hours should be of particular interest to macroeconomists: if people are willing to substitute leisure over the phases of their life cycle, they are likely to be willing to substitute over business-cycle frequencies as well. Mulligan presents regressions of the logarithm of hours on the logarithm of wages by age group, an exercise which has been carried out many times before. The paper discusses six potential adjustments to the standard exercise. The main contribution is his attempt to put actual data to use in estimating the effects of these adjustments. The six adjustments are (1) including older workers in the estimation, (2) including nonemployment as an hours choice, (3) using data from a time-diary study as a potentially more accurate source of hours information, (4) incorporating on-the-job training in the calculation of the hourly wage, (5) allowing for taxes, and (6) adjusting for composition bias. All of these are potentially important adjustments, and I found it instructive to see what difference they make. To facilitate my discussion of these six adjustments, I have created a data set of mean hours and wages by age group from the 1980 Census comparable to Mulligan's CPS sample. Quantitatively, the most important adjustments are the first four, so I will discuss them in some detail.

2.1 INCLUDING OLDER WORKERS

Both wages and hours vary relatively little for workers between the ages of 35 and 55. Thus, in standard analyses of life-cycle data, most of the variation in hours and wages comes from the difference between prime-age and young workers. Since hours and wages differ for older workers as well, this seems potentially a good reason for exploiting this additional variation in the data. In practice, I am rather skeptical that the hours choices of older workers teach us much about the intertemporal substitution elasticity. Mulligan tries to address two potential problems for workers past the retirement age: the fact that social security changes the incentives workers face, and the problem that the older workers for whom we observe a wage are a highly selected group. Mulligan uses data from the 1980 Census by assigning older workers the wages of younger full-time workers in the same occupation and schooling group and then comparing the imputed wages of those retiring with those who continue working. This calculation of the composition bias adjusts for selective retirement between groups but not for possible biases arising from within group selection.

The fact that the social security system changes the after-tax wage is incorporated in the tax calculations in the paper. But Mulligan acknowledges that it is difficult to collapse the multitude of constraints and implicit taxes into a single tax rate relevant for the cohort averages. More importantly, the tax calculation does not incorporate the fact that workers are first eligible to receive social security benefits at age 62 and Medicare at age 65. This omission is perfectly consistent with the model, because benefit availability should not matter for the hours decisions of a "life-cycling" worker, since benefits are part of life-cycle wealth. But social security and Medicare wealth are hard to borrow against to finance leisure earlier in life, and prudent consumers tend to be reluctant to make use of the borrowing opportunities that are available. This constraint is relevant, because many individuals do not own substantial assets other than durable goods even at ages close to retirement. The median financial net worth of households with a male head age 55 to 61 in the 1983 Survey of Consumer Finances is $5,000. Including housing wealth, the median net worth is $94,000. I believe that some of the spikes in retirement rates at ages 62 and 65 are explained by the presence of the social security system. Costa's (1995) work is a case in point. She finds that the availability of army pensions for Union veterans after the Civil War substantially changed the retirement behavior of those who qualified for these pensions, suggesting that the presence of old-age benefits matters for retirement decisions and that the effect does not operate through wages.

Mulligan discusses another major difference between the old and the young, which is the fact that the young are healthier. This is important to the degree that health affects tastes for leisure directly. He finds little empirical evidence for a direct effect of health on hours choices. He also cites historical evidence to support his claim that health may not have much of a direct effect on labor-supply behavior. The fact that older men seemed to be in much worse health around the turn of the century but worked more than the elderly do now is hardly convincing evidence that health does not influence the taste for leisure. Americans are far richer now and therefore may find it far easier to finance leisure at times when it is particularly valuable. The social security disability and old-age pension programs make this easy even for individuals who have not provided for these circumstances on their own.

I am also unconvinced by the evidence presented by Mulligan on the effect of health on hours choices. The Census also asks questions about disabilities which limit the household member's ability to work or which prevent him from working. These disability questions are available for all respondents, and therefore they do not have to be imputed for the age groups below age 51 as with data used by Mulligan. In the first three rows of Table 1 I report the estimated elasticities from Mulligan's paper (column 1) and my reestimates with the Census (column 2) for the various age ranges he looks at. These estimates use hours for all men, not just those working, since much of the variation in hours for older men comes from the employment margin. I will have more to say on the distinction between workers and nonworkers below. The point estimate

Table 1   ESTIMATES OF THE INTERTEMPORAL ELASTICITY
OF SUBSTITUTION FOR VARIOUS AGE GROUPS
AND SPECIFICATIONS

			Census estimates		
Row	Age Group	Mulligan's estimates (1)	No Additional Controls (2)	Controlling Disability Limits Work (3)	Controlling Disability Prevents Work (4)
		Geometric-Average Wage			
1	25–55	0.57	0.59 (0.02)	0.49 (0.03)	0.46 (0.03)
2	24–64	1.41	1.11 (0.11)	0.30 (0.20)	0.18 (0.12)
3	24–79	2.86[a]	2.91 (0.18)	3.67 (0.35)	1.73 (0.45)
		Arithmetic-Average Wage			
4	25–55		0.59 (0.03)	0.50 (0.05)	0.46 (0.04)
5	24–64		1.11 (0.15)	−0.02 (0.20)	0.02 (0.13)
6	24–79		3.60 (0.47)	2.04 (0.94)	−0.47 (0.56)

Each entry represents the coefficient from a separate regression of the log of mean annual hours for an age cell on the mean of the log of the hourly wage for the age cell (in rows 1–3) or on the log of the mean of the hourly wage for the age cell (in rows 4–6). All regressions also include a constant and a linear term in age. Regressions in column (3) also control for the fraction of the age group reporting a disability which limits the kind or amount of work a person can do. Regressions in column (4) also control for the fraction of the age group reporting a disability which prevents a person from working on a job. All cell means are computed from the 1980 Census of Population 5% PUMS. Standard errors are reported in parentheses.
[a]This estimate is not reported in the published version of Mulligan's paper and is taken from a previous draft.

for the age group 25–55 is almost exactly the same, while our estimates differ a bit for the samples including older men.

If I include the fraction of an age group who report a disability which either limits or prevents work (columns 3 and 4 of Table 1), some of the estimated elasticities fall substantially. Unlike Mulligan, I find no significant intertemporal substitution effects for the age group 24–64 once health status of the age group is controlled for. For the age group 24–79, the estimated elasticities remain substantial, but the estimates differ by a factor of 2 depending on the exact definition of the disability variable. This is despite the fact that the raw correlation of the two disability measures in the sample is 0.99! This makes me quite skeptical whether we are able to control adequately for the effect of health in these regressions.

My skepticism is heightened by the fact that these regressions seem rather sensitive to changes in the functional form used. When the arithmetic average of the wage (i.e. the log of the average wage) is used as a regressor instead of the geometric average (i.e. the average of the log wages), I find substantially lower estimates for the elasticity once older groups are included. This result is again in contrast to Mulligan's estimates in his Table 3. The difference between the two wage measures results from the fact that the geometric-average wage declines much more strongly for workers over age 60, thus producing an age–wage profile which tracks the age–hours profile much more closely when older workers are included. This means that there is less need for the health indicators to explain the behavior of hours for the elderly. While the specification using the geometric-average wage may be more sensible, I find it more comforting that these functional form issues are not of importance for the age group below 55.

Mulligan concludes that retirement might be a life event particularly suitable for the study of intertemporal substitution. I find the complications introduced by using older workers overwhelming. Since the results are very sensitive to important specification issues, I feel that it is much safer to rely on the age group below 55. I will focus the rest of my comments on them.

2.2 INCLUDING NONEMPLOYMENT

Not working at all during the year is a valid choice of hours, and studies of intertemporal substitution have often neglected this margin because we do not observe the wages of nonworkers. But the male employment rate is clearly hump-shaped over the life cycle. In 1980, it was 93% at age 25, peaked around 95% for men in their thirties, and drops to 86% at age 55. Thus, the employment rate varies most for workers in their late forties and fifties, a period when wages are rather stable. The combination implies that including nonworkers raises the estimated substitution elasticity substantially because a little wage variation has to account for a lot of hours variation. But I doubt that this is the full story. An important reason why men do not work during their prime-age years (apart from unemployment, which rarely lasts an entire year) is, again, health. The fraction of workers reporting a disability which prevents them from working rises from 1.4% at age 25 to 10% at age 55. In fact, this fraction has a correlation with the employment rate of -0.95. Rows 1 and 2 of Table 2 compare the estimates of the intertemporal substitution elasticity for working men and for all men including nonworkers, controlling for

Table 2   ESTIMATES OF THE INTERTEMPORAL ELASTICITY OF
SUBSTITUTION FOR THE AGE GROUP 25–55 FOR VARIOUS
SPECIFICATIONS

			Census Estimates		
Row	Specification	Mulligan's Estimates (1)	No Additional Controls (2)	Controlling Disability Limits Work (3)	Controlling Disability Prevents Work (4)
1	Employed workers' hours and wages	0.37	0.36 (0.02)	0.38 (0.03)	0.37 (0.03)
2	All men's hours, employed workers' wages	0.57	0.59 (0.03)	0.50 (0.05)	0.46 (0.04)
3	As in row 2, but using CPS ORG usual weekly hours		0.56 (0.02)	0.52 (0.05)	0.49 (0.05)
4	As in row 2, but using CPS ORG weekly hours last week		0.61 (0.03)	0.59 (0.05)	0.55 (0.05)
5	As in row 4, but using CPS ORG hourly earnings		0.79 (0.04)	0.62 (0.05)	0.61 (0.05)
6	As in row 4, but using CPS ORG hourly earnings adj. for overtime		0.83 (0.05)	0.64 (0.04)	0.61 (0.05)
7	As in row 6, but wages adj. for learning by doing using Shaw est.		0.44 (0.02)	0.38 (0.02)	0.38 (0.03)

Each entry represents the coefficient from a separate regression of the log of mean annual hours for an age cell on the log of the mean hourly wage for the age cell. All regressions also include a constant and a linear term in age. Regressions in column (3) also control for the fraction of the age group reporting a disability which limits the kind or amount of work a person can do. Regressions in column (4) also control for the fraction of the age group reporting a disability which prevents a person from working on a job. All cell means are computed from the 1980 Census of Population 5% PUMS. Standard errors are reported in parentheses.

the fractions reporting a disability.[1] These health variables do not matter for men below age 55 who are working (row 1), while they reduce the estimates somewhat once we use hours for all men.

2.3 MISREPORTING OF HOURS AND WAGES

Answers to "usual weekly hours" questions in the Census Bureau surveys are well known to produce spikes at 40 hours, particularly for men. It seems plausible to me that some rounding by respondents masks actual hours fluctuations over the life cycle. I also agree with the idea of including nonwork investment activities, like job search in the measured

1. The estimates in Table 2 use the arithmetic average of the wage. I switch to this variable here because this makes some of the later adjustments I wish to make much easier.

hours. Hence, the time-diary data which Mulligan uses should in principle allow better inferences on the intertemporal substitution elasticity. Unfortunately, the available time-diary sample is small and therefore produces noisy means for the hours measure. This is very visible in Mulligan's Figure 1. A salient feature in these data among the group 25–55 years old are two outliers with low hours of about 1200 at age 54 and about 900 at age 55. The observations for the next few ages are higher again and lie between 1500 and 2000 hours. The data imply that the typical man at age 55 who is employed at all worked less than 20 hours a week. I find this implausible, given that the same age group reports *more* than 40 hours in the CPS and Census. I doubt that the average worker in this group spends more than 20 hours a week at the doctor or having coffee breaks. I stress this issue because it is these two observations which more than double Mulligan's estimate of the intertemporal elasticity of substitution. When I replace annual hours for 54-year-olds by 1200 and for 55-year-olds by 900 in the Census data, my estimates change from 0.59 to 1.32 for the specification using hours for all men including nonworkers. Comparing this with Mulligan's numbers of 0.57 and 1.36 makes clear that these two data points drive the result. Moreover, the *t*-statistic on the substitution elasticity falls from 23 to 4 when I make this change, indicating that OLS agrees with me that these two data points are very different from the rest of the sample.

Realizing that sampling error is important in the diary data and may affect the estimates, Mulligan uses three other methods to adjust the CPS data for possible reporting bias. He assumes that respondents may report hours between the norm and the truth (the compression model) or that some respondents report the norm rather than the truth (the liars model). Both models are plausible, but their use requires either knowledge of or an assumption about the degree of misreporting. Mulligan gauges this quantity by comparing the standard deviation of hours by age group in the CPS and in the diary data for the ages 25–55. Of course, we know that for those ages the two outliers for 54- and 55-year-olds in the diary data will have a big effect on the estimated standard deviation. Therefore, these exercises do not address my concern with the diary data either. The final method to adjust the CPS data is to discard everybody reporting 40 hours. This idea relies on the strong assumption that every report of 40 hours is erroneous. If this is incorrect, and some men actually work 40 hours a week, even when their wages change, then this adjustment will lead to an overestimate of the intertemporal substitution elasticity. Since there are important institutional reasons which imply that 40-hour responses may be roughly correct, we have reason to doubt these estimates.

Coffee breaks apart, why do weekly hours fluctuate for male workers? We know that part-time work is rare for men before they reach retirement age. For salaried workers, hours may vary, but this variation should have no particular effect on pay during the current period. A potential source in variation in weekly hours that remains is overtime by hourly workers, even though Mulligan's indivisible-labor model ignores this possibility if a work session is a day or longer. The questions in the Census or CPS annual demographic supplement are ill suited to pick up these variations. So I went to the 1979 merged Outgoing Rotation Group (ORG) files of the CPS and recorded data on "hours worked last week." These data come from throughout the year, and recall bias for this question should be much less important than in the surveys asking about the previous year. Thus, these data are likely to give a more accurate picture of deviations of hours from their usual level, although I agree that they are inferior to the continuous recording done in diary studies. I constructed annual hours by multiplying the CPS hours last week for the age group with their weeks worked from the Census. I also did the same construction with the "usual weekly hours" variable from the CPS. This latter variable should give an answer very similar to the annual hours from the Census. The result is shown in row 3 of Table 2, and a comparison with row 2 reveals that this is in fact true for the estimated elasticity, although usual hours from the CPS tend to be somewhat lower than usual hours from the Census. Using hours last week raises the estimated elasticity a bit, but not dramatically (row 4). Like the diary hours, using hours last week produces an annual hours measure which is below the Census measure for older workers, but there is not much difference for younger workers. In addition, the differences are not large: about 50 hours a year for workers aged 55. Thus, I believe that the adjustment due to the diary hours goes in the right direction, but I am not convinced of the magnitudes shown by Mulligan.

If hours are measured incorrectly, the measurement of the wage is also affected. Mulligan tries to correct the wage measure by using the diary hours to compute the hourly wage and instruments this measure with the wage constructed from the CPS alone. Since the first stage of this regression does not fit very well, the whopping elasticity estimate of above 6 is not very informative. The sampling distribution of the just-identified IV estimator has fat tails when the correlation of the instrument with the endogenous regressor is low, so that it easily produces crazy estimates.

Combining information from the Census and the CPS allows us to exploit the superior wage measure from the CPS. I calculated hourly wages as earnings last week divided by usual weekly hours for salaried workers and used the reported hourly wage for hourly workers. At least for hourly workers, this wage measure should be much more accurate than dividing annual earnings by annual hours, even those collected from a diary study. Row 5 in Table 2 shows that using this CPS wage measure raises the estimated elasticity by 10 to 30%. Once we are considering hours fluctuations due to overtime, we should also adjust wages for this. An hourly worker working more than 40 hours a week has to be paid time and a half for the overtime hours according to the Fair Labor Standards Act. For a work session where a worker is in the overtime range, this becomes the relevant wage for the decision about hours. I assume that hourly workers report the straight-time wage in the CPS and label every hourly worker reporting more than 40 hours last week as working overtime (thus neglecting multiple job holding). The wage of these workers is 1.5 times the reported wage. This adjustment makes little difference, as can be seen in row 6 of Table 2.

2.4 ON-THE-JOB TRAINING

Not all hours at work are actually spent in productive activities. Some time may be spent accumulating more human capital. This means that the wage for an hour of actual production is higher than the hourly wage rate reported by a worker. Since accumulation of human capital tends to be concentrated during the early years of a worker's life, making this adjustment flattens the wage profile, and therefore increases the estimated elasticity of substitution. Mulligan's Table 1 shows that the elasticity estimate rises from 0.57 to 0.61 when training hours from the time-diary data are used, or to 0.76 when the estimated hours from Heckman, Lochner, and Taber (1998) are used. I am actually surprised that either adjustment makes so little difference.

A number of assumptions go into this adjustment. We should only deduct hours of work which are not compensated by the employer. Thus, hours spent in firm-specific training, a large part of which may be paid for by the employer, should not necessarily be deducted. The assumptions in the paper with respect to the issue are actually relatively conservative, since most on-the-job training seems to be general (see Loewenstein and Spletzer, 1997). However, there is some empirical evidence suggesting that employers also seem to pay for a good part of general training (see, e.g., Barron, Berger, and Black, 1997). Acemoglu and Pischke (1999) provide a theoretical rationale for this finding: If labor markets are not competitive, and general training raises the rents which employers may capture from the workers, then employers are willing to invest in general skills. As a consequence, I suspect that Mulligan's adjustment is an upper bound for the effect of general training, because employers may well pay their workers even for most hours spent in general training.

Mulligan works with the standard training model of Gary Becker and Jacob Mincer, in which learning only takes place when the worker does not engage in productive activities. An alternative, and probably complementary, approach is the learning-by-doing model, which implies that it is an additional hour actually spent at work which makes the worker more productive. This also means that the relevant value of an hour of work has to be adjusted upwards when skill accumulation takes place. The relevant price is not just the current wage but also the discounted effect of the additional hour on all future wages, weighted appropriately by the hours worked in the future. We would expect that this has the same effect of making the correct wage profile flatter and therefore raising the estimated elasticity of substitution. The implications of this model for intertemporal substitution have been studied by Shaw (1989). However, she allows the effect of an hour of work today on wages next year to depend on the current wage. She finds that a high current wage enhances learning by doing, so that her estimates actually imply a steeper and more concave profile for the true value of an hour of work, because most learning by doing takes place during the high-wage years when individuals are in their late thirties and forties. Using her estimates of the human-capital production function, I imputed the corrected value of an hour of work using the cohort means from the Census and CPS. This is a crude way of doing things. It would be much preferable to do this calculation with the micro data and aggregate up, because the relationship between the wage next period and today's hours is rather nonlinear. This can only be done with a panel, so I ignore Jensen's inequality and feed average hours and wages into this function anyway. The results are displayed in row 7 of Table 2. The intertemporal elasticity of substitution falls by over a third. I do not want to defend these estimates as a better adjustment of the effects of training. I rather view them as an illustration of what can happen when some different estimates on human-capital formation are used in place of the ones Mulligan focuses on. I think we have too little empirical knowledge about the form of the human-capital production function and the relative importance of different channels of on-the-job training, so that it remains rather unclear whether adjusting for training actually raises or lowers the elasticity of substitution.

Career concerns or rat races among young workers generate behavior very similar to the learning-by-doing model. If more hours mean higher output, and employers use output to make inferences about the ability of workers (to set future wages), then an additional hour worked today will result in a payoff in the future. Since career concerns become less important with age, hours choices are more distorted for the young. Unfortunately, there seems to be no simple way of adjusting for the resulting distortion in the hours. This is because in equilibrium employers take the behavior of the workers into account in setting wages. They reward inferred ability, not the fact that associates in law firms and assistant professors have tried to jam the signal on ability by overly hard work. This means that, without a lot of structure, observed wages and hours by themselves will contain no information on how important career concerns are. But career concerns likely imply a higher intertemporal elasticity of substitution than we will typically estimate.

2.5 OTHER ADJUSTMENTS AND SUMMARY

The remaining adjustments are empirically much less important, at least in the group of workers below retirement age. One is for taxes. Reported wages are before taxes. As an individual's earnings rise with age, he or she gets pushed into higher tax brackets. So the after-tax wage profile will be flatter, once more generating a (slightly) higher elasticity.

Since we included nonworkers in the hours calculation, we have to address the potential composition bias resulting from the fact that we do not observe wages for these workers. This bias may differ by age. I like the way Mulligan uses panel data to get at the composition bias. This is again most important for older workers, because employment rates at young ages vary less dramatically. I have followed an alternative strategy myself, which is to assume that nonworkers are individuals with low potential earnings. Consequently, I assigned them the 10th-percentile wage within their schooling, race, and age cell. Like Mulligan's adjustment, this approach also produced lower elasticities, but the difference was equally minor.

Overall, I agree much more with the ideas underlying the specific adjustments made to the life-cycle estimates by Mulligan than with some of the empirical estimates he obtains. I find the results from the adjustments which make the biggest difference, using older workers and using diary data, the most dubious. I agree that many of the adjustments will raise the estimated elasticity. But based on those where we have reliable data, the elasticity seems to be more like 0.6 than 0.3, not out of the ballpark of previous estimates. All this said, it still remains an open question whether the hours choices of individuals over their life cycle really reflect intertemporal substitution.

3. *The Termination of AFDC Benefits*

The second empirical exercise in the paper is very different from the first. It examines the change in labor-supply behavior of women when their AFDC benefits end because the youngest child turns 18. AFDC rules impose a substantial tax rate up to 100% on the earnings of benefit recipients, thus making work much less attractive before the youngest child is age 18. In order to estimate the elasticity of intertemporal substitution implied by this change in effective wages, Mulligan compares the hours of women who received AFDC benefits when their youngest child was 17, at the times when the child was 15 and 19. For example, in the most restricted sample, average hours go up by 37 log points. Wages have changed by $-\ln(1 - \text{tax rate})$, or -0.51 when the tax rate is 0.4. Dividing these two numbers, you get the substitution elasticity of 0.73 in the bottom right-hand corner of Mulligan's Table 5. Some mothers in the sample will have received AFDC when their child was 15, and some will not. This means that the change in the implicit tax rates differs for these women. Mulligan assumes an average tax rate for the whole group. It might seem preferable to use the micro-level heterogeneity in these tax rates to estimate the effect of intertemporal substitution. But these tax rates depend on labor-supply behavior, and Mulligan's method filters out the variation which is solely due to the AFDC rules. This is effectively an application of instrumental variables.

What is unfortunate is that we are not given more information about the average tax rate, because the estimated elasticity depends fairly strongly on the assumed rate. This could be done in principle by calculating the actual benefit reduction rate faced by the individuals in the micro data. As a first approximation, I would neglect complications such as the costs of obtaining earnings disregards in this exercise. Nevertheless, the PSID probably does not have enough information to do this, because surveys are only done once a year. The Survey of Income and Program Participation (SIPP) collects monthly data on employment, income, and participation in government programs and might be more suited for such an analysis. It would also allow the researcher to incorporate participation in other government transfer programs which are tied to the presence of a child in the household, primarily housing benefits. Burtless (1990) suggests that the effective marginal tax rate resulting from the combination of programs might well be as high as 0.8 or 0.9, much above the base value of 0.5 assumed by Mulligan. I therefore suspect that the more appropriate calculations in Mulligan's Table 5 are the ones with the higher tax rates, producing the lower elasticities.

Uncertainty about the estimated elasticity also results from the small sample sizes in the PSID (unfortunately, I suspect that pooling all the SIPP panels would yield just about as many, or as few, observations). For the employment rates in Mulligan's Table 4 it is possible to calculate standard errors from the information in the table. For the most restrictive sample in column 5, the employment rate when the child is 15 rises from 0.35 with a standard error of 0.07 to 0.43 with a standard error of 0.06, not a significant change. I imagine that the magnitudes of standard errors on the hours would look similar. It would therefore be useful to have these results corroborated in other samples before we draw strong conclusions.

Even if we accept the finding as a fact that women raise their annual hours by 37% when their AFDC benefits end, there is still the question of whether this is really a response to a change in the value of work, and therefore due to intertemporal substitution. Looking at consumption changes to corroborate this interpretation is clever. Mulligan finds that women reduce their food and housing expenditures by 22 cents for each dollar of AFDC income they lose, close to Gruber's (1996) finding of 30 cents based on within-state changes in benefit levels. The benefit changes Gruber analyzed should produce wealth effects, since they were presumably unanticipated by recipients. Thus, the consumption response in Mulligan's sample seems rather large.

But alternative explanations to forward-looking behavior are consistent with a small consumption response as well. Other sources of income, such as help from family and friends, may replace the previous AFDC income and therefore help smooth consumption. The child itself may start going to work between age 15 and 19 and contribute to the income of the family. Some mothers start work or raise their hours, as we have seen, and their earnings help keep their consumption up. But this behavior may be purely myopic and have nothing to do with intertemporal substitution. Another potential test of a forward-looking versus a myopic explanation would be to compare the consumption and labor-supply responses of mothers in states with different benefit levels. The benefit level should not matter for the intertemporal substitution story (only the tax rate matters, which is set federally). But women in a high-benefit state like California may be in for more of a shock when their benefits run out than their compatriots in a low-benefit state like Texas. Unfortunately, I cannot think of a data set large enough to generate decent sample sizes for this by state. But until I see some further evidence, I also remain skeptical that what we see in the behavior of welfare mothers is intertemporal substitution.

REFERENCES

Acemoglu, D., and J.-S. Pischke (1999). The structure of wages and investment in general training. *Journal of Political Economy* 107(3), forthcoming.
Barron, J. M., M. C. Berger, and D. A. Black (1997). *On-the-Job Training.* Kalamazoo, MI: W.E. Upjohn Institute for Employment Research.
Burtless, G. (1990). The economist's lament: Public assistance in America. *Journal of Economic Perspectives* 4(1):57–78.
Costa, D. (1995). Pensions and retirement: Evidence from Union army veterans. *Quarterly Journal of Economics* 110(2):297–319.
Gruber, J. (1996). Cash welfare as a consumption smoothing mechanism for single mothers. Cambridge, MA: National Bureau of Economic Research. NBER Working Paper 5738.
Heckman, J. J., L. Lochner, and C. Taber (1998). Explaining rising wage inequality: Explorations with a dynamic general equilibrium model of labor earnings with heterogeneous agents. *Review of Economic Dynamics* 1(1):forthcoming.
Loewenstein, M. A., and J. R. Spletzer (1997). General and specific training: Evidence and implications. Bureau of Labor Statistics. Manuscript.
Shaw, K. L. (1989). Life-cycle labor supply with human capital accumulation. *International Economic Review* 30(2):431–456.

Discussion

John Shea suggested that the exclusion of family size and composition from the analysis could be a significant omission. He also pointed out that the countervailing income and substitution effects of wage changes on labor supply weaken the *a priori* case for a high elasticity of labor supply. He mentioned evidence from studies of cab drivers, whose behavior apparently reflects a substitution effect but also an income effect, as reflected in a weekly income target. Mulligan replied that his model can give new insights into the interaction of substitution and income effects, noting for example that, in his model, an increase in the real wage will lead individuals to increase the number of work sessions but reduce average session length.

David Laibson raised the issue of liquidity constraints, the existence of which may confound efforts to estimate the elasticity of intertemporal substitution. For example, labor supply peaks in midlife, which is also the time when family consumption needs are highest.

John Cochrane pointed out possible selection problems in the use of the sample of elderly workers. For example, the observed decline in hours and wages after age 65 could reflect a situation in which only lower-productivity individuals continue to work, as they cannot afford to retire.

Responding to a comment by Pischke, Mulligan argued that the way that human-capital accumulation is financed isn't critical; what is important is that the rate of accumulation is higher for younger workers, which should be interpreted as a higher implicit wage for those workers. More generally, Mulligan stressed that it was not the intention of his paper to consider all possible explanations for observed lifetime patterns of hours and wages. Rather, the idea was to see how far we can get by extending earlier research that takes the life-cycle model seriously.

Pierre-Olivier Gourinchas
PRINCETON UNIVERSITY, NBER, AND C.E.R.A.S.

Exchange Rates and Jobs: What Do We Learn from Job Flows?

1. Introduction

This paper investigates the effect of real-exchange-rate movements on net and gross job reallocation in the U.S. manufacturing sector. Interpreting real-exchange-rate shocks as reallocation shocks, it then draws implications for modern business-cycle theories. Real exchange rates measure the relative price of domestic and foreign baskets of goods. Their fluctuations are pronounced and very persistent. Figure 1 reports the U.S. effective real and nominal exchange rates from 1972 to 1996. Most striking over this period, is the 40% appreciation of the dollar from 1980 to 1985, followed by a no less spectacular depreciation that lasted until the early 1990s. Using disaggregated quarterly data for the U.S. manufacturing from 1972 to 1988, I argue that such movements in relative prices induce a sizable job reallocation, both across and within narrowly defined tradable industries. To preview the paper's main results, the benchmark estimation yields an average 0.27% contraction in tradable employment over the three quarters following a mild 10% appreciation of the real exchange rate. This contraction is brought about through a simultaneous destruction of 0.44% and creation of 0.17% of tradable jobs.

Most importantly, these results are obtained after controlling for the potential endogeneity of the real exchange rate. In effect, this paper makes use of the substantial autonomous component driving exchange-rate movements to identify movements along the tradable industry fac-

I thank Ben Bernanke, Ricardo Caballero, Bob Hall, Mike Horvath, Jonathan Parker, Paul Romer, Julio Rotemberg, Tom Sargent, and the participants at the Stanford Graduate School of Business weekly lunch and Economics Department macro lunch for their comments. The usual disclaimer applies.

Figure 1 U.S. NOMINAL AND REAL EFFECTIVE EXCHANGE RATE INDEX
(1980:1=1)

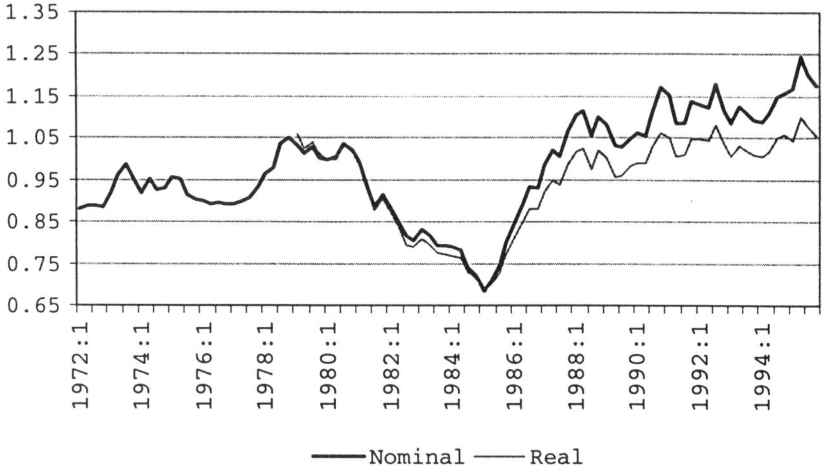

Nominal ——— Real

Source: IFS (series neu and reu).

tor demand curves. As a result, it can rule out supply or technology shocks as an alternative explanation for the results.

Investigating the dynamic response to exchange-rate shocks, this paper also finds that exchange-rate innovations induce less persistence than aggregate or monetary shocks and represent altogether a smaller source of fluctuations.

The simultaneous increase in job creation and job destruction has important implications. First, it indicates an increase in excess reallocation—the *churn*—during appreciation episodes. I find that excess job reallocation induced by a 10% appreciation represents 0.34% of tradable employment. Conversely, when the currency is depreciated, traded sector industries experience a *chill*, with lower job creation and destruction rates. Second, interpreting real-exchange-rate shocks as reallocation shocks, this paper provides useful information on how reallocative shocks propagate through the economy. Reallocation shocks have long been assumed to increase simultaneously *aggregate* job creation and destruction. The novel finding here is that relative-price shocks induce a *positive* comovement at the four-digit industry level. This suggests a cleansing effect that forces both entry and exit margins to comove positively.

The theoretical part of the paper explores the ability of a prototypical two-sector nonrepresentative business-cycle model to replicate both the aggregate and sectoral results. Since aggregate job creation and destruction comove negatively in the data, there is a tension between positive comovements at the industry level and negative ones at the aggregate level.

The next section provides a detailed motivation. Section 3 presents the empirical results and methodology, and Section 4 develops a two-sector matching model similar in spirit to that of Mortensen and Pissarides (1994).

2. Motivation

Figure 1 delivers three messages. First, changes in the nominal exchange rate account for the lion's share of real-exchange-rate fluctuations. Second, the magnitude of the fluctuations can be enormous. Lastly, in due time, those deviations appear to be reversed.

Such large movements raise two important questions. First and paramount, what is the source of these fluctuations? Second, how do firms respond to these shifts in relative prices? I address these questions in the following subsections.

2.1 ON EXCHANGE-RATE ENDOGENEITY

Exchange-rate movements are not exogenous. In a trivial way, the nominal exchange rate is the result of the confrontation of a relative demand for, and a relative supply of, currencies. Understanding the determinants of each side of this market has, and still is, the holy grail of international finance. In the long run, the current account has to be stabilized. At shorter horizons, the nominal exchange rate responds to domestic and foreign monetary conditions. Prices also adjust, as domestic firms may decide to stabilize their export prices in foreign currency (exchange-rate pass-through). Both variables, along with the nominal exchange rate, are determined in a dynamic equilibrium. In standard intertemporal models of exchange-rate determination, this implies that movements in the real exchange rate reflect the response of the economy to some fundamental impulses: domestic and foreign monetary policy, supply, and technology shocks, or aggregate demand. Rather than tracing the impact of the exchange-rate shock itself, a natural course of action would consist in evaluating the relative importance of the various impulses directly (Betts and Devereux, 1997; Chari, McGrattan, and Kehoe, 1996; Backus, Kehoe, and Kydland, 1995).

Instead, this paper starts with the premise that real-exchange-rate movements contain an important autonomous component. Before going any further, it is necessary to motivate this approach. A large body of empirical work has aimed to characterize the relationship between the real exchange rate and its fundamental determinants, for instance productivity differentials or real-interest-rate differentials (de Gregorio, Giovannini, and Wolf, 1994). It is widely recognized that this quest has, so far, yielded disappointing results. As Meese and Rogoff (1983) have forcefully demonstrated, the forecasting ability at short to medium horizons (1 quarter to 2 years) of the most refined models is poor compared to that of a more parsimonious random walk representation. The simple Mundell–Fleming–Dornbusch model linking real-exchange-rate depreciation to real interest rates differential does not appear to be supported by the data (Campbell and Clarida, 1987, Meese and Rogoff, 1988), and the empirical evidence in Clarida and Gali (1994) suggests that monetary shocks account for only a third of the variance of real-exchange-rate one-year-ahead forecast errors. At longer horizons (4 years), Mark and Choi (1997) find more encouraging results and conclude that monetary models retain some predictive power.[1]

Further, numerous empirical studies suggest that deviations of the real exchange rate from its time-varying equilibrium are not permanent, yet very persistent, with a half-life commonly estimated between 2.5 and 5 years [see Froot and Rogoff (1995) and Rogoff (1996) for a survey]. As emphasized by Rogoff (1996), the slow rate at which exchange-rate deviations fade away is hard to reconcile with their extreme short-run noisiness. In particular, monetary shocks or productivity shocks are unlikely to be the most important source of short-run fluctuations. Overall, this indicates that additional sources of fluctuations, beyond the standard determinants postulated in models of exchange-rate determination, are at play and indeed dominate over the short to medium term.

Such considerations constitute this paper's starting point: exchange-rate fluctuations contain an empirically important, if conceptually elusive, source of fluctuations that is independent of the other determinants of the economy (monetary and fiscal policy, technology, etc.). In other words, I use autonomous fluctuations in real exchange rates to identify disaggregated industries' factor demand.

2.2 ON MICRO ADJUSTMENT, AGGREGATE AND REALLOCATION SHOCKS

The real exchange rate represents the relative price of two baskets of goods. Like any relative price, movements in the real exchange rate direct

1. Mark (1995) also finds significantly better long-horizon (4 years) forecasting power for the nominal exchange rate using a fundamental equation that incorporates domestic and foreign output and money supply.

resources to and from specific sectors of the economy. One would, in general, expect large fluctuations in relative prices to have major implications on the relative quantities supplied and demanded. The levels of production, prices and markups, profit margins, and input demands and—for exporters—the decision to enter or exit foreign markets may all be affected by fluctuations in exchange rates. In the traditional two-sector model with a representative firm in each sector, competitive and frictionless markets, domestic competition for scarce factors of production induces, *ceteris paribus*, a reallocation of factors *across* sectors: following an appreciation of the currency that translates into a lower price for tradables, jobs are destroyed, workers fired, and capital dismantled in the traded goods sector, while jobs are created, the same workers hired, and the same machines reassembled in the nontraded goods sector. Inputs are continuously reallocated between sectors so as to maintain the economy on its production possibility frontier at all times.

Most previous studies focused on this *net* factor reallocation [Campa and Goldberg (1996) on investment, Branson and Love (1988), Goldberg and Tracy (1998), Burgess and Knetter (1996) on employment], on pricing-to-market and sectoral pass-through (Knetter, 1993), or on the static comparison of reallocation levels for exporters and nonexporters (Bernard and Jensen, 1995a).[2]

Nonconvexities and heterogeneity enrich this picture substantially. Consider first the entry–exit decision in the presence of irreversible adjustment costs, and uncertainty about the future value of the exchange rate. Firms may decide to stay invested in a foreign market—and absorb fluctuations in the exchange rate on their profit margin—or to postpone entry in the hope that adverse exchange-rate movements might be reversed in the near future. Similar arguments apply to the decision to hire workers, invest in new machines, upgrade capital, or set prices. Typically, the optimal policy will be one of inaction interspersed with brief adjustment episodes [a generalized (S,s) policy]. In a representative firm setting, this optimal inaction region blurs the link between exchange-rate movements and reallocation of factors of production. Firms will only enter or leave a market when the exchange rate has deviated sufficiently far from equilibrium. This indicates a nonlinearity presumably hard to document on aggregate

2. Bernard and Jensen (1995b) analyze the entry–exit decision of U.S. manufacturing exporters using plant-level data from the Annual Survey of Manufactures (ASM). They conclude that entry costs are relatively small and plant characteristics are crucial. However, by design they limit their analysis to the binary decision exporter–nonexporter. This precludes looking at import-competing firms. Moreover, as Bernard and Jensen (1995a) discuss, the export measure reported in the ASM only captures direct exports. They calculate that the ASM reported exports only account for 70% of exports measured by the Foreign Trade Division at ports of export.

data and history dependence (hysteresis). Irreversibilities were advanced as a potential explanation for the continued U.S. trade and current account deficit after 1985. Krugman (1989) concluded provocatively that real exchange rates fluctuate wildly exactly because they do not matter.

However, this conclusion is only valid if the pattern of microeconomic adjustment carries over from the plant or firm level to the sectoral or aggregate one. As recent theoretical research demonstrates in the context of price setting or investment dynamics (Caballero, 1992; Caplin and Leahy, 1991; Caballero, Engel, and Haltiwanger 1997), this assumption is often not warranted. Heterogeneity across production units contemplating an entry–exit decision will typically tend to smooth out at the aggregate level any sharp microeconomic nonlinearities.

One-sector nonrepresentative agent models of reallocation have been recently developed which build upon the rich empirical evidence on microeconomic nonconvexities and heterogeneity (Mortensen and Pissarides, 1994; Ramey and Watson, 1997; Caballero and Hammour, 1996; Hall, 1997b). These models emphasize the importance of both entry and exit margins for understanding critical features of the business cycle uncovered by Davis and Haltiwanger (1990). First, generically, both entry and exit margins are active simultaneously: gross flows are substantially larger than net flows. Second, job destruction plays an essential role in aggregate fluctuations and tends to be concentrated during brief episodes that coincide with sharp downturns in economic activity. Job creation, by contrast, is substantially less volatile over the course of the business cycle. In short, recessions are times of large job destruction and mild decline in job creation. The general challenge, so far, has been to build a theory of aggregate fluctuations that matches these stylized facts.

While existing models all share to some degree the same features, their dynamic and welfare implications differ vastly. In Mortensen and Pissarides (1994) and Cooper, Haltiwanger, and Power (1994), firms want to reallocate workers across employment opportunities or engage in nonproduction activities—like search—when aggregate productivity declines. Recessions are times of *cleansing* of the productive structure. In turn, they are also the best times for firms to enter and try to hire new workers. This cleansing effect of recessions explains why destruction is very concentrated, but also implies that destruction and creation are tightly synchronized.[3] As a result, unemployment deviations will typically tend to be short-lived.[4]

In Caballero and Hammour (1996), the presence of convex creation

3. See Caballero and Hammour (1996) for a discussion of the importance of timing assumptions for the correlation between job creation and job destruction.
4. See Cole and Rogerson (1996) for developments on this point.

costs, in conjunction with contractual inefficiencies, decouples creation and destruction, implying a large buildup of inefficient unemployment in periods of recession. However, match separation is still *ex post* efficient, and agreed upon by both the worker and firm. The contractual inefficiency distorts both the first and second moments of the gross flow series and generates countercyclical reallocation.

This reorganization view of recessions is criticized by Ramey and Watson (1997), who argue that recessions do not appear to be good times for job losers. In their model, workers and firms are engaged in a dynamic version of the prisoner's dilemma. While renegotiation is possible, the key assumption is that the match becomes nonviable as soon as one party deviates. Thus matches can be terminated following a negative productivity shock, even though the surplus is still positive, as it becomes harder to prevent either party from deviating. Their model emphasizes the importance of the "fragile" matches that accumulate close to the cutoff.

Den Haan, Ramey, and Watson (1997) present and calibrate a dynamic general equilibrium model with costly capital adjustment, similar in spirit to Mortensen and Pissarides (1994). Their model emphasizes the interaction between endogenous job destruction and capital accumulation as a source of additional persistence. As more jobs are destroyed, the marginal product of capital decreases. The endogenous response of the economy is a decline in investment, to restore the marginal product of capital. However, lower investment triggers secondary waves of separation that further depress the marginal product of capital and induce considerably more unemployment persistence.

Hall (1997b) also points out the theoretical and empirical importance of the discount rate for the economics of the shutdown margin. In his model, firms will decide to liquidate their inventories and reduce their workforce simultaneously when the value of output is high and expected to decline. In general equilibrium, recessions are associated with a high Arrow–Debreu "time-zero" price of output, or equivalently, with a high interest rate.

These models are quite successful at explaining how aggregate shocks can match the Davis–Haltiwanger (1990) stylized facts. Yet, they restrict their attention to the dynamic response to *aggregate* productivity or demand shocks. A natural question, within that framework, is the extent and pattern of excess reallocation induced by exchange-rate movements. While real-exchange-rate movements may exert pressure to relocate factors of production *across* sectors, they will also influence the pattern of reallocation *within* narrowly defined sectors and industries. This paper, analyzes *inter-* and *intra*sectoral dynamic reallocation patterns in response to both aggregate and reallocation shocks.

Moreover, existing empirical work using structural VAR-based variance decompositions generally concludes that standard impulses (technology shocks, government expenditures, or monetary policy) do a poor job of explaining the volatility of aggregate output (Cochrane, 1994; Hall, 1997a, 1997b). Reallocation shocks—usually interpreted as the result of sectoral-specific technology shocks, or relative demand shifts—have long been another prime candidate to explain aggregate fluctuations, following the seminal work of Lilien (1982).[5] Davis and Haltiwanger (1996), using gross job flows and long-run restrictions to identify the relative importance of aggregate and reallocative shocks in the U.S. economy, conclude that the latter represent the major source of job reallocation. Campbell and Kuttner (1996) reach a similar conclusion looking at fluctuations in sectoral employment shares. On the other hand, Caballero, Engel, and Haltiwanger (1997), using micro data on employment adjustment, conclude that the bulk of average-employment and job-destruction fluctuations is accounted for by aggregate rather than reallocation shocks, while job creation reacts strongly to allocative shocks.[6]

Both arguments suggest that a first order of business consists in establishing more structural correlations between primitive disturbances and measures such as gross flows. Davis and Haltiwanger (1997) explore this avenue in the context of oil shocks. This paper presents an attempt in the same direction using exchange-rate fluctuations as the main driving force, and attempts to uncover the nature and importance of these adjustment patterns using a rich disaggregated data set of U.S. manufacturing plants.

To do so, I trace back sectoral fluctuations to exogenous movements in the real exchange rate and then develop a prototypical two-sector nonrepresentative-agent business-cycle model (with tradable and nontradable goods) to explore the ability of the model to replicate salient features of the data. In practice, the problem consists in mapping gross flow movements to exogenous real-exchange-rate fluctuations.

This is difficult for two different, but related, reasons. First, as noted above, exchange rates move in reaction to changes in monetary or aggregate conditions, making inference difficult. It is precisely in order to avoid similar problems that a number of papers use oil shocks as an exogenous source of disturbance (Davis and Haltiwanger, 1997; Campbell and Kuttner, 1996). Second, as Bernanke, Gertler, and Watson (1997) argue, in the context of oil shocks, the economy's response to exchange-rate innovations may also reflect the endogenous response of monetary

5. See Lilien (1982), Abraham and Katz (1986), and Blanchard and Quah (1989).
6. In the context of nonrepresentative agent models, reallocation shocks are often modeled as a mean-preserving spread on the cross-section distribution of idiosyncratic shocks, in a one-sector economy.

policy to the initial disturbance. While the original impulse can be thought of as exogenous, it is not possible, without additional identification assumptions, to separate the direct effect of exchange-rate shocks from the expected monetary policy response. The more likely it is that monetary policy reacts to the original disturbance, the more severe this problem is. Arguably, it may not be too much of a problem in the case of the United States, to the extent that monetary policy is set largely independently of the exchange rate.[7] I will allow for exchange-rate innovations to feed back on monetary policy, so that the responses should be thought of as a combination of the response to exchange innovations and the expected implied monetary response.

3. Exchange Rates and Gross Flows

This section investigates the response of gross and net employment flows to exchange-rate fluctuations. This requires an operational definition of tradables and nontradables, a measure of gross flows, and a real exchange rate. I start with a description of the data construction, then discuss the empirical specification and results. I look at both net and gross employment changes, using quarterly disaggregated data for U.S. manufacturing from 1972 to 1988. The focus on manufacturing is largely dictated by the availability of gross flow data. While this excludes services, arguably an important component of nontradables, it will soon become apparent that finely disaggregated manufacturing industries exhibit substantial variation in international exposure that allows identification of exchange-rate effects.

3.1 THE DATA

3.1.1 Tradable and Nontradable Industries I first allocate four-digit industries into a traded, a nontraded, and a residual group. This exercise aims at measuring the exchange-rate exposure of disaggregated U.S. manufacturing industries. Campa and Goldberg (1995) identify three distinct channels through which an industry is exposed to exchange-rate fluctuations: export revenues as a share of the industry's revenues, the extent of import competition, and lastly the cost of imported inputs. I abstract from the last measure, which would require use of an input–output

---

7. Since 1985 and the abrupt policy shift of the Reagan administration, the Fed has intervened more systematically on foreign exchange markets, sometimes in concert with partner central banks. These interventions, however, are mostly *sterilized,* implying an offsetting action at the open-market window and unchanged money supply or interest rates.

table, and concentrate on export shares and import penetration ratio.[8] While the definition of traded good industries is relatively straightforward (if we observe sufficient levels of trade in some good, then it must be traded), this is not the case for nontradables. An industry might be fully integrated internationally, yet experience very low levels of exports and imports. Luckily, this problem is only likely to lead to the spurious classification of some tradable industries as nontradable, which biases the results towards zero.[9] Using the NBER trade database, I adopt the following operational definition of tradable and nontradable industries. First, I calculate for each four-digit industry and every year in the sample the export share and import penetration ratios. Then I classify an industry as traded if *either* the export share exceeds 13% *or* the import penetration ratio exceeds 12.5% *in all the years of the sample*. Conversely, an industry is classified as nontraded when either (1) the export share is lower than 1.3% and the import penetration ratio is lower than 6.8% *in all years in the sample* or (2) the export share is lower than 5.8% and the import penetration is less than 0.8% *in all years in the sample*. All other sectors are discarded.[10] This selection criterion ensures that sectors experiencing a transition from very closed to very open or vice versa are excluded from the sample. 48 sectors are initially identified as nontraded and 69 as traded, out of a total of 450 four-digit manufacturing sectors. Based on the NBER trade database, I further exclude all sectors without detailed information on exports and imports by country of destination or origin. The final list includes 35 nontraded sectors and 68 traded ones. Tradable industries are further classified as exporters or import-competing according to their export share and import penetration ratios. Out of the 68 traded industries (with some overlap), 34 are classified as exporters and 39 as import-competing sectors.[11]

Nontradables are concentrated primarily in nondurables, where they represent around 23% of employment. By comparison, nontradables rep-

8. There are reasons to believe that omitting imported inputs may not bias the results seriously, since the direction of the effect is likely to be the same as for nontraded industries, that is, an appreciation leads to a relative gain in profitability through a decline in input costs. The bias is likely to be more serious if industries classified as traded based on their output are in fact very cost-sensitive to exchange-rate fluctuations.

9. An alternative would be to compare domestic and foreign prices. Foreign prices for exported and imported goods are relatively difficult to find.

10. The values for the export shares and import penetration ratios cutoffs are similar to the ones used in Davis, Haltiwanger, and Schuh (1996).

11. The list of industries with their SIC code, average export share, import penetration, and share of the two-digit industry labor force is reported in an appendix available from the author or on the Web: **http://www.princeton.edu/~pog/RER-home.html.**

Table 1   CHARACTERISTICS OF NONTRADED AND TRADED EXPORTERS
AND IMPORT-COMPETING FIRMS

			Traded		
Variable	All	Nontraded	All	Exporters	Import-Competing
Capital:					
Per production worker	89.92	75.51	102.47	125.29	95.93
Per worker	63.16	50.20	70.23	82.02	69.51
Investment:					
Per production worker	27.75	20.70	43.74	55.07	33.15
Per worker	19.56	14.95	29.62	35.62	23.96
Employment:					
Production workers	29.14	31.65	27.32	31.49	21.24
Total	40.46	49.13	41.37	53.93	26.48
Shipments	4784	5784	5689	5985	4920
TFP (%)	0.57	0.46	0.48	0.65	0.41
Materials intensity (%)	51.41	51.46	52.97	51.23	54.03
Energy intensity (%)	2.56	2.18	2.41	2.13	2.77
Wages:					
Production workers	19.42	18.33	20.06	23.23	17.53
Total	22.01	20.70	23.03	26.76	19.96

Capital, investment, shipments, and wages: thousands of 1987 dollars. Employment: thousands. Materials intensity: materials expenditures/shipment. Energy intensity: energy expenditures/shipment.
Source: NBER productivity database and author's calculations.

resent only 6.6% of durable manufacturing employment. Overall, nontradable goods are either perishable goods (such as food products and newspapers) or heavy durable goods (such as concrete, bricks, or stone) for which transportation costs are prohibitive. Conversely, tradables tend to be concentrated in durable goods industries, with an average share of durables employment of 21.4%. Major exporting two-digit industries, measured in terms of employment, include nonelectrical machinery (SIC 35), with a 41% share of export industries employment, transportation equipment (SIC 37, 27%), and instruments (SIC 38, 8%). Overall, import-competing industries represent quite a small fraction of total manufacturing employment (around 11%) and tend to be concentrated in paper (SIC 26), with a 14% share of import-competing industries employment, leather (SIC 31, 15%), and especially motor vehicles (SIC 3711, 31%).[12]

Table 1 reports some characteristics for industries grouped according

12. See the appendix available on the web.

to the previous classification.[13] We observe that traded-goods producers tend, on average, to be more capital-intensive, to pay higher wages, to be smaller, and to have slightly higher total factor productivity. Looking at exporting versus import-competing sectors, we observe that exporters pay higher wages, tend to be larger in terms of shipments or number of employees, and are more capital-intensive and more productive (as measured by total factor productivity).

3.1.2. Gross Flows Quarterly sectoral data on job creation and job destruction are tabulated by Davis and Haltiwanger (1990) for both two-digit and four-digit industries.[14] These data are constructed from the Census's Longitudinal Research Database, and cover U.S. manufacturing over the period 1972:2–1988:4.[15]

Using the previous classification, I first aggregate gross flows for traded, nontraded, exporter, and import-competing sectors. Table 2 reports descriptive statistics for the resulting gross and net flows. The main points are as follows. First, net employment growth is negative for all groups, reflecting the declining importance of manufacturing employment in the U.S. economy. This downward trend is especially marked for import-competing industries, with an average quarterly employment decline of 0.62%. Second, defined tradables and nontradables represent roughly similar shares of total manufacturing employment, around 13%. This indicates that the bulk of manufacturing employment cannot be classified as either traded or nontraded according to our criterion. Third, for all sectors, job destruction exhibits more volatility than job creation. Furthermore, creation and destruction are proportionately more volatile for tradable industries. Taken together, these results indicate larger turbulence in the traded goods sector. This paper explores the link between this turbulence and exchange-rate exposure. Lastly, as pointed out by Foote (1995), one should expect industries with a marked downward employment trend to exhibit a larger volatility of job destruction, as the exit margin is "hit" more frequently while the industry shrinks. One

---

13. The data referred to in the previous footnote are taken from the NBER productivity database. See Bartelsman and Gray (1996) for a description.

14. I thank John Haltiwanger for providing the sectoral data through his ftp site.

15. This data set is now widely used in macro and labor studies, and I refer the reader to Davis, Haltiwanger, and Schuh (1996) for a detailed description. Two points are worth noting. First, the timing of quarters is nonstandard, with quarter 1 of year t running from November of year $t - 1$ to February of year t. Second, the SIC underwent substantial changes in 1987. Davis and Haltiwanger's data report sectoral job creation and destruction using the SIC72 classification for 1972–1986 and the SIC87 classification for 1987–1988. The last two years of data were spliced into the SIC72 classification using the concordance table provided in Bartelsman and Gray (1996).

Table 2 GROSS FLOWS BY SECTORS

Sector	Job Creation				Job Destruction			
	Mean	Standard Deviation	Min.	Max.	Mean	Standard Deviation	Min.	Max.
Nontraded	5.48	0.79	4.04	7.54	5.67	1.02	3.46	8.61
Traded	5.36	0.96	3.16	7.50	5.76	1.68	3.04	10.85
Exporters	4.82	1.06	2.55	7.51	5.00	1.69	2.29	10.05
Import-comp.	6.01	1.55	2.86	9.84	6.64	2.68	3.44	16.27
	Excess Reallocation				Net Employment Growth			
	Mean	Standard Deviation	Min.	Max.	Mean	Standard Deviation	Min.	Max.
Nontraded	10.16	1.20	6.93	12.50	−0.19	1.29	−3.88	2.80
Traded	9.38	1.53	6.09	13.76	−0.39	2.28	−7.69	3.41
Exporters	8.08	1.83	4.58	15.01	−0.18	2.21	−6.21	3.64
Import-comp.	10.29	2.19	5.72	16.46	−0.62	3.26	−10.42	4.06
	Manufacturing Employment Share							
	Mean	Standard Deviation	Min.	Max.				
Nontraded	12.11	0.45	11.32	12.95				
Traded	14.54	0.32	13.70	15.27				
Exporters	8.48	0.62	7.29	9.59				
Import-comp.	6.41	0.60	5.36	7.50				

Source: Gross flows from Davis and Haltiwanger, LRD; and author's calculations.

finds indeed that the job destruction rate is both higher and more volatile for import-competing industries.

3.1.3. Real Exchange Rate The last ingredient for the analysis is the real exchange rate. I use an *industry-based* definition of the real exchange rate, constructed as a trade-weighted log average of bilateral WPI-based real exchange rates. The trade weights are industry-specific and constructed from the NBER trade database, which includes, for each four-digit industry, annual data on shipments, exports, and imports, disaggregated by country of destination (exports) or origin (imports). The industry-specific log real exchange rate is then a weighted average of the WPI-based log real exchange rate against *that sector's* major trading partners.[16]

16. For the purpose of this paper, I define the major trading partners by calculating the average export/import shares of total export/import for each industry and destination/origin country. Country *i* is considered a major trading partner for industry *j* if either (1)

For the appropriate sectors, both an export- and an import-based sectoral real exchange rate are created in this fashion. A similar methodology is also used to construct real exchange rate indices for each of the two-digit industries and for nontradable industries, whenever data on exports and imports are available.[17]

Figure 2 reports the real-exchange-rate index for some two-digit industries. At this level of aggregation, the figure reveals a similar broad pattern in all industries, with a significant real appreciation during the first half of the eighties corresponding to the nominal appreciation of the dollar, and a rapid depreciation from 1985 onwards. Note however, that the figures do exhibit substantial variation in terms of timing and amplitude. For instance, furnitures (SIC 25) experienced a rapid real depreciation between 1972 and 1977, while textiles' real exchange rate (SIC 22) remained relatively unchanged until late 1980. This sectoral variation will help identification.

3.2 EMPIRICAL RESULTS

In this subsection, I consider first the reduced-form response of gross and net flows to exchange-rate movements. Issues of simultaneity are discussed and controlled for. I then present dynamic structural estimation based on a VAR decomposition.

3.2.1 Reduced-Form Estimation One can think of the approach of this subsection as mapping an industry factor demand curve from movements in the real exchange rate. I start with the direct estimation results for net and gross job flows and then discuss simultaneity issues and instrumentation.

NET EMPLOYMENT CHANGES Given the definitions adopted, nontraded industries play the role of a control group: their international exposure is limited, and their response to exchange-rate fluctuations should be minimal. On the other hand, an appreciation of the real exchange rate should induce a reallocation of factors away from the traded-good sector. That

---

country i is among the largest trading partners accounting for the first 50% of exports/imports for industry j or (2) trade with country i represents more than 10% of exports/imports, on average over the sample period. The real exchange rate is then constructed as a log average using export/import shares as weights. For each industry, the real exchange rate is normalized to 100 in 1987:4. Data on WPI and nominal exchange rates were obtained from the International Financial Statistics Database. China, Iraq, Hong Kong, Taiwan, and the United Arab Emirates were deleted as trading partners, since no reliable data on the bilateral real exchange rate were available.

17. Trade data on all four-digit sectors were used to construct weights at the two-digit level.

Figure 2 SIC-2 LOG REAL EXCHANGE RATE

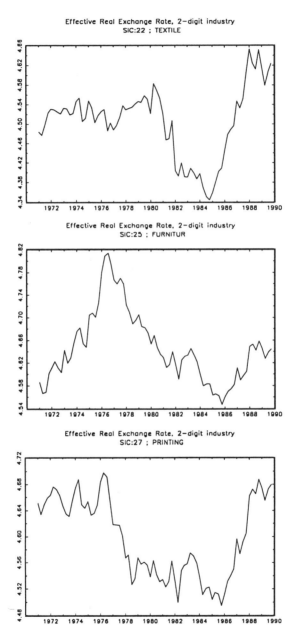

1987:4 = 1n 100.

is, each traded industry's employment level should respond negatively to an appreciation of its real exchange rate. In turn, the decline in employment can result from a decline in job creation or an increase in job destruction. At the aggregate level, there is overwhelming evidence that the adjustment takes place along the exit margin.

I investigate each question in turn. Starting with net employment changes, I evaluate the amount of intersectoral reallocation that is induced by the exchange rate. I then turn to the gross flows.

Consider the following specification:

$$\hat{E}_{it} = \alpha_i + \beta(L)\lambda_{it} + \gamma(L)Z_t + \epsilon_{it}, \tag{1}$$

where $\hat{E}_{it}$ is the net employment growth in industry i between time $t - 1$ and t, and λ_{it} is the deviation from trend of the industry specific log real exchange rate. Z_t contains aggregate variables likely to influence both the real exchange rate and employment growth. I include in Z_t total manufacturing employment growth $\hat{E}_t$, to capture the effect of aggregate shocks, as well as the federal funds rate i_t. Finally, $\beta(L)$ and $\gamma(L)$ are lag polynomials. They are allowed to vary across groups: nontraded, traded, exporters, and import-competing. The results are presented in panel A of Table 3.

Under the null hypothesis that all variations in employment growth are unrelated to real-exchange-rate fluctuations, the real exchange rate should have no explanatory power. The table indicates that a depreciated exchange rate has a small effect on tradable employment growth.[18] A 10% depreciation of the exchange rate (a high value of λ) leads to an increase of tradable manufacturing employment of 0.27%.[19] Nontradable employment appears unresponsive to exchange-rate movements (with a sum of coefficients equal to 2.18 and a standard error of 1.88). However, note that the point estimates for tradable and nontradable are close together and one cannot reject the hypothesis that they are equal. Further, comparing export and import-competing industries, it appears that the effect comes mostly through an employment increase in import-competing industries. These reduced-form results indicate a limited amount of intersectoral reallocation. Looking at individual coefficients, it appears that employment growth increases for the first 2 quarters, then declines.

---

18. Note that equation (1) is a growth-level relation with the industry employment growth on the left-hand side and the real-exchange-rate deviation from trend on the other side.
19. A caveat on reading the regression results: a coefficient of β for the real-exchange-rate coefficient implies that a 1% depreciation will increase employment growth by $\beta/100\%$. A coefficient of α on aggregate employment growth implies that a 1% increase in growth rates will increase sectoral employment growth by $\alpha\%$.

Table 3   EMPLOYMENT RESPONSE TO REAL-EXCHANGE-RATE
DEVIATIONS

Sector:	Two-digit		Traded						Nontraded	
			All		Exports		Import comp.			
Regressor	Timing	Coeff.	SE	Coeff.	SE	Coeff.	SE	Coeff.	SE	Coeff.	SE
				Panel A: Direct Estimation							
λ_t	Cont.	1.40	1.65	4.97	2.47	2.72	3.32	4.58	3.18	6.24	3.38
	1 lag	−0.64	2.29	5.47	3.40	2.60	4.70	8.24	4.32	−3.13	4.45
	2 lags	−0.37	1.76	−7.73	2.58	−4.28	3.49	−9.84	3.31	−0.92	3.49
	Sum:	0.39	0.76	2.71	1.13	1.03	1.38	2.96	1.03	2.18	1.88
$\hat{E}_t$	Cont.	0.68	0.03	0.66	0.06	0.48	0.07	0.77	0.08	0.52	0.08
	1 lag	0.01	0.04	0.08	0.06	0.12	0.08	0.03	0.08	0.02	0.08
	2 lags	0.17	0.03	0.28	0.05	0.37	0.07	0.18	0.07	0.06	0.07
	Sum:	0.85	0.04	1.02	0.07	0.98	0.10	0.98	0.10	0.60	0.10
i_t	Cont.	0.05	0.03	0.05	0.05	0.18	0.07	−0.08	0.07	−0.03	0.07
	1 lag	−0.12	0.03	−0.05	0.06	−0.10	0.08	0.01	0.08	−0.06	0.08
	2 lags	0.02	0.03	0.01	0.06	−0.07	0.07	0.04	0.08	0.07	0.07
	Sum:	−0.06	0.02	0.01	0.03	0.01	0.05	−0.03	0.04	−0.01	0.04
				PANEL B: 2SLS							
λ_t	Cont.	6.34	1.76	−0.42	2.41	1.65	3.03	−3.15	3.23	3.81	3.89
	1 lag	−6.15	2.05	5.34	2.86	1.96	3.61	8.48	3.84	−3.68	4.62
	2 lags	0.21	1.67	−3.44	2.34	−3.12	2.95	−4.86	3.14	0.12	3.85
	Sum:	0.39	1.47	1.47	1.87	0.49	2.24	0.47	2.58	0.25	3.12
$\hat{E}_t$	Cont.	0.70	0.03	0.64	0.06	0.47	0.07	0.76	0.08	0.51	0.08
	1 lag	0.01	0.04	0.06	0.06	0.12	0.08	0.01	0.09	0.02	0.08
	2 lags	0.17	0.03	0.29	0.05	0.37	0.07	0.19	0.07	0.07	0.07
	Sum:	0.88	0.04	1.00	0.08	0.96	0.10	0.96	0.11	0.60	0.11
i_t	Cont.	0.04	0.03	0.03	0.05	0.16	0.07	−0.10	0.07	−0.03	0.07
	1 lag	−0.11	0.03	−0.05	0.06	−0.09	0.08	0.01	0.08	−0.07	0.08
	2 lags	0.03	0.03	0.01	0.06	−0.06	0.07	0.01	0.08	0.07	0.08
	Sum:	−0.04	0.02	−0.02	0.03	−0.01	0.05	−0.08	0.05	−0.03	0.05

The tables shows the response of employment growth to deviations of the real exchange rate from trend for each sector (λ), change in total manufacturing employment growth ($\hat{E}$), and the federal funds rate i_t. The coefficients are constrained to be equal across sectors, except for a constant (not shown). The first column reports the results for all two-digit industries. The remaining columns report the result for four-digit tradables, exporters, import-competing, and nontradables. Panel A reports fixed-effect estimation. Panel B instruments the real exchange rate with the Hall–Ramey instruments (Hall, 1988): military expenditure growth, crude-oil price growth, political party of the President. Observations are quarterly, 1972:2 to 1988:4.
Source: Net employment change from Davis and Haltiwanger (1990), LRD; real exchange rate: author's calculations.

Table 4 JOB-DESTRUCTION RESPONSE TO REAL-EXCHANGE-RATE DEVIATIONS

Sector:	Two-digit			Traded					Nontraded	
				All		Exports		Import comp.		
Regressor	Timing	Coeff.	SE	Coeff.	SE	Coeff.	SE	Coeff.	SE	Coeff.	SE
		Panel A: Direct Estimation									
λ_t	Cont.	−2.88	1.25	−4.26	1.82	−1. 56	2.39	−4.99	2.40	−5.27	2.22
	1 lag	−2.13	1.74	−8.65	2.51	−7.19	3.39	−10.23	3.25	0.58	2.93
	2 lags	3.43	1.34	8.46	1.91	6.06	2.52	10.27	2.49	4.21	2.30
	Sum:	−1.58	0.57	−4.44	0.83	−2.68	0.99	−4.95	1.15	−0.47	1.24
$\hat{E}_t$	Cont.	−0.45	0.02	−0.40	0.04	−0.26	0.05	−0.50	0.06	−0.33	0.05
	1 lag	−0.03	0.03	−0.10	0.05	−0.11	0.06	−0.10	0.06	−0.01	0.06
	2 lags	−0.16	0.02	−0.23	0.04	−0.27	0.04	−0.16	0.05	−0.06	0.05
	Sum:	−0.65	0.03	−0.73	0.05	−0.65	0.07	−0.75	0.08	−0.39	0.07
i_t	Cont.	−0.07	0.02	−0.10	0.04	−0.20	0.05	−0.01	0.05	−0.01	0.05
	1 lag	0.08	0.02	0.06	0.04	0.09	0.05	0.02	0.06	0.03	0.05
	2 lags	0.01	0.02	0.01	0.04	0.05	0.05	−0.01	0.06	−0.01	0.05
	Sum:	0.01	0.01	−0.03	0.02	−0.05	0.03	0.01	0.03	0.01	0.03
		Panel B: 2SLS									
λ_t	Cont.	−0.69	1.36	−2.02	1.76	−4.05	2.11	0.38	2.45	1.21	2.57
	1 lag	0.98	1.59	−4.99	2.09	−4.72	2.52	−5.59	2.91	−1.38	3.05
	2 lags	−1.58	1.28	1.46	1.72	3.45	2.06	1.68	2.38	2.49	2.54
	Sum:	−1.29	1.13	−5.54	1.37	−5.31	1.56	−3.53	1.95	2.33	2.06
$\hat{E}_t$	Cont.	−0.46	0.02	−0.40	0.04	−0.27	0.05	−0.50	0.06	−0.33	0.05
	1 lag	−0.02	0.03	−0.08	0.05	−0.11	0.06	−0.06	0.06	0.01	0.06
	2 lags	−0.17	0.02	−0.24	0.04	−0.27	0.05	−0.19	0.05	−0.08	0.05
	Sum:	−0.65	0.03	−0.73	0.06	−0.65	0.07	−0.76	0.08	−0.41	0.07
i_t	Cont.	−0.05	0.02	−0.07	0.04	−0.16	0.05	0.03	0.05	−0.01	0.05
	1 lag	0.07	0.02	0.05	0.04	0.08	0.05	0.02	0.06	0.04	0.05
	2 lags	0.01	0.02	0.01	0.04	0.03	0.05	0.01	0.06	0.01	0.05
	Sum:	0.02	0.02	−0.01	0.03	−0.05	0.03	0.05	0.04	0.04	0.03

Table is analogous to Table 3.

The coefficients on total manufacturing employment growth $\hat{E}_t$ are large and significant, and their sum is close to 1 for all sectors but nontraded, indicating that shocks that affect total manufacturing employment growth are reflected almost one for one into sectoral employment growth. Somewhat surprisingly, it appears that monetary policy does not markedly influence industry employment growth, once we control for fluctuations in total manufacturing employment.[20]

To summarize, the results indicate limited intersectoral reallocation of labor in response to exchange rates. We turn now to the next question: is the increase in employment coming from an increase in job creation, a decrease in job destruction, or a combination?

GROSS EMPLOYMENT CHANGES   To answer this question, I now run the same specification, replacing industry net employment growth successively with job destruction rates and job creation in equation (1). The results are presented in panel A of Tables 4 and 5.

The results indicate the following:

- Gross flows in the nontraded good sector are insensitive to exchange-rate movements. They are, however, very sensitive to aggregate shocks, as captured by total manufacturing employment growth. Thus our definition of nontradable seems relevant as a control group.
- Traded sectors' job destruction rates are quite sensitive to exchange-rate movements. A 10% real depreciation destroys 0.44% of tradable employment. With an average quarterly job destruction rate around 5.3%, this represents a very sizeable response to relatively minor exchange-rate fluctuations.
- Job destruction in both sectors covaries negatively and significantly with aggregate shocks.
- Irrespective of the type of shock, job destruction is more responsive than job creation in all sectors.
- Tradable job creation declines mildly in response to a depreciation of the exchange rate (−0.17% for 10% depreciation) and increases in response to a positive aggregate shock.
- Import-competing industries appear more sensitive to exchange-rate fluctuations than exporters.

20. In unreported regressions, I also included the Hamilton oil price index (Hamilton, 1995) or a commodity price index as another control. The results were unchanged, and the oil price index was never significant. Results are also unchanged if one uses the spread between 6-month commercial paper and 6-month T-bills instead of the federal funds rate. Similar results are also obtained when using the import-based real exchange rate or using the absolute level of the real exchange rate instead of the deviations from trend.

Table 5 JOB-CREATION RESPONSE TO REAL-EXCHANGE-RATE
DEVIATIONS

Sector:	Two-digit			Traded						
				All		Exports		Import comp.		Nontraded
Regressor	Timing	Coeff.	SE	Coeff.	SE	Coeff.	SE	Coeff.	SE	Coeff.	SE
			Panel A: Direct Estimation								
λ_t	Cont.	−1.43	0.99	0.71	1.44	1.16	2.04	−0.41	1.79	0.97	2.16
	1 lag	−2.86	1.37	−3.17	1.99	−4.58	2.90	−1.99	2.43	−2.54	2.85
	2 lags	3.20	1.05	0.72	1.51	1.77	2.15	0.42	1.86	3.29	2.24
	Sum:	−1.09	0.45	−1.73	0.60	−1.64	0.65	−1.98	0.56	1.71	1.31
$\hat{E}_t$	Cont.	0.22	0.02	0.26	0.03	0.22	0.04	0.28	0.04	0.19	0.05
	1 lag	−0.02	0.02	−0.02	0.04	0.01	0.05	−0.07	0.05	0.01	0.06
	2 lags	0.01	0.02	0.06	0.03	0.09	0.04	0.02	0.04	−0.01	0.05
	Sum:	0.21	0.02	0.29	0.04	0.33	0.06	0.23	0.06	0.20	0.07
i_t	Cont.	−0.03	0.02	−0.05	0.03	−0.02	0.04	−0.08	0.04	−0.04	0.05
	1 lag	−0.04	0.02	0.01	0.03	−0.04	0.05	0.03	0.04	−0.03	0.05
	2 lags	0.02	0.02	0.02	0.03	−0.02	0.04	0.02	0.04	0.06	0.05
	Sum:	−0.05	0.01	−0.03	0.02	−0.04	0.03	−0.04	0.03	−0.01	0.03
			Panel B: 2SLS								
λ_t	Cont.	5.61	1.05	−2.44	1.39	−2.40	1.84	−2.77	1.79	5.02	2.49
	1 lag	−5.11	1.23	0.35	1.65	−2.76	2.19	2.89	2.14	−5.05	2.96
	2 lags	−1.37	0.99	−1.97	1.35	0.33	1.80	−3.18	1.75	2.62	2.46
	Sum:	−0.86	0.88	−4.07	1.07	−4.83	1.36	−3.05	1.43	2.58	1.99
$\hat{E}_t$	Cont.	0.24	0.02	0.24	0.03	0.21	0.04	0.25	0.04	0.18	0.05
	1 lag	−0.01	0.02	−0.02	0.04	0.01	0.05	−0.05	0.05	0.03	0.05
	2 lags	−0.01	0.02	0.05	0.03	0.09	0.04	0.01	0.04	−0.01	0.04
	Sum:	0.22	0.03	0.27	0.04	0.31	0.06	0.20	0.06	0.19	0.06
i_t	Cont.	−0.02	0.02	−0.04	0.03	0.01	0.04	−0.07	0.04	−0.04	0.04
	1 lag	−0.04	0.02	0.01	0.03	−0.01	0.05	0.02	0.04	−0.03	0.05
	2 lags	0.04	0.02	0.01	0.03	−0.04	0.04	0.02	0.04	0.07	0.05
	Sum:	−0.02	0.01	−0.03	0.02	−0.05	0.02	−0.03	0.03	0.01	0.03

Table is analogous to Table 3.

This last point indicates that gross flows depict a somewhat different picture than net flows for exporters and import-competing industries. In export-oriented industries, an appreciation is associated with a substantial increase in job destruction and creation that leaves, on net, employment unchanged.

The apparent similarity between the point estimates of net employment for traded and nontraded sectors disappears when looking at gross flows. The contrast between the two groups indicates that the results are not driven by a response to aggregate disturbances. Further, it appears that the dynamic adjustment to a relative price shock is quite different from the adjustment to an aggregate shock. Following an aggregate shock, job creation and destruction move in *opposite directions*. However, following an exchange-rate shock, job creation and destruction move *in the same direction*. While reallocative shocks are often assumed to induce a simultaneous increase in aggregate job creation and destruction, it is worthwhile to note that the simultaneous move occurs *within* the tradable sector, while the intersectoral channels sometimes emphasized in the literature. A similar result is obtained by Davis and Haltiwanger (1997) in response to oil shocks.

By contrast, a positive aggregate shock increases job creation by 0.29 (0.20) in the traded (nontraded) sector and a decline in job destruction of 0.73 (0.39).

How much does each margin contribute to industry employment adjustment? Clearly, given our estimates, job destruction plays the major role, with job creation as a follower. The results also indicate that excess reallocation, or *churn*, will increase when the exchange rate appreciates, and decrease when the currency depreciates. Hence, the next point:

- Appreciations are associated with increased turbulence on the labor market. Job creation, destruction, and excess reallocation increase. Conversely, during depreciation phases, the tradable sector chills as creation and destruction rates fall.

Note that the paper does not draw any welfare implications at this stage, and that this chill does not follow a burst of destruction as in Caballero and Hammour (1998).

SIMULTANEITY AND CHOICE OF INSTRUMENTAL VARIABLES   The preceding empirical analysis suggests that an appreciation of the real exchange rate that lowers the relative price of tradables is associated with a simultaneous increase in destruction and creation that results in a net employment loss. An alternative possibility is that both the appreciation and the

Figure 3 RELATIVE-TECHNOLOGY SHOCKS

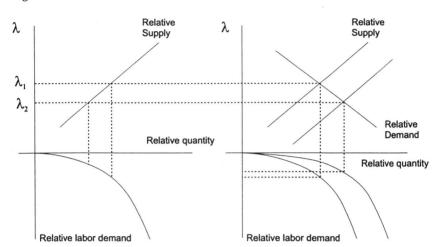

increase in gross flows result from a technological shift at the industry level. To see clearly the contrast between the two interpretations, consider Figure 3. This paper's interpretation is that there is a stable industry relative-supply curve (upper left diagram) that is mapped through exogenous shifts in the relative price λ, i.e., the real exchange rate. Associated with this stable supply curve is a stable relative-factor-demand curve (lower left diagram).[21] In this rendition, an appreciation is associated with a decline in λ, in relative output, and in relative employment. An alternative interpretation (right diagrams) would assert that there is a stable demand curve, and that the relative-supply curve shifts in response to relative-technology shocks. A positive relative-technology shock in tradables shifts out the relative-supply curve, leading to a decline in λ (an appreciation) from λ_1 to λ_2 and an increase in relative output. In terms of net job flows, this relative-technology shock may decrease relative employment in the traded sector, as illustrated in the lower right diagram.[22] While job creation may increase, job destruction

21. In the context of a specific factor model, for instance, assume that $Y_T = z_T L_T^\alpha K_T^{1-\alpha}$ and $Y_N = z_N L_N^\alpha K_N^{1-\alpha}$ where K_T and K_N denote sector-specific capital and z_T and z_N sector-specific productivities. Then clearly $Y_T / Y_N = (z_T / z_N) (L_T / L_N)^\alpha (K_T / K_N)^{1-\alpha}$. The lower panel describes this relationship for given relative productivities and relative capital.

22. Take the limit case described in Baumol, Blackman, and Wolff (1985): suppose the economy produces only cars and live concerts and preferences are Leontieff. Relative technological progress in car production would lead to an overall decline in the number of workers in the car industry and an increase in the share of the labor force producing live concerts.

may increase as well if old and unproductive production units are cleansed. In the latter case, the link between exchange rate and reallocation is spurious and simply reflects the response to sectoral relative-technology shocks. Note however that relative-demand shocks do not generate the same pattern, since a relative-demand shock would lead to a simultaneous depreciation (an increase in λ) and a relative increase in traded goods output and tradable employment.

There are two possible lines of defense for the previous result that I now present. First, there is a subtle difference between the real exchange rate that matters in Figure 3 and the one used in the regressions. Relative-technology shocks will undoubtedly influence the relative price of traded and nontraded goods.[23] Instead, the previous results used a WPI-based real exchange rate. Relative-technology shocks at the four-digit level are unlikely to affect the real exchange rate constructed in this fashion. This, in effect, amounts to instrumenting the real-exchange-rate measure in a way that minimizes the role of relative-technology shocks. Fluctuations in the real exchange rate will thus capture mostly variations in the nominal exchange rate.

For those still unconvinced, another solution consists in explicitly instrumenting the real exchange rate λ_{it} in (1), using shifters of the relative demand schedule. Clearly, one will then only measure employment movements induced by the shifters themselves and mediated through changes in the real exchange rate, and one may miss the response to autonomous movements of the real exchange rate. To the extent that these relative demand shifts are uncorrelated with supply shifts and affect the real exchange rate, however, it is still a valid exercise. As a crude attempt, I report estimates using the Hall–Ramey set of instruments (see Hall, 1988): the growth rate of military expenditures, the growth rate of the crude oil price, and the political party of the President.[24] Military expenditures are likely to be the best instrument for our purpose, since they tend to be fairly concentrated in a few manufacturing industries.

Panel B in Tables 3–5 present 2SLS estimates. Comparing the results with the simple fixed-effect estimates, it is immediate that employment growth becomes nonsignificant for all groups. Looking at gross flows, we see that job creation appears to respond more strongly to exchange rates. A 10% depreciation leads to a decline of 0.40% in job creation in

23. Indeed, plots of the relative price of traded versus nontraded goods constructed from the shipment deflators of the NBER Productivity Database reveal a strong and downward trend in the price of traded goods, in accordance with the faster productivity growth in those sectors.

24. The set of instruments is common to all sectors. Yet the coefficients from the first stage are industry-dependent. A better solution, not investigated in this paper, would use sector-specific demand shifters, along the lines of Shea (1993).

traded industries. Overall, the results indicate that there is a strong response of gross flows, less so for net flows. The absence of a net effect may also suggest that the grouping remains too coarse for an analysis of exchange-rate movements.

3.2.2 Dynamic Analysis The preceding results describe an economy that reacts on average and with some lags to exchange-rate movements. This section takes a more rigorous approach towards controlling for possible endogeneity of the exchange rate by using sectoral VARs, along the lines of Davis and Haltiwanger (1997).

I estimate a VAR for each four-digit industry classified as traded or nontraded. The VAR for sector j contains an aggregate bloc with the Hamilton oil price index s_t, the total manufacturing job creation and destruction for all sectors but sector j (denoted JC_t^{-j} and JD_t^{-j}) and the quality spread between 6-month commercial paper and 6-month T-bills, m_t.[25] This definition of aggregate flows ensures that idiosyncratic shocks to sectoral flows will not influence aggregate flows for large sectors. The VAR also includes the sectoral real exchange rate λ_{st} as well as sectoral job creation and destruction JC_{st} and JD_{st}. I make the following assumptions:

1. the sectoral gross flows do not affect either aggregate variables or the sectoral real exchange rate;
2. aggregate variables are block Wold-causally ordered and prior to the sectoral ones;
3. the real exchange rate is Wold-causally ordered after the aggregate variables and before the sectoral flows;
4. the covariance matrix of structural innovations is block-diagonal.

Note that under these assumptions the real exchange rate is only restricted not to influence aggregate variables within the quarter. Given the possible feedback from the real exchange rate, the assumption that sectoral flows are independent of the real exchange rate only ensures that they do not indirectly affect aggregate variables.[26]

---

25. The Hamilton net oil price measure is the maximum of 0 and the difference between the log level of the crude-oil price for the current month and the maximum value of the logged crude-oil price over the previous 12 months. The spread captures monetary policy. Unreported results using the federal funds rate as the instrument of monetary policy yield essentially unchanged results.

26. Given these assumptions, and unlike Davis and Haltiwanger (1997), the set of aggregate innovations is sector-dependent. In practice, the results are virtually unchanged if we assume instead that the real exchange rate does not influence aggregate variables at all lags. In addition, Davis and Haltiwanger (1997) decompose oil price movements into positive and negative components. It is comforting, however, to find that oil shocks play a similar role in this decomposition and theirs.

Formally, denoting by Z_t the first four aggregate variables of the seven-variable vector (in that order), and by S_t the sectoral job creation and destruction rates, the VAR system is written

$$Z_t = \sum_{i=1}^{p} (\psi_{zz,i} Z_{t-i} + \psi_{z\lambda,i} \lambda_{st-i}) + B_{zz} \epsilon_{z,t},$$

$$\lambda_{st} = \sum_{i=1}^{p} (\psi_{\lambda z,i} Z_{t-i} + \psi_{\lambda\lambda,i} \lambda_{st-i}) + B_{\lambda z} \epsilon_{z,t} + \epsilon_{\lambda,t},$$

$$S_{st} = \sum_{i=1}^{p} (\psi_{sz,i} Z_{t-i} + \psi_{s\lambda,i} \lambda_{st-i} + \psi_{ss,i} S_{st-i}) + B_{sz} \epsilon_{z,t} + B_{s\lambda} \epsilon_{\lambda,t} + B_{ss} \epsilon_{s,t},$$

where p is the order of the VAR, ψ_{ij} and B_{ij} are matrices of the appropriate dimensions, and ϵ_t is a vector of structural innovations.[27]

Under the assumption of block recursivity, it is possible to evaluate the contribution of each block to the variance of forecast errors. The variance decomposition of the forecast errors is important for evaluating the role of exchange-rate shocks at the sectoral level. Tables 6–7 report the employment-weighted average variance decomposition at 1, 4, and 8 quarters for industry job creation and destruction rates as well as the exchange rate.[28]

First one observes that exchange-rate innovations represent a substantial fraction of the forecast error variance of the exchange rate itself, further substantiating the assumption that exchange rates contain an important autonomous component. Around 65% of the eight-step-ahead forecast error variance is attributed to the exchange-rate innovation. By contrast, monetary innovations account for only 9 to 14% of the variance. The tables also indicate that exchange-rate movements contribute a nonnegligible amount to the overall gross flow fluctuations, around 3% during the first quarter, and reaching 8 to 12% after 8 quarters. The standard errors indicate that this share is significant. Most of the fluctuations remain explained by sectoral shocks and aggregate fluctuations contributed by the innovations to aggregate job creation and destruction.

These results indicate that autonomous exchange-rate fluctuations are a significant force behind industry evolutions. Somewhat more surprisingly, the results also indicate that nontraded industries seem only slightly less sensitive to exchange-rate movements.

27. In practice, given the relatively small sample, I take $p = 4$. By assumption (2), the matrix B_{zz} is lower block-triangular with 1's on the diagonal.

28. The standard errors are obtained by two-stage bootstrapping. Bias-corrected estimates are obtained after 500 iterations. Standard errors are obtained after 100 additional iterations. For each iteration, the entire matrix of residuals for all sectors simultaneously is sampled with replacement in order to preserve the cross-sectional correlation.

Table 6 VARIANCE DECOMPOSITION I

Shock: Qtr.	Oil		Aggregate		Spread		Exch. Rate		Sectoral	
	Coeff.	SE	Coeff.	SE	Coeff.	SE	Coeff.	SE	Coeff.	SE

<table>
<tr><td colspan="11" align="center">Nontraded</td></tr>
<tr><td colspan="11" align="center">Job Creation</td></tr>
<tr><td>1</td><td>4.02</td><td>1.98</td><td>13.46</td><td>2.88</td><td>2.38</td><td>1.43</td><td>3.42</td><td>1.07</td><td>76.73</td><td>3.60</td></tr>
<tr><td>4</td><td>6.84</td><td>1.90</td><td>18.31</td><td>2.66</td><td>7.31</td><td>1.63</td><td>6.93</td><td>0.96</td><td>60.85</td><td>2.77</td></tr>
<tr><td>8</td><td>9.42</td><td>1.87</td><td>20.33</td><td>2.49</td><td>8.27</td><td>1.64</td><td>8.14</td><td>1.04</td><td>53.84</td><td>2.41</td></tr>
<tr><td colspan="11" align="center">Job Destruction</td></tr>
<tr><td>1</td><td>5.04</td><td>2.07</td><td>13.25</td><td>3.77</td><td>4.87</td><td>1.92</td><td>2.40</td><td>0.79</td><td>74.44</td><td>3.57</td></tr>
<tr><td>4</td><td>8.56</td><td>1.65</td><td>18.21</td><td>2.73</td><td>8.78</td><td>2.08</td><td>6.19</td><td>1.11</td><td>58.26</td><td>2.78</td></tr>
<tr><td>8</td><td>13.01</td><td>1.64</td><td>19.70</td><td>2.51</td><td>10.74</td><td>2.13</td><td>7.33</td><td>1.10</td><td>49.21</td><td>2.53</td></tr>
<tr><td colspan="11" align="center">Exchange Rate</td></tr>
<tr><td>1</td><td>2.40</td><td>1.85</td><td>7.48</td><td>3.62</td><td>3.56</td><td>2.29</td><td>86.56</td><td>4.57</td><td></td><td></td></tr>
<tr><td>4</td><td>3.27</td><td>2.61</td><td>11.54</td><td>4.31</td><td>5.79</td><td>3.09</td><td>79.40</td><td>4.87</td><td></td><td></td></tr>
<tr><td>8</td><td>7.39</td><td>3.67</td><td>14.06</td><td>4.48</td><td>9.17</td><td>3.93</td><td>69.38</td><td>5.26</td><td></td><td></td></tr>
<tr><td colspan="11" align="center">Traded</td></tr>
<tr><td colspan="11" align="center">Job Creation</td></tr>
<tr><td>1</td><td>2.61</td><td>1.58</td><td>9.93</td><td>2.38</td><td>2.64</td><td>1.25</td><td>3.70</td><td>1.20</td><td>81.13</td><td>2.61</td></tr>
<tr><td>4</td><td>8.57</td><td>2.08</td><td>17.45</td><td>2.43</td><td>7.35</td><td>1.61</td><td>8.02</td><td>1.11</td><td>58.61</td><td>1.92</td></tr>
<tr><td>8</td><td>11.57</td><td>2.14</td><td>21.12</td><td>2.23</td><td>9.16</td><td>1.64</td><td>9.81</td><td>1.01</td><td>48.34</td><td>1.70</td></tr>
<tr><td colspan="11" align="center">Job Destruction</td></tr>
<tr><td>1</td><td>3.83</td><td>1.70</td><td>11.37</td><td>2.19</td><td>2.89</td><td>1.26</td><td>2.94</td><td>1.17</td><td>78.97</td><td>2.73</td></tr>
<tr><td>4</td><td>11.33</td><td>2.21</td><td>14.56</td><td>2.25</td><td>10.54</td><td>1.58</td><td>9.76</td><td>0.95</td><td>53.80</td><td>2.53</td></tr>
<tr><td>8</td><td>15.83</td><td>2.51</td><td>17.38</td><td>2.13</td><td>13.07</td><td>1.91</td><td>11.01</td><td>0.84</td><td>42.72</td><td>2.12</td></tr>
<tr><td colspan="11" align="center">Exchange Rate</td></tr>
<tr><td>1</td><td>3.13</td><td>2.45</td><td>10.16</td><td>2.37</td><td>4.08</td><td>1.61</td><td>82.63</td><td>3.31</td><td></td><td></td></tr>
<tr><td>4</td><td>3.93</td><td>2.22</td><td>13.06</td><td>3.37</td><td>7.89</td><td>2.34</td><td>75.13</td><td>3.97</td><td></td><td></td></tr>
<tr><td>8</td><td>5.54</td><td>2.81</td><td>13.47</td><td>4.68</td><td>14.27</td><td>2.92</td><td>66.71</td><td>4.53</td><td></td><td></td></tr>
</table>

The table reports the average variance decomposition for a sectoral seven-variable VAR including Hamilton's oil price index, total manufacturing job creation and destruction, a 6-month quality spread, the industry-specific real exchange rate, and industry job creation and destruction.
Source: Gross flows: LRD; spread, oil price, and real exchange rate: IFS and author's calculations.

Table 7   VARIANCE DECOMPOSITION II

Shock:	Oil		Aggregate		Spread		Exch. Rate		Sectoral	
	Coeff.	SE	Coeff.	SE	Coeff.	SE	Coeff.	SE	Coeff.	SE
					Exporters					
					Job Creation					
1	3.35	2.00	9.87	2.86	3.10	1.73	4.34	1.55	79.33	3.15
4	7.54	2.42	18.59	2.70	6.32	2.26	8.44	1.47	59.10	2.13
8	11.66	2.46	23.93	2.50	7.68	2.21	10.07	1.39	46.66	2.01
					Job Destruction					
1	4.76	2.12	11.85	2.64	2.83	1.37	2.91	1.43	77.65	3.18
4	9.90	2.06	14.98	2.46	11.69	1.91	12.30	1.38	51.13	2.54
8	14.86	2.64	17.44	2.43	14.78	2.41	12.75	1.24	40.18	2.17
					Exchange Rate					
1	3.72	2.30	11.27	3.08	3.95	2.01	81.06	3.88		
4	3.97	2.41	14.07	4.05	7.47	2.61	74.48	4.75		
8	5.46	3.14	14.37	5.72	14.36	3.41	65.81	5.41		
					Import-Competing					
					Job Creation					
1	1.72	2.78	9.93	4.05	2.11	1.73	3.04	1.86	83.20	4.25
4	9.81	3.10	15.75	3.53	8.76	1.80	7.67	1.55	58.01	3.03
8	11.37	3.00	17.19	3.35	11.13	1.86	9.55	1.34	50.76	2.68
					Job Destruction					
1	2.46	2.27	10.73	3.34	2.88	2.80	3.01	1.98	80.90	4.80
4	13.08	3.45	13.92	3.54	8.78	2.37	6.47	1.48	57.74	3.81
8	16.93	3.22	17.13	3.14	10.54	2.28	8.76	1.25	46.65	3.21
					Exchange Rate					
1	2.37	4.33	8.61	2.64	4.27	2.28	84.75	4.87		
4	3.81	3.23	11.48	4.25	8.66	2.94	76.06	4.76		
8	5.60	3.48	12.04	5.34	14.55	3.07	67.82	5.25		

The table reports the average variance decomposition for a sectoral seven-variable VAR including Hamilton's oil price index, total manufacturing job creation and destruction, a 6-month quality spread, the industry-specific real exchange rate, and industry job creation and destruction.
Source: Gross flows: LRD; spread, oil price, and real exchange rate: IFS and author's calculations.

Turning to the dynamic response of gross and net flows, Figure 4 reports the normalized cumulated average impulse response of job creation (thin line), job destruction (dashed line), and (implicitly) net employment growth (thick solid line) to the spread shocks, supply shocks, and real-exchange-rate shocks (columns) for the traded, nontraded, exporter, and import-competing sectors (rows). Complete identification is obtained by imposing a Cholesky ordering.[29] Starting with the second column, one observes that a unit standard deviation in the spread variable has a substantial and long-lasting effect on net and gross employment. Employment declines, as a result of a mild decline in job creation and a sharp increase in job destruction in all sectors. Employment growth bottoms out after 8 to 10 quarters. These impulse responses resemble what we know about the effect of monetary policy shocks on job creation and destruction (see Davis and Haltiwanger, 1996).

Turning to the response to real-exchange-rate shocks, observe first that the amplitude is smaller. An unexpected depreciation of the real exchange rate increases employment growth in all traded industries. About 4 quarters following a positive 1-standard-deviaton real-exchange-rate shock, employment growth is 1.40% higher in export sectors and roughly 0.75% higher in import-competing sectors. Job destruction declines significantly in both sectors by roughly similar amounts. However, the results indicate very different dynamics of job creation in the export and import-competing sectors. While job creation is mildly positive in the export sector following a depreciation and turns negative after 8 quarters, job creation falls significantly after only 4 quarters in import competing industries. The contrast between a monetary shock and an exchange-rate shock is most striking for import-competing firms: while job creation and job destruction move in opposite directions in response to a spread shock, they appear to comove positively in response to exchange-rate innovations. This result is further confirmed by looking at the response to oil price shocks (first column) for that sector: job creation increases by 1.5% and job destruction by 2.4% following a normalized increase in oil prices.

Table 8 reports the cumulative 8- and 16-step impulse responses to the oil, spread, and exchange-rate shocks.

First note that job destruction is more volatile than job creation in response to almost all shocks considered. Furthermore, the response to *reallocation* shocks (real-exchange-rate and oil shocks) differs markedly from the response to monetary shocks for import-competing sectors,

---

29. Since I do not look into the dynamic response to aggregate and sectoral job creation and destruction, the results are robust to the identification procedure.

Figure 4 AVERAGE NORMALIZED CUMULATED RESPONSE FUNCTIONS TO OIL, MONETARY, AND REAL-EXCHANGE-RATE SHOCKS.

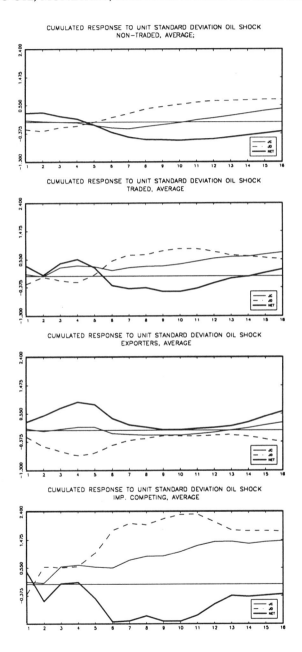

Figure 4 (continued)

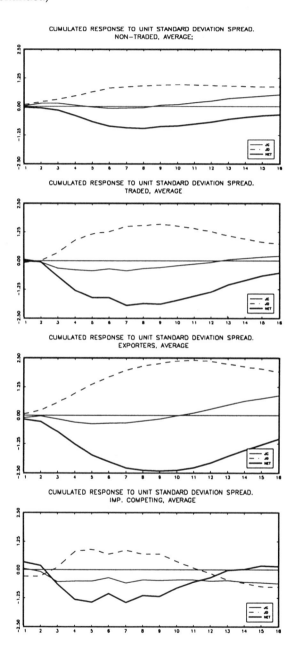

Figure 4 (continued)

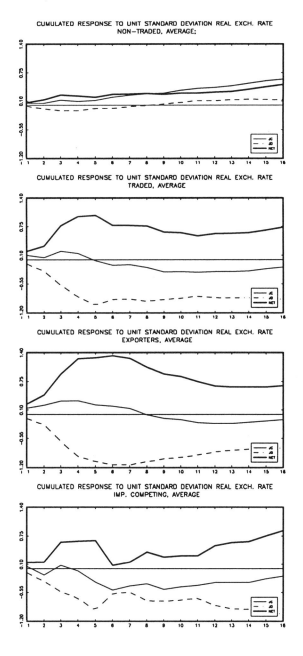

Table 8 CUMULATIVE IMPULSE RESPONSES

8 Quarters

| | Job Creation | | | | | | Job Destruction | | | | | |
| | Oil | | Spread | | Exchange | | Oil | | Spread | | Exchange | |
Sector	Coeff.	SE	Coeff.	SE	Coeff.	SE	Coeff.	SE	Coeff.	SE	Coeff.	SE
Nontraded	-0.22	0.10	-0.05	0.07	0.24	0.06	0.29	0.13	0.88	0.11	-0.05	0.07
Traded	0.31	0.19	-0.43	0.16	-0.13	0.12	0.70	0.35	1.54	0.22	-1.12	0.18
Exporters	-0.15	0.16	-0.33	0.15	0.16	0.09	-0.29	0.25	2.09	0.21	-1.47	0.11
Import-competing	0.89	0.33	-0.55	0.26	-0.48	0.22	1.97	0.65	0.80	0.65	-0.64	0.35
Motor vehicles, 3711	3.29	1.32	-1.50	0.40	-1.37	0.52	5.43	1.45	0.08	1.25	-2.28	0.65
Aircraft, 3721	-0.42	0.17	-0.65	0.18	0.33	0.23	0.07	0.21	2.20	0.23	-0.49	0.21

16 Quarters

| | Job Creation | | | | | | Job Destruction | | | | | |
| | Oil | | Spread | | Exchange | | Oil | | Spread | | Exchange | |
Sector	Coeff.	SE	Coeff.	SE	Coeff.	SE	Coeff.	SE	Coeff.	SE	Coeff.	SE
Nontraded	0.48	0.12	0.57	0.13	0.59	0.11	0.72	0.15	0.90	0.16	0.14	0.14
Traded	0.79	0.37	0.31	0.28	-0.21	0.22	0.62	0.51	0.74	0.43	-1.12	0.26
Exporters	0.25	0.21	0.95	0.20	-0.19	0.15	-0.22	0.26	1.83	0.26	-0.99	0.16
Import-competing	1.47	0.76	-0.51	0.55	-0.18	0.45	1.71	1.03	-0.68	0.85	-1.25	0.52
Motor vehicles, 3711	3.49	1.45	-3.04	0.55	-1.21	0.58	4.32	1.65	-4.86	1.65	-1.58	0.74
Aircraft, 3721	-0.04	0.45	0.02	0.53	-0.78	0.42	-0.06	0.36	2.33	0.45	-1.00	0.40

The table reports the average 8- and 16-step cumulative impulse responses of sectoral job creation and destruction to an oil price shock, a monetary policy shock, and a real-exchange-rate shock.
Source: Gross flows: LRD; spread, oil price, and real exchange rate: IFS and author's calculations.

and less so for export sectors. An appreciation triggers a wave of job separations (0.64% for a normalized appreciation after 8 quarters), but also an associated increase in job creation (0.48%). By contrast, a tightening of monetary policy increases job destruction by 0.80% and decreases job creation by 0.55%. Export industries exhibit a more traditional pattern in response to an appreciation, with a slight decline in job creation (0.16%) and a substantial increase in job destruction (1.47%).

To shed some additional light on this result, the table further presents the cumulated impulse response for motor vehicles (SIC 3711) and aircraft (SIC 3721). Each sector represents the largest sector of the import-competing and export industries, respectively, with an employment share of 30.87% and 12.60%.[30] Both sectors largely reproduce the average results, with, in particular, a substantial positive comovement of job creation and destruction in the automobile industry. While it is beyond the scope of this paper to analyze sectoral dynamics in detail, it is worth noting that this specific pattern could result from the establishment of Japanese-owned car factories in the United States in the eighties, following the appreciation of the U.S. currency. However, there is more to the results than simply the automobile industry. 21 out of the 39 import-competing industries—representing 72% of import-competing employment—exhibit a pattern similar to the average.[31] By contrast, 12 out of the 34 export industries—representing only 36% of employment—exhibit positive comovement between job creation and destruction after 8 quarters.

The positive sectoral comovement is also obtained by Davis and Haltiwanger (1997) in their study of the effect of oil shocks. While those authors do not emphasize this point, they interpret the positive comovement as an indication of the reallocative nature of oil shocks, within narrowly defined industries. The results presented in Table 8 confirm their analysis and extend it to real-exchange-rate fluctuations.

I now summarize the paper's main findings so far:

- There are substantial variations in openness and international exposure within the U.S. manufacturing sector. Using a classification based on export shares and import penetration ratios, we find that tradable-goods firms are more productive, are more capital-intensive, and pay higher wages. Further, within tradables, import-competing firms are less productive, are less capital intensive, and employ fewer workers.
- Looking at the SIC composition of the traded and nontraded groups,

---

30. See the on-line appendix available at **http://www.princeton.edu/~pog/RER-home.html**.
31. If one excludes the automobile industry, the number remains 60% of employment.

nontradables are concentrated in nondurables (food and printing) as well as heavy durables, for which transportation costs are presumably prohibitive (concrete, bricks). Import-competing industries represent a relatively small share of the overall manufacturing employment and tend to be concentrated in paper, leather, and motor vehicles.

- Exchange-rate fluctuations do affect tradable industries. According to this paper's benchmark estimates, a 10% depreciation of the real exchange rate boosts employment by 0.27%, combining a decline in job destruction of 0.44% and a decline of job creation of 0.17%.

- Job destruction appears more volatile than job creation, confirming a now well-established stylized fact for U.S. manufacturing as a whole.

- Although the impact of real exchange rates is significant, they constitute a relatively minor source of gross and net employment fluctuations, accounting for roughly 10% of the forecast error in sectoral gross flows.

- More strikingly, job creation and job destruction appear to comove positively in response to reallocation shocks, especially in import-competing industries. A similar result is obtained, although not emphasized, by Davis and Haltiwanger (1997) in the context of oil shocks.

- Thus, for the typical tradable industry, appreciation episodes are times of turbulence, while depreciations are times of chill, with lower job creation and destruction.

Previous empirical studies have documented extensively the negative comovements in job creation and destruction following aggregate perturbations. The new finding here is that reallocative disturbances can induce sizable positive comovements of sectoral flows. The next section aims at exploring the extent to which existing models of reallocation can account for both set of facts simultaneously. While the positive sectoral comovements are reminiscent of a cleansing mechanism, I will argue that the cleansing effect will generically be stronger in response to aggregate shocks than to sectoral ones, in direct contradiction with the evidence so far.

4. Models of Reallocation and Sectoral Correlations

To gain intuition for the previous statement, and in preview of the formal model, suppose that an economy can produce two goods, tradables and nontradables. Production units in this economy are buffeted by three types of shocks: aggregate, reallocation, and idiosyncratic shocks. The reallocation shock takes the form of a shock to the relative price of tradables in terms of nontradables—one possible definition of the real exchange rate—but this is not essential for our results. Assume also, not unrealistically, that it takes time to match workers and jobs. To make things even simpler, assume that the economy is efficient, so that the competitive equilibrium coincides with the solution to the central planner's problem.[32]

With such an environment as our background, I now turn to the equilibrium sectoral dynamics and the timing of entry and exit. Suppose, to start with, that the economy is hit by a negative aggregate productivity shock. By definition, all units, irrespective of their specialization, are worse off. The value of production declines in both sectors, compared to nonmarket activities such as search. This makes it a good time to cleanse the productive structure by releasing labor for more productive matches. This is the essence of the cleansing approach to recessions (Cooper, Haltiwanger, and Power 1994; Cohen and Saint-Paul 1992). Since the planner would want to minimize the amount of time the average worker spends unemployed in the efficient equilibrium, job creation will increase strongly on the tail of job destruction. Unemployment will be short-lived, and gross flows will tend to be positively correlated. We can also look at the same dynamics through a competitive lens: The increase in creation occurs through a decline in the opportunity cost of employment. As destruction picks up and unemployment rises in both sectors, workers become less picky about their employment opportunities, thus inducing the subsequent surge in creation.

Consider now the response to a decline in the relative price of tradables. The planner will want to reallocate workers from the tradable sector to the nontradable. The value of tradable good production declines relative to both nonmarket activities and nontradable production. As before, labor is released in the tradable sector, and as before, the planner will want to minimize the amount of time that the worker spends idle. That is easier this time around, since the nontradables sector is experiencing a boom. In other words, the efficient response is an *intersectoral* reallocation. In particular, there is no need to increase creation in the tradable sector. The very nature of a reallocation shock is such that one sector of the economy can pick up the slack. In the decentralized equilibrium, we will observe that the opportunity cost of employment remains mostly unchanged. What does this all imply for the correlation of sectoral gross flows? Although aggregate gross creation and destruction may still be positively correlated, the correlation of sectoral flows will *have* to be smaller.

32. In search models such as the one presented shortly, the decentralized equilibrium is efficient when the congestion and search externalities balance out exactly (Hosios, 1990).

While the preceding intuition assumed that the economy was efficient, the decentralized equilibrium will carry over the same features.
What is essential here is that other sectors of the economy can assume
the slack following reallocation shocks, preventing the opportunity cost
of employment from adjusting downward.

4.1 THE MODEL

4.1.1 Consumers I make the following assumptions. Time is discrete.
The domestic economy consists of two sectors: tradables and
nontradables. The demand side of the economy is characterized by a
representative agent with risk-neutral preferences over both goods:

$$U_0 = E_0 \left[\sum_{t=0}^{\infty} \beta^t C_t \right], \tag{2}$$

where β is the discount factor and C_t is a constant elasticity of substitution consumption index defined as

$$C_t = \left[\gamma^{1/\phi} \left(x_t^d \right)^{(\phi-1)/\phi} + (1-\gamma)^{1/\phi} y_t^{(\phi-1)/\phi} \right], \qquad \phi > 0, \quad 0 < \gamma < 1, \tag{3}$$

where ϕ is the elasticity of substitution between tradable x_t^d and
nontradables y_t. These preferences yield standard isoelastic demand for
each good. Normalizing the price of nontraded goods to 1, and denoting
by p_t the price of traded goods, I define the price of the consumption
index C_t as $q_t = [1 - \gamma (1 - p_t^{1-\phi})]^{1/(1-\phi)}$.

p_t is exogenous and fluctuates stochastically. An increase in p_t represents an increase in the relative price of tradables, that is, a depreciation of
the real exchange rate.[33] I assume that p_t follows a discrete Markov process
with n_p states and transition matrix Q_p, where $Q_p(j, i) = \Pr(p_{t+1} = p_i | p_t = p_j)$.
Both goods are nonstorable, but agents can borrow and lend tradable
goods internationally at a gross interest rate R_t. With an outstanding stock
of international debt B_t (in tradables), the budget constraint is

$$p_{t+1} B_{t+1} = \frac{q_{t+1}}{\beta q_t} (p_t B_t + H_t - q_t C_t),$$

where, given the assumption of risk neutrality, $q_{t+1}/\beta q_t$ is the reciprocal of
the pricing kernel for tomorrow's nontradables. H_t denotes total current
income (labor and dividends) received by the representative agent.

---

33. A change in p_t forces a reallocation of resources between the traded and nontraded
    sectors. Therefore, in what follows, I refer to p_t indifferently as the relative-price or
    reallocation shock.

4.1.2 Technology and Matching The elementary unit of production is the combination of a worker and a technology, so that one should think of firms and plants as representing many simultaneous production units.[34] I assume that the technology is Leontieff with one worker producing $A^x(z + \epsilon_i)$ units of traded good or $A^y (z + \epsilon_i)$ units of nontraded goods, where z represents an aggregate productivity shock that affects units in both sectors identically and ϵ_i is an idiosyncratic shock. A^j represents the average labor productivity in sector j. Aggregate shocks follow a discrete Markov process with n_z states, a transition matrix Q_z, and an unconditional mean of 1.

The state variables for this economy consist of the aggregate and the relative-price shocks as well as the cross-sectional distribution of firm-specific productivities in both sectors. As is common in this type of model, I will concentrate on an equilibrium in which all aggregate variables except employment are independent of the cross-section distribution. Define $s = (z,p)$; then s follows a Markov process with transition matrix Q derived from Q_p and Q_z. The total number of states is $n_s = n_z n_p$.

As in Mortensen and Pissarides (1994), I assume that idiosyncratic shocks follow a Poisson process with arrival rate λ. The new value of ϵ is drawn from a fixed distribution $G(\epsilon)$ with support $[\epsilon_l, \epsilon_u]$.[35]

Denoting by v_t^x and v_t^y the numbers of vacancies posted in the tradable and nontradable sectors, respectively, the numbers of matches formed in the two sectors are equal to $m(u_t, v_t^x)$ and $m(u_t, v_t^y)$, where m is a constant-returns-to-scale matching function.[36] There is no on-the-job search, and workers need to be unemployed first before finding a new job. I define the job matching probability as $\pi_t = m_t/v_t$ and the worker matching probability as $\mu_t = m_t/u_t$. Under the CRS assumption, one can characterize the job finding rates in each sector, π_t^j, as a function of that sector's labor-market tightness $\theta_t^j = v_t^j/u_t$: $\pi_t^j = \pi(\theta_t^j) = m (1/\theta_t^j, 1)$. Similarly, $\mu_t^j = m (1, \theta_t^j)$ $= \theta_t^j \, \pi (\theta_t^j)$. The overall probability of finding a job at time t is $\mu_t^x + \mu_t^y$. Under this specification, workers cannot arbitrage between traded- and nontraded-sector jobs.[37] I assume the following obvious properties: $\lim_{\theta \to 0} \pi(\theta) = 1$, $\lim_{\theta \to 0} \theta \pi (\theta) = 0$, and $0 \le \eta (\theta) = - \theta \pi'(\theta)/\pi(\theta) \le 1$. The last property ensures that $\pi' (\theta) \le 0$ and $(\theta \pi (\theta))' \ge 0$, so that an increase in labor-market tightness decreases the worker arrival rates and increases

---

34. Clearly, this abstracts from any vertical aspects of the production process: a firm is the horizontal combination of many identical production units except for the realization of their idiosyncratic shock.
35. Under this assumption, new idiosyncratic shocks are independent of old ones, yet the process exhibits persistence.
36. Under that specification, one extra vacancy posted in one sector does not affect the worker's arrival rate in the other sector.
37. See Moen (1997) for a model where workers can decide which pool they apply to.

the job arrival rates. Prospective employers post vacancies at a cost ν per period, in units of the good produced in that sector.[38] Lastly, newly formed matches are the most productive with $\epsilon = \epsilon_u$, and firms enter the traded sector as long as profits are positive.[39]

4.1.3 Market Clearing   Denote by $E_t^j(\epsilon)$ the cross section of employment in sector j at time t. The following market clearing conditions hold:

$$E_t^x = \int E_t^x(\epsilon)\, d\epsilon, \tag{4}$$
$$E_t^y = \int E_t^y(\epsilon)\, d\epsilon, \tag{5}$$
$$u_t = 1 - E_t^y - E_t^x, \tag{6}$$
$$y_t + \nu u_t \mu_t^y = \int A^y(z_t + \epsilon)\, E_t^y(\epsilon)\, d\epsilon, \tag{7}$$
$$x_t + \nu u_t \mu_t^x = \int A^x(z_t + \epsilon)\, E_t^x(\epsilon)\, d\epsilon. \tag{8}$$

The first two equations express sectoral employment from the cross section in each sector. With a labor force normalized to 1, equation (6) is the larbor-market equilibrium. Lastly, equations (7)–(8) express the market clearing conditions for tradables and nontradables. The term $\nu u_t \mu_t^j$ represents the search and hiring costs incurred at time t in sector j. Finally, under the free-entry condition, and assuming that workers pool income and financial resources, there is no distributed dividend and total income is simply

$$H_t = \int [w_t^x(\epsilon)\, E_t^x(\epsilon) + w_t^y(\epsilon)\, E_t^y(\epsilon)]\, d\epsilon = p_t x_t + y_t.$$

Plugging that into the representative agent's budget constraint, one obtains

$$p_{t+1} B_{t+1} = \frac{q_{t+1}}{\beta q_t} \left[p_t B_t + p_t \left(x_t - x_t^d \right) \right]. \tag{9}$$

The second term in the brackets, $p_t(x_t - x_t^d)$, is the trade balance at time t, expressed in units of nontradables.

4.2 THE COMPETITIVE EQUILIBRIUM

To characterize the competitive equilibrium, I now derive standard asset equations for a representative firm. Consider a production unit in sector

---

38. The vacancy cost can be thought of as forgone output.
39. The assumption that all firms enter "at the top" is common in the literature. It is not crucial in our context, but it simplifies employment dynamics, since all entrants are identical. It captures the idea that production units become—stochastically—obsolete over time.

j matched with a worker and facing an idiosyncratic shock ϵ in state s at the beginning of the period. Should employment be continued, the value of the match to the firm, $\tilde{J}_s^j(\epsilon)$, is equal to

$$\tilde{J}_s^j(\epsilon) = p_s^j A^j(z_s + \epsilon) - w_s^j(\epsilon)$$
$$+ \beta \sum_{s'} Q_{ss'} \frac{q_s}{q_{s'}} \left((1 - \lambda) J_{s'}^j(\epsilon) + \lambda \int J_{s'}^j(\epsilon') \, dG(\epsilon') \right). \tag{10}$$

The first two terms on the right-hand side represent the flow profits to the firm in the current period, where $p^y = 1$ and $p^x = p$. The remaining terms represent the option value associated with keeping the production unit active. I describe each term in turn. First the aggregate state may change from s to s' with probability $Q_{ss'}$. Second, the unit gets a new draw of its idiosyncratic productivity ϵ' with probability λ or keeps its current productivity level ϵ. In either case the firm will get an optimal value $J_{s'}^j$. Lastly, the value of the firm tomorrow, in terms of nontradables, is discounted using the state-contingent pricing kernel $\beta q_s / q_{s'}$.

The value to the firm of the match today is then

$$J_s^j(\epsilon) = \max \left\langle \tilde{J}_s^j(\epsilon), V_s^j \right\rangle.$$

The value of a vacancy V_s^j can be determined similarly:

$$V_s^j = \max \left\langle -\nu p_s^j + \beta \sum_{s'} Q_{ss'} \frac{q_s}{q_{s'}} \left[\pi_s^j J_{s'}^j(\epsilon_u) + (1 - \pi_s^j) V_{s'}^j \right], 0 \right\rangle. \tag{11}$$

Posting a vacancy in sector j costs νp_s^j. With probability π_s^j the vacancy is filled and the unit starts producing next period in state s' with an idiosyncratic shock ϵ_u. Otherwise the vacancy remains unfilled with value $V_{s'}^j$. Since it is costless to stop posting the vacancy, the firm will only post if $V_s^j > 0$.

When entry occurs, the value of a vacancy must be zero in either sector: $V_s^j = 0$ for all states s. Substituting into (11), we have

$$\frac{\nu p_s^j}{\pi_s^j} = \beta \sum_{s'} Q_{ss'} \frac{q_s}{q_{s'}} J_{s'}^j(\epsilon_u). \tag{12}$$

This is the *entry condition*. It states that the expected cost of a vacancy is equal to the expected profit from the new match.[40]

---

40. Note that $1/\pi$ is the expected duration until a match is found.

Turning to the workers, denote by $W_s^j(\epsilon)$ the value of holding a job in sector j when the aggregate state is s and the idiosyncratic shock is ϵ. The continuation value inside the match, $\tilde{W}_s^j(\epsilon)$, is determined as

$$\tilde{W}_s^j(\epsilon) = w_s^j(\epsilon) + \beta \sum_{s'} Q_{ss'} \frac{q_s}{q_{s'}} \left((1 - \lambda) \, W_{s'}^j(\epsilon) + \lambda \int W_{s'}^j(\epsilon') \, dG(\epsilon') \right). \quad (13)$$

The worker gets a wage $w_s^j(\epsilon)$. Next period with probability λ a new idiosyncratic shock is drawn from the distribution G. The worker ends the relationship as soon as $\tilde{W}_s^j(\epsilon)$ falls below the value of being unemployed, U_s:

$$W_s^j(\epsilon) = \max \left\langle \tilde{W}_s^j(\epsilon), \, U_s \right\rangle$$

Lastly, an unemployed worker finds a job opportunity in the traded (the nontraded) sector with probability μ_s^x (μ_s^y). The value of being unemployed is therefore

$$U_s = \beta \sum_{s'} Q_{ss'} \frac{q_s}{q_{s'}} [(1 - \mu_s^x - \mu_s^y) \, U_{s'} + \mu_s^x W_{s'}^x(\epsilon_u) + \mu_s^y W_{s'}^y(\epsilon_u)]. \quad (14)$$

Since the production unit must incur search costs before it can hire a new worker, there are quasi rents associated with the match. I assume that the surplus is divided according to the Nash bargaining rule with a share δ accruing to the worker and a share $1 - \delta$ to the firm. This implies that all separations are *ex post* efficient as workers, and firms maximize the joint surplus generated by the match, $S_s^j(\epsilon)$:

$$S_s^j(\epsilon) = J_s^j(\epsilon) + W_s^j(\epsilon) - U_s.$$

Using the Nash bargaining rule, and rewriting the asset equation for both the worker and the firm, one obtains

$$\tilde{S}_s^j(\epsilon) = p_s^j A^j (z_s + \epsilon)$$
$$+ \beta \sum_{s'} Q_{ss'} \frac{q_s}{q_{s'}} \left((1 - \lambda) \, S_{s'}^j(\epsilon) + \lambda \int S_{s'}^j(\epsilon') \, dG(\epsilon') \right.$$
$$\left. - \delta \, [\mu_s^x S_{s'}^x(\epsilon_u) + \mu_s^y S_{s'}^y(\epsilon_u)] \right), \quad (15)$$
$$S_s^j(\epsilon) = \max \left\langle \tilde{S}_s^j(\epsilon), \, 0 \right\rangle.$$

Lastly, one can rewrite the free-entry conditions as

$$\pi_s^j = \frac{\nu p_s^j}{\beta(1 - \delta) \sum_{s'} Q_{ss'} (q_s/q_{s'}) S_{s'}^j (\epsilon_u)}.$$ (16)

Defining $\bar{S}$ as the collection of surplus functionals $S_1^x, \ldots, S_{N_s}^x$, $S_1^y, \ldots, S_{N_s}^y$, equation (16) can be implicitly inverted to obtain the job arrival rate μ_s^x, μ_s^y as a function of the surplus functions $\bar{S}$. One can then construct the operator $T(\bar{S})$ according to the right-hand sides of (15) and (16). An equilibrium is defined as a fixed point of the operator T. Clearly, the proposed equilibrium does not depend on the cross-section distribution of idiosyncratic productivities, as was claimed initially.

With a production function that is linear in ϵ, it is easy to show that the equilibrium surplus functions are piecewise linear, are increasing in ϵ, and satisfy the cutoff property. One can then characterize the solution in terms of a cutoff vector for each sector, $\{\epsilon_s^x, \epsilon_s^y\}_{s=1}^{ns}$, such that $S_s^j (\epsilon_s^j) = 0$.

The following proposition fully characterizes the competitive equilibrium:

PROPOSITION 1   *The surplus functions $\{S_s^x, S_s^y\}_{s=1}^{ns}$ satisfy the cutoff property and are piecewise linear. Moreover, the cutoff for each sector $\{\epsilon_s^x, \epsilon_s^y\}_{s=1}^{ns}$ fully determine the surplus functions. Lastly, the cutoffs solve*

$$p^j A^j \left(z_s + \epsilon_s^j \right) = \beta\delta \sum_{s'} Q_{ss'} \frac{q_s}{q_{s'}} [\mu_s^x S_{s'}^x (\epsilon_u) + \mu_s^y S_{s'}^y (\epsilon_u)]$$

$$- \beta \sum_{\epsilon_s^j > \epsilon_{s'}^j} Q_{ss'} \frac{q_s}{q_{s'}} (1 - \lambda) S_{s'}^j (\epsilon_s^j)$$

$$- \beta \sum_{s'} Q_{ss'} \frac{q_s}{q_{s'}} \lambda \int_{\epsilon_{s'}^j}^{\epsilon_u} S_{s'}^j (\epsilon') \, dG (\epsilon'),$$ (17)

where the job arrival rates μ_s^j are determined by (16).

The cutoff equations (17) characterize the *exit condition*. The left-hand side of (17) represents the lowest acceptable flow of sales from the match in state s. The first term on the right-hand side represents the opportunity cost of employment, that is, the expected gain from search: with probability $\mu_s^j Q_{ss'}$ the unemployed worker finds a job in sector j in aggregate state s'. The worker then gets a fraction δ of the surplus $S_{s'}^j$. The term on the second line represents the option value associated with the realization of an aggregate or reallocation shock that lowers the cutoff ϵ^x and therefore increases the value of the existing match while the idiosyncratic component remains unchanged. Finally, the last term represents the option value associated with the realization of a new idiosyncratic shock ϵ' together with a change in the state variable to s'. As in Mortensen and Pissarides (1994), the lowest acceptable flow profit is lower than the opportunity cost, as both the worker and the firm are willing to incur a loss today in anticipation of a future improvement in the value of the match.

This proposition reduces enormously the dimensionality of the problem. Instead of solving for a fixed point of the mapping T, we are looking for a set of $2n_s$ cutoff that solve the nonlinear system (17).

Let's gather a few remarks about the equilibrium. First note that the model does not force an identical response in the two sectors to aggregate shocks. If the average tradables labor productivity pA^x (in terms of nontradables) exceeds the average nontradables labor productivity A^y, then the response to an aggregate productivity shock z will have reallocative effects: following a positive shock, resources will be reallocated away from nontraded good production towards good production. Clearly, if $pA^x = A^y$, both sectors respond identically to aggregate shocks.

Consider now the response to relative-price shocks, arguably the novel feature of this model. Inspecting the definition of the surplus function (15), the first thing to notice is that the relative price enters twice. First, it directly affects the current profits of the traded sector production units. Second, it also changes the price index and the discount factor for future profits, $\beta q_{s'}/q_{s'}$, since under our assumptions an increase in the price of tradables increases the aggregate price index. For an easier interpretation, define $R_{ss'} = q_{s'}/\beta q_{s'}$. $R_{ss'}$ is the (implicit) state-contingent real interest rate in terms of nontradables. Evidently, the real interest rate will be high when the price of tradables is expected to increase, or equivalently, when there is an expected depreciation. This form of interest-rate parity has to hold in this model under the assumption of risk neutrality.

A higher interest rate decreases the value of production units in both sectors and may trigger a shutdown. Hall (1997b) has emphasized the empirical and theoretical importance of fluctuations in the real interest rate on the shutdown margin. While the current model emphasizes mostly fluctuations in current profits as a source of aggregate dynamics, it is worth pointing out that expected variations in the price of one good generically affect the discount rate faced by producers of the remaining goods.

Finally, I characterize the dynamics of the labor market. The timing is as follows. At the beginning of period t, employment level is E_t^j in sector j. Clearly, $E_t^j = \int_{\epsilon_s^j}^{\epsilon_u} E_t^j(\epsilon) \, d\epsilon$, where the state in period $t - 1$ was $\hat{s}$. A new aggregate state s is realized. Consequently, all units with a productivity level ϵ

below ϵ_s^j are scrapped, and the workers return to unemployment. Among the remaining units, $E_t^j - \int_{\epsilon_l^j}^{\epsilon_s^j} E_t^j(\epsilon)\, d\epsilon$, a fraction $\lambda G(\epsilon_s^j)$ experience a new idiosyncratic shock ϵ with a value below the new cutoff. Workers who are unemployed at the beginning of period t are assumed to search for a new job—and potentially be rematched—within the period. A fraction μ_s^j of those unemployed finds a job at productivity level ϵ_u. In summary:

$$E_{t+1}^j(\epsilon) = \begin{cases} (1 - \lambda)E_t^j(\epsilon) + \lambda G'(\epsilon)\left(E_t^j - \int_{\epsilon_l}^{\epsilon_s^j} E_t^j(\tilde{\epsilon})\, d\tilde{\epsilon}\right) & \text{for } \epsilon_s^j < \epsilon < \epsilon_u, \\ (1 - \lambda)E_t^j(\epsilon) + \lambda G'(\epsilon)\left(E_t^j - \int_{\epsilon_l}^{\epsilon_s^j} E_t^j(\tilde{\epsilon})\, d\tilde{\epsilon}\right) \\ \quad + \mu_s^j\Big[-[1 - \lambda G(\epsilon_s^x)]\left(E_t^x - \int_{\epsilon_l}^{\epsilon_s^x} E_t^x(\tilde{\epsilon})\, d\tilde{\epsilon}\right) \\ \quad -[1 - \lambda G(\epsilon_s^y)]\left(E_t^y - \int_{\epsilon_l}^{\epsilon_s^y} E_t^y(\tilde{\epsilon})\, d\tilde{\epsilon}\right)\Big] & \text{for } \epsilon = \epsilon_u, \\ 0 & \text{for } \epsilon \le \epsilon_s^j. \end{cases} \tag{18}$$

The total job creation in sector j is thus

$$\mu_s^j\left[1 - [1 - \lambda G(\epsilon_s^x)]\left(E_t^x - \int_{\epsilon_l}^{\epsilon_s^x} E_t^x(\tilde{\epsilon})\, d\tilde{\epsilon}\right)\right.$$
$$\left. -[1 - \lambda G(\epsilon_s^y)]\left(E_t^y - \int_{\epsilon_l}^{\epsilon_s^y} E_t^y(\tilde{\epsilon})\, d\tilde{\epsilon}\right)\right].$$

However, the observed job creation does not take into account jobs that are rematched within the period, within the same sector. The *observed* job creation in sector j is thus

$$JC_t^j = \mu_s^j\left[1 - E_t^x - E_t^y + \int_{\epsilon_l}^{\epsilon_s^i} E_t^i(\tilde{\epsilon})\, d\tilde{\epsilon} + \lambda G(\epsilon_s^i)\left(E_t^i - \int_{\epsilon_l}^{\epsilon_s^i} E_t^i(\tilde{\epsilon})\, d\tilde{\epsilon}\right)\right]. \tag{19}$$

The last two terms inside the brackets (indexed by i) refer to the jobs destroyed in sector i and rematched in sector j within the period. Similarly, the observed job destruction is given by[41]

$$JD_t^j = (1 - \mu_s^j)\left[\int_{\epsilon_l}^{\epsilon_s^j} E_t^j(\epsilon)\, d\epsilon + \lambda G(\epsilon_s^j)\left(E_t^j - \int_{\epsilon_l}^{\epsilon_s^j} E_t^j(\epsilon)\, d\epsilon\right)\right]. \tag{20}$$

4.3 SPECIFICATION AND CALIBRATION

The purpose of this section is to evaluate the ability of the model to replicate salient features of the data. To do so, I follow the tradition in the business-cycle literature and "calibrate" the model against sample moments. The two sources of aggregate fluctuations in the model are the productivity shocks z and relative-price shocks p.

To calibrate the real exchange-rate shocks, I fit an AR(1) process to the log of the industry-specific real exchange rate in the sample. The average

41. Given our definitions, $E_{t+1}^j = E_t^j + JC_t^j - JD_t^j$.

estimated autoregression coefficient across traded sectors is 0.916 with a standard deviation of the exchange-rate innovations equal to 0.035.[42] I take this average AR representation as characterizing the exchange rate process. Assuming that the innovations are normally distributed, I use the Tauchen–Hussey (1991) method to obtain an equivalent three-state Markov transition matrix with an identical Wold representation. I obtain

$$p = \begin{pmatrix} 0.8597 \\ 1 \\ 1.163 \end{pmatrix}, \qquad Q_p = \begin{pmatrix} 0.916 & 0.084 & 0 \\ 0.021 & 0.958 & 0.021 \\ 0 & 0.084 & 0.916 \end{pmatrix}.$$

A similar method is applied to convert an AR process for aggregate productivity into a three-state Markov chain. However, fitting an AR1 process to the quarterly deviations from a linear trend of log manufacturing output per hour yields a correlation coefficient of 0.914 with a standard deviation of the innovations of 0.009. This implies a standard deviation of aggregate innovations about 4 times smaller than that of the exchange rate. I view such large differences as implausible, especially given the small contribution of real exchange rates to the forecast MSE in the empirical section. It should be clear that one cannot hope to replicate the aggregate dynamics if the major source of fluctuations is coming from the reallocation shocks. Instead, I assume that reallocation and aggregate shocks represent similar sources of fluctuations, so that $z = p$ and $Q_z = Q_p$.

Next, I parametrize the matching function in a standard fashion:

$$m\,(u_t,\, v_t) = \min\,(k\,u_t^\eta v_t^{1-\eta},\, u_t,\, v_t).$$

This specification imposes that the worker and job matching probabilities are less than one. η represents the elasticity of the matching function with respect to unemployment while k is a scaling parameter. Blanchard and Diamond (1989) estimate an aggregate matching function and find mild support for a constant-return specification with $\eta = 0.4$. Their measure of new hires includes flows into employment from unemploy-

---

42. A similar estimation in deviations from a linear trend yields an average autoregression coefficient of 0.90 with a standard deviation for the innovations of 0.034. A Philips–Perron test allowing autocorrelation of the residuals at 12 lags rejects the unit-root hypothesis for three sectors: cordage and twine (SIC 2298) with a serial correlation of 0.81, leather gloves and mittens (SIC 3151) with 0.79, and dolls (SIC 3942) with 0.658. Given the small-sample lack of power of unit-root tests, the nonrejection of the unit-root hypothesis is not particularly worrying. Studies using longer sample periods and/ or multiple countries typically find a statistically significant mean reversion rate between 2.5 and 5 years, equivalent to a larger implied autoregression coefficient between 0.933 and 0.965.

ment, flows from out of the labor force, and employment minus recalled workers. These authors find that the flows into employment from out of the labor force are roughly of the same magnitude as the flows into employment from unemployment.[43] Den Haan, Ramey, and Watson (1997) and Cole and Rogerson (1996) have also pointed out that part of the out-of-the-labor-force population must be included when calibrating worker matching probabilities. Otherwise, worker matching probabilities based on unemployment duration (on average 21 weeks) yield a far too rapid adjustment of the unemployment rate to its steady-state value.

The average job destruction rates in the traded and nontraded sectors are $\rho^x = 0.0576$ and $\rho^y = 0.0567$ respectively (see Table 2). To obtain the average worker matching probabilities, observe that in steady state the number of jobs created $\mu^x u$ must equate the number of jobs destroyed $\rho^x E^x$. The second term reflects the number of workers that are rematched within the quarter. In steady state it must be equal to the number of jobs created: $\mu^x u$. A similar equation holds for the nontraded sector. From Blanchard and Diamond (1990), one gets an estimate of the ratio of unmatched to matched workers, $u/(E^x + E^y)$, of around 12%, where out-of-the-labor-force workers are considered as part of the pool of unmatched workers. Lastly, since tradable and nontraded employment represent respectively 14.54% and 12.11% of total manufacturing employment, I estimate the ratio $E^x/(E^x + E^y) = 0.5455$.[44] One can then solve for the average worker matching probabilities in both sectors, finding $\mu^x = 0.262$ and $\mu^y = 0.215$.

To calibrate the taste parameters γ and ϕ, I first arbitrarily set ϕ equal to 1 so that γ represents the share of current expenditures on tradables. Using the definition of the trade balance, the ratio of trade balance to output is equal to

$$\frac{TB}{px + y} = \frac{x - \frac{\gamma}{1-\gamma} y}{px + y}.$$

The average ratio of trade balance to GDP is equal to -1.28% over the sample period 1972–1988. This allows us to pin down γ, the share of traded goods in expenditures. Note that γ indirectly affects the strength

43. Blanchard and Diamond (1989) adjust the CPS flow data using the Abowd–Zellner (1985) technique. However, they report that using the Poterba–Summers correction yields very different results, with flows from out of the labor force representing only 28% of the flows into employment from unemployment. In what follows I adopt their baseline specification.
44. This implicitly assumes that the ratio is 54% for the entire economy.

of the interest-rate effect discussed previously. A smaller γ implies less variation in the price index and therefore a smaller fluctuation in the real interest rate in response to exchange-rate shocks. While γ pins down the relative importance of tradables and nontradables in consumption, one also needs to calibrate the relative importance of both sectors in production. For lack of a direct estimate of the average relative productivity of traded and nontraded goods, I assume in what follows that $A^x = A^y$.

The discount rate β is set so that the annualized interest rate is equal to 4%; the idiosyncratic shocks ϵ are distributed uniformly with mean 0 on $[-\epsilon_u, \epsilon_u]$, where the range ϵ_u will be calibrated to the match the average standard deviation of the job destruction series in both sectors.

Table 9 reports the main parameters together with the moments that need to be matched.[45]

4.4 SIMULATION AND DISCUSSION OF THE RESULTS: THE ROLE OF THE OPPORTUNITY COST OF EMPLOYMENT

For the calibrated values of the parameters, Table 10 reports the cutoff as well as the job and worker matching probabilities.[46]

We observe a few points. First, the cutoff declines in the tradable sector as both the relative price and the aggregate productivity improve. In the nontraded sector, the cutoff increases with the reallocation shock and decreases with the aggregate shock. Similarly, we observe that the job matching probabilities increase in the tradable sector with positive aggregate and reallocation shocks, implying a decline in the job matching rate. Destruction rates in this model, can be read off directly from the change in the cutoff. Suppose, to simplify, that the economy has enough time to reach its ergodic distribution $\bar{E}^j(\epsilon)$ between shocks. Then, following an adverse shock that shifts the state from s to s', approximately $\int_{\epsilon_s^j}^{\epsilon_{s'}^j} \bar{E}^j(\epsilon) \, d\epsilon$ jobs are destroyed if $\epsilon_s^j < \epsilon_{s'}^j$.

The interesting question is what happens to job creation. From Table 10, we know that an adverse shock, whether aggregate or reallocation, lowers the worker matching rate. Going from the highest to the lowest aggregate productivity state, the matching rate drops by 20%, from 0.268 to 0.219 in each sector. This decline in matching rates can result from an increase in unemployment or a decline in vacancies posted. Its effect is clearly to dampen the opportunity cost of employment. In turn, a decline in the opportunity cost of employment indicates that it is profitable

---

45. The parameters are estimated by the simulated method of moments. I use a sample of length 2000 and delete the first 500 observations to reduce dependence on initial conditions. Since there is no growth in the model, the correlation structure is estimated in levels. With eight moments and six parameters, the estimation is overidentified.

46. The states are in a lexicographic order with the aggregate shock first.

Table 9 CALIBRATION

Parameter	Symbol	Value
Consumers		
Discount rate	β	0.99
Elasticity of substitution between x and y	ϕ	1.00
Share of traded goods x	γ	0.532
Technology		
Average productivity, tradables	A^x	0.028
Average productivity, nontradables	A^y	0.028
Arrival rate of idiosyncratic shocks	λ	0.184
Range of idiosyncratic shock	ϵ_u	1.879
Search cost per period	ν	0.006
Matching		
Elasticity of the matching function	η	0.40
Worker share of surplus	δ	0.40
Matching function scale parameter	k	0.086

	Value	
Moment	Data	Model
Trade balance output ratio	−0.0128	−0.016
Unemployment	0.12	0.126
Worker matching probability (traded)	0.262	0.262
Worker matching probability (nontraded)	0.215	0.223
Standard deviation of job creation (traded)	0.0096	0.013
Standard deviation of job creation (nontraded)	0.0080	0.012
Mean job destruction (traded)	0.057	0.091
Mean job destruction (nontraded)	0.056	0.089

Parameters estimated by simulated method of moments, sample length: 2000.
Source: Author's calculations.

to try to hire labor. This mechanism is central to all reorganization models of the business cycle: reallocation occurs efficiently when the opportunity cost of reorganization is lowest, i.e. when nonmarket activities, such as search, are relatively more productive. The subsequent large increase in unemployment lowers the opportunity cost of labor and triggers massive entry, so that unemployment is both large and very short-lived. The result is a strong synchronization between entry and exit margins. Central to this argument is the feedback mechanism from the destruction margin to the opportunity cost of employment, which in turn activates the entry margin.

Table 10   CUTOFFS AND MATCHING PROBABILITIES

| | | | Tradable | | | Nontradable | | | Overall |
| | | | | Job Match-ing | Worker Match-ing | | Job Match-ing | Worker Match-ing | Worker Match-ing |
State	Aggregate	Relative Price	Cutoff			Cutoff			
1	0.8597	0.8597	−0.434	0.046	0.219	−0.191	0.043	0.246	0.464
2	0.8597	1.0000	−0.314	0.044	0.234	−0.314	0.044	0.234	0.467
3	0.8597	1.1631	−0.191	0.043	0.247	−0.439	0.046	0.219	0.465
4	1.0000	0.8597	−0.397	0.045	0.226	−0.128	0.042	0.256	0.482
5	1.0000	1.0000	−0.266	0.043	0.243	−0.266	0.043	0.243	0.485
6	1.0000	1.1631	−0.133	0.042	0.257	−0.400	0.045	0.226	0.483
7	1.1631	0.8597	−0.347	0.044	0.235	−0.054	0.040	0.268	0.503
8	1.1631	1.0000	−0.204	0.042	0.253	−0.203	0.042	0.253	0.506
9	1.1631	1.1631	−0.058	0.040	0.268	−0.351	0.044	0.235	0.503

The table reports the cutoffs and the matching probabilities in the traded and nontraded sectors.
Source: Author's calculations.

Consider now the case of a reallocation shock. If anything, the feedback mechanism must be *less* effective. The reason for this is that the opportunity cost of labor remains abnormally high, from the point of view of the depressed sector, since the reallocation shock increases entry in the other sector. One can clearly see this effect at work by looking at the last column of Table 10, reporting the overall worker matching rate $\mu_s^x + \mu_s^y$. The overall matching rate varies substantially in response to aggregate shocks, from a low of 0.46 to a high of 0.50, but remains almost entirely unaffected by changes in the relative price. To see why this is the case, suppose we adopt the perspective of the central planner.[47] Following a reallocation shock, the optimal response consists in reallocating labor *between* sectors, since one sector is expanding and the other one is contracting. The opportunity cost of labor remains muted, so that there is less of a feedback on the entry margin. In turn, this implies that we should observe less of a correlation between job creation and destruction at the intrasectoral level.

To confirm this intuition, Table 11 reports the dynamic correlation between job creation and destruction at both the aggregate and the sectoral level, from the data and from simulations of the calibrated model. It is important to note that the calibrated parameters do not

---

47. As usual, since the sole source of inefficiency in this economy is the search externalities, efficiency can be restored if $\delta = \eta$. See Hosios (1990). The cutoff and matching probabilities are mostly unchanged if I impose $\delta = \eta = 0.5$.

attempt to replicate the dynamic correlation between job creation and destruction. As a result, it is perhaps not too surprising that the model does not replicate the overall correlation between creation and destruction (the simulation predicts a correlation of 0.35 in the presence of both shocks and 0.17 in the presence of aggregate shocks only). This failure indicates a stronger reallocation mechanism in the model than in the data: job creation picks up on the tail of job destruction. The table further decomposes the correlation into the components resulting from the aggregate and reallocation shocks respectively. The correlation of *total* job creation and destruction rates in response to reallocation shocks is similar to that in response to aggregate shocks. This is the effect discussed by Lilien (1982): a reallocation shock increases job creation in one sector and job destruction in the other, leading to a positive comovement in the overall job creation and destruction rates. However, this aggregate positive comovement masks a lower comovement at the *sectoral* level. The contemporaneous correlation between job creation and destruction in the traded (and nontraded) sectors is 0.17 in the case of aggregate shocks

Table 11   DYNAMIC CORRELATION OF JC^j_{t+k}, JD^j_t

Sector	Origin	*Correlation*						
		$k=-3$	-2	-1	0	1	2	3
Aggregate	Data	−0.24	−0.12	−0.27	−0.35	−0.06	0.27	0.25
	Agg.	0.09	0.11	0.14	0.17	0.76	0.57	0.41
	Real.	−0.10	−0.13	−0.15	0.17	0.75	0.41	0.17
	Both	0.02	0.08	−0.01	0.35	0.68	0.39	0.20
Nontraded	Data	−0.09	−0.03	0.01	0.02	0.013	0.15	0.31
	Agg.	0.09	0.11	0.14	0.17	0.76	0.57	0.41
	Real.	−0.24	−0.27	−0.28	−0.43	−0.02	−0.08	−0.12
	Both	−0.03	−0.09	−0.17	−0.35	0.11	0.02	−0.08
Traded	Data	−0.14	−0.24	−0.38	−0.43	0.002	0.0001	0.006
	Agg.	0.09	0.11	0.14	0.17	0.76	0.57	0.41
	Real.	−0.18	−0.21	−0.23	−0.36	0.15	0.09	0.02
	Both	−0.21	−0.14	−0.17	−0.25	0.13	0.07	0.08
Exporters	Data	−0.46	−0.35	−0.34	−0.24	−0.14	0.05	0.16
Import-competing	Data	−0.24	−0.12	−0.27	−0.35	−0.07	0.27	0.25

The table reports the dynamic correlation at various leads and lags between sectoral and aggregate job creation and destruction rates. Simulation results obtained from 100 simulations.
Source: LRD and author's calculations.

but falls to -0.36 (respectively, -0.43) in the case of allocative disturbances. Reallocative shocks in this model trigger an intersectoral reallocation response, as opposed to an intrasectoral reallocation.

The lower within-sector correlation points to the difficulty faced by the model: if the model aims at replicating the negative comovements in response to aggregate shocks (and negative overall comovements), the opportunity-cost channel must be sufficiently weak. However, in that case, a relative-price shock will also lead to a negative correlation of within sector gross flows. Lastly, Figure 5 reports the impulse response to an aggregate and a relative-price shock, as generated by the model.[48] The figure reports the response to a decrease in aggregate productivity and a real depreciation. An aggregate shock imparts similar dynamics in both the traded and nontraded sectors, with a surge in job destruction (the dashed line) followed by a mild increase in job creation (the thin solid line). By contrast, a depreciation triggers a surge of job destruction in the nontraded goods sector and a simultaneous increase in job creation in the traded goods sector. While the aggregate effect is a strong positive comovement of job creation and destruction, the sectoral gross flows move clearly in opposite directions.

Observe also that the problem is not solved by decoupling job creation and destruction in response to aggregate shocks. If anything, this implies an even lower algebraic correlation between sectoral flows.

This result indicates the difficulty faced by this type of model: to generate a positive comovement between sectoral job creation and job destruction, it needs to generate a positive comovement between job creation and destruction in response to an aggregate shock. The tension between the two requirements indicates some other mechanism is required. Clearly, while a great deal of effort has been spent on the dynamics of the shutdown margin, we need to think more actively about the dynamics of the entry margin and recoveries. The results in the paper point to a difference in the dynamic response that cannot be accommodated within the current framework.

5. Conclusion

This paper has aimed at uncovering the relationship between factor adjustment and real-exchange-rate fluctuations. Concentrating on gross job flows in the U.S. manufacturing sector, it was found that exchange-rate movements affect significantly both net and gross factor realloca-

---

48. The impulse response is generated by assuming that the system is initially in steady state.

Figure 5 NORMALIZED IMPULSE RESPONSE FUNCTIONS TO AGGREGATE
AND SECTORAL SHOCKS: SIMULATED MODEL

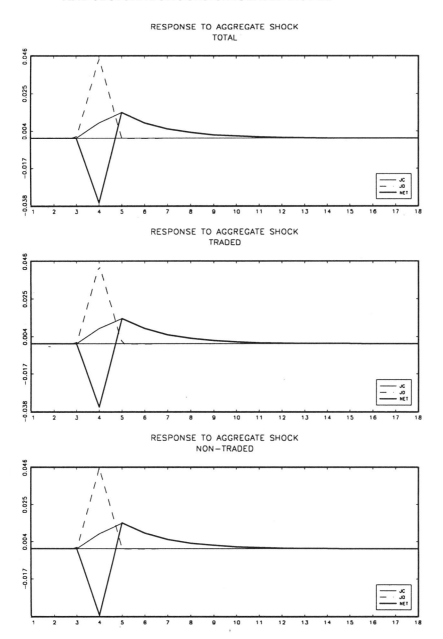

Figure 5 (continued)

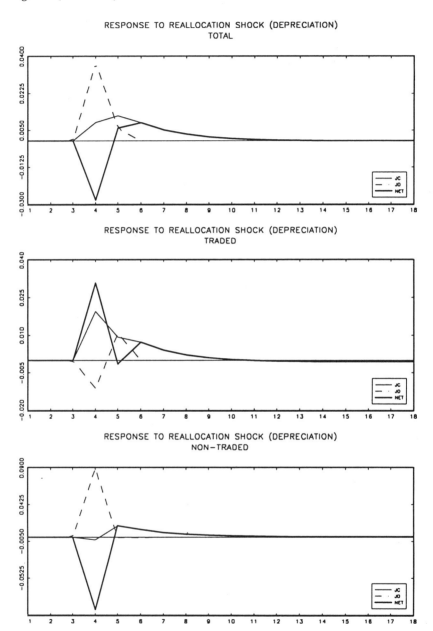

tion. In the paper's benchmark estimation, a 10% appreciation of the real exchange rate translates into a contraction in tradables employment of roughly 0.3%, through a simultaneous increase in job destruction and job creation. The effect is mostly concentrated in import-competing industries, which exhibit much higher exchange-rate sensitivity. While these effects are significant, it also appears that exchange-rate shocks do not constitute a major source of fluctuations at the sectoral level. We found only roughly 9 to 11% of the 8-quarters-ahead forecast MSE accounted for by real-exchange-rate movements.

Perhaps more strikingly, the results indicate a pattern of adjustment in response to reallocative shocks essentially different from the response to aggregate shocks. While aggregate dynamics are characterized by a strong decoupling between job creation and destruction, reallocative shocks [oil shocks in Davis and Haltiwanger (1997) or real-exchange-rate shocks in this paper] induce positive comovements in sectoral gross flows. In the context of real exchange rates, appreciations are times of turbulence, with a joint increase in creation and destruction, whereas depreciations are times of chill.

Lastly, this paper has presented a canonical two-sector business-cycle model with employment reallocation and argued that the pattern found in the data is hard to replicate in current models or reallocation. This should provide fertile ground for further theoretical and empirical investigations.

REFERENCES

Abowd, J., and A. Zellner. (1985). Estimating gross labor force flows. *Journal of Economic and Business Statistics* 3 (June):254–283.

Abraham, K., and L. Katz. (1986). Cyclical unemployment: Sectoral shifts or aggregate disturbances. *Journal of Political Economy*, November.

Backus, D., P. Kehoe, and F. Kydland. (1995). International business cycle: Theory and evidence. In *Frontiers of Business Cycle Research*, T. Cooley (ed.). Princeton University Press.

Bartelsman, E., and W. Gray. (1996). The NBER Manufacturing Productivity Database. Cambridge, MA: National Bureau of Economic Research. NBER Working Paper, October.

Baumol, W., S. Blackman, and E. Wolff. (1985). Unbalanced growth revisited: Asymptotic stagnancy and new evidence. *American Economic Review*, September.

Bernanke, B., M. Gertler, and M. Watson. (1997). Systematic monetary policy and the effects of oil price shocks. *Brookings Papers on Economic Activity*, Fall.

Bernard, A., and B. Jensen. (1995a). Exporters, jobs and wages in U.S. manufacturing, 1976–1987. *Brookings Papers on Economic Activity, Microeconomics*.

———, and ———. (1995b). Why some firms export: Experience, entry costs, spillovers and subsidies. Cambridge, MA: Massachusetts Institute of Technology, Mimeo. December.

Betts, C., and M. Devereux. (1997). The international monetary transmission mechanism: A model of real exchange rate adjustment under pricing-to-market. Mimeo.

Blanchard, O., and P. Diamond. (1989). The Beveridge curve. *Brookings Papers on Economic Activity* 1.

———, and D. Quah. (1989). The dynamic effects of aggregate demand and supply disturbances. *American Economic Review,* September.

———, and ———. (1990). The cyclical behavior of the gross flows of U.S. workers. *Brookings Papers on Economic Activity* 2.

Branson, W., and J. Love. (1988). U.S. manufacturing and the real exchange rate. In *Misalignment of Exchange Rates: Effects on Trade and Industry,* R. Marston (ed.). NBER, University of Chicago Press.

Burgess, S., and M. Knetter. (1996). An international comparison of employment adjustment to exchange rate fluctuations, Cambridge, MA: National Bureau of Economic Research. NBER Working Paper 5861, December.

Caballero, R. (1992). A fallacy of composition. *American Economic Review,* December.

———, and M. Hammour. (1996). On the timing and efficiency of creative destruction. *Quarterly Journal of Economics,* August.

———, and ———. (1998). Improper churn: Social costs and macroeconomic consequences. Cambridge, MA: Massachusetts Institute of Technology. Mimeo.

———, E. Engel, and J. Haltiwanger. (1997). Aggregate unemployment dynamics: Building from microeconomic evidence. *American Economic Review,* March.

Campa, J., and L. Goldberg. (1995). Investment, exchange rates and external exposure. *Journal of International Economics,* May.

———, and ———. (1996). Investment, pass-through and exchange rates: A cross-country comparison, Federal Reserve Bank of New York, June.

Campbell, J., and R. Clarida. (1987). *The Dollar and Real Interest Rates: An Empirical Investigation.* Carnegie-Rochester Series on Public Policy.

Campbell, J., and K. Kuttner. (1996). *Macroeconomic Effects of Employment Reallocation.* Carnegie-Rochester Series on Public Policy.

Caplin, A., and J. Leahy. (1991). State-dependent pricing and the dynamics of money and output. *Quarterly Journal of Economics* 106 (August).

Chari, V. V., E. McGrattan, and P. Kehoe. (1996). Monetary policy and the real exchange rate in sticky price models of the international business cycle. Mimeo.

Clarida, R., and J. Gali. (1994). *Sources of Real Exchange-Rate Fluctuations: How Important Are Nominal Shocks?* Carnegie-Rochester Series on Public Policy.

Cochrane, J. (1994). *Shocks.* Carnegie-Rochester Series on Public Policy, December.

Cohen, D., and G. Saint-Paul. (1992). Uneven technical progress and job destructions. Center for Economic Policy. Research Discussion Paper 979, June.

Cole, H., and R. Rogerson. (1996). Can the Mortensen–Pissarides matching model match the business cycle facts? Federal Reserve Bank of Minneapolis. Research Department Staff Report 224, December.

Cooper, R., J. Haltiwanger, and L. Power. (1994). Machine replacement and the business cycle: Lumps and bumps. Mimeo, July.

Davis, S., and J. Haltiwanger. (1990). Gross job creation and destruction: Microeconomic evidence and macroeconomic implications. in *NBER Macroeconomics Annual,* O. Blanchard and S. Fischer (eds.). Cambridge, MA: The MIT Press, pp. 123–185.

———, and ———. (1996). Driving forces and employment fluctuations. NBER Working paper 5775, September.

———, and ———. (1997). Sectoral job creation and destruction responses to oil price changes and other shocks. Mimeo.

———, ———, and S. Schuh. (1996). *Job Creation and Destruction*, Cambridge, MA: The MIT Press.

de Gregorio, J., A. Giovannini, and H. Wolf. (1994). International evidence on tradables, nontradables inflation. *European Economic Review*, March.

Den Haan, W., G. Ramey, and J. Watson. (1997). Job destruction and propagation of shocks. San Diego: University of California. Mimeo.

Foote, C. (1995). Trend employment growth and the bunching of job creation and destruction. Cambridge, MA: Harvard University. Mimeo.

Froot, K., and K. Rogoff. (1995). Perspectives on PPP and long run real exchange rates. In *Handbook of International Economics, Vol. 3*, G. Grossman and K. Rogoff (eds.). Amsterdam: North-Holland.

Goldberg, L., and J. Tracy. (1998). Real exchange rates: Implications for U.S. industry and regional labor markets. Federal Reserve Bank of New York. Mimeo, February.

Hall, R. (1988). The relation between price and marginal cost in U.S. industry. *Journal of Political Economy*, December.

———. (1997a). Macroeconomic fluctuations and the allocation of time, *Journal of Labor Economics*, January.

———. (1997b). The temporal concentration of job destruction and inventory liquidation: A theory of recessions. Stanford University. Mimeo, September.

Hamilton, J. (1996). This is what happened to the oil price macroeconomy relationship. *Journal of Monetary Economics*, October.

Hosios, A. (1990). On the efficiency of matching and related models of search and unemployment. *Review of Economic Studies*, April.

Knetter, M. (1993). International comparisons of pricing-to-market behavior. *American Economic Review*, June.

Krugman, P. (1989). *Exchange-Rate Instability*. Lionel Robbins Lectures Series. Cambridge, MA: The MIT Press.

Lilien, D. (1982). Sectoral shifts and cyclical unemployment. *Journal of Political Economy*, August.

Mark, N. (1995). Exchange rates and fundamentals: Evidence on long horizon predictability. *American Economic Review* 85 (March):201–218.

———, and D.-Y. Choi. (1997). Real exchange rate prediction over long horizons. *Journal of International Economics*, August.

Meese, R., and K. Rogoff. (1983). Empirical exchange rate models of the seventies: Do they fit out of sample? *Journal of International Economics*, February, pp. 3–24.

———, and ———. (1988). Was it real? The exchange rate–interest differential relation over the modern floating-rate period. *Journal of Finance*, September.

Moen, E. (1997). Competitive search equilibrium. *Journal of Political Economy* 105 (April).

Mortensen, D., and C. Pissarides. (1994). Job creation and destruction in the theory of unemployment. *Review of Economic Studies* 61 (July), 397–415.

Ramey, G., and J. Watson. (1997). Contractual fragility, job destruction and business cycles. *Quarterly Journal of Economics* 112 (August), 873–912.

Rogoff, K. (1996). The purchasing power parity puzzle. *Journal of Economic Perspectives*. June.

Shea, J. (1993). Do supply curves slope up? *Quarterly Journal of Economics* 108 (February), 1–32.

Tauchen, G., and R. Hussey. (1991). Quadrature-based methods for obtaining approximate solutions to nonlinear asset pricing models. Duke University, Mimeo, March.

Comment

DAVID BACKUS
Stern School of Business, New York University; and NBER

1. Introduction

Despite the implication that I've become one of the old men of the profession, I'm pleased to be here. Gourinchas has written an interesting and ambitious paper. Interesting because it looks at a good issue: the relation between employment and the substantial exchange-rate fluctuations we've seen over the last 25 years. Ambitious because the theoretical framework is state-of-the-art, and because the history of attempts to relate exchange rates to real variables is littered with wreckage.

2. Sargent's Law

This history was put into context for me by Tom Sargent. Ten or twelve years ago, Pat Kehoe and I were visiting Stanford. We met Tom for coffee and described our unsuccessful attempts to find a systematic relation between movements in exchange rates and GDP. I think of his response as Sargent's law: When you mix prices and quantities, the results stink. (This isn't an exact quote, but you get the idea.) Economics is filled with examples that make his point. 1960s-era macroeconomics, by and large, related quantities to quantities—the consumption function, for example. It worked great, in the sense that the quantities were highly correlated with each other. But when they added prices, as in cost-of-capital variables for investment equations, there were problems: the relation suggested by theory between (say) investment and the cost of capital was hard to detect in the data. Similarly, modern finance explains prices with prices, and it works pretty well, too. But when we add quantities, as in consumption-based asset pricing models, the data protest loudly. From this perspective, our experience with exchange rates doesn't seem so unusual.

This history serves as a warning to anyone who would like to document a strong statistical relation between exchange rates and real variables. There are, nevertheless, some very good reasons to do it anyway.

One is that the economic mechanism is often most clearly reflected in the relation between exchange rates and quantities. Another is that exchange rates highlight novel features of the economy. In this paper, the idea is that exchange rates are a convenient example of an exogenous (meaning uncorrelated with almost everything) reallocative shock. Finally, I think exchange rates are interesting in their own right. For all of these reasons, I find Gourinchas's paper extremely well motivated.

3. Predecessors

Before getting to the paper, let me give you a quick review of earlier work relating exchange rates to real variables. One of the most striking is Baxter and Stockman's (1989) study of exchange-rate regimes. After an exhaustive exploration of the IFS database, they conclude that there is no significant difference in the behavior of real variables across regimes: fixed and floating exchange-rate regimes are pretty much the same with respect to aggregate variables. An equally influential study is Frankel and Rose (1995), who summarize an enormous body of work as saying that high-frequency exchange-rate movements are unrelated to virtually any fundamental economic variable. The behavior of exchange rates, in their view and others', is something of a mystery (hence the term "exogenous"). A third line of research concerns effects on stock prices, which I regard as most notable for the amount of effort required to find a "significant" statistical relation. In short, it has proved to be extremely difficult to find nonzero correlations between exchange rates and other variables.

The first glimmer of hope comes from Campa and Goldberg (1995, 1997, 1998), whose work I have followed with interest for some time. Campa and Goldberg note that external exposure varies dramatically across industries and over time. Over the last 25 years, for example, industries have moved from net importers to net exporters and the reverse, and the extent of foreign competition has varied as well. An example is Figure 1, where we see that in SIC 35 (machinery) the share of imported inputs rose by a factor of 3, the fraction of sales by foreign firms increased by a factor of 5, and the share of domestic output sold abroad varied substantially, all over the last two decades. More relevant to this discussion, perhaps, is that these patterns show little similarity across industries. Once differences across industries and time are accounted for, Campa and Goldberg find strong effects of exchange rates on investment, somewhat smaller effects on wages, and nonzero but weak effects on employment.

Figure 1 VARIATION IN EXPOSURE (SIC 35: MACHINERY)

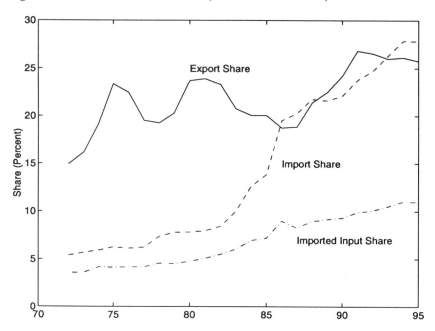

Source: Campa and Goldberg (1997).

4. The Paper

Gourinchas makes two distinct contributions: he takes a systematic look at the statistical relations between exchange rates and job flows, and constructs a dynamic model to account for them. My executive summary is this: (i) The effects of exchange rates on employment are small, but (ii) there are significant, small effects on net job flows, and larger effects on gross flows. All told, exchange-rate movements account for 5–7% of the variance of job creation and destruction. (iii) Job creation and destruction move the same way: appreciation raises both, and in this sense leads to labor-market turbulence. (iv) This last feature is not easy to mimic in a model.

One might quibble with parts of the evidence, but on the whole it agrees with earlier work: exchange-rate fluctuations play a relatively small role in the allocation of labor across firms and industries. My primary concern is the emphasis on (iii), which I worry is a fairly subtle, and perhaps fragile, feature of the data.

Perhaps the most ambitious part of the paper is the model. My initial reaction is that the model focuses on the wrong issue: Since exchange-rate fluctuations play such a small role in allocating labor, why try to model their effects? But the modeling is interesting enough in its own right to warrant attention for other reasons. The main reason, to me, is that the dynamics of the labor market are inherently interesting, whether they are related to exchange rates or not. The issue is how to formalize the allocation process. Gourinchas's model is a good start, but a number of questions come to mind:

Can we model the allocation of labor separately from that of capital? My experience has been that capital formation has a substantial—and frequently counterintuitive—effect on overall dynamics, and perhaps that is true here, too. We also gain an additional channel by which exchange-rate movements might affect the economy, one with a stronger statistical basis.

How important is the choice of matching technology? My impression is that this kind of technology, in which matching is simply the result of vacancies and unemployment, fails to reproduce many of the dynamic features of labor markets. Perhaps something like Jovanovic's (1979) model would be worth exploring.

Can we get more out of the shock process? The shock process is a relatively simple Markov chain. Even within this structure, I wonder whether we could get different responses by allowing the spread of the distribution to vary substantially across states.

None of these are complaints—more signs that the approach is interesting, and worth pursuing along new directions.

5. Are Exchange-Rate Movements Big?

I'd like to conclude with a question implicit in Gourinchas's empirical work: Are exchange-rate movements big? I'm used to thinking of the post-Bretton Woods movements in currency prices as large, but this paper and others make me wonder whether this is right. The issue is what yardstick we use to judge magnitude. Certainly log changes in exchange rates have greater variance than log changes in (say) real GDP, so in that sense exchange-rate movements are large. Alternatively, we might note that the variation is a little less than we see for equity prices: annualized volatility is about 15% for the S&P 500, and about 11% for major currencies against the U.S. dollar. By this comparison, exchange-rate movements aren't so big. This paper shows quite clearly, I think, that exchange-rate movements are small relative to other shocks driving the sectoral reallocation of labor. The work of Campa and Goldberg also suggests that there may be large effects on particular sectors or firms, but the weight of earlier work on aggregates tells us exchange rates are not a major source of aggregate fluctuations.

REFERENCES

Baxter, M., and A. Stockman. (1989). Business cycles and the exchange rate regime: Some international evidence. *Journal of Monetary Economics* 23:377–400.
Campa, J., and L. Goldberg. (1995). Investment in manufacturing, exchange rates, and external exposure. *Journal of International Economics* 38:297–320.
———, and ———. (1997). The evolving external orientation of manufacturing industries. *Economic Review of the Federal Reserve Bank of New York* 3:53–81.
———, and ———. (1998). Employment versus wage adjustment and exchange rates: A cross-country comparison. Stern School of Business, New York University. Manuscript.
Frankel, J., and A. Rose. (1995). An empirical characterization of nominal exchange rates. In *Handbook of International Economics, Volume III*, G. Grossman and K. Rogoff (eds.). Amsterdam: North-Holland.
Jovanovic, B. (1979). Job matching and the theory of labor turnover. *Journal of Political Economy* 87:972–990.

Comment

RUSSELL COOPER
Boston University

1. Introduction

This paper studies a number of issues that are relevant for understanding both the nature of job flows and the response of the U.S. economy to shocks created by interactions with other countries. This is clearly a very ambitious project, one that could define a research program for a group rather than be the topic of a single research paper. Nonetheless, Gourinchas touches all of the key bases in this paper and provides a basis for further study in a number of areas.

The paper bears on the following questions:

Is reallocation an important aspect of job flows?
Do real-exchange-rate movements constitute a key source of reallocation?
What does a model of the reallocation process imply for the specification of open economy macro models in general?

My comments start with the motivation for this paper and then are structured around these three questions.[1]

2. Motivation

Why should a traditional macroeconomist care about a paper on real exchange rates and job flows? It is often too easy to ignore the fact that the U.S. economy is influenced by shocks that arise from sources external to our borders. The traditional search for sources of fluctuations focuses on technology shocks and policy variations and ignores the possibility that disturbances arising in other countries may be reflected in our domestic levels of economic activity.

This paper provides a partial challenge to that view. The idea is that by looking at the impact of exchange-rate movements on job flows we can potentially learn about two important topics.

First, it could be that for some industries, real-exchange-rate movements constitute an empirically relevant source of fluctuations. Second, even when real-exchange-rate movements are relatively small, they are still useful for tracing out the process of job reallocation. This is particularly true if by studying the impact of real-exchange-rate changes we are able to identify certain structural aspects of the adjustment process that can be used to study the impact of other, perhaps more quantitatively important, shocks. From this perspective these real-exchange-rate shocks may produce small fluctuations but considerable economic information.

In the end, and perhaps not too surprisingly, real-exchange-rate movements appear not to be a main source of fluctuations. Further, the empirical exercises, while pointing to some significant comovements of job creation and destruction, fail to identify structural aspects of the adjustment process. Thus it is not clear how much one can infer about the general nature of the labor and capital adjustment processes from this exercise.

Still, this paper is extremely impressive in both its depth and its breadth. Reaching its intellectual target, while quite appealing, is no easy task. So despite not providing convincing evidence on the importance of real exchange rates, this paper sets the basis for further study in this area.

3. Is Reallocation a Large Piece of Aggregate Fluctuations?

Sources of fluctuation are generally classified as either aggregate or sectoral in nature. With regard to aggregate shocks, it is common to con-

---

1. My comments presented at the conference were more directed at details of the paper. My goal here is to address the arguments of the paper in a more general manner.

sider variations in technology, monetary policy, fiscal policy, and expectations as the sources. Of course, these same shocks can be sectoral in nature as well, insofar as they influence sectors differentially.

Evaluating these sources of shocks is, of course, a full-time job in macroeconomics. A persuasive analysis is one that first identifies these shocks and then, in the context of a dynamic equilibrium model, matches relevant aspects of the data. Likewise, models that stress sectoral shocks are subject to the same standards.

One of the primary empirical hurdles in evaluating sectoral models is the fact that sectors generally move together. Positive sectoral comovements in output, employment, and productivity have been documented in a number of studies. While this type of evidence is often taken as indicative of aggregate shocks, positive comovements can be created in a model with sectoral shocks *if* there is some type of complementarity (either through technology or the structure of demands) that links sectors together.

Still, there are a number of interesting features of sectoral-shock models. First, there are numerous candidates for sectoral shocks. Included would be aggregate shocks, such as shocks to government spending, that affect sectors asymmetrically. Further, oil price shocks may affect sectors in a differential manner, as in Davis and Haltiwanger (1997).

Second, once one moves away from aggregate data, there is a wealth of statistical information that can be brought into the discussion. The research summarized in Davis, Haltiwanger, and Schuh (1996) highlights a broad set of facts concerning the nature of job flows over time and across firms. These "facts" are now well known: job creation is mildly procyclical, job destruction is strongly countercyclical, and reallocation (the sum of creation and destruction) is countercyclical. This last fact gives rise to the theme that recessions are a time for reorganization, since job reallocation rises significantly in periods of low economic activity.

Along with the time-series dimension of job flows is the incredible richness of the cross-sectional diversity. Even in bad economic times, it is not unusual to have a number of plants expanding activity. Further, it is not clear that disaggregation to even the four-digit level is sufficient to create a homogeneous set of plants. Simply put, the heterogeneity across plants is not easily captured by controlling for the obvious characteristics such as sector, age, or size.

To fix these ideas, consider a simple investment model, studied, for example, by Cooper and Haltiwanger (1998). While this model does not have all of the richness of the theory presented by Gourinchas, it is a simple device for exploring some of the key points.

The optimization problem of a firm (which is taken to be equivalent to a plant for this discussion) reduces to the choice of replacing/augmenting or retaining its capital (k). If capital is retained, then it is productive, yielding a profit flow (net of the costs of all adjustable factors) given by $\pi(A,\xi,k)$, where A represents a common shock and ξ is a firm-specific shock. In the subsequent period the firm has a lower capital stock, due to physical depreciation and obsolescence (given by ρ below).

If capital is replaced and/or augmented, then the firm bears both convex and nonconvex adjustment costs. For the nonconvex costs, the profit flow is reduced by a factor of λ and the firm must incur costs of investment, given by F below, independent of the size of the investment expenditure. In addition, the model allows for convex costs of adjustment, captured by a cost-of-adjustment function specified below.

The gains to investment arise from the increased capital at the firm in the following period. This may appear as simple additions to the existing stock of capital or the replacement of old machines with new ones, yielding a vintage-type model as in Cooper, Haltiwanger, and Power (1995). For our purposes here this distinction is not a critical point.

Letting $V(A,\xi,k)$ represent the value of a firm given the state (A,ξ,k), the formal representation of this problem is

$$V(A,\xi,k) = \max(V^a(A,\xi,k), V^i(A,\xi,k)),$$

where the superscript a refers to "action" and i to "inaction." The values associated with these actions are given by

$$V^a(A,\xi,k) = \max_{k'} [\pi(A,\xi,k)(1 - \lambda) - F - C(k,k') + \beta EV(A',\xi',k')],$$

and

$$V^i(A,\xi,k) = \pi(A,\xi,k) + \beta EV(A',\xi',\rho k).$$

The solution of this dynamic optimization problem yields two policy functions. One describes the state contingent probability of investment, $h(A,\xi,k)$, and the other the level of investment contingent upon acting, $I(A,\xi,k)$. The properties of these policy functions are quite dependent upon the nature of the adjustment costs and the serial correlation of the driving processes.

As argued in Cooper, Haltiwanger, and Power (1995), lumpy investment (created by the nonconvex aspect of adjustment costs) will be procyclical when shocks to profitability are highly serially correlated and when the costs of action are largely independent of the level of current profitability. So, using the model specified above, procyclical activity is more likely to arise when the (A,ξ) shocks are positively serially correlated and the adjustment cost is borne mainly through a large F and not a large λ. Conversely, adjustment is likely to occur in low-profitability states when adjustment costs entail large opportunity costs, as through a large value of λ and less persistent shocks.[2] Thus this type of model can deliver the theme that "recessions are a time for reorganization," but this result depends critically on underlying parameters.

We can use this model to exposit some of the key themes raised by Gourinchas. Clearly there is a bit of a gap between this formulation and his, since Gourinchas talks about job flows and exchange rates and this model has neither.[3] Further, to his credit, Gourinchas has more of a general equilibrium structure. Clearly, then, my exposition does not substitute for a careful reading and evaluation of his model.

In the mapping between investment and labor, a relabeling of the variable k cheaply converts the model from one of investment to costly adjustment in the stock of workers. In this latter interpretation, hours per worker and capital rentals could then be viewed as the flexible factors which are already included in the optimization problem leading to the reduced-form profit function. Alternatively one can argue that adjustments in the stock of machines lead to job flows, so that an understanding of investment leads to a theory of job flows.[4]

Second, what are the shocks here relative to those studied by Gourinchas? Ignoring aggregate shocks for the moment, fluctuations in investment and jobs can arise from two sources: sectoral shocks and idiosyncratic shocks. So, being a bit more specific with labels for the shocks in the optimization problem, let A_{it} be the shock to profitability in sector i in period t, and ξ_{ijt} the idiosyncratic shock to firm j in sector i in period t. The first type of shock creates reallocation across sectors, while the second type underlies the heterogeneity of job creation, destruction, and investment activity at the firm (plant) level within a sector. In principle, real-exchange-rate movements would appear as both a firm-specific and a sectoral shock.

With this classification of shocks in mind, what types of behavior does the model produce? If the primitives are such that activity is procyclical, then there will be a set of relatively high values of the shocks, (A, ξ), such that positive investment arises if the state is within this set, given the existing stock of capital. There will also be a set of realizations of the

2. In Cooper and Haltiwanger (1993), profitability movements occurred due to deterministic seasonal two-cycles, so that adjustment occurred in periods of low profitability, given time to build of one period.
3. To be clear, job flows and exchange rates are at the heart of the empirical exercise. The theory model presented in Section 4 of the paper has a technology that does not distinguish capital and labor, with shocks coming from relative prices.
4. On this point see Abel and Eberly (1997) and Cooper and Haltiwanger (1998).

shocks with disinvestment. In the remainder of states, there will be inaction.

Within a sector, an optimal policy of this form will create dispersion in activity across firms due to the idiosyncratic shocks. In principle, the model can be parametrized in a way that mimics the observed heterogeneity across plants observed in, for example, the LRD. So, in the language of Davis, Haltiwanger, and Schuh (1996), there will be job creation (capital accumulation) at some high-profitability plants and job destruction (disinvestment) at others, in all sectors of the economy.

These sectoral shocks create a basis for plants within a sector to move together. Again, assuming that activity is procyclical, a sector experiencing a high-profitability shock will undertake investment activity either by expanding existing capacity or by introducing new techniques and products (machine replacement). On the job-flow side, these expanding sectors will be creating jobs, assuming either that employment is complementary with capital or that the fixed factor in the model is labor.

Sectoral shocks may also create reallocation across sectors. This arises naturally from the effects of reduced factor demands by one sector leading to variations in factor prices that lead to increased factor demands by other sectors. This reallocation process is potentially complicated by considering the actual process of worker flows. As discussed in Section 4.4 of his paper, the richer search and matching model analyzed by Gourinchas has this property of reallocation across sectors in response to a relative-price shock. The difficult element, as noted in his remarks as well, is generating reallocation within a sector in these models.

Intrasectoral reallocation might be created by shocks that lead to a mean-preserving spread across plants. In this case, given the distribution of capital holdings, an increase in the variance of the distribution of idiosyncratic shocks will simultaneously increase both creation and destruction within a sector, since more plants are pushed outside of the region of inactivity in (A, ξ) space. This leads one to consider whether shocks, such as real-exchange-rate movements, can lead to changes in the distribution of the profitability of investment and employment opportunities.[5]

With this type of model in mind, we can turn to the evidence of the effects of various shocks on job and capital flows. The key points will be isolating sectoral or reallocative shocks and tracing their implications for job creation and destruction as well as investment activity.

---

5. Using plant-level data to investigate this type of mechanism seems quite promising. Caballero, Engel, and Haltiwanger (1997) use their characterization of "employment shortages" to construct an idiosyncratic shock series for a panel of plants in the LRD. This allows them to uncover some time-series evolution in the distribution of idiosyncratic shocks.

4. Are Real-Exchange-Rate Movements a Key Source of Reallocation?

One of the primary contributions of Gourinchas's paper is to add to the accumulation of evidence on reallocation shocks and their impact on employment. A previous paper, by Davis and Haltiwanger (1997), looks at the impact of oil price shocks on job creation and destruction. From their evidence, the reallocative component of oil price shocks leads to positive comovement in job destruction and job creation. Further, Davis and Haltiwanger find that much of the reallocation appears within rather than between sectors. Finally, there is a distinctive dynamic pattern. The immediate impact of an adverse oil price shock is for employment to fall with reallocation emerging over a longer period of time.

The paper by Gourinchas parallels Davis and Haltiwanger's study except for the nature of the reallocation shock. Clearly, the approach of Gourinchas is to view real-exchange-rate movements as partly a source of reallocation between plants and sectors that differ in their sensitivity to this variable. To conduct such a study, one must first isolate real-exchange-rate movements and then find some metric for distinguishing groups of plants in terms of their responsiveness to these movements.

As Gourinchas is using four-digit SIC data, his approach is to split the sample into a group of plants that is sensitive to real-exchange-rate movements and one that isn't. The selection is based on trade exposure, measured by either export shares or import penetration. Given the isolation of 69 out of 450 sectors, Gourinchas then constructs a sectoral measure of real-exchange-rate movements, which is used to identify the response of the sector's employment to variations in real exchange rates.

Using this measure of sectoral real exchange rates, two empirical exercises are undertaken. The first, as reported in Gourinchas's Tables 3 to 5, regresses net employment growth, job creation rates, and job destruction rates in each sector on an aggregate measure of net employment growth and the sectoral real exchange rates. Gourinchas finds that net employment is relatively insensitive to real-exchange-rate shocks within the groups of exporting and import-competing firms.[6]

The decomposition of these effects into job creation and destruction in the subsequent tables indicates a significant response of these flows within sectors to real-exchange-rate shocks. These results clearly have the sign pattern associated with reallocation shocks: job destruction and job creation move together within a sector over the three quarters. Fur-

6. In fact, none of the individual coefficients from the regressions summarized in Table 3 are significant, though their sum is different from zero.

ther, the movements of the export sectors and those identified as import competitors are quite similar.

There must be quantitatively disperse movements across plants that underlie these movements within a sector in response to these real-exchange-rate shocks. Interestingly, there is no apparent response from the nontraded goods sector and hence no general equilibrium spillovers of the type discussed in the model presentation above.

The second exercise is quite close to the approach taken by Davis and Haltiwanger: use a VAR to distinguish the innovations to real-exchange-rate movements and then trace out their impact on job flows. The details of this (including the assumptions needed) are spelled out in the paper. The main finding of this approach (see Table 8) is that while sometimes statistically significant, the effects of exchange-rate movements on employment are small. From this table, one does see that there is some evidence of reallocation. The effects seems largest in particular isolated industries, such as motor vehicles, leading to more interest in detailed studies of particular sectors.[7] Further, as Gourinchas notes there is something a bit puzzling about the results created by the VAR analysis: the responses of the nontraded and traded sectors to real-exchange-rate movements are comparable.

Overall, the quantitative analysis documents the role of real-exchange-rate shocks as a source of reallocation. While not a large source of fluctuations in job flows, movements in the real exchange rates do create some statistically significant movements in job destruction and creation that have the pattern of reallocative shocks.

5. Should We Respecify Open-Economy Models?

While not touched upon in Gourinchas's paper, there is a large literature that falls under the heading of *open-economy real-business-cycle* (ORBC) models. Papers in this tradition, such as Backus, Kehoe, and Kydland (1992), Baxter and Crucini (1993), and Stockman and Tesar (1995), consider multicountry stochastic growth models in which there are both country-specific and sector-specific shocks. In equilibrium, of course, these shocks influence real exchange rates and, in monetary models, the nominal exchange rate as well.

There are clearly two differences between these models and that presented in the last section of the paper by Gourinchas. First, the ORBC models are completely specified and are general-equilibrium in nature.

---

7. In fact, it would have been useful to complement this evidence with graphs of real-exchange-rate movements and job flows for particular industries.

In principle this is a great advantage, since it allows one to trace the effects of certain types of shocks on equilibrium outcomes, generally summarized by impulse response functions. In contrast, the model presented by Gourinchas talks about real-exchange-rate shocks, but, of course, they are not exogenous shocks. To the extent that the variation in the real exchange rate comes from, say, a disturbance to technology, it should affect decisions on job creation and destruction beyond the effects highlighted in Gourinchas's analysis.

Second, the model explored by Gourinchas has the distinct advantage relative to the ORBC models of specifying a richer adjustment process. This is important and not just for purposes of "realism." One of the ways in which the ORBC models fail to fit the data is precisely in terms of capital flows. Specifically, in many of these analyses, capital flows too quickly across national boundaries, yielding negative correlations in output across countries. This is of course simply the international analogue of negative comovements created by sector-specific shocks.

From the perspective of the ORBC models, the issue is how to build frictions in the adjustment of capital across international borders. In some of these exercises, explicit transactions costs are imposed. This has the desirable effect of reducing these flows, but leaves open the source of the frictions.

One could imagine constructing a model much closer to that proposed by Gourinchas in which the costs of adjustment appear through labor-market frictions. To the extent that machines need workers to operate them, the frictions in the labor market provide a simple impediment to the flow of capital. The difficult part is the construction of general equilibrium models in which there is a distribution of capital vintages.[8]

So, from this viewpoint, I see a natural merger of these research lines. The gain to the Gourinchas model would be to make the real exchange rate endogenous. The gain to the ORBC model is a more realistic specification of the factor adjustment process.

6. Conclusions

This is a very thoughtful and carefully crafted paper. While it is not clear that it provides convincing evidence that real-exchange-rate movements are an important part of the fluctuations story, it lends support to the view that they are an important source of reallocation. As we continue to study the sources of uncertainty and their implications for factor flows both across and within sectors, studies such as this will

8. For progress along these lines see, for example, Gilchrist and Williams (1998).

provide the needed evidence and modeling to understand a wide range of observations.

REFERENCES

Abel, A., and J. Eberly (1997). The mix and scale of factors with irreversibility and fixed costs of investment, Cambridge, MA: National Bureau of Economic Research. NBER Working Paper 6148.
Backus, D., P. Kehoe, and F. Kydland (1992). International real business cycles. *Journal of Political Economy* 100:745–775.
Baxter, M., and M. Crucini. (1993). Explaining savings–investment correlations. *American Economic Review* 83:416–436.
Caballero, R., E. Engel, and J. Haltiwanger. (1997). Aggregate employment dynamics: Building from microeconomic evidence. *American Economic Review* 87:115–137.
Cooper, R., and J. Haltiwanger. (1993). The aggregate implications of machine replacement: Theory and evidence. *American Economic Review* 83:360–382.
———, and ———. (1998). On the nature of adjustment costs for capital and labor. Boston University. Mimeo.
———, ———, and L. Power. (1995). Machine replacement and the business cycle: Lumps and bumps, Cambridge, MA: National Bureau of Economic Research. NBER Working Paper 5260 (revised 1997).
Davis, S., and J. Haltiwanger. (1997). Sectoral job creation and destruction responses to oil price changes and other shocks. University of Chicago. Mimeo, May.
———, ———, and S. Schuh. (1996). *Job Creation and Destruction*. Cambridge, MA: The MIT Press.
Gilchrist, S., and J. Williams. (1998). Putty-clay and investment: A business cycle analysis. Boston University. Mimeo.
Stockman, A., and L. Tesar (1995). Tastes and technology in a two country model of the business cycle: Explaining international comovements. *American Economic Review* 85:168–185.

Discussion

Gourinchas began the discussion by responding to some comments of the discussants. He emphasized that the purpose of the paper was not to claim that exchange rates are a major driving force behind job flows, but rather to use the observed effects of exchange-rate shocks to improve our understanding of the transmission mechanism in general. He defended the use of an empirical specification in levels rather than growth rates, arguing that using growth rates would obscure the dynamic response of job creation and destruction to a one-time depreciation or appreciation. Finally, he argued that focusing on the statistical significance of sums of coefficients (as opposed to individual coefficients) in the basic regressions of Tables 3–5 was justified by the likely importance of adjustment costs and expectational effects.

Michael Klein noted that Gourinchas's time-series approach is a useful complement to the cross-sectional approach of Davis, Haltiwanger, and Schuh. He suggested that larger effects of exchange rates might be found in annual data, because of delayed responses by firms. Gourinchas pointed out that with the use of annual data the sample would be quite small in the time-series dimension.

John Shea thought the finding of positive comovement of job creation and job destruction in response to reallocative shocks to be the most interesting of the paper and he asked whether this result could be confirmed for other reallocative shocks. One possibility would be to use sector-specific demand shocks based on input–output relations, as in Shea's own work. Gourinchas noted that a positive correlation of sectoral job creation and destruction had been found for the case of oil shocks by Davis and Haltiwanger.

Henning Bohn raised the issue of durability of output. He noted that the theoretical model considers only nondurable goods, but that in the data tradable goods tend to be durable and nontradable goods tend to be nondurable. Bohn expressed the concern that the sectoral differences found in the paper might reflect differences in durability of output rather than tradability. Gourinchas replied that exporting and import-competing sectors both produce mostly durable goods, but that their responses to exchange-rate shocks appear to be different.

Robert Shimer suggested that sectoral specificity of workers' skills might be an important factor limiting intersectoral movement following a reallocative shock. Gourinchas agreed that this factor would reduce the absolute value of the expected negative correlation between job creation and destruction following a reallocative shock, but by itself it cannot account for the positive correlation found in the data.

Simon Gilchrist and Charles Himmelberg
BOSTON UNIVERSITY AND NBER, AND COLUMBIA UNIVERSITY

Investment: Fundamentals and Finance

1. Introduction

It is well recognized that financial variables such as cash flow and cash stocks are robust and quantitatively important explanatory variables for investment in reduced-form equations estimated with firm-level data. Following the seminal work of Fazzari, Hubbard, and Petersen (1988), a large body of recent empirical work attributes these findings to capital-market imperfections [see the extensive survey by Hubbard (1998)]. This literature argues that when access to external debt and equity is costly, internally available funds provide a cheaper source of financing, thus increasing the desired level of investment. Such cost premiums for external finance are generally explained by appealing to models with asymmetric information and agency problems.

Despite the volume of empirical work in this literature, financing-based interpretations of the explanatory power of cash flow and other financial variables in investment equations remain controversial.[1] Even among economists who agree that firms face some degree of financial frictions, there remains substantial disagreement over the magnitude of such frictions and whether they are large enough to affect investment behavior. The controversy can be traced to two distinct but related problems with identification. The first problem is that financial variables may contain information about future returns to capital. In a forward-looking

We thank Charles Calomiris, Russel Cooper, Jan Eberly, Bernd Fitzenberger, Bill Gentry, Mark Gertler, Bob Hodrick, Glenn Hubbard, Cornelia Kullman, Chris Mayer, John Shea, and Kristen Willard for helpful comments and suggestions and the NSF for financial support. We are especially grateful for excellent comments from Ben Bernanke, David Gross, Julio Rotemberg, and Ken West. We are also grateful to seminar participants at Boston University, the CEPR/DFG/ZEW Conference on Industrial Structure and Input Markets, Columbia, CREST, Georgetown, the Federal Reserve Bank of Boston, the Federal Reserve Bank of New York, and the 1998 NBER Macro Annual Conference.
1. See, for example, Kaplan and Zingales (1997) and Fazzari, Hubbard, and Petersen (1996).

model, investment depends on marginal Q, the present value of expected future marginal returns to capital. This present value is the "fundamental" to which investment should respond, even in the absence of capital-market imperfections. Any variable that helps predict marginal Q should appear as a state variable in the firm's decision rule for investment, and should therefore have explanatory power for investment. The ratio of cash flow to capital is obviously closely related to the return on capital, so from the perspective of models based on forward-looking fundamentals, if other variables in the regression (like Tobin's Q) do not fully specify the expected marginal value of capital, it is not surprising that cash flow appears in reduced-form regression models. The same logic makes it difficult to interpret the role of other financial variables such as cash stocks and leverage as well.

The second identification problem relates to the distinction between the *marginal* return to capital and the *average* return to capital. In the absence of financial-market imperfections, the present value of expected future marginal profitability of capital (MPK) should be the sole determinant of investment at the firm level. Lacking good measures of the marginal return to capital, the empirical investment literature often relies on the *average* return to capital—the ratio of profits to capital—as a proxy for the marginal return. Unfortunately, this proxy also provides a good measure of the financial health of the firm, which, in the presence of financial-market imperfections, should also influence investment. By not carefully distinguishing between the present value of marginal and average returns, the existing empirical investment literature potentially confounds the influence of investment fundamentals with the effect of financial factors that reflect premiums on external finance.

In Gilchrist and Himmelberg (1995), we attempted to resolve the first of these identification problems by using a vector autoregression to model the forward-looking role of cash flow in a structural model for investment. Using firm-level data, we confirmed that the predictive power of cash flow for future MPK in a model with perfect capital markets could account for a significant portion of the overall explanatory power of cash flow for investment. But we also found evidence against the model. Like previous studies that used Tobin's Q to control for the expected return to investment, we found that investment is "excessively sensitive" to cash flow, that is, more sensitive to cash flow than the neoclassical model of investment information would predict. We concluded that financial-market imperfections were a likely source of the model's rejection, but our modeling framework was not sufficiently general to assign a structural interpretation to investment's excess sensitivity to cash flow.

In this paper, we attempt to resolve the second identification problem by extending the empirical framework used in our previous work to a (linearized) structural model of investment that explicitly incorporates financial frictions. Like our previous work, this empirical framework uses panel-data vector autoregressions (VARs) to construct expectations of the future marginal profitability of capital. Unlike our previous work, however, we introduce financial frictions into the model, and we develop improved measures of the marginal profitability of capital (MPK) that sharpen the distinction between MPK and financial factors. By combining better measures of MPK with our extended model, we substantially improve our ability to identify and quantify the influence of financial factors on investment decisions.

Although panel-data VARs have not been widely used by previous researchers to describe investment behavior, we believe they can be a useful tool for summarizing the data and testing structural model assumptions.[2] We consider two strategies for using VARs to model investment. First, we use VARs to summarize the dynamic relationship among investment, MPK, and cash flow. By imposing a recursive structure on the contemporaneous shocks of the model (a standard identification technique in VAR analysis), we identify shocks to cash flow that are orthogonal to MPK. The impulse response functions for this model show that the orthogonalized shocks to cash flow elicit a substantial and prolonged response from investment. Moreover, the cash-flow shock predicts either zero or negative response to MPK. This result implies that the response of investment to cash flow cannot be attributed to revisions in the expected return to capital. Indeed, the negative response of MPK implies (counterfactually) that investment should fall rather than rise in response to the cash-flow shock. This evidence is difficult to reconcile with a model in which cash flow's influence on investment is entirely attributable to nonfinancial fundamentals.

Our second strategy uses panel-data VARs to impose structural restrictions on the investment equation derived from a model with costly external finance. The use of VARs to estimate structural investment models was introduced into the empirical investment literature by Abel and Blanchard (1986), and was subsequently applied to panel data by Gilchrist and Himmelberg (1995). The modeling contribution in this paper is to show that putting financial frictions in the model introduces a state-dependent discount factor that depends on the firm's balance-sheet condition. Because it is not possible to solve this model analyti-

---

2. The two applications of panel-data VARs to firm-level investment of which we are aware are Whited (1992) and Himmelberg (1990).

cally, we work with a linearized version that is amenable to VAR methods. This structure allows us to identify the sensitivity of investment to changes in the expected marginal value of capital. With financial frictions in the model, we show that investment should also display excess sensitivity to the present value of financial variables because these variables influence the future shadow cost of funds used to discount future MPK.

In our empirical results, we find that investment is responsive to both fundamental and financial factors, as predicted by the existence of financial frictions. This response is both statistically and economically significant—for the average firm in our sample, our estimates show that financial factors increase the overall response of investment to an expansionary shock by 25% over the first few years following the initial impulse.

Although the average firm in our sample shows a quantitatively significant response to financial factors, we also find that financial factors play little, if any, role in determining the investment behavior of bond-rated firms. Because bond-rated firms account for a large fraction of overall investment activity (on the order of 50% in manufacturing), this reduces the role of financial factors for aggregate investment, at least during normal times. While non-bond-rated firms are quantitatively less important for aggregate investment, they are more labor-intensive and are influential in the determination of inventory dynamics.[3] To the extent that non-bond-rated firms rely on external funds to finance both labor inputs and inventory investment, our evidence that such firms do indeed face capital market imperfections suggests that financial factors will have important influences through these channels as well.[4]

2. Investment, MPK, and Cash Flow: Simple VAR Evidence

In this section we begin by discussing the importance of measuring MPK as accurately as possible. We then briefly discuss the estimation of panel-data vector autoregressions and argue the merits of using VARs as summary statistics that provide a full, dynamic description of the relationship among investment, MPK, and financial variables. Finally, we suggest a recursive ordering of the VAR that allows us to identify the component of cash-flow innovations that is orthogonal to the MPK shock. We report

3. See Carpenter, Fazzari, and Peterson (1997).
4. Sharpe (1993) shows the importance of financial constraints for employment dynamics. Kashyap, Lamont, and Stein (1994), Carpenter, Fazzari, and Peterson (1997), and Gertler and Gilchrist (1994) provide evidence for inventory dynamics, and Himmelberg and Peterson (1994) estimate the effect of financial frictions on R&D spending.

impulse response functions for investment based on this ordering, and argue that the results provide evidence of a financing role for cash flow. These results motivate a more structural econometric investigation, which we provide in Section 3.

2.1 MEASURING MPK

Suppose a firm has a Cobb–Douglas production function $y = Ak^{\alpha_k}n^{\alpha_n}x^{\alpha_x}$, where A is the total factor productivity, y is output, k and n are quasifixed capital stocks, and x is a variable factor input. We allow for nonconstant returns to scale by assuming $\alpha_k + \alpha_n + \alpha_x = 1 + \gamma$, where γ is the return-to-scale parameter. We allow for multiple quasifixed factors because we are concerned about the empirical implications of ignoring omitted quasifixed factors. The idea here is that k represents the stock of fixed property, plant, and equipment, while n represents R&D capital and other intangible assets. The assumption of a single variable input is without loss of generality. Assuming that the firm faces an inverse demand curve $p(y)$, variable factor prices w, and fixed costs F, the profit function is defined by

$$\pi(k, n, w, F) = \max_{x>0} p(y)y - wx - F$$
$$\text{s.t.} \quad y = Ak^{\alpha_k}n^{\alpha_n}x^{\alpha_x}. \tag{2.1}$$

This specification of the profit function allows fixed costs F to be time-varying. For example, if n represents the stock of the firm's R&D workers, which are quasifixed factors due to hiring and firing costs, the F could represent the wages paid to these workers.

By applying the envelope theorem, the marginal profitability of fixed capital, denoted by MPK, is readily shown to be

$$\text{MPK} \equiv \frac{\partial \pi}{\partial k} = \theta \left(\frac{s}{k} \right), \tag{2.2}$$

where $\theta = (1 + \eta^{-1})\alpha_k$, $\eta \equiv (\partial y/\partial p)p/y < -1$ is the (firm-level) price elasticity of demand,[5] α_k is the capital share of output from the Cobb–Douglas specification, and $s = py$ is the firm's sales. Equation (2.2) shows that, up to a scale parameter,[6] the ratio of sales to capital measures the

5. Note that if firms are profit maximizers, they will produce on the elastic portion of the demand curve, so that $\eta < -1$.
6. If the effect of corporate taxes is included, then the tax-adjusted expression for MPK takes the form $\text{MPK} = (1 - \tau)\theta(s/k)$, where τ is the corporate tax rate on profits. Our estimates of θ allow variation in τ over industries but not over time. Time variation in tax rates would, to some degree, be captured by our year dummies. We plan to explore the effects of taxes in more detail in future work.

Table 1   TWO-DIGIT SIC ESTIMATES OF $\hat{\theta}_j$

		$\hat{\theta}_j$					$\hat{\theta}_j$	
SIC	Obs.	Sales	OI	SIC	Obs.	Sales	OI
20	1112	0.036	0.387	30	670	0.040	0.373
21	34	0.027	0.171	31	153	0.017	0.233
22	549	0.035	0.376	32	420	0.069	0.571
23	332	0.017	0.185	33	821	0.063	0.612
24	298	0.044	0.489	34	958	0.040	0.375
25	373	0.031	0.330	35	2161	0.036	0.328
26	562	0.077	0.598	36	2123	0.039	0.304
27	700	0.042	0.300	37	1062	0.037	0.353
28	1504	0.051	0.334	38	1411	0.036	0.313
29	469	0.097	0.722	39	398	0.032	0.301

marginal profitability of fixed capital.[7]

Because it is unreasonable to assume that manufacturing firms in different industries face the same price elasticity of demand, η, or the same capital share of sales, α_k, we construct industry-level estimates of θ. We assume that firms are, on average, at their equilibrium capital stocks. Ignoring adjustment costs, this says the marginal profitability of capital should roughly equal the cost of capital, that is, $MPK_{it} = r_{it} + \delta_{it}$, where r_{it} and δ_{it} are the risk-adjusted discount rate and depreciation rate of capital, respectively. Substituting $\theta_j(s/k)_{it}$ for MPK_{it} and averaging over all firms $i \in I(j)$ and years $t \in T(i)$ in industry j suggests that a reasonable estimate of θ_j is given by

$$\hat{\theta}_j = \left(\frac{1}{N_j}\sum_{i\in I(j)}\sum_{t\in T(i)} (s/k)_{it}\right)^{-1} \frac{1}{N_j}\sum_{i\in I(j)}\sum_{t\in T(i)} (r_{it}+\delta_{it}),$$

where N_j is the number of firm–year observations for industry j. In practice, we assume that $(1/NT)\sum_{i\in I(j)}\sum_{t\in T(i)} (r_{it} + \delta_{it}) = 0.18$ for all industries.[8]

To show the degree to which θ varies across two-digit industries, columns 3 and 7 in Table 1 report the values of $\hat{\theta}_j$. The table shows that the value of $\hat{\theta}_j$ ranges from .017 to 0.097. The assumptions $\alpha_k = 0.06$ and $\eta = -4.0$ imply a value of $(1 + \eta^{-1})\alpha_k = 0.045$. These values seem

---

7. This derivation ignores the difference between production and sales. For the smaller subset of firms in Compustat that report finished goods, the correlation between production-to-capital ratio and sales-to-capital ratio exceeds 0.99. In light of this fact and because of the limited availability of data on finished goods, we opted to measure MPK using the sales-to-capital ratio.

8. We experimented with different values for $(1/NT)\sum_{i\in I(j)} \sum_{t\in T(i)} (r_{it} + \delta_{it})$, including the calculation of industry-specific depreciation rates. In practice, this adds very little variation to the estimated value of θ_j, but this is probably an issue that future work could profitably explore in more depth.

plausible, suggesting that our estimates of $\hat{\theta}_j$ reported in Table 1 are reasonable. We therefore construct estimates of the marginal profit using

$$\text{MPK1}_{it} = \hat{\theta}_j \frac{S_{it}}{k_{it}} .$$

In the results reported in the paper, this is our preferred measure of MPK, which we refer to as MPK1. The summary statistics reported in Table 2 indicate that MPK1 has a mean of 0.200, with an interquartile range of 0.121 to 0.240.

2.2 WHY IT IS LESS DESIRABLE TO MEASURE MPK USING OPERATING INCOME

Previous authors have measured MPK using the ratio of operating income to capital. For example, using aggregate data for U.S. manufactur-

Table 2   VARIABLES: ACRONYMS, DEFINITIONS, AND SUMMARY STATISTICS

Acronym	Description/Compustat Definition	Mean (S.D.)	Min	25%	50%	75%	Max
				Percentiles			
MPK1	Sales-based marginal profitability of capital (see text)	0.200 (0.125)	0.019	0.121	0.170	0.241	1.37
MPK2	Operating-income-based marginal profitability of capital (see text)	0.164 (0.131)	−0.410	0.090	0.1521	0.241	2.04
S/K	Sales/capital $=x_{12}/k_8(t-1)$	5.03 (3.36)	0.518	2.86	4.27	6.21	30.4
OI/K	(Operating income)/capital $=x_{13}/k_8(t-1)$	0.467 (0.392)	−1.23	0.237	0.419	0.637	3.86
CF/K	(Cash flow)/capital $=(x_{18}+x_{14})/x_8(t-1)$	0.291 (0.291)	−0.976	0.148	0.274	0.427	2.44
I/K	(Gross investment)/capital $=x_{30}/k_8(t-1)$	0.227 (0.175)	0.013	0.119	0.185	0.280	1.56
CE/K	(Cash and equivalents)/capital $=x_1/k_8(t-1)$	0.271 (0.372)	0.00	0.045	0.129	0.344	4.13
FW/K	(Financial working capital)/capital $=(x_4-x_5+x_3)/x_8(t-1)$	0.218 (0.548)	−1.00	−0.092	0.122	0.441	2.98
TD/K	(Total debt)/capital $=(x_{34}+x_9)/x_8(t-1)$	1.01 (0.825)	0.001	0.481	0.764	1.27	7.64
TQ	Tobin's Q $=(x_{25}x_{199}+10x_{19}+x_{181})/x_6$	1.47 (0.955)	0.170	0.972	1.17	1.48	12.0

The notation x_{99} refers to Compustat data item 99, etc.

ing, Abel and Blanchard (1986) used the average profitability of capital to measure MPK. In Gilchrist and Himmelberg (1995), we constructed a similar measure with firm-level data by using the ratio of operating income to capital. In hindsight, we think the assumptions necessary to make this approximation—zero fixed costs and perfect competition—are unreasonable at the firm level.[9] The sales-based measure described in the previous section is our preferred measure, for reasons which we explain in this section.

Working from the firm's objective function in equation (2.1), an alternative representation of the marginal profit is

$$\frac{\partial \pi}{\partial k} = \varphi \left(\frac{\pi}{k} + \frac{F}{k} + \eta^{-1} \frac{py}{k} \right), \tag{2.3}$$

where $\varphi = \alpha_k/(\alpha_k + \alpha_n - \gamma)$.[10] With accounting data, we observe π/k and py/k, but not F. Hence, to use equation (2.3), we must assume fixed costs are zero, so that $F = 0$. Moreover, η and φ cannot be separately identified without access to additional data, so it is also necessary to at least assume that η^{-1} is constant across industries; more conventionally, perfect competition is assumed, so that $\eta^{-1} = 0$. Under these assumptions, a measure of MPK based on operating income is given by

$$\frac{\partial \pi}{\partial k} = \varphi \frac{\pi}{k} . \tag{2.4}$$

Just as we used industry estimates of θ_j to adjust the sales-to-capital ratio, we implement equation (2.4) using industry estimates of the capital share of variable profits, φ_j. Thus, a second measure of MPK is given by

$$MPK2_{it} = \hat{\varphi}_j \frac{oi_{it}}{k_{it}},$$

9. In defense of Abel and Blanchard (1986), one advantage of using aggregate data is the availability of prices and wages, which make it possible to construct variable costs. At the firm level, however, only total costs are available, so variable costs are unmeasurable unless we assume fixed costs are zero.

10. The derivation of equation (2.3) follows from the first-order condition for variable inputs, $(1 + \eta^{-1})\alpha_x py = wx$. The returns-to-scale parameter γ is defined so that the factor shares sum to $1 + \gamma$, i.e., $\alpha_x + \alpha_k + \alpha_n = 1 + \gamma$, so that constant returns would imply $\gamma = 0$. Substituting for α_x in the first-order condition and rearranging, we find $(1 + \eta^{-1})(\alpha_k + \alpha_n - \gamma)py = (1 + \eta^{-1})py - wx$. Using $\pi + F = py - wx$, this can be written

$$(1 + \eta^{-1})\alpha_k py = \frac{\alpha_k}{\alpha_k + \alpha_n - \gamma}(\pi + F + \eta^{-1}py).$$

Dividing both sides by k gives the desired result. Note that if $\gamma = 0$, then $\varphi = \alpha_k/(\alpha_k + \alpha_n)$ is simply the capital share of quasifixed inputs.

where oi_{it} denotes operating income.

It is important to stress that for our purposes, MPK2 is less desirable than MPK1. This is because the accuracy of MPK2 requires the added assumptions of zero fixed costs and perfect competition, whereas MPK1 does not. In other words, MPK2 is a noisier measure of MPK. But the most important shortcoming of MPK2 is that the noise component is correlated with cash flow, and thus MPK2 could spuriously attribute cash-flow fluctuations to changes in MPK. This distinction is obviously important, because MPK is what matters for fundamental explanations, whereas cash flow is more likely to matter for financial reasons. The empirical results in this paper exploit this difference.

2.3 MEASURING CASH FLOW

Our accounting definition of cash flow is net income before extraordinary items plus depreciation. Equivalently, cash flow is operating income before depreciation and minus taxes, minus interest payments, plus nonoperating income, plus special items. To provide a feel for relative magnitudes, Table 3 reports the aggregate income sheet for the Compustat universe of manufacturing firms in 1988.

With respect to the terms in Equation (2.3), *py* corresponds to sales, while $wx + F$ corresponds to cost of goods sold plus selling, general, and administrative expenses. It is therefore not possible with accounting data to disentangle variable and fixed costs. This is one of the reasons we gave in the previous section for preferring MPK1 over MPK2.

In equation 2.3, the difference between marginal and average profits introduced scope for identifying changes in cash flow distinct from changes in MPK. Our definition of cash flow provides additional sources of independent variation from MPK, because it treats taxes payable and

Table 3 AGGREGATE INCOME STATEMENT IN 1988 (PERCENTAGE OF SALES)

Sales	
−Cost of goods sold	67.6
−Selling, general, and administrative expenses	17.6
Operating income before depreciation	14.9
−taxes payable	3.6
−interest payments	2.2
+(−) Nonoperating income	1.8
+(−) Special items	0.0
Cash flow	10.9
−depreciation	5.0
Net income before extraordinary items	5.9

interest payments as fixed charges.[11] In addition, as the table shows, many firms generate internal funds from financial investments and other nonoperating assets. These funds provide a third source of cash-flow variation, which is distinct from MPK variation.

Our definition of cash flow is only partly correlated with operating income, which in turn is only partly correlated with MPK. This is an important empirical distinction which previous authors (including Gilchrist and Himmelberg, 1995) have failed to exploit. We exploit this difference below to distinguish the investment response to pure cash-flow shocks from the response to mere MPK shocks.

2.4 PANEL-DATA VECTOR AUTOREGRESSIONS

It is uncommon to see VARs estimated with panel data, and VARs have not been widely used in the investment literature, so we provide a brief discussion of the (minimal) econometric assumptions for their estimation with panel data. Without loss of generality, consider the following VAR(1) with fixed firm effects and year effects:

$$y_{it} = A y_{it-1} + f_i + d_t + u_{it},$$

where A is a $k \times k$ matrix of slope coefficients, f_i is a $k \times 1$ vector of (unobserved) firm effects, and d_t is $k \times 1$ vector of year effects (to be estimated). In this paper, y_{it} will generally consist of a $k \times 1$ vector of firm-level state variables and decision variables that will include variables like investment, MPK, and cash flow. More generally, this notation will be used to describe the companion form of a VAR(p) model for y_{it}. In either case, the matrix of parameters A is redefined accordingly.

A VAR model provides a surprisingly flexible framework for describing the dynamic relationship among firm-level panel data. For one, the inclusion of the time effects d_t accommodates aggregate shocks to y_{it} that are common across firms. Thus, to the extent that there may be common movements to interest rates or other macroeconomic conditions that are not captured by lagged y_{it}, these factors will be captured by time dummies. In addition, under the assumption that $E(u_{it}) = 0$ and $E(u_{it}u'_{it}) = \Omega_i$ (and conditional on $\{d_t\}_{t=1}^T$, where the d_t's are parameters that will be estimated), y_{it} has unconditional mean and variance given by $E(y_{it}) = (I - A)^{-1}f_i$ and $\text{Var}(y_{it}) = (I - A)^{-1}\Omega_i(I - A)^{-1}$. Thus, while the model imposes the same slope coefficients A across firms, it imposes no restrictions on the unconditional mean and variance of y_{it}. This is an important feature

---

11. We do not need to assume that current interest and tax payments are strictly predetermined. Rather, we only assume that to the extent they are endogenous, they are determined by factors independently of the decision to invest.

of the model, since the unconditional means and variances of most firm-level variables display substantial cross-sectional heterogeneity.

The estimation of panel-data VARs has been discussed by Holtz-Eakin, Newey, and Rosen (1988), among others, and they show that panel data pose no particular problem for the estimation of VARs. In fact, asymptotic results are, if anything, easier to derive for panel data than for time series. We mention this because it is still common to encounter confusion (usually among macroeconomists) over the feasibility of estimating a time-series model (such as a VAR) using only a few years of data. Because the sampling properties depend on the number of cross-sectional observations, not the number of time-series observations, it is technically possible, for example, to estimate an AR1 on a panel with as few as 3 years of data, although it is preferable to have panels with 5 or more years (because this increases the availability of instruments required for the estimation technique described below). All that is required is that the slope coefficients be the same across observations in the cross section. Estimation does not require homogeneity of the intercepts or the variances of the error terms. More details on the econometrics are included in the appendix.

2.5 THE DATA

Our data set is a firm-level panel of annual data on firms drawn from the Compustat universe of manufacturing firms from 1980 to 1993. We sampled every available firm–year observation during this time period without regard to whether the firm was in existence for the length of the time period; that is, we did *not* require a balanced panel. We then removed observations for which the data required to construct the variables in Table 2 were not available. We also imposed outlier rules on the Table 2 variables by removing observations that fell below the first or above the 99th percentile. Rules of this sort are both common and necessary when working with large panels, because some firms have very small (measured) capital stocks, and these cause large outliers when capital appears in the denominator as a scaling variable.[12]

12. To deal with large discrete changes in firm identity due to large mergers, acquisitions, and divestitures, we deleted observations which had large outliers in the amount by which the percentage change in the capital stock differed from the gross investment rate net of depreciation. For robustness issues, when estimating structural models, we considered financial variables that were ratios of both capital and debt. Because these financial variables have more dispersion in the tails, the forecasting equations used in our structural estimates were in some cases less precise without more stringent outlier rules for these variables. We therefore imposed the additional requirements that the ratios CE/debt and FW/K be within $(-1,3)$. These rules are approximately equivalent to trimming the tails of these variables at the 2% level.

2.6 IDENTIFICATION USING RECURSIVELY ORDERED VECTOR AUTOREGRESSIONS

When interpreting the effect of cash flow on investment, the primary identification problem is to distinguish the information revealed about future MPKs from the information revealed about the financial condition of the firm. One way to make this distinction is by using a *structural* VAR, which imposes restrictions on the contemporaneous shocks but not on the coefficients of lagged variables. In our empirical specification, we estimate a three-variable, two-lag VAR that controls for fixed firm and year effects. The VAR variables are I/K, the ratio of gross investment to capital; MPK, the marginal profit of capital (based on sales as described in the previous section); and CF/K, the ratio of cash flow to capital. In the context of this VAR system, there are two issues that affect the interpretation of cash flow in the investment equation as evidence of a financing effect.

The first issue, of which the literature has long been aware, is that even after conditioning on lagged investment and MPK, lagged cash flow can still contain information about the future marginal profitability of capital. In this case, the responsiveness of investment to cash flow simply reflects the fact that we are estimating a forward-looking decision rule, and that CF/K belongs in the information set. The second issue is that it is difficult to identify the effects of contemporaneous cash-flow shocks on investment. To deal with this issue, we postulate a causal relationship among contemporaneous shocks that is obtained from a standard Cholesky decomposition using the ordering I/K, MPK, CF/K. This ordering allows for the possibility that I/K shocks contemporaneously cause movements in cash flow and MPK, but assumes there is no feedback (contemporaneously) from MPK shocks to I/K, or from cash flow to MPK.

This ordering is particularly interesting for investigating the effect of cash flow's financing role because orthogonal cash-flow shocks, by construction, contain no information about current MPK. While this represents progress toward identifying pure cash-flow effects, it does not confront the first issue. That is, while our orthogonal cash-flow shocks are uncorrelated with current MPK, they may nonetheless be correlated with *future* MPK. Thus, when using the impulse response functions to interpret the dynamic response of investment to orthogonal cash-flow shocks, it is important to inspect the dynamic response of MPK for evidence that the cash-flow shock predicts future marginal profits.

We report the impulse response of investment to both MPK shocks and cash-flow shocks, where the residuals are orthogonalized using the

Table 4 SELECTED IMPULSE RESPONSE FUNCTIONS

Shock	Variable	*Response*						
		$T=0$	$T=1$	$T=2$	$T=3$	$T=4$	$T=5$	$T=6$
MPK	$(I/K)_{it}$	0.00	0.021	0.01	0.004	0.002	0.001	0.00
	$MPK1_{it}$	0.041	0.031	0.02	0.012	0.008	0.005	0.003
	$(CF/K)_{it}$	0.079	0.054	0.028	0.016	0.009	0.005	0.003
Cash flow	$(I/K)_{it}$	0.00	0.034	0.02	0.011	0.006	0.003	0.001
	$MPK1_{it}$	0.00	0.003	−0.001	−0.003	−0.003	−0.003	−0.002
	$(CF/K)_{it}$	0.184	0.074	0.034	0.014	0.005	0.001	0.00

Impulse response functions based on a two-lag VAR for investment, MPK, and cash flow. Impulse response functions show the response to a one-standard-deviation shock.

decomposition described above. The top part of Table 4 reports the impulse response of all three variables to the MPK shock. As expected, investment, MPK and cash flow all rise in response to such a shock, with the effect persisting over a two- to three-year horizon before returning slowly to steady state.

The bottom part of Table 4 reports the response of investment to a cash-flow shock that is orthogonal to MPK. In this case investment responds positively to cash flow (the magnitude of response here is actually slightly larger than for the MPK shock), despite the fact that the marginal profitability of capital falls in response to such a shock. Thus, while fundamentals are falling, investment is rising. These results suggest that the positive investment response to cash flow is not caused by the predictive content of cash flow for future investment opportunities. Indeed, the negative response of future MPK implies that the impulse response for investment understates the full magnitude of the financing effect.[13]

In summary, reduced-form VAR analysis shows that investment re-

---

13. It is possible that, in addition to financial factors, cash flow also captures information about cost shocks that are not reflected in our sales-based fundamental. Under the assumption of Cobb–Douglas production, our measure of MPK captures the influence of both cost shocks and demand shocks on the marginal profitability of capital. If there are large deviations from Cobb–Douglas production, however, then cost shocks may be an issue. To investigate this possibility, we augmented our VAR framework by adding the ratio of cost of goods sold to capital (COG/K) as another variable in the VAR. We then considered a shock to cash flow that was orthogonal to I/K, MPK, and COG/K. We still obtain the result that investment responds positively to cash flow even though fundamentals are falling. Indeed, the quantitative results from this exercise are very close to those reported in Table 4. Thus, it seems unlikely that unmeasured variations in costs are driving this result.

sponds to both fundamentals (as measured by MPK) and financial factors (as measured by cash flow). The positive investment response to cash-flow shocks cannot be attributed to rising profit opportunities using our measure of the marginal profitability of capital, and is therefore most likely to be explained by financial frictions that generate excess sensitivity of investment to cash-flow shocks. While these results suggest that financial factors influence investment at the firm level, this exercise is limited in its ability to provide an economic description of the exact channel through capital-market imperfections influence investment dynamics. To say more, it is necessary to consider the more structural approach provided in the next section.

3. A Model of Investment with Financial Frictions

In this section we develop a model of investment with financial frictions that is similar to models that have been explored in the literature. The goal here is not to show how financial frictions can be integrated into the standard investment model, but to show how the resulting model, which is nonlinear, can be linearized to obtain a tractable dynamic system of equations that describe the joint evolution of investment, MPK, and financial variables. This framework includes the standard Q model of investment as a special case.

Let $\Pi(K_t, \xi_t)$ denote the maximized value of current profits taking as given the beginning-of-period capital stock, K_t, and a profitability shock, ξ_t. For the time being, we make no assumptions regarding the nature of returns to scale or competition in the product and factor markets, other than to assume that the profit function is concave and bounded. The time to build and install one unit of capital is one period,[14] where δ is the rate of capital depreciation and I_t is the investment expenditure, so that the capital stock evolves according to the equation $K_{t+1} = (1 - \delta)K_t + I_t$. Finally, as is common in the literature, we assume that $C(I_t, K_t)$ is the resource cost of installing I_t units of capital.[15] For simplicity, the numeraire is the price of capital.

14. The true time to build is probably somewhere closer to six months, for which we have no corresponding assumption using annual data. In the absence of a strong empirical motive, a good theoretical reason for assuming one-period time to build is that it simplifies the inversion of the marginal adjustment cost function.
15. Future research could investigate alternative adjustment cost technologies designed to deal with asymmetries and nonconvexities, such as those developed by Abel and Eberly (1994, 1996) and Caballero (1997). Under one such alternative specification of adjustment costs, Caballero and Leahy (1996) show why average Q may be theoretically more effective than marginal Q for explaining investment. Recent papers by Goolsbee and Gross (1997) and Caballero and Engel (1998) provide empirical evidence on the importance of such factors.

A simple way to incorporate financial frictions is to assume that the marginal source of external finance is debt, and to assume that risk-neutral debt holders demand an external finance premium, $\eta_t = \eta(K_t, B_t, \xi_t)$, which in general depends on the entire state vector of the firm, and is increasing in the amount borrowed ($\partial\eta/\partial B > 0$). The idea is that highly leveraged firms have to pay an additional premium to compensate debt holders for increased costs due to information problems (e.g., *ex post* monitoring costs and/or moral hazard costs). While previous researchers have derived this premium in equilibrium,[16] it is sufficient for our purposes to postulate the existence of such a function, and to assume that this function is increasing in the debt level. Hence, we assume that the gross required rate of return on debt is $(1 + r_t) [1 + \eta(K_t, B_t, \xi_t)]$, where r_t is the risk-free rate of return.

We have in mind that B_t summarizes the firm's net financial liabilities (bank debt, trade debt, cash holdings, etc.). This is the simplest possible model of financial assets and liabilities. In our empirical work, we consider several alternative definitions of B_t, one measure being long-term debt minus the net short-term financial assets of the firm, i.e., long-term debt minus financial working capital. Alternative specifications of B_t and $\eta(K_t, B_t, \xi_t)$ could be easily investigated.[17]

To guarantee that debt (and not equity) is the firm's marginal source of finance, we need either to assume a binding non-negativity constraint on dividends, or to assume that equity holders prefer to have dividends paid out rather than reinvested. One way to make this operational is to assume a utility function for dividends (e.g. Gross, 1997). This assumption is particularly useful when constructing numerical solutions to the model, because it avoids corner solutions. For our purposes, however, it is sufficient to display a model that generates a *shadow cost* of equity, and the simplest way to this is to assume that dividends cannot be negative (i.e., that marginal equity is prohibitively expensive).

For simplicity, assume a constant price of new capital goods, normalized at unity, and let $(1 + r_t)^{-1}$ be the *ex ante* one-period discount factor used to value period-$t + 1$ dividends at time t. Then the manager's problem is

$$V(K_t, B_t, \xi_t) = \max_{\{I_{t+s}, B_{t+s+1}\}_{s=0}^{\infty}} D_t + E_t \sum_{s=1}^{\infty} \left(\prod_{k=1}^{s} (1 + r_{t+k})^{-1} \right) D_{t+s}$$

subject to

16. For example, Moyen (1997) derives an equilibrium debt premium generated by default costs.

17. Future research on the underlying sources of capital-market frictions could usefully guide future empirical work by suggesting appropriate functional forms for η and λ.

$$D_t = \Pi(K_t, \xi_t) - C(I_t, K_t) - I_t + B_{t+1} - (1 + r_t)[1 + \eta(B_t, K_t, \xi_t)]B_t,$$
$$K_{t+1} = (1 - \delta)K_t + I_t,$$
$$D_t \geq 0,$$

where E_t is the exceptions operator conditional on the time-t information set Ω_t.

To see the effect of financial frictions, let λ_t be the Lagrange multiplier for the non-negativity constraint on dividends. The multiplier λ_t indicates the shadow value of paying a negative dividend, and can thus be interpreted economically as the shadow cost of internally generated funds. The role of this shadow cost in the firm's investment decision is exposed by deriving the Euler equation for investment[18]:

$$1 + \frac{\partial C(I_t, K_t)}{\partial I_t}$$
$$= E_t \left\{ \frac{1}{1 + r_t} \left(\frac{1 + \lambda_{t+1}}{1 + \lambda_t} \right) \left[\frac{\partial D_{t+1}}{\partial K_{t+1}} + (1 - \delta) \left(1 + \frac{\partial C(I_{t+1}, K_{t+1})}{\partial I_{t+1}} \right) \right] \right\}. \quad (3.1)$$

If $\lambda_{t+1} = \lambda_t = 0$ and $\eta_t = 0$, then the shadow cost of internal funds is one, and the Euler equation is identical to the one provided by the perfect-capital-markets model. In the presence of financial market imperfections, however, $\lambda_t = \lambda(K_t, B_t, \xi_t)$ and $\eta_t = \eta(K_t, B_t, \xi_t)$ are state-dependent and time-varying.[19] The first-order condition for debt requires that

$$E_t \left[\frac{1 + \lambda_{t+1}}{1 + \lambda_t} \left(1 + \eta_{t+1} + \frac{\partial \eta_{t+1}}{\partial B_{t+1}} B_{t+1} \right) \right] = 1.$$

The marginal cost of debt determines the shadow cost of funds today vs. tomorrow (i.e., λ_t vs. λ_{t+1}), and hence provides a time-varying discount factor that depends on the level of net financial liabilities, B_t (among

18. A number of papers in the literature estimate this Euler equation directly by assuming a parametric form for the shadow cost term: Himmelberg (1990), Whited (1992), Hubbard and Kashyap (1992), Hubbard, Kashyap, and Whited (1995), and Jaramillo, Schianterelli, and Weiss (1996).

19. While it is not necessary to resolve such issues for our empirical specification, it is interesting to ask under what conditions the premium on external funds is likely to be stationary. For simplicity, suppose η_{t+1} doesn't depend on θ_{t+1}, so that we can ignore the expectations operator (B_{t+1} and K_{t+1} are known at time t). Then in steady state, a constrained firm would have $\lambda_t = \lambda_{t+1}$, which implies $(\partial \eta / \partial B)B + \eta = 0$. Since $\partial \eta / \partial B > 0$, we would observe $B > 0$ only if $\eta < 0$. This is possible if, for example, the premium η is net of tax advantages or agency benefits. That is, despite the positive marginal premium on debt, the average premium might be negative. In a more general model, a steady-state equilibrium with $\partial \eta / \partial B > 0$ could be maintained by modeling managers as "impatient." In Bernanke, Gertler, and Gilchrist (1998), for example, exogenous firm "failure" generates this behavior.

other state variables). This point is general and does not depend in any specific way on our particular dividend assumption.

3.1 A LINEARIZED EMPIRICAL FRAMEWORK

Let $c(I_t, K_t)$ denote the *marginal* adjustment cost function, and let MPK_t denote the marginal profit function net of adjustment costs and financing costs.[20] For simplicity, assume the discount rate r_t is constant over time and over firms (in the discussion below, we explain how this assumption could easily be relaxed). Then the first-order conditions for the above model with financial frictions can be written

$$1 + c(I_t, K_t) = E_t \sum_{s=1}^{\infty} \left[\prod_{k=1}^{s} \frac{1-\delta}{1+r} \left(\frac{1 + \lambda_{t+k}}{1 + \lambda_{t+k-1}} \right) \right] \mathrm{MPK}_{t+s}$$

$$= E_t \sum_{s=1}^{\infty} \left(\frac{1-\delta}{1+r} \right)^s \left(\prod_{k=1}^{s} \frac{1 + \lambda_{t+k}}{1 + \lambda_{t+k-1}} \right) \mathrm{MPK}_{t+s}$$

$$= E_t \sum_{s=1}^{\infty} \beta^s \Theta_{t,t+s} \mathrm{MPK}_{t+s}$$

where the discount factor has been factored into a deterministic component, $\beta = (1-\delta)/(1+r)$, times a stochastic component $\Theta_{t,t+s} \Pi_{k=1}^{s} (1 + \lambda_{t+k})/(1 + \lambda_{t+k-1})$, which in general will be a function of firm-level variables.

Since the mean of $\Theta_{t,t+s}$ should be near one, we can use a first-order Taylor approximation around $E(\Theta_{t,t+s}) \simeq 1$ and $E(\mathrm{MPK}_{t+s}) \simeq \gamma$ to write

$$\Theta_{t,t+s} \mathrm{MPK}_{t+s} \simeq \gamma_0 + \gamma \Theta_{t,t+s} + \mathrm{MPK}_{t+s}.$$

Furthermore, we can approximate the expression for $\Theta_{t,t+s}$ to get

$$\Theta_{t,t+s} = \prod_{k=1}^{s} \frac{1 + \lambda_{t+k}}{1 + \lambda_{t+k-1}}$$

$$\simeq 1 + \sum_{k=1}^{s} \frac{\lambda_{t+k} - \lambda_{t+k-1}}{1 + \lambda_{t+k-1}}$$

$$\simeq \mathrm{const} + \sum_{k=1}^{s} \phi \mathrm{FIN}_{t+k},$$

where we have assumed that $(\lambda_{t+k} - \lambda_{t+k-1})/(1 + \lambda_{t+k-1}) = \phi_0 + \phi \mathrm{FIN}_{t+k}$ is a linear approximation representing the dependence of the shadow discount term on a financial state variable represented by FIN_{t+k}. This functional form assumption for $\Theta_{t,t+s}$ obviously allows us to specify FIN either as net financial liabilities (i.e., B_t), in which case the predicted sign of ϕ is negative, or as net financial assets (i.e., $-B_t$), in which case the predicted

20. In our empirical work, we ignore the marginal reduction of financing costs in our construction of MPK because it is a small effect relative to $\partial \Pi / \partial K$.

sign of ϕ is positive. In our empirical work, we prefer to work with net financial assets.

Note that with additional notation, we could have allowed the stochastic component of the discount factor, $\Theta_{t,t+s}$, to include a time-varying discount factor, r_t. Then the above linearization would include an additional term capturing the effect of r_t. In our empirical work, the inclusion of time dummies in our panel-data regressions accommodates time-varying discount rates. By the same logic, allowing for firm fixed effects accommodates firm-specific discount rates attributable to differences in the average firm-level "beta" as well as differences in the average level of the firm's external finance premium.

It is useful at this point to briefly consider what would constitute a plausible range of values of ϕ for our model. One way to do this is to consider a plausible range of variation for the premium on external funds across firms. Letting σ_r represent the standard deviation of the net external finance premium, our model suggests that $\sigma_r \simeq \phi\sigma_{\text{Fin}}$. Calomiris and Himmelberg (1998) report that the standard deviation for underwriting spreads for seasoned equity issues is 5.8%. For annual data, the measured premium on average loan rates can easily vary by 5 percentage points across firms, or over time for a given firm. Thus a range of 5% to 10% seems reasonable for the *marginal* premium on external funds. In our empirical work below, we use the ratio of cash and equivalents to capital as one measure of FIN_t. This variable has a standard deviation of 0.37, implying that a ballpark figure for ϕ is on the order of 0.1 to 0.3.

Substituting the above approximations for $\Theta_{t,t+s}\text{MPK}_{t+s}$ and $\Theta_{t,t+s}$ into the present value and collecting constant terms yields

$$
\begin{aligned}
1 + c(I_t, K_t) &= E_t \sum_{s=1}^{\infty} \beta^s \Theta_{t,t+s} \text{MPK}_{t+s} \\
&= \text{const} + \gamma E_t \sum_{s=1}^{\infty} \beta^s \Theta_{t,t+s} + E_t \sum_{s=1}^{\infty} \beta^s \text{MPK}_{t+s} \\
&= \text{const} + \gamma\phi E_t \sum_{s=1}^{\infty} \sum_{k=1}^{s} \beta^s \text{FIN}_{t+k} + E_t \sum_{s=1}^{\infty} \beta^s \text{MPK}_{t+s}.
\end{aligned}
$$

Estimation requires a functional form for adjustment costs. Following standard practice, we assume that $C(I_t, K_t)$ is quadratic in I_t/K_t, so that marginal adjustment costs are linear in I_t/K_t. We also extend the specification to include a technology shock ω_t. Thus, the marginal adjustment cost function is assumed to be

$$
c(I_t, K_t) = \text{const} + \alpha^{-1}(I/K)_t - \omega_t.
$$

Under this specification of the adjustment cost technology, the relationship between investment, the present value of future FIN_t, and the present value of future MPK_t is given by

$$(I/K)_t = \text{const} + \alpha\gamma\phi E_t \sum_{s=1}^{\infty} \sum_{k=1}^{s} \beta^s \, FIN_{t+k} + \alpha E_t \sum_{s=1}^{\infty} \beta^s \, MPK_{t+s} + \omega_t. \tag{3.2}$$

The standard Q-model of investment is a special case of the above model where $\phi = 0$, and the model is typically estimated using Tobin's Q as a proxy for the present value of future marginal profits, i.e., $Q_t = E_t \Sigma_{s=1}^{\infty} \beta^s MPK_{t+s}$. With financial frictions, however, Tobin's Q-values not only future MPK, but also changes in the expected financial status of the firm, $E_t \Sigma_{s=1}^{\infty} \Sigma_{k=1}^{s} \beta^s FIN_{t+k}$. Thus Tobin's Q would appear to be a poor choice for estimating investment models when the goal is to identify financial frictions.[21] We elaborate on this point in Section 4. As an alternative to using Tobin's Q, we propose the method used by Abel and Blanchard (1986) and Gilchrist and Himmelberg (1995), which constructs present-value terms by estimating a VAR for the vector of state variables that help to forecast MPK_t and FIN_t.

3.2 THE EXPECTED PRESENT VALUE OF MPK AND FINANCIAL FACTORS USING VAR FORECASTS

In our notation, we now add the subscript i to index firm-level variables. To construct this expectation using a VAR model of the firm's state vector, let x_{it} be a vector containing current and lagged values of MPK_{it}, FIN_{it}, and any other variables containing information that can be used to forecast the future marginal profitability of investment.[22] This information $x_{it-1} \subseteq \Omega_t$ is available at time t when the firm i makes its investment decision. We assume that these variables follow an autoregressive process, and to simplify notation, we write this VAR in companion form as

$$x_{it} = Ax_{it-1} + u_{it},$$

21. Under some specifications of the external finance premium, it is possible to show that Tobin's Q remains a sufficient statistic for investment (see Chirinko, 1993). This further shows why Tobin's Q is a poor choice for estimating investment models when the goal is to detect and quantify the importance of financing constraints. For further evidence on this point, see the simulation results reported by Gomes (1997).

22. The variables included in the forecast VAR should not include lagged investment. In theory, it is feasible and even desirable to include lagged investment in the forecast VAR, but doing so makes it much more difficult to impose the cross-equation restrictions. This is a difficult methodological issue on which we are currently working and which we hope to explore in a future paper.

and we assume $E(u_{it}|x_{it-1}) = 0$. By recursive substitution, the conditional expectation of x_{it+s} given x_{it-1} is easily seen to be

$$E[x_{it+s}|x_{it-1}] = A^{s+1}x_{it-1}.$$

Let MPK_{it} be the first element of x_{it}, and let FIN_{it} be the second element. If we let c_j denote a vector of zeros with a one in the jth position, then $MPK_{it} = c_1'x_{it}$ and $FIN_{it} = c_2'x_{it}$. Using this notation, the expected present value of MPK is given by

$$
\begin{aligned}
PV_{it}^{MPK} &= E_{it} \sum_{s=1}^{\infty} \beta^s \, MPK_{it+s} \\
&= \sum_{s=1}^{\infty} \beta^s E[MPK_{it+s}|x_{it-1}] \\
&= c_1' \sum_{s=1}^{\infty} \beta^s A^{s+1} x_{it-1} \\
&= c_1'(I - \beta A)^{-1}\beta A^2 x_{it-1}.
\end{aligned}
$$

Analogously, using our notation $FIN_{it} = c_2'x_{it}$, the expected present value of financial factors is given by[23]

$$
\begin{aligned}
PV_{it}^{FIN} &= E_t \sum_{s=1}^{\infty} \sum_{k=1}^{s} \beta^s \, FIN_{t+k} \\
&= \sum_{s=1}^{\infty} \sum_{k=1}^{s} \beta^s \, E[FIN_{it+k}|x_{it-1}] \\
&= c_2' \sum_{s=1}^{\infty} \sum_{k=1}^{s} \beta^s A^{k+1} x_{it-1} \\
&= c_2'(1 - \beta)^{-1}(I - \beta A)^{-1}\beta a^2 x_{it-1}.
\end{aligned}
$$

These present-value formulae allow us to specify a structural reduced-form model of investment that is linear in x_i:

$$(I/K)_{it} = \text{const} + \alpha(PV_{it}^{MPK}) + \alpha\gamma\phi(PV_{it}^{FIN}) + f_i + d_t + \omega_{it}, \tag{3.3}$$

The terms f_i and d_t represent fixed firm and year effects that are controlled for in the estimation. The residual satisfies the moment condition $E[\omega_{it}x_{it-s}] = 0$ for all s, so all lagged values of x_{it} are valid for estimation.

---

23. Here we make use of the result that $\sum_{s=1}^{\infty}\beta^s \sum_{k=1}^{s} A^k = (1 - \beta)^{-1}(I - \beta A)^{-1}\beta A$.

4. Model Implications and a Discussion of the Recent Investment Literature on Financing Constraints

The empirical framework in the previous section shows that in a (linearized) model with financial frictions, investment is a function of both (1) the expected present value of future MPKs, or *fundamental Q*, and (2) the expected present value of future financial state variables of the firm, or *financial Q*. That is,

$$(I/K)_t = \underbrace{\alpha E_t \sum_{s=1}^{\infty} \beta^s \text{MPK}_{t+s}}_{\text{fundamental } Q} + \underbrace{\alpha \gamma \phi E_t \sum_{s=1}^{\infty} \sum_{k=1}^{s} \beta^s \text{FIN}_{t+k}}_{\text{financial } Q}.$$

Although the above equation has not been used in past research, it nevertheless explains the intuition underlying many of the empirical specifications in the literature surveyed by Hubbard (1998). Specifically, it shows that investment equations based only on fundamental Q contain an omitted variable in the error term, so that investment will appear to be excessively sensitive to any explanatory variable (e.g., cash flow) that helps to predict current or future values of FIN_t. This equation also shows that investment can be excessively sensitive even to nonfinancial variables such as sales growth, provided such variables help to forecast future financial conditions.

While it is easy in theory to see why investment should be excessively sensitive to variables that are correlated with financial Q, it is difficult in practice to assign econometric interpretations to the explanatory variables in a reduced-form regression. The interpretation of cash flow, for example, is not obvious, because it could predict fundamental Q as well as financial Q. By the same logic, the role of Tobin's Q is theoretically ambiguous, because Tobin's Q measures the average value of capital, and this is closely related to financial Q in some theoretical models. In Gertler (1992), for example, the firm's net worth determines the degree to which external investors can write contracts that reduce moral hazard on the part of insiders, and thus determines the severity of financing constraints. In his model, or in any model where the specification of the financial friction depends on net worth, Tobin's Q will contain information about both fundamental Q and financial Q, and will therefore be difficult to interpret in the absence of more model structure.[24]

24. There are additional problems in the empirical literature that are usefully viewed in the context of the above model. First, as we argued in Gilchrist and Himmelberg (1995), there are reasons to believe that Tobin's Q is a poor proxy for fundamental Q. For example, if firms enjoy market power, or if firms employ multiple quasifixed factor inputs, or if Tobin's Q is measured with noise, then Tobin's Q will not be a sufficient

A recent paper by Cummins, Hassett, and Oliner (1997) provides a useful illustration of this problem. In their paper, the idea is to use analysts' earnings forecasts to construct fundamental Q. They use data obtained from IBES, which provides forecasts at one-year and two-year horizons, $f1_{it}$ and $f2_{it}$, as well as forecasts of the expected annual growth rate, g_{it}, of earnings in years 3 through 5. Assuming a discount rate β, they approximate the present value of earnings by assuming that earnings continue to grow at the rate g_{it} for 10 years. Thus, they assume the present value of earnings is well approximated by[25]

$$PV_{it}^{EARN} = \beta\, f1_{it} + \beta^2 \left(\sum_{s=0}^{8} \beta^s (1 + g_{it})^s \right) f2_{it}.$$

Defining "fundamental Q" as PV_{it}^{EARN}/K_{it}, they regress investment on this measure of fundamental Q and current earnings and report that investment displays no "excess sensitivity" to current earnings.[26] But does PV_{it}^{EARN}/K_{it} measure fundamental Q or financial Q? Our model makes it clear that identification requires two separate terms; at best, PV_{it}^{EARN}/K_{it} combines these two Q-variables into one term. Indeed, PV_{it}^{EARN}/K_{it} is conceivably a better measure of financial Q than of fundamental Q,

---

statistic for fundamental Q, and investment will display excess sensitivity to any variable (including financial variables) that contains forecast information for the future marginal profitability of capital. In other words, poor proxies for fundamental Q may spuriously give rise to excess cash-flow sensitivity and thus overstate the importance of financial Q. For this reason, the literature has generally placed more emphasis on the fact that cash-flow sensitivity tends to be greater for firms that are more likely to face financial frictions on the basis of some *a priori* measure (such as size, dividend payout, or access to public debt markets). Even so, the interpretation of excess cash-flow sensitivities remains controversial. See the critique by Kaplan and Zingales (1997) and the rebuttal by Fazzari, Hubbard, and Petersen (1996).

25. Strictly speaking, they do not report this equation, but this is what we infer based on our reading of the verbal description in their paper.

26. In addition to their conceptual failure to distinguish between fundamental Q and financial Q, we have some doubts about the robustness of their empirical results. We have examined the IBES data ourselves, and in contrast to the claims made by Cummins, Hassett, and Oliner, we do not find that the inclusion of earnings forecasts eliminates the explanatory power of cash flow and other balance-sheet variables. We have not yet been able to trace the sources of this discrepancy, but one possible explanation may be the fact that Cummins, Hassett, and Oliner use IBES earnings per share (EPS) and shares outstanding to construct current total earnings. This is problematic, because the number of shares reported by IBES corresponds to the number outstanding on the date of the *forecast* and does not correspond to the number outstanding on the date of the *fiscal year end*. Stock splits and other share adjustments make this calculation impossible. When we use Compustat cash flow and earnings measures instead of IBES earnings, we find no evidence to suggest that earnings forecasts are sufficient statistics for investment. In the end, however, the robustness of their results is a red herring. Our main objection is conceptual, because the present value of earnings is a good measure of financial Q.

because the only difference between earnings and cash flow is depreciation, whereas it is a long way from earnings to MPK1 (see the discussion in Section 2.1.1, and the income sheet reported in Section 2.2).

5. Empirical Results on the Structural Model

In this section of the paper we explore the extent to which investment responds to fundamental Q versus financial Q in our structural model. We begin our analysis using the full sample. We then look at how our results vary across subsamples where the data are split based on indicators that capture a firm's likely degree of access to finance.

The estimates of equation (3.3) described in the previous section are constructed as follows. First, a VAR(2) is specified with the following vector of variables: MPK1, MPK2, and the state variable FIN_{it} measuring the firm's financial status. Because MPK1 depends on sales, and MPK2 depends on operating income, the VAR system includes information on both revenues and profits as well as financial factors. The instrument set includes lags one and two each of the variables used in the forecasting system. For the regressions that do not include a PDV of financial factors, we include the cash and equivalents to capital ratio in the forecasting system. Second, this VAR is used to construct the fundamental Q, $\text{PV}_{it}^{\text{MPK}}$, and the financial Q, $\text{PV}_{it}^{\text{FIN}}$:

$$\text{PV}_{it}^{\text{MPK}} = c_2'(I - \beta A)^{-1}\beta A^2 x_{it-1},$$
$$\text{PV}_{it}^{\text{FIN}} = c_3'(1 - \beta)^{-1}(I - \beta A)^{-1}\beta A^2 x_{it-1}.$$

Finally, investment is regressed on $\text{PV}_{it}^{\text{MPK}}$ and $\text{PV}_{it}^{\text{FIN}}$ using the same set of instrumental variables as those used when estimating the VAR. All regressions are run using the forward mean-differencing transformation described in the appendix.

We consider two alternative definitions of the state variable measuring financial Q: the ratio of cash and equivalents to capital, $(\text{CE/K})_{it}$, and the ratio of financial working capital minus long-term debt to capital, $(\text{FW/K} - \text{LD/K})_{it}$.[27] The first definition captures the short-term liquid asset position of the firm. It thus reflects the amount of savings inside the firm. It also reflects the share of assets that is most easily used as collateral. The second variable measures the leverage position of the firm, net of current liquid assets. A distinct advantage of both of these variables is that they measure financial stocks rather than financial flows. Because finan-

---

27. We define "financial working capital" as current assets minus current liabilities plus inventories. Exact definitions are provided in Table 2.

Table 5 FULL-SAMPLE RESULTS

Variable	Estimated Parameter Value					
	Sales-Based MPK			OI-Based MPK		
PV_{it}^{MPK}	1.48	1.16	1.27	1.22	1.07	1.1
	(0.261)	(0.229)	(0.237)	(0.233)	(0.218)	(0.216)
$PV_{it}^{CE/K}$	—	0.056	—	—	0.05	—
	—	(0.008)	—	—	(0.011)	—
$PV_{it}^{FW/K}$	—	—	0.048	—	—	0.035
	—	—	(0.008)	—	—	(0.01)
R^2	0.356	0.385	0.394	0.377	0.401	0.398
P	0.00	0.00	0.00	0.007	0.118	0.009
N_{obs}	8520	8520	8520	8520	8520	8520

Adjusted standard errors in parentheses (see appendix).

cial stocks are less directly linked to the marginal profitability of capital, their present values are more likely orthogonal to PV_{it}^{MPK} than are present values that are constructed from financial flows.[28]

5.1 FULL-SAMPLE RESULTS

Table 5 reports estimates of parameters corresponding to α and $\alpha\gamma\phi$ in equation (3.3). For comparison purposes, we report results using the two alternative definitions of PV_{it}^{MPK} based on the two alternative measures of MPK. As described in Section 2, the first definition is based on the ratio of sales to capital, while the second definition is based on the ratio of operating income to capital. These results are estimated under the assumption that the time to build is one period, and the information set used by the firm is based on time-$(t-1)$ information. The first three columns contain results using the sales-based MPK, and the last three

28. We also investigated a third specification of financial Q using cash flow, $(CF/K)_{it}$, as the financial state variable. This specification of financial Q was a robust explanatory variable in all of the specifications that we tried. Unfortunately, it was also highly correlated with our measure of fundamental Q, just as one might have anticipated from our theoretical discussion of MPK in Section 2.2. As a consequence of this collinearity, the coefficient on fundamental Q in these regressions was typically insignificant and occasionally even negative. We obviously do not view this as evidence that adjustment costs are negative. Rather, we view this as evidence of model misspecification caused by the fact that financial Q was picking up information about fundamental Q. As we explain in the text, when we used stock measures of the firm's financial status, this was not a problem. We consider additional theoretical work on the financial side of the model to be an important direction for future research because this could help resolve this specification choice.

columns contain results using MPK based on operating income. This table reveals one of the major results in the paper: Fundamental Q does very well in explaining the investment data. In particular, the coefficients on $\mathrm{PV}_{it}^{\mathrm{MPK}}$ suggest rapid adjustment speeds and hence reasonable adjustment costs.

Despite the success of the sales-based measure of fundamental Q in explaining investment, investment is still highly responsive to financial factors. In all cases, financial Q is an important determinant of investment. With standard errors adjusted for the fact that the present-value terms are generated from previous regressions, the t-statistics are on the order of 3–8 for all three variables reported in the first three columns of Table 5.[29]

Besides reporting coefficient values, Table 5 also reports two diagnostic statistics: the P-value from a chi-squared test of orthogonality between error terms and instruments, and the R^2 from the regression. The orthogonality tests reject the model overwhelmingly and suggest model misspecification, even when financial factors are included. As we show below, this model misspecification is due to firms that are most likely to face severe financial constraints.

We now consider the results using fundamental Q constructed from the operating-income-based measure of MPK. In the full-sample results (Table 5, columns 4–6), it appears to make little difference whether our measure of MPK is based on sales or operating income. We obtain similar coefficients for adjustment costs, and approximately the same R^2. The fact that the coefficients on fundamental Q are fairly close across both measures suggests that we are using the correct normalizations of sales to capital and operating income to capital ratios when constructing MPK measures.

5.2 RESULTS BASED ON SAMPLE SPLITS

We now consider how our results vary across subsamples of firms when the subsamples are designed to sort firms by their ability to access financial markets. The traditional argument for performing subsample splits in the literature is that not all firms have the same degree of access to financial markets. The response of investment by firms with costly access is more likely to be sensitive to financial factors than that of firms with cheap access to external financial markets. Sample splitting thus provides a way to test for the presence of financial factors, even with imperfect measures of investment fundamentals. For example, large

---

29. The standard-error correction that results from generated regressors raised the standard errors by approximately 75–100%.

firms and firms that have issued public debt or have established commercial-paper programs are likely to have established lines of credit that may be drawn down during periods of low profitability. As a result, the investment policy of such firms may not be responsive to swings in balance-sheet conditions. By not taking such differences into account, we may not obtain an accurate description of the importance of financial factors in investment. Also, to the extent that we can identify a subset of firms that do not face financial frictions, and for whom the baseline investment model without financial frictions fits well, we can be more confident that our underlying investment model is correct. Such a result would imply that the presence of financial factors does not simply capture an undetermined source of model misspecification.

When splitting the sample, we consider three alternative criteria. The first criterion sorts firms according to whether or not they have an S&P bond rating. Because most firms that issue public debt obtain a bond rating, this effectively sorts the full sample into firms that have issued public debt in the past, versus those that have not. Calomiris, Himmelberg, and Wachtel (1995) argue that public-debt issuance is a good indication that a firm has low-cost access to capital markets, because firms with serious adverse selection or moral hazard problems are forced to rely on intermediated finance such as bank debt and private placements. Because the population of public-debt issuers is relatively stable over time, this selection criterion has the advantage of being relatively exogenous with respect to the time-series variation in the data. It has the disadvantage of only capturing a subset of the best-quality firms.

The other two criteria that we use to split the sample are the dividend payout ratio and firm size. The dividend payout ratio was originally used by Fazzari, Hubbard, and Petersen (1988) and has been employed in a number of additional studies. The size split has also been used extensively to distinguish between *constrained* and *unconstrained* firms (Gertler and Gilchrist, 1994; Carpenter, Fazzari, and Petersen 1996). The rationale for splitting the sample according to dividend policy is that when firms declare dividends, they endogenously reveal that they have a low shadow value of internal funds. For a number of reasons, firm size is another common way of identifying firms with low external-financing premiums. For one, it is plausible that costs of obtaining funds contain a significant fixed-cost component. The presence of such increasing returns suggests that small firms face higher costs of obtaining external funds than large firms. In addition, size is a proxy for age and other unobservable firm attributes that affect the degree to which public information about the firm's investment projects is available. Among publicly traded firms, smaller, newer firms are less likely to be tracked by analysts and less likely to have been through multiple equity or debt offerings that result in substantial production of public information.

While the bond-rating categorization is based on a zero–one variable (rating versus no rating), both the dividend payout ratio and size are continuous. Because we wish to distinguish firms with cheap access to credit from firms that face potential credit frictions whose investment will be responsive to financial state variables, we divide the sample conservatively and classify firms who are in the top one-third of the dividend payout or size distribution as likely to be unconstrained.[30]

For each sample split, we allow the VAR forecasting system to vary across the constrained and unconstrained subsamples. By allowing the VAR forecasting system to vary across subsamples we correct for any systematic differences in forecasting properties that may bias results. We report the results using both the sales-based MPK and the operating-income-based MPK, and consider the cash-and-equivalents variable as our financial state variable. The regression results for this exercise are reported in Tables 6 and 7.

The results from the sample-splitting exercise provide strong evidence that financial factors are important determinants of investment, principally for firms classified as constrained. Table 6 reports the results for the bond-rating split, using both the sales-based and operating-income-based measures of MPK. Using either definition of MPK, firms with a bond rating show no sensitivity of investment to financial factors. Thus all of the contribution of financial factors in explaining investment comes through firms without bond ratings. The orthogonality conditions for the baseline investment model are not rejected for firms classified as unconstrained. This result implies that the underlying investment model does well at explaining the data, in the absence of financial frictions. In addition, adding the financial factor adds very little in terms of explanatory power as measured by R^2 for unconstrained firms. For firms without bond ratings, the coefficients on financial factors increase by 40% relative to the full sample results.

Table 6 also shows that, for bond-rated firms, the sales-based MPK measure does a much better job explaining investment than the operating-income-based MPK. In particular, the coefficient on fundamental Q is much higher and the model is not rejected when using a sales-based

30. Because we compute the 66th percentile for the dividend payout and size variables before dropping firms because of missing values, we end up with slightly different sample sizes than the one-third–two-thirds split of the original sample. The actual values used are a ratio of common dividends to capital greater or less than 0.05 and real sales greater or less than $364 million. Real sales were constructed using the GDP deflator. This cutoff for real sales is close to the value of $250 million used by Gertler and Gilchrist (1994) in their study of small versus large manufacturing firms.

Table 6   BOND RATED VERSUS NON-BOND-RATED FIRMS

	Estimated Parameter Value					
Variable	Bond Rating			No Bond Rating		
	Sales-Based MPK					
PV_{it}^{MPK}	1.32	1.26	1.21	1.55	1.24	1.32
	(0.603)	(0.622)	(0.536)	(0.399)	(0.353)	(0.36)
$PV_{it}^{CE/K}$	—	0.003	—	—	0.07	—
	—	(0.01)	—	—	(0.015)	—
$PV_{it}^{FW/K}$	—	—	0.006	—	—	0.049
	—	—	(0.021)	—	—	(0.013)
R^2	0.419	0.428	0.426	0.318	0.342	0.358
P	0.889	0.789	0.743	0.00	0.00	0.00
N_{obs}	1720	1720	1720	4420	4420	4420
	Operating-Income-Based MPK					
PV_{it}^{MPK}	0.318	0.254	0.357	1.22	1.02	0.993
	(0.205)	(0.175)	(0.218)	(0.364)	(0.34)	(0.313)
$PV_{it}^{CE/K}$	—	0.013	—	—	0.063	—
	—	(0.009)	—	—	(0.018)	—
$PV_{it}^{FW/K}$	—	—	−0.006	—	—	0.04
	—	—	(0.021)	—	—	(0.014)
R^2	0.418	0.45	0.436	0.339	0.357	0.354
P	0.025	0.018	0.034	0.058	0.082	0.01
N_{obs}	1720	1720	1720	4420	4420	4420

Adjusted standard errors in parentheses (see appendix).

MPK. These findings suggest that our sales-based MPK captures most of the information about fundamentals in the absence of credit frictions.

Table 7 reports results for alternative sample splits using the sales-based measure of fundamentals (similar conclusions are reached using MPK based on operating income). Small firms are clearly more responsive to financial factors than large firms. For the dividend split, the differences across subsamples are not so obvious. There is less of a difference in estimates of ϕ for low- vs. high-dividend firms, once one corrects for the fact that the coefficient estimate on fundamental Q is much lower for high-dividend firms.

5.3 GOODNESS OF FIT AND ROBUSTNESS EXERCISES

We conducted a variety of robustness exercises that are not reported in the tables. First, we investigated the robustness of our results across industries. While it is not possible to estimate separate investment equations for each industry, it is possible to consider a more homogeneous sample than the full set of manufacturing firms considered above. For robustness, we reestimated all the regressions reported in Table 5 for a sample that is limited to durable-goods industries only (two-digit SICs between 3200 and 3999). The argument for doing this exercise is that the durable-goods industries are much more homogeneous than the nondu-

Table 7   ALTERNATIVE SAMPLE SPLIT CRITERIA

Variable	Estimated Parameter Value					
	High Dividend Payout			Low Dividend Payout		
PV_{it}^{MPK}	0.422	0.215	0.516	1.84	1.44	1.57
	(0.2)	(0.117)	(0.234)	(0.428)	(0.384)	(0.362)
$PV_{it}^{CE/K}$	—	0.038	—	—	0.085	—
	—	(0.007)	—	—	(0.014)	—
$PV_{it}^{FW/K}$	—	—	0.031	—	—	0.062
	—	—	(0.013)	—	—	(0.011)
R^2	0.31	0.385	0.363	0.37	0.401	0.41
P	0.00	0.022	0.023	0.00	0.00	0.00
N_{obs}	2900	2900	2900	5240	5240	5240
	Large Firm			Small Firm		
PV_{it}^{MPK}	0.714	0.513	0.616	1.35	1.28	1.39
	(0.174)	(0.18)	(0.173)	(0.325)	(0.326)	(0.357)
$PV_{it}^{CE/K}$	—	0.012	—	—	0.096	—
	—	(0.006)	—	—	(0.015)	—
$PV_{it}^{FW/K}$	—	—	0.014	—	—	0.052
	—	—	(0.009)	—	—	(0.011)
R^2	0.56	0.553	0.553	0.278	0.303	0.317
P	0.063	0.016	0.014	0.00	0.00	0.00
N_{obs}	3260	3260	3260	5140	5140	5140

Adjusted standard errors in parentheses (see appendix).

rables industries. In addition, these industries may have different time-series properties that would be better captured by their own set of time dummies. If so, the forecasting equations obtained from the VAR may perform better. This exercise provides very similar results to those obtained in Table 5. For the durables subsample, fundamental Q provides considerable explanatory power for investment and reasonable estimates of adjustment costs. Nonetheless, present values of financial state variables are still important determinants of investment, in both economic and statistical terms.

The second exercise we perform is to check for robustness by excluding the smallest firms in the sample. Because size and bond rating are correlated, it is useful to know if the results based on sample splits are purely a size effect, generated by the smallest firms in the sample. For a variety of reasons, such firms may respond differently to both fundamental Q and financial Q. To examine this issue, we reconsidered the bond-rating splits after dropping all firms with total assets less than $100 million in real terms (1992 dollars). As one would expect, the financial effect is somewhat weaker when one drops the small firms. We nonetheless still find substantial differences in response between non-bond-rated and bond-rated firms, with bond-rated firms showing no response to financial Q, and non-bond-rated firms showing an economically and statistically significant response. This finding implies that while size is important, it is nonetheless the case that some medium-size firms do not have perfect access to debt and equity markets, and these account for an important component of the overall degree of excess sensitivity measured in the data.

The final exercise we consider is to include lagged investment in the empirical specification. The convex adjustment cost structure developed in this paper suggests that only the fundamentals and financial variables should explain investment and that lagged investment should not matter. Empirically, however, lagged investment may matter for three reasons. First, the adjustment cost structure could be richer than what we have modeled. If this is the case, the model may exhibit more inertia than one would expect absent such misspecification. Second, it is possible that investment itself helps forecast the future fundamentals and/or financial factors, in which case our present value constructs would be measured with an error that is correlated with lagged I/K. Finally, it is possible that the model is well specified but that shocks exhibit serial correlation, in which case the presence of lagged investment would reveal such correlation.

Our empirical results uniformly reject the hypothesis that lagged investment does not matter for current investment, even after controlling for both fundamentals and financial factors. The coefficient on lagged investment is on the order of 0.1–0.2 and highly significant. While this result suggests model misspecification, it is also the case that including lagged investment has little effect on the estimated parameter values and does not reduce the importance of financial factors in the investment equation.[31]

To further investigate the role of lagged investment, we estimated a VAR forecasting system that included investment as one of the system variables. With this specification, lagged investment is then explicitly included in our construction of present-value forecasts. Without imposing model consistency between the forecasting system and the empirical specification of the structural investment equation, we re-estimated the investment equation, allowing lagged investment to enter freely on the right-hand side. Other than raising the coefficient on lagged investment somewhat, this exercise produced little change in any of the coefficient estimates, implying that investment's ability to forecast future MPK and financial variables does not explain the presence of lagged investment. In future work, it would be useful to further investigate the role of alternative explanations like richer adjustment costs and serially correlated shocks. Finally, it is worth noting that lagged investment is a significant explanatory variable in more standard Q regressions as well. Thus, this form of model misspecification does not result from our particularly empirical specification, but is instead endemic to a wide variety of empirical specifications of investment equations.[32]

5.4 THE EMPIRICAL CONTRIBUTION OF FINANCIAL FACTORS

Having estimated the basic model, and having considered a variety of robustness issues, we now use the structural coefficients to gauge the likely empirical contribution of the financial factors to investment. We do this by shocking the VAR used to construct the forecast and tracing out the time path for both fundamental Q and financial Q. To obtain the time path of investment, we feed these two Q-values into the investment

31. To be more precise, omitting lagged investment from both the regressors and the instruments produced very similar coefficients to regressions that include lagged investment as both a regressor and instrument. The main difference in results is that the coefficients on both fundamental and financial terms rise somewhat to offset the inertia introduced by lagged investment in the empirical specification. As a result, the dynamic responses of the models look very similar, whether or not one includes lagged I/K on the right-hand side.

32. While this is especially true of panel data, it also tends to be true for aggregate data as well (see Abel and Blanchard (1986) for example). Kiyotaki and West (1996) provide a notable counterexample with their empirical model of investment using aggregate postwar Japanese data. In particular, they attribute all of the explanatory power of lagged investment to its ability to predict future fundamentals.

Table 8   DYNAMIC INVESTMENT RESPONSE TO FUNDAMENTAL VERSUS
FINANCIAL Q

	Response					
Variable	$T=0$	$T=1$	$T=2$	$T=3$	$T=4$	$T=5$
MPK_{it}	0.046	0.032	0.019	0.011	0.006	0.004
$(\text{CE}/\text{K})_{it}$	0.042	0.029	0.018	0.011	0.007	0.004
$\hat{\alpha}_1 \text{PV}_{it}^{\text{MPK}}$	0.033	0.019	0.011	0.007	0.004	0.002
$\hat{\alpha}_1 \text{PV}_{it}^{\text{MPK}} + \hat{\alpha}_1 \hat{\gamma} \phi \text{PV}_{it}^{\text{CE}/\text{K}}$	0.041	0.024	0.014	0.008	0.005	0.003
Excess response (%)	0.245	0.261	0.275	0.288	0.299	0.308

specification using the parameter values reported in column 2 of Table 5.[33] To gauge the contribution of financial factors, we do this exercise both with and without financial Q. The results are reported in Table 8.

A one-standard deviation shock raises MPK1 by 0.046 units. The ratio of cash and equivalents to capital increases by slightly more than 0.04 units as balance sheets are strengthened in the wake of the expansionary shock. The response of fundamental Q implies an increase in the investment rate next period of 0.033. Adding in the contribution of financial Q raises the overall response of investment to 0.041. Thus in the first period, financial Q adds an additional 25% to the baseline response obtained from shutting down movements in the present value of cash and equivalents. In the next few periods, we also obtain 25–30% magnification. Thus, the financial effect has a substantial contribution to the overall investment response of the average firm.

Using a combination of the coefficient estimates and the impulse response to financial Q, we can compute the implied response to the one-period return that generated the additional movement in investment relative to the baseline model. With $\beta = 0.8$, $\gamma = 0.2$, and an estimate of α around unity, our estimate of ϕ is approximately 0.2.[34] In the initial period, financial Q rises by approximately 0.04. This implies that the one-period return rose by 80 basis points in the first period, before slowly returning to steady state. Given the fact that the average postwar spread between the prime rate and T-bill is 2%, and bank loans are often quoted at 1–2% above or below prime depending on credit quality, this strikes us as a moderate response for the premium on external funds.

33. The model with lagged investment produces similar results.
34. This estimate is very much in line with our ballpark figures of 0.1–0.3 discussed above.

6. Conclusions

In this paper, we argue that by combining careful measurement of MPK with structural VAR methods, it is possible to improve on existing methods for identifying the financing role of cash flow and other financial variables in reduced-form investment equations. We examine two strategies for imposing structure on VARs to identify the effect of financial factors on investment.

In our first strategy, we use a recursive ordering to structure the contemporaneous relationship among shocks in the VAR. This allows us to identify shocks to cash flow that are orthogonal to current MPK. Such shocks elicit a sustained response from investment over a three-year period. Such shocks also predict a fall in future MPK, suggesting that cash flow matters above and beyond its ability to predict investment fundamentals. Because the future response of MPK to an orthogonal cash-flow shock is negative, the investment response likely understates the effect that cash flow has on investment via lower financing costs.

In our second strategy, we estimate a linearized version of a structural model of investment that embeds financial frictions. This structural framework shows that investment depends not only on the present value of the future marginal profitability of capital (MPK), which we call "fundamental Q," but also on the present value of future shadow values of internal funds, which we call "financial Q." In contrast to previous work on financing constraints using firm-level panel data, we first explicitly relate these shadow values to observable financial state variables and then use VARs to construct the present-value terms corresponding to both fundamental Q and financial Q.

Our empirical results using the structural model show that for a wide variety of specification choices, investment is responsive to both fundamental Q and financial Q. We argue that the values of the estimated structural parameters are reasonable on *a priori* grounds, and that the estimated effect of financial factors on investment is quantitatively significant. For the average firm in our sample, financial factors amplify the overall investment response to an expansionary shock by 25%, relative to a baseline model where such effects are shut down. Consistent with the theory underlying financial-market imperfections, small firms and firms without bond ratings show the strangest response to financial factors, while bond-rated firms show little if any response. Because bond-rated firms account for 50% of aggregate manufacturing investment, our results suggest that the overall amplification of manufacturing investment is somewhat less than 25%.

Appendix

This appendix briefly describes the econometrics used in the paper. First, it describes our approach to estimating panel-data VARs, and second, it describes the adjusted standard-error calculations required by our two-step procedure for estimating the structural parameters of the investment equation. Our approach to estimating panel-data VARs follow Holtz-Eakin, Newey, and Rosen (1988), Arellano and Bond (1991), Keane and Runkle (1992), and Arellano and Bover (1995), among others, which consider the treatment of fixed firm effects in the presence of predetermined but not strictly exogenous explanatory variables. Our treatment of the generated regressor problem introduced by our two-step estimation technique follows Newey (1984).

A.1 ESTIMATING VECTOR AUTOREGRESSIONS USING PANEL DATA

Let $y_{it} = \{y_{it}^1, \ldots, y_{it}^M\}'$ be an $M \times 1$ vector of variables observed in panel data, where i indexes cross-section observations and t indexes time-series observations. Then the mth equation of a P-lag VAR can be written as

$$y_{it}^m = x_{it}'b^m + \alpha_i^m + \gamma_t^m + u_{it}^m,$$

where $x_{it} = \{y_{it-1}', \ldots, y_{it-p}'\}'$ is an $MP \times 1$ vector of lagged endogenous variables (the same for each equation of the VAR), b^m is an $MP \times 1$ vector of slope coefficients, α_i^m is a fixed firm effect, γ_t^m is an aggregate shock (time dummy), and u_{it}^m is an idiosyncratic shock satisfying

$$E(u_{it}^m | f_i^m, \gamma_t^m, x_{it}, x_{it-1}, x_{it-2}, \ldots) = 0.$$

This conditional moment implies $E(x_{it}'u_{it+s}^m) = 0$ for all $s \geq 0$. If the model did not include fixed firm and year effects, we could use OLS to obtain estimates of b^m for all m. However, the presence of unobserved fixed effects (which, by virtue of the lagged dependent variable, are correlated with x_{it}) requires panel-data techniques for obtaining consistent estimates of b^m. To deal with fixed year effects is trivial; we can either estimate dummy variables or, more simply, transform the above model again to deviations from year-specific means. In the exposition below, we assume that y_{it}^m and x_{it} have already been transformed to remove year effects.

To remove the fixed effects α_i^m, we transform the model to deviations from forward means. Let $\bar{y}_{it}^m$ and $\bar{x}_{it}$ denote the means constructed from the future values of y_{it}^m and x_{it} available in the data, and let $\tilde{y}_{it}^m$ and $\tilde{x}_{it}$ denote the data transformation given by

$$\tilde{y}_{it}^m = w_{it}(y_{it}^m - \bar{y}_{it}^m),$$
$$\tilde{x}_{it} = w_{it}(x_{it} - \bar{x}_{it}),$$

where $w_{it} = \sqrt{(T_i - t)/(T_i - t - 1)}$, and T_i denotes the last year of data available (among the nonmissing observations) for observation i. Note that in the last year of the data for observation i, the transformation is unavailable (there are no future values for the construction of $\bar{y}_{it}^m$ and $\bar{x}_{it}$), so this observation is set to missing. This transformation sets α_i^m to zero, so the transformed model is

$$\tilde{y}_{it}^m = \tilde{x}_{it}'b^m + \tilde{u}_{it}^m.$$

If the original error term u_{it}^m is homoscedastic, this transformation preserves homoscedasticity, and does not induce serial correlation. This transformation preserves instruments, because all current and lagged values of x_{it} remain uncorrelated with the tranformed error term: $E(x_{it-s}\tilde{u}_{it}^m) = 0$ for all $s \geq 0$. These moment conditions suggest the use of an efficient GMM estimator for b^m. In theory, many instruments (all lags of x_{it}) are potentially available in the sample. In practice, to avoid finite-sample problems, we use only current values of x_{it}. That is, we assume $z_{it} = x_{it}$. Combining moment conditions for all equations, our GMM estimator is based on $E(\tilde{u}_{it} \otimes z_{it}) = 0$.

This model can be expressed in matrix notation as follows. Let $\tilde{y}^m = \{\tilde{y}_{11}^m, \tilde{y}_{12}^m, \ldots \tilde{y}_{NT_N}^m\}'$ denote the stacked vector of observations on $\tilde{y}_{it}^m$ for the mth equation, stacking only observations for which $\tilde{y}_{it}^m$, $\tilde{x}_{it}$, or $\tilde{z}_{it}$ are not missing for any m. Similarly, let Z, $\tilde{X}$, and $\tilde{u}^m$ be the stacked observations on z_{it}', x_{it}', and u_{it}^m, respectively. Then the model for the observations in the data (expressed in differences from forward means) can be written

$$\tilde{y}^m = \tilde{X}b^m + \tilde{u}^m.$$

To write the expression for the GMM estimates of the $M^2P \times 1$ vector of slope coefficients $b = \{b^{1'}, \ldots, b^{M'}\}'$, stack the moments from all M equations to form the $ML \times 1$ vector of moment conditions $E(\tilde{u}_{it} \otimes z_{it}) = 0$, where $\tilde{u}_{it} = \{\tilde{u}_{it}^1, \ldots, \tilde{u}_{it}^M\}'$. Let y be the $MN^* \times 1$ vector $y = \{\tilde{y}^{1'}, \ldots, \tilde{y}^{M'}\}'$ formed by stacking the vectors of observations on the M equations, and let $X = I_M \otimes \tilde{X}$, $Z = I_M \otimes \tilde{Z}$, and $W = (Z'Z)^{-1}$. It turns out, then, that the vector of slope coefficients b is

$$\hat{b}_{\text{GMM}} = (X'ZWZ'X)^{-1}X'ZWZ'y,$$

where W is a positive semidefinite weighting matrix. The efficient GMM estimator is obtained by choosing $W = \hat{V}_1^{-1}$, where $\hat{V}_1$ is a consistent estimate of the asymptotic covariance of the sample moments, $(1/N^*)$ $\sum_{i=1}^{N} \sum_{t=1}^{T_i} (\tilde{u}_{it} \otimes z_{it})$. A convenient estimator of V is

$$\hat{V}_1 = \frac{1}{N^*} \sum_{i=1}^{N} \sum_{t=1}^{T_i} (\hat{u}_{it} \otimes z_{it})(\hat{u}_{it} \otimes z_{it})',$$

where $N^* = \sum_{i=1}^{N} T_i$ is the total number of observations in the (unbalanced) panel, T_i denotes the number of nonmissing time-series observations available for firm i, and $\hat{u}_{it}$ is the residual estimate of the transformed error term $\tilde{u}_{it}$, constructed using a consistent preliminary estimate of b (two-stage least squares). Note that it is not necessary to include auto-covariance terms in the expression for $\hat{V}_1$, since, by assumption, $E(\tilde{u}_{it} \tilde{u}_{it-s}'|z_{it}, \ldots, z_{it-s}) = 0$ for all $s > 0$.

Finally, a robust estimate of the asymptotic covariance of b_{GMM} is given by

$$\text{Est Var}(\hat{b}_{\text{GMM}}) = (\tilde{X}'ZWZ'\tilde{X})^{-1}\tilde{X}'Z\check{V}_1 Z'\tilde{X}(\tilde{X}'ZWZ'\tilde{X})^{-1},$$

where $\check{V}_1$ is an estimated like $\hat{V}_1$ using estimates of the transformed residuals derived from the GMM estimate $\hat{b}_{\text{GMM}}$.

A.2 ESTIMATING THE INVESTMENT EQUATION USING GENERATED REGRESSORS BASED ON THE VAR ESTIMATES

Given the GMM estimates $\hat{b}_{\text{GMM}}$ of a VAR system that includes a measure of the marginal profitability of capital, MPK_{it}, and a financial state variable FIN_{it}, we can use a second-stage regression to obtain structural estimates of the parameters for the cost of adjustment and shadow discount rate functions. Consistent estimates of the slope coefficients are easily obtained using GMM. However, the use of generated regressors implies that the usual standard error estimates are inconsistent. This subsection reviews the details of the second-state estimator and provides standard-error estimates that are consistent in the presence of generated regressors.

The investment model in the paper is

$$(I/K)_{it} = \alpha_0 + \alpha_1 (\text{PV}_{it}^{\text{MPK}}) + \alpha_1 \gamma \phi(\text{PV}_{it}^{\text{FIN}}) + f_i + d_t + \omega_{it},$$

where $\text{PV}_{it}^{\text{MPK}}$ and $\text{PV}_{it}^{\text{FIN}}$ are present-value terms that are linear in x_{it} but (highly) nonlinear in b. Let $f(b)$ be an $MP \times 2$ matrix defined so that multiplication of $\tilde{x}_{it}$ by $f(b)'$ produces a 2×1 vector of present-values terms, $f(b)'\tilde{x}_{it} = \{\text{PV}_{it}^{\text{MPK}}, \text{PV}_{it}^{\text{FIN}}\}'$. Using the notation from the main text, the first column of $f(b)$ is given by $c_2[I - \beta A(b)]^{-1} bA(b)^2$, and the second column of $f(b)$ is given by $c_3(1-\beta)^{-1}[I - \beta A(b)]^{-1} bA(b)^2$, where the notation $A(b)$ reflects the fact that the companion matrix A is a function of the VAR parameters b.

Letting $i_{it} = (I/K)_{it}$, $\tilde{q}_{it} = f(b)'\tilde{x}_{it}$, and $a = \{\alpha_1, \alpha_2\gamma\phi\}'$, we can write the above investment model as

$$i_{it} = q'_{it}a + f_i + d_t + \omega_{it}.$$

Using forward-mean differences to remove year and firm effects (as discussed in the previous subsection), we can write the transformed model as

$$\tilde{i}_{it} = \tilde{q}'_{it}a + \tilde{\omega}_{it}.$$

For identification, we assume $E(\omega_{it}| f_i, \gamma_t, x_{it}, x_{it-1}, x_{it-2}, \ldots) = 0$. This implies that the same vector of instruments z_{it} used in the estimation of the VAR is also valid for the estimation of the investment equation. If we let i and Q be the matrices of stacked observations on i_{it} and q_{it}, respectively, then a GMM estimator for a is given by

$$\hat{a}_{GMM1} = (Q'Z\hat{V}_2^{-1}Z'Q)^{-1}Q'Z\hat{V}_2^{-1}Z'i,$$

where $\hat{V}_2 = 1/N^* \Sigma_{i=1}^N \Sigma_{t=1}^{T_i} (\hat{\omega}_{it} \otimes z_{it})(\hat{\omega}_{it} \otimes z_{it})'$, and where $\hat{\omega}_{it}$ is the residual estimate of the transformed error term, $\tilde{\omega}_{it}$, constructed using the first stage estimate of a.

Recall that $\hat{a}_{GMM1}$ is estimated using generated regressors. Hence, the above expression for $\hat{V}_2$ does not consistently estimate the asymptotic covariance of the second-stage sample moments, because it fails to take account of the implicit variation in $\hat{\omega}_{it}$ induced by $\hat{b}$. A consistent estimator that does take account of this variation is

$$\hat{V}_3 = \frac{1}{N^*} \sum_{i=1}^N \sum_{t=1}^{T_i} r_{it} r'_{it},$$

where

$$r_{it} = (\hat{\omega}_{it} \otimes z_{it}) - Z'X\hat{G}P_1(\hat{u}_{it} \otimes z_{it})$$
$$P_1 = (X'Z\hat{V}_2^{-1}Z'X)^{-1}X'Z\hat{V}_2^{-1}$$
$$\hat{G} = \frac{\partial}{\partial b}[f(\hat{b})\hat{a}].$$

Consistent standard-error estimates for $\hat{a}_{GMM1}$ are given by

$$\text{Est Var}(\hat{a}_{\text{GMM1}}) = (\tilde{X}'Z\hat{V}_2^{-1}Z'\tilde{X})^{-1}\tilde{X}'Z\hat{V}_3Z'\tilde{X}(\tilde{X}'Z\hat{V}_2^{-1}Z'\tilde{X})^{-1}.$$

The availability of $\hat{V}_3$ suggests a second, potentially more efficient GMM estimator for a, namely,

$$\hat{a}_{\text{GMM2}} = (Q'Z\hat{V}_3^{-1}Z'Q)^{-1}Q'Z\hat{V}_3^{-1}Z'i.$$

Consistent standard error estimates for $\hat{a}_{\text{GMM2}}$ are given by

$$\text{Est Var }(\hat{a}_{\text{GMM2}}) = (\tilde{X}'Z\hat{V}_3^{-1}Z'\tilde{X})^{-1}\tilde{X}'Z\hat{V}_4Z'\tilde{X}(\tilde{X}'Z\hat{V}_3^{-1}Z'\tilde{X})^{-1},$$

where $\hat{V}_4$ is estimated using the expression for $\hat{V}_3$, but where $\hat{\omega}_{it}$ and $\hat{a}$ are calculated using $\hat{a}_{\text{GMM2}}$. The estimates reported in the main text are based on this estimator.

A derivation of the above results is available from the authors on request. See also Newey (1984).

REFERENCES

Abel, A. B., and O. Blanchard. (1986). The present value of profits and cyclical movements in investments. *Econometrica* 54:249–273.
———, and J. C. Eberly. (1994). A unified model of investment under uncertainty. *American Economic Review* 84:1369–1384.
———, and ———. (1996). Investment and q with fixed costs: An empirical analysis. Wharton School, University of Pennsylvania. Working Paper.
Arellano, M., and S. Bond. (1991). Some tests of specification for panel data: Monte Carlo evidence and an application to employment equations. *Review of Economic Studies* 58:277–297.
———, and O. Bover. (1995). Another look at the instrumental variable estimation of error component models. *Journal of Econometrics* 68:29–51.
Bernanke, B., M. Gertler, and S. Gilchrist. (1998). The financial accelerator in a quantitative business cycle framework. Forthcoming in *Handbook of Macroeconomics,* Michael Woodford and John Taylor (eds.).
Caballero, R. J. (1997). Aggregate investment. Cambridge, MA: National Bureau of Economic Research. NBER Working Paper 6264.
———, and E. M. R. A. Engel. (1998). Nonlinear aggregate investment dynamics: Theory and evidence. Cambridge, MA: Working Paper. M.I.T.
———, and J. V. Leahy. (1996). The demise of marginal q. Cambridge, MA: National Bureau of Economic Research. NBER Working Paper 5508.
Calomiris, C. W., and C. P. Himmelberg. (1998). Investment banking costs as a measure of the cost of access to external finance. Columbia University. Working Paper.
———, ———, and P. Wachtel. (1995). Commercial paper, corporate finance, and the business cycle: A macroeconomic perspective. *Carnegie-Rochester Conference Series on Public Policy* 42:203–250.
Carpenter, R. E., S. Fazzari, and B. Petersen. (1997). Inventory investment,

internal-finance fluctuations, and the business cycle. *Brookings Papers on Economic Activity* 2:75–122.

Chirinko, R. S. (1993). Business fixed investment spending: A critical survey of modelling strategies, empirical results, and policy implications. *Journal of Economic Literature* 31(4):1875–1911.

Cummins, J. G., K. A. Hassett, and S. D. Oliner. (1997). Investment behavior, observable expectations, and internal funds. New York University. Working Paper.

Fazzari, S. M., R. G. Hubbard, and B. C. Petersen. (1988). Financing constraints and corporate investment. *Brookings Papers on Economic Activity* 1:141–195.

———, ———, and ———. (1996). Financing constraints and corporate investment: Response to Kaplan and Zingales. Cambridge, MA: National Bureau of Economic Research. NBER Working Paper 5462.

Gertler, M. (1992). Financial capacity and output fluctuations in an economy with multiperiod financial relationships. *Review of Economic Studies* 59:455–472.

———, and S. Gilchrist. (1994). Monetary policy, business cycles and the behavior of small manufacturing firms. *Quarterly Journal of Economics* 109:309–340.

Gilchrist, S., and C. P. Himmelberg. (1995). Evidence on the role of cash flow for investment. *Journal of Monetary Economics* 36:541–572.

Gomes, J. (1997). Heterogeneity in macroeconomics: Essays on investment behavior and unemployment dynamics. University of Rochester. Unpublished Ph.D. Dissertation.

Goolsbee, A., and D. B. Gross. (1997). Estimating adjustment costs with data on heterogeneous capital goods. University of Chicago. Working Paper.

Gross, D. B. (1997). The Investment and financing decisions of liquidity constrained firms. University of Chicago. Working Paper.

Himmelberg, C. P. (1990). Essays on the relationship between investment and internal finance. Northwestern University. Unpublished Ph.D. Dissertation.

———, and B. Petersen. (1994). R&D and internal finance: A panel study of small firms in high-tech industries. *Review of Economics and Statistics* 76(1):38–51.

Holtz-Eakin, D., W. Newey, and H. S. Rosen. (1988). Estimating vector autoregressions with panel data. *Econometrica* 56:1371–1395.

Hubbard, R. G. (1998). Capital market imperfections and investment. *Journal of Economic Literature* 36(1):193–225.

———, and A. Kashyap. (1992). Internal net worth and the investment process: An application to U.S. agriculture. *Journal of Political Economy* 100(3):506–534.

———, ———, and T. Whited. (1995). Internal finance and firm investment. *Journal of Money, Credit and Banking* 27(3):683–701.

Jaramillo, F., F. Schianterelli, and A. Weiss. (1996). Capital market imperfections before and after financial liberalizations: An Euler equation approach to panel data for Ecuadorian firms. *Journal of Development Economics* 51:367–386.

Kaplan, S. N., and L. Zingales. (1997). Do financing constraints explain why investment is correlated with cash flow? *Quarterly Journal of Economics* 109(3): 565–592.

Kashyap, A., O. Lamont, and J. Stein. (1994). Credit conditions and the cyclical behavior of inventories. *Quarterly Journal of Economics* 109:565–592.

Keane, M. P., and D. E. Runkle (1992). On the estimation of panel data models with serial correlation when instruments are not strictly exogenous. *Journal of Business and Economic Statistics* 10:1–9.

Kiyotaki, N., and K. D. West. (1986). Business fixed investment and the recent business cycle in Japan. In *NBER Macroeconomics Annual 1996*. Cambridge, MA: The MIT Press.

Moyen, N. (1997). Dynamic investment decisions with a tax benefit and a default cost of debt. University of British Columbia. Working Paper.

Newey, W. K. (1984). A method of moments interpretation of sequential estimators. *Economics Letters* 14:201–206.

Sharpe, S. (1993). Financial market imperfections, firm leverage, and the cyclicality of employment. *American Economic Review* 84(4), 1060–1074.

Whited, T. (1992). Debt, liquidity constraints, and corporate investment. *Journal of Finance* 47(4):1425–1459.

Comment

DAVID B. GROSS
University of Chicago

Understanding investment has always been one of the central goals of macroeconomics. Unfortunately, the neoclassical model does not do a very good job in describing the empirical investment behavior of individual firms. This nice paper by Gilchrist and Himmelberg is part of the large literature which invokes financial-market imperfections to better explain microeconomic investment decisions. One of the key issues in this area is disentangling changes in economic fundamentals from changes in the firm's financial position. Do balance-sheet variables like cash flow have an independent effect on investment, or are both investment and cash flow simply correlated with the firm's underlying state variable? Improvements in economic fundamentals, such as the marginal product of capital (MPK), directly increase investment through the standard neoclassical channel while at the same time improving the firm's financial position. Hence, even if financial markets are perfect, financial variables will be correlated with investment. Initially, this literature used Tobin's q to control for fundamentals and argued that financial variables are still important in explaining investment. However, since empirical estimates of q are most likely highly mismeasured, variables like cash flow may still be capturing the effects of fundamentals on investment rather than imperfect financial markets.

Gilchrist and Himmelberg attempt to solve this problem by obtaining a better measure of economic fundamentals. Instead of using average q, the authors show that for a certain set of production functions, the sales-to-capital ratio will be proportional to the firm's MPK. They then use their preferred measure of economic fundamentals in two specifications. First, they run panel data VARs in I/K, MPK, and CF/K to argue that orthogonal shocks to cash flow matter even after controlling for the marginal product of capital. Second, they linearize a model of investment with financial-market imperfections where firms' discount rates are parametrized as a reduced-form function of balance-sheet variables. The model generates linear regressions similar to the ones used in the earlier financial-market imperfections literature:

$$\frac{I}{K} = \beta_0 + \beta_1 \text{EPDV(MPK)} + \beta_2 \text{EPDV(FIN)}$$

where EPDV denotes the expected present discounted value and FIN is a financial indicator. In this specification, following Abel and Blanchard (1986), economic fundamentals as measured by marginal q are determined by forecasting expected future values of the MPK. Since the forecasts of MPK and the financial variables are based on lags of investment, MPK, and financial variables, this specification is similar to the previous VAR regressions except that the dynamic structure has been constrained by theory.

The results from both specifications are quite nice. The financial variables are significant for small firms and firms without bond ratings, even controlling for fundamentals. Economic fundamentals also are significant, and unlike results using average q, they are economically important. This is an important achievement which should give more confidence in these types of specifications. However, I will argue that the improved performance of the authors' measure of fundamentals should not be surprising and may not be capturing what we originally expected.

The key issue in this paper is appropriately measuring economic fundamentals. Otherwise, the authors could have continued to use average q with stock-market data like most of the literature. What exactly are economic fundamentals? Under the null hypothesis with no financial-market imperfections, economic fundamentals represent the state variable of the firm's investment problem. Gilchrist and Himmelberg follow the financial-market-imperfection literature by arguing that this theoretical state variable is marginal q or EPDV(MPK). Note, however, that marginal q is the correct state variable only in problems with quadratic (or some other convex) adjustment costs. There is a growing empirical literature which argues that quadratic adjustment costs are a poor assumption for investment at the microeconomic level. Instead, at the level of the firm or plant, investments are intermittent and lumpy, consistent with nonconvex adjustment cost functions such as fixed costs of investment. Caballero and Leahy (1996) show that with nonconvex adjustment costs, marginal q is not the appropriate state variable for the firm's problem. In fact, average q is more correlated than marginal q with investment. If marginal q is not the firm's true state variable, then financial variables could be statistically significant in the data, without any financial-market imperfections.

Even if marginal q as measured using the expected future MPK is the correct state variable, there are several difficulties. The authors measure the MPK as

$$\text{MPK} = \theta \left(\frac{\text{sales}}{K} \right)$$

where the constant of proportionality

$$\theta \equiv (1 + \tfrac{1}{\eta})\alpha_k = \frac{r + \delta}{\text{industry average (sales}/K)}$$

is allowed to vary across industries. These identifying assumptions for θ, while true for Cobb–Douglas production functions with a constant elasticity demand curve, are very strong and likely to introduce measurement error just as in the original criticism leveled at average q. For example, there is no reason to believe that θ is constant over time and within an industry. In addition, to solve for θ for an industry, it is assumed that the average marginal product of capital within the industry is just the user cost, $r + \delta$. However, this is not true in general for most specifications of adjustment costs. It is also not true if there are financial-market imperfections, since constrained firms will act as if they faced a higher discount rate than the market rate for unconstrained firms. While the high discount rate is not a problem under the null hypothesis, the authors use this measure of fundamentals to interpret their linearized model of financial imperfections.

The most problematic issue with the construction of fundamentals in this paper is the interpretation of a quantity-based measure such as sales rather than a forward-looking asset price such as stock returns or interest rates. It is well known that including almost any firm-level quantity variable has strong predictive power in investment regressions, while including variables related to the user cost does not work as well. By adding a quantity-based measure such as sales, are we really capturing the expected marginal return on investment, or are we capturing accelerator effects? This question is similar to an earlier debate in the investment literature in which strong interest-rate elasticities for investment were found by substituting output for the interest rate in the firm's first-order condition for investment. These results were not robust to using interest rates directly.

It is certainly possible that quantity measures, such as sales, have less measurement error than price measures, such as average q or the user cost, for measuring economic fundamentals. The problem with arguing that the marginal product of capital is proportional to sales is one of interpretation. How do you separate the effects of fundamentals from financial explanations when financial-market imperfections are the main story behind accelerator models? Models with financial-market imperfections predict that the average product of capital (APK) or other measures of profits should be important for investment in addition to the marginal product. Even in the authors' model, the APK and the MPK will be highly correlated:

$$\text{APK} = \theta_2 \left(\frac{\text{sales}}{K} \right) - \frac{F}{K}$$

Similarly, it is difficult to separate the partial effects of sales and cash flow in the regression

$$\frac{I}{K} = \beta_0 + \beta_1 \text{EPDV} \left(\frac{\text{sales}}{K} \right) + \beta_2 \text{EPDV} \left(\frac{\text{CF}}{K} \right).$$

Since profits or cash flow is equal to sales minus costs, do we really believe that shocks to sales capture economic fundamentals while shocks to costs are only related to financial effects? The authors argue that there is some variation in cash flow which is not related to fundamentals. However, there is also some variation in cash flow which is related to fundamentals, and in sales which is related to the firm's financial condition. As a result, I think of both sales and cash flow as noisy estimates of both fundamentals and financial effects.

Even though it may be difficult to separate fundamentals from financial effects through direct measurement, there is still a lot of potential in this approach. In particular, I encourage the authors to follow the methodology used in their previous paper, Gilchrist and Himmelberg (1995). Rather than trying to distinguish the MPK from cash flow, the authors focused on the strength of this method—dynamics. Using the same variable for both fundamentals and financial effects, it is possible to test for financial effects by looking at whether investment has excess sensitivity to current variables:

$$\frac{I}{K} = \beta_0 + \beta_1 \text{EPDV} \left(\frac{\text{CF}}{K} \right) + \beta_2 \frac{\text{CF}}{K}.$$

Does current cash flow or, even better, the stock of cash predict investment even after controlling for the EPDV of future profits?

In future work, adding more structure to the alternative model of financial-market imperfections should yield differential predictions to help test the validity of financial explanations for investment. In my past work, for example, I showed (Gross, 1997) that imposing liquidity constraints leads to strong nonlinearities in the predicted effects of financial variables, which are confirmed in the data. It would be even more useful to explicitly model the information or agency problem which generated the financial-market imperfection in the first place. It may be too much to ask for an empirically tractable, theoretically justified model of financial-market imperfections which allows for nonconvex adjustment costs and can deal with the heterogeneity present in real-world data. However, it will be difficult to fully understand the microeconomics of investment without such a model.

REFERENCES

Abel, A. B., and O. Blanchard. (1986). The present value of profits and cyclical movements in investments. *Econometrica* 54:249–273.
Caballero, R. J., and J. V. Leahy. (1996). The demise of marginal *q*. Cambridge, MA: National Bureau of Economic Research. NBER Working Paper 5508.
Gilchrist S., and C. P. Himmelberg. (1995). Evidence on the role of cash flow for investment. *Journal of Monetary Economics* 36:541–572.
Gross, D. B. (1997). The investment and financing decisions of liquidity constrained firms. University of Chicago. Mimeo.

Comment

KENNETH D. WEST
University of Wisconsin

1. Introduction

In this stimulating paper, Gilchrist and Himmelberg (hereafter, GH) use Compustat data to test and quantify the effect of financial factors on investment. I like the paper's innovative willingness to estimate and test a structural model with financial frictions. In my view, this is a welcome advance on a common practice of estimating a model without such frictions and testing whether the model fails in ways consistent with financial frictions. By specifying precisely and completely how financial frictions affect investment, GH can quantify the effects of those frictions,

I thank the National Science Foundation and the Graduate School of the University of Wisconsin for financial support, and John Jones for helpful comments and discussions.

and get a sense for whether still richer models are required to adequately explain investment.

I divide my comments into two parts. First is a summary of the literature on borrowing constraints and investment. Then follows a discussion of the structural model (Sections 3–5 in GH). I conclude that the present paper leaves some important questions unanswered. While I am receptive to GH's interpretation, in the end I do not find it compelling.

2. *Borrowing Constraints and Investment*

In typical parametrizations of the models of Hall and Jorgenson (1967) and Tobin (1969), investment is determined by the ratio of output to the cost of capital or by stock-market-based measures of Tobin's Q, perhaps along with lags of these variables or of investment itself. For want of a better term, I will refer to such variables as the *traditional* determinants of investment. At least since Meyer and Kuh (1957), however, it has been recognized that cash flow is a good predictor of aggregate investment. Clark (1979) concluded that cash flow and output together predict better than do the neoclassical determinants, a finding broadly consistent with the somewhat weaker role for cash flow found in the more recent study by Kopcke (1993).

In a pioneering paper, Fazzari, Hubbard, and Petersen (1988) established a complementary set of results with individual firm data. They ran investment regressions in which right-hand-side variables included some traditional determinants of investment as well as cash flow. They found that cash flow had a statistically significant effect on investment for firms that one might expect to be financially constrained, namely, ones with low dividend payouts. As documented in Hubbard's (1998) survey, many subsequent studies have found that measures of liquidity, such as cash flow or debt, are statistically significant predictors of investment for firms displaying low dividends, no bond rating, or some other presumed signals of financial illiquidity. While a literature has risen in reaction, arguing that in one or another dataset the empirical evidence in fact does not suggest that financial factors are important (e.g., Hayashi, 1997; Kaplan and Zingales, 1997; Cummins, Hassett, and Oliner, 1998), it is my judgment that there now exists a strong case that financial variables have information about investment not contained in the traditional measures.

The predictive power of cash flow suggests a difference between internal and external costs of funds. Indeed, it has been shown formally that in the presence of informational frictions, such as imperfect or costly monitoring of a firm's behavior by a lender (Townsend, 1979; Myers and Majluf, 1984), the shadow value of internal funds will be larger than that of external funds, at least some of the time. Cash flow will therefore likely affect investment, even after controlling for traditional determinants.

In my opinion, however, the empirical literature has not made a good case that informational frictions in fact rationalize the empirical importance of financial variables.[1] It is well recognized that misspecification of the parametric form of the traditional model, or inappropriate accounting for unobservable disturbances or for the informational role of financial variables, could cause spurious significance of financial variables, significance that would disappear if the frictionless model were appropriately specified.

Support for the view that financial frictions rather than misspecification are key could come from establishing that the estimates on financial factors fall in a tight range predicted by an underlying theoretical model, that a model with financial frictions does not reject tests of overidentifying restrictions, that no variables beyond those posited by the model have substantial explanatory power for investment, and so on. To my knowledge, little research in this literature attempts to do so. Instead, the bulk of the literature that I am familiar with evaluates (and usually rejects) a null neoclassical model. No doubt this is in large part because quantitatively tractable models of financial frictions are difficult to come by. Nonetheless, this approach yields diminishing returns for people who, like me, are already persuaded that cash flow and other financial variables help predict the investment of firms that display signs of illiquidity.

I therefore am very receptive to Gilchrist and Himmelberg's effort to formulate and evaluate a model with financial frictions.

3. Gilchrist and Himmelberg's Model

Sections 3–5 of GH specify, estimate, and test a model of investment in the presence of financial frictions—that is, the null model is one with financial frictions (though a frictionless model is nested within the null model).

Specifically, this part of GH:

1. Nor, even assuming that these frictions in fact do account for the econometric results, does this or related literature establish that the frictions have nontrivial effects on aggregate output, although it has been shown that such frictions potentially have aggregate effects (Carlstrom and Fuerst, 1997; Kiyotaki and Moore, 1997; Jones, 1998). But further discussion of that point will take us pretty far from the GH paper.

1. Constructs a present value called *fundamental Q*—a specific example of what I called a "traditional" measure above—by positing a parametric functional form, linearizing, and using data on output, capital, and other variables, as in Abel and Blanchard (1986). Fundamentals depend only on the marginal profit of capital (MPK) and, in contrast to Abel and Blanchard (1986) and many other papers, not on discount factors (i.e., not on user costs of capital), which are assumed not to vary.

2. Approximates the effects of financial frictions by (i) showing that these will manifest themselves in time-varying discount factors; (ii) linearizing to separate the discount factor from the frictionless fundamentals; (iii) assuming the linearized term is also linear in observable financial data, namely, cash and equivalents, or working capital less long-term debt.

3. Regresses investment on lagged investment, fundamental *Q*, and the present value of financial frictions (*financial Q*). The finding is that financial frictions are both statistically and economically important.

As a mechanical matter, the regressions are novel essentially in entering the financial variable in a constrained form, as a present value; the common procedure in this literature is simply to add a variable like cash and equivalents to whatever variables are included by virtue of the traditional model under examination. The important novelty is a willingness to maintain, at least tentatively, that the addition of the financial variable results in a complete model for investment. GH acknowledge that the model in fact does miss an important aspect of investment behavior, in that the data want lagged investment on the right-hand side (Section 5.3), and they make rationalizing this extra term a high priority for future research. But they also clearly feel that the present specification documents strong economic and statistical effects from financial frictions.

While I do find GH's results suggestive, I am not as convinced as are GH that they have documented strong effects. In explaining this viewpoint, I will not promote an alternative interpretation of their results, still less provide a different point estimate of the quantitative effects of financial frictions. Rather, I want to raise some questions, which, until answered, suggest caution in interpreting GH's findings. These questions include:

1. In their theoretical development, GH assume that in the absence of financial frictions the discount rate is constant across firms and time (Section 3.1); had they carried through the algebra with time-varying discount rates, there would have been an additional term, involving

the present value of future values of discount rates (see Abel and Blanchard, 1986). The presence of time dummies in the empirical work implicitly allows time variation in discount rates that is common to all firms; the presence of a fixed effect means one can interpret such variation as occurring around a firm-specific mean discount rate. (That is, these dummies allow for time variation in discount rates that is perfectly correlated across firms, with each firm possibly having a different mean discount rate.) But firm-specific variation (i.e., imperfect correlation across firms) is swept into the regression disturbance. And we have a raft of finance studies indicating that discount rates vary across firms. Such variation may affect the estimates on the coefficients on the two present values included by GH. If the variation is largely uncorrelated with the GH present values (perhaps this is the case for most firms presumed to be financially unconstrained in Tables 5 and 6), the GH interpretation is still legitimate. But if the variation is correlated with the included present values (perhaps firms that are financially constrained undertake riskier projects), omitted-variable bias will invalidate the GH procedure. So: how are the estimates and interpretation affected by cross-sectional variation in discount factors stemming from traditional forces (rather than from financial frictions)?

2. When lagged investment is added to the GH equation, the term proves significant, but, the authors tell us, the point estimates on the two present values change little. It is, however, premature to conclude, as the authors seem to, that once the model is expanded to formally allow for lagged investment, the statistical or economic importance of the two present values will change little. This is because in the expanded model the present values will be calculated in a different way, implying that the present model's regressions contain noisy measures of the relevant objects. If one rationalizes the lag with costs of adjustment or serially correlated shocks, the relevant regression will involve a lag of investment and two present values, and the two present values will be different from the ones presently included. (For example, with costs of adjustment, a certain quadratic will be factored, with forward solution of the unstable root to this quadratic affecting the present value calculation.) If, instead (or in addition), one rationalizes the lag with an information role for investment—that is, the firm forecasts the present values using data not available to the econometrician—the regression will still involve only two present values, but once again the two will be different from the ones presently included (see Kiyotaki and West, 1996). So: what happens when

the model is extended to rationalize the predictive power of lagged investment?

3. GH state that their linearization implies that the external finance premium is proportional to their measure of financial liquidity (either cash and equivalents, or working capital less long-term debt), with a factor of proportionality ϕ. They also conclude that the regression estimate of ϕ is pretty much consistent with a back-of-the-envelope calculation. I could not quite follow the details of this calibration, so I will not comment except to state such a check on the reasonableness of the estimate is an important one. An additional check is suggested by the model's implication that one can read interest-rate spreads off the measure of financial liquidity. If one backs out a series of spreads (presumably identified only up to the addition of a constant), what does the series look like, and how does it compare to observed data on lending rates?

I look forward to the answers to questions such as these in the next paper in the Gilchrist Himmelberg's research program.

REFERENCES

Abel, A., and O. J. Blanchard. (1986). The present value of profits and cyclical movement in investment, *Econometrica* 54(2):249–274.

Carlstrom, C. T., and T. S. Fuerst. (1997). Agency costs, net worth and business fluctuations: A computable general equilibrium analysis. *American Economic Review* 82:430–450.

Clark, P. K. (1979). Investment in the 1970s: Theory, performance and prediction. *Brookings Papers on Economic Activity* 1979(1):73–113.

Cummins, J. G., K. A. Hassett, and S. Oliner. (1998). Investment behavior, observable expectations, and internal funds. New York University. Manuscript.

Fazzari, S. R., R. G. Hubbard, and B. Petersen. (1988). Financing constraints and corporate investment. *Brookings Papers on Economic Activity* 1, 141–195.

Hall, R. E., and D. Jorgenson. (1967). Tax policy and investment behavior. *American Economic Review* 53, 391–414.

Hayashi, F. (1997). The main bank system and corporate investment: An empirical reassessment. Cambridge, MA: National Bureau of Economic Research. NBER Working Paper 6172.

Hubbard, R. G. (1998). Capital market imperfections and investment. *Journal of Economic Literature* XXXVI:193–225.

Jones, J. (1998). Firm finance with collateral constraints: Business cycle implications. University of Wisconsin. Manuscript.

Kaplan, S. N., and L. Zingales. (1997). Do investment–cash flow sensitivities provide useful measures of financing constraints? *Quarterly Journal of Economics* 112:169–215.

Kiyotaki, N., and J. Moore. (1997). Credit cycles. *Journal of Political Economy* 105, 211–248.

———, and K. D. West. (1996). Business fixed investment and the recent business cycle in Japan. In *NBER Macroeconomics Annual, 1996*, B. Bernanke and J. Rotemberg (eds.), Cambridge, MA: The MIT Press, pp. 277–323.

Kopcke, R. A. (1993). The determinants of business investment: Has capital spending been surprisingly low? *New England Economic Review*, 3–31.

Meyer, J. R., and E. Kuh. (1957). *The Investment Decision*, Cambridge, MA: Harvard University Press.

Myers, S. C., and N. Majluf. (1984). Corporate financing and investment decisions when firms have information that investors do not have. *Journal of Financial Economics* 13(2):187–221.

Tobin, J. (1969). A general equilibrium approach to monetary theory. *Journal of Money, Credit and Banking* 1, 15–29.

Townsend, R. M. (1979). Optimal contracts and competitive markets with costly state verification. *Journal of Economic Theory* 21(2):265–293.

Discussion

Much of the discussion focused on the adequacy of the baseline model, particularly the use of the sales-to-capital ratio as a measure of the marginal profitability of fixed capital. Janice Eberly pointed out that the proportionality of profitability and sales requires that variable factors, such as labor, be adjustable instantaneously. If there are costs of adjusting labor, then shocks to wages (for example) will affect profitability and cash flow without having a short-run effect on output. On a related issue, Fabio Schiantarelli noted that, if there are costs of adjusting the capital stock, the net marginal profitability of capital depends on the investment-to-capital ratio as well as sales. Jason Cummins asked about the omission of inventories from the analysis. Charles Himmelberg replied to Cummins that, possibly because of the use of annual data, it makes little difference empirically whether inventories are included, that is, either sales or production can be used as the measure of profitability. More generally, Himmelberg defended the baseline model by pointing out that it seems to work well empirically for bond-rated firms, which are less likely to be financially constrained. Deviations from the baseline model are thus reasonably interpreted as arising from financial factors.

A second issue was the possible effects of unmodeled heterogeneity among firms. Cummins suggested that the restriction that the data-generating process for shocks is identical across firms is unrealistic. He noted that financial analysts produce earnings forecasts using firm-specific models. He reported that, in his own work with coauthors, the use of firm-specific earnings expectations reduced the measured effect of cash-flow variables significantly. Himmelberg disputed the result that earnings expectations measures "drive out" cash-flow variables from investment equations, indicating that this was not the case for the specifications used in the present paper. He also argued that earnings expectations might be interpreted as projections of whether the firm can repay its debt, that is, as an indicator of financial condition, rather than as forecasts of long-term profitability. Also on the theme of heterogeneity, Benjamin Friedman proposed that investment–cash-flow relationships might be quite different at the firm level than at the industry level. For example, a firm might be impelled to invest by an increase in competitive pressure, resulting in a negative relationship of current cash flow and future investment for the firm, even though that relationship might well be positive for the industry as a whole.

Econometric issues also received some discussion. Stephen Oliner proposed the use of a larger set of instruments to reduce problems of endogeneity.

John Shea
UNIVERSITY OF MARYLAND AND NBER

What Do Technology Shocks Do?

1. Introduction

The real business cycle (RBC) approach to short-run fluctuations, pioneered by Kydland and Prescott (KP) (1982) and Long and Plosser (LP) (1983), has dominated the academic business-cycle literature over the last decade and a half. KP and LP were seminal in several respects. First, they reintroduced the Schumpeterian idea that stochastic technological progress could generate business cycles. Second, they argued that one could explain fluctuations using a frictionless neoclassical framework in which business cycles are optimal and therefore require no smoothing by policymakers. Third, they argued that business cycles could and should be explained using dynamic stochastic general equilibrium models in which preferences and production are explicitly spelled out in a way consistent with microeconomic first principles, such as optimizing behavior.

The RBC literature has broadened considerably since KP and LP. Recent research has introduced frictions such as imperfect competition (e.g., Rotemberg and Woodford, 1995), increasing returns to scale (e.g., Farmer and Guo, 1994), and price stickiness (e.g., Kimball, 1995), as well as alternative sources of shocks, such as government spending (e.g., Christiano and Eichenbaum, 1992), monetary policy (e.g., Christiano and Eichenbaum, 1995), and animal spirits (e.g., Schmitt-Grohe, 1997). The idea that business cycles should be analyzed using explicit dynamic stochastic general equilibrium models seems destined to be the main lasting contribution of KP and LP's work.

Meanwhile, the profession has largely ignored the empirical question of what role technology shocks actually play in business cycles. I believe that this is unfortunate, for four reasons. First, the idea that new prod-

I thank Kortum and Susanto Basu for providing their data, and the editors and participants, as well as seminar participants at Brown, for helpful comments.

ucts and processes are introduced at a time-varying rate is inherently plausible, at least at the disaggregated industry level. Second, much recent research exploring the effects of frictions on business-cycle propagation still assumes that cycles are driven by technology shocks (e.g., Cogley and Nason, 1995; Horvath, 1997; Carlstrom and Fuerst, 1997). It would be useful to know if this modeling strategy has any empirical foundation. Third, while few would argue any more that technology shocks are the *only* source of business cycles, it would still be useful to know if technology shocks can explain *some* part of fluctuations, particularly given that monetary, oil price, and other observable shocks seem unable to account for a large fraction of observed cyclical variation in output (Cochrane, 1994). Finally, even if technology shocks are not responsible for a large share of volatility, the response of the economy to technology could help distinguish between competing views of the economy's propagation mechanisms. In the baseline one-sector flexible-price RBC model, technology shocks shift out the production possibilities frontier, inducing short-run increases in investment, labor, and materials. In multisector models, industry technology shocks reduce input prices to downstream sectors, inducing increases in downstream input and output. Meanwhile, Galí (1996) and Basu, Fernald, and Kimball (1997) demonstrate that favorable technology shocks may reduce input use in the short run if prices are sticky; intuitively, if prices do not fall, output will be unchanged and inputs must fall to accommodate improved total factor productivity (TFP). Thus, one can potentially distinguish between sticky and flexible price models by examining whether technology shocks increase or decrease input use.

To date, the empirical case for technology has largely been made indirectly, by showing that plausibly calibrated models driven by technology shocks can produce realistic patterns of volatility and comovement. Of course, these quantitative exercises, while informative, do not tell us what technology shocks actually do. Two pieces of more direct evidence are that measured TFP is procyclical and that aggregate output potentially has a unit root, suggesting that at least some output shocks are permanent. However, it is now well known that neither of these facts proves that technology is important to business cycles. Observable nontechnology shocks cause procyclical movements in TFP, consistent with imperfect competition, increasing returns to scale, procyclical factor utilization, or procyclical reallocation of factors to high productivity sectors (e.g., Hall, 1988; Evans, 1992; Burnside, Eichenbaum, and Rebelo, 1995; Basu and Fernald, 1997). Meanwhile, demand shocks can have permanent effects on output in endogenous growth models (e.g., Stadler, 1990); and in any case, a unit root is consistent with transitory shocks driving an arbitrarily large fraction of short-run variation (Quah, 1989).

This paper takes a more direct approach to assessing what technology shocks do, an approach inspired by the large literature estimating the impact of monetary policy shocks on the economy (e.g., Christiano, Eichenbaum, and Evans, 1998). Using annual panel data for 19 U.S. manufacturing industries from 1959 to 1991, I employ vector autoregressions (VARs) to document the dynamic impact of shocks to two observable indicators of technological change: research and development (R&D) spending, and patent applications. R&D measures the amount of input devoted to innovative activity, while patent applications measure inventive output. Previous studies (e.g., Griliches and Lichtenberg, 1984; Lichtenberg and Siegel, 1991; Scherer, 1993), as well as results reported below, suggest that variation in R&D and patenting is related to long-run variation in productivity growth across firms and industries. Moreover, industry-level R&D and patents display nontrivial short-run fluctuations, as can be seen in Figure 1, which plots log real R&D and log patent applications by industry of manufacture and use for the U.S. aerospace industry. If technological progress is truly stochastic, then fluctuations in R&D should in part reflect variation in the perceived marginal product of knowledge, while fluctuations in patents should in part reflect shocks to the success of research activity. I use these fluctuations to estimate how a typical industry's inputs and TFP respond over time to technology shocks, and to quantify the share of industry volatility due to technology shocks. I estimate the impact of both own technology shocks and technology shocks in upstream input-supplying industries.

To be sure, fluctuations in R&D and patent applications may not be due to technology shocks alone. Griliches (1989), for instance, argues that patenting fluctuations in the U.S. are in part responses to factors such as changes in patent law and changes in the efficiency and resources of the U.S. Patent Office. Both R&D and patent applications, meanwhile, are a type of investment, and as such they may respond endogenously to output shocks, either because of financial-market constraints or because current shocks are positively correlated with the future marginal product of capital. My preferred VAR specifications address these concerns by including time dummies in the regressions and by placing the technological indicators last in the Choleski ordering used to decompose the VAR innovations into orthogonal components. The time dummies remove fluctuations in R&D and patent applications due to aggregate factors unrelated to true technological progress, such as changes in the number of patent examiners, provided that these factors affect all industries equally. My impulse responses therefore measure the

Figure 1 TECHNOLOGY INDICATORS IN THE AEROSPACE INDUSTRY

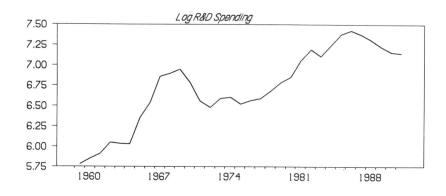

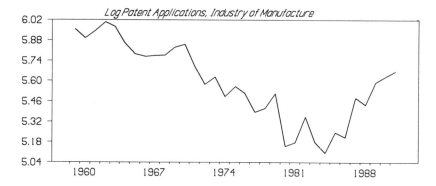

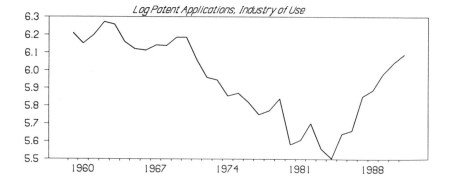

impact of industry-specific technology shocks on industry-specific fluctuations in inputs and TFP, while my variance decompositions estimate
the contribution of technology shocks to idiosyncratic industry fluctuations. Placing technology last in the ordering, meanwhile, defines technology shocks as the component of R&D or patenting orthogonal to both
lagged technology and lagged and contemporaneous inputs and TFP.
Empirically, innovations to industry output are positively correlated
with innovations to both R&D and patent applications; placing technology last assumes that this contemporaneous comovement reflects an
accelerator mechanism running from industry activity to technology,
rather than an instantaneous impact of technology shocks on output.
This assumption seems inherently plausible given the likely lags between R&D spending, invention, and diffusion of a new technology
(Gort and Klepper, 1982).

My main empirical findings are as follows. First, favorable technology
shocks—increases in the orthogonal components of R&D and patents—
tend to increase input use, especially labor, in the short run, but to reduce
inputs in the long run. Second, technology improvements tend to encourage substitution towards capital relative to materials and labor, as well as
substitution towards nonproduction labor relative to production labor.
These results are consistent with recent cross-sectional studies establishing a complementary long-run relationship between technological change
and equipment (Delong and Summers, 1991) and skilled labor (Berman,
Bound, and Griliches, 1994). Third, favorable technology shocks do not
significantly increase measured TFP at any horizon, and indeed in some
cases reduce TFP. This suggests that procyclical movements in TFP have
little to do with the introduction of new products and processes. Fourth,
technology shocks explain only a small share of idiosyncratic industry
volatility of inputs and TFP at business-cycle horizons. This result is bad
news for technology-shock-driven models, particularly given that
industry-specific technology shocks are likely to explain industry-specific
volatility better than aggregate volatility (Horvath, 1997). However, my
results could be consistent with models in which technology contributes
to low-frequency fluctuations (e.g., Jovanovic and Lach, 1997); or with
models in which the important "real" shocks come from strikes, weather,
cartel behavior, and so on; or with models in which "technology shocks"
are not due to stochastic scientific and engineering developments, but to
stochastic movements in management techniques or industrial organization that cause a given set of inputs to be more or less efficient. Finally, I
find that technology improvements are more likely to raise TFP and reduce prices in industries characterized by process innovations than in
industries dominated by product innovations. This suggests that my fail-

ure to find strong effects of technology on TFP may be due in part to the failure of available price data to capture productivity gains caused by quality improvements and new product introductions.

Two other recent papers (Galí, 1996; Basu, Fernald, and Kimball, 1997) also investigate the short-run impact of technology shocks, in both cases using aggregate data. Galí estimates a structural vector autoregression for labor productivity and labor input in the United States, identifying technology shocks by assuming that only technology affects long-run productivity. Basu, Fernald, and Kimball correct industry-level TFP for variations due to increasing returns to scale, imperfect competition, and cyclical factor utilization, and then measure aggregate technology as an appropriately weighted average of sectoral technology. Interestingly, Galí (1996) and Basu, Fernald, and Kimball (1997) both find that favorable technology shocks reduce input use in the short run, consistent with sticky prices but contrary to my results.

These two papers represent a distinct advance over existing literature. Nevertheless, one might disagree with their methodologies for measuring technological change. Galí's approach rests heavily on the assumption that demand shocks cannot affect productivity in the long run. This assumption is inconsistent both with endogenous growth models and with models in which recessions cleanse the economy by wiping out low-productivity firms (e.g., Caballero and Hammour, 1994, 1996). Cleansing models, in particular, predict that favorable demand shocks will reduce long-run productivity, and Galí himself has in the past argued for such an interpretation of the data (Galí and Hammour, 1992). Interestingly, my impulse response functions suggest that input innovations lead to short-run increases in TFP, consistent with increasing returns or procyclical utilization, but long-run decreases in TFP, consistent with cleansing models.

Basu, Fernald, and Kimball's approach does not rely on long-run restrictions. It does, however, rely on the idea that TFP fluctuations are valid measures of stochastic technological progress at the two-digit industry level, once one corrects for increasing returns, imperfect competition, and cyclical factor utilization. This idea seems plausible, but it is not necessarily true, given that fluctuations in "corrected" sectoral TFP could still be due to nontechnology sources such as measurement error, within-sector factor reallocations, or inadequate corrections for increasing returns or cyclical utilization. Basu, Fernald, and Kimball's methodology would be more convincing if their corrected measure of technology could be linked to some sort of outside measure of technological progress, such as anecdotal evidence on the timing of particular technical changes in particular industries.

The remainder of the paper proceeds as follows. Section 2 describes the data. Section 3 examines long-run and contemporaneous relationships between technological progress and my measures of innovative activity, largely to connect my work to previous studies. Section 4 presents evidence from VARs, and Section 5 concludes.

2. Data Description

My goal is to examine the time-series interactions between measures of technological change, such as patents and R&D, and measures of economic activity. Ideally, I would estimate these interactions using aggregate data for a single country, following the empirical literature on monetary policy. However, this approach is not feasible in my case. The only readily available data for patents and R&D are annual rather than quarterly or monthly, implying short aggregate time series. Even if higher-frequency data could be constructed, it is not clear that they would be useful, since the impact of technological change on the economy is likely to operate at a somewhat lower frequency than the impact of monetary shocks. To obtain sufficient degrees of freedom to estimate the impact of technology shocks with reasonable precision, I use panel data for 19 manufacturing industries covering 1959–1991, exploiting the fact that technological developments are not perfectly synchronized across industries. An alternative, worth pursuing in future work, would be to use annual aggregate data for a panel of countries, or for panels of both countries and industries.

Data on R&D by industry are taken from the National Science Foundation's annual survey of U.S. firms. I examine only company-financed R&D. Previous research using cross sections of industries and firms (e.g., Terleckyj, 1975; Lichtenberg and Siegel, 1991) has shown that long-run productivity growth is related to company-financed R&D, but not to federally financed R&D, suggesting that public R&D dollars are spent inefficiently or that they are spent in areas, such as defense or space exploration, where productivity measurement is difficult. I convert nominal R&D to 1991 dollars using the GDP deflator, then convert real R&D flows to an R&D capital stock, following Griliches (1973) and most other subsequent research. I employ a linear capital accumulation equation, assuming a 15% annual depreciation rate and setting the 1959 stock equal to the 1959 flow divided by 0.15 plus the industry's average R&D growth over the sample period; these assumptions are standard in recent literature (e.g., Lach, 1995; Keller, 1997). The empirical results are similar if I use real R&D flows instead of R&D stocks. As a timing convention, I include R&D spending in year t in the R&D stock for year

Table 1   SAMPLE MEANS

Industry	R&D	R&D Growth	Manuf. Patents	Manuf. Patent Growth	Use Patents	Use Patent Growth
Food (SIC 20)	879.1	4.62	311.2	0.63	1085	0.06
Textiles (SIC 22–23)	185.5	3.57	620.9	1.17	994	−0.81
Lumber (SIC 24–25)	152.0	4.81	605.9	0.08	597	−0.05
Paper (SIC 26)	611.7	5.53	482.4	0.04	490	0.08
Industrial chemicals (SIC 281–282, 286)	3211.7	2.80	3758.8	0.75	2518	0.47
Drugs (SIC 283)	2629.4	7.75	825.5	5.90	1100	2.73
Other chemicals (other SIC 28)	1053.0	5.27	2517.4	0.54	1261	0.70
Petroleum (SIC 29)	1812.4	2.82	1745.5	−1.30	1659	0.22
Rubber (SIC 30)	693.2	4.01	1586.0	1.03	1348	1.45
Stone (SIC 32)	574.5	3.05	506.8	1.60	557	0.76
Metals (SIC 33)	835.9	1.51	373.1	0.30	795	0.06
Metal prods. (SIC 34)	684.1	2.06	3737.6	0.18	1979	0.24
Computers (SIC 357)	5172.6	6.66	1114.3	2.70	1333	3.09
Other nonelec. equip. (other SIC 35)	2102.3	5.08	10966.1	−0.15	4084	−0.33
Electronics & commun. equip. (SIC 366–367)	5018.4	6.65	5629.4	1.51	4456	1.76
Other electric equip. (Other SIC 36)	2043.7	0.99	4154.1	0.41	2779	0.43
Aerospace (SIC 372, 376)	4022.4	4.81	276.9	−1.22	392	−0.77
Autos & other transp. equip. (SIC 37)	5701.8	4.37	1972.1	−0.28	2787	−0.09
Instruments (SIC 38)	3100.3	7.42	3626.7	2.33	1268	1.59

t, so that I can interpret the correlations between R&D and other variables as reflecting a contemporaneous response of R&D to industry activity. I use data for 19 manufacturing industries; these are listed in Table 1 along with sample means of real R&D flows in millions of dollars and the growth rate of the R&D stock. The largest flows of company R&D are found in automobiles, electronics, and computers; the fastest-growing R&D stocks are in drugs, electronics, computers, and instruments. Note that my baseline sample omits nonmanufacturing industries as well as some manufacturing industries (tobacco, printing and publishing, leather, and miscellaneous manufacturing) whose R&D data are lumped together by the NSF. The share of overall R&D accounted for by these sectors is trivial for most of my sample period.

I must mention two problems with these data. First, to avoid disclosure of individual firms' operations, the NSF suppresses some industry-year observations. In virtually all such cases, the NSF suppresses either company-financed or total (including federally financed) R&D, but not both, so that I can interpolate gaps in company R&D using growth of total R&D. Second, the NSF data are collected at the company level. All R&D spending performed by a company is assigned to the industry in which the company had the most sales, even if part of the R&D was conducted in establishments belonging to another industry. Given that R&D is typically performed in large conglomerated firms, the assignment of R&D to particular industries is presumably subject to error. Particularly troubling is the fact that a given firm's industry classification can change over time as its pattern of sales changes, creating the possibility of large movements in measured industry-level R&D spending unrelated to actual changes in spending at the establishment level. Griliches and Lichtenberg (1984) attempt to overcome this problem by using R&D data grouped by applied product field rather than by industry of origin. Unfortunately, the reporting requirements of the NSF's product field survey were burdensome on participating firms, leading to spotty coverage. The survey was reduced from annual to biannual beginning in 1978, and was discontinued in 1986.

Patent data for U.S. industries are not routinely available. The reason is that the U.S. Patent Office assigns new patents to technological fields, but not to industries. Estimating patents by industry for the U.S. thus requires a mapping from technological fields into industries. The most satisfactory mapping available is the Yale Technology Concordance (YTC), described by Kortum and Putnam (1997). This concordance uses the fact that the Canadian patent office assigns patents to technological fields, to industries of manufacture, and to industries of use; for instance, a new farm tractor invented in an aerospace establishment would be assigned to the agricultural machinery sector (industry of manufacture) and to agriculture itself (industry of use). The YTC estimates mappings between technological field and industries of manufacture and use using the Canadian data, then applies the Canadian mapping to U.S. patents by technological field. For this study, I use annual data on U.S. patent applications grouped both by industry of manufacture and by industry of use, generously provided by Sam Kortum. I convert the annual flows of patents to stocks using the same method as for R&D; the empirical results again are similar if I use flows instead of stocks. Note that patents grouped by date of application are superior to patents grouped by date of grant, both because application presumably coincides with the economic viability of an innovation, and because historically there have been long and variable lags between application and granting in the United States, caused in part by changes in the resources of the U.S. Patent Office (Griliches, 1989).

I must again acknowledge potential problems with these data. First, the assignment of U.S. patents to industries is presumably not perfect, as the mapping between technological fields and industries probably varies between the U.S. and Canada as well as over time. Kortum and Putnam (1997) show that the estimated Canadian mapping forecasts Canadian industry patents out of sample reasonably well, alleviating these concerns somewhat but not entirely. Second, the distinction in the data between industry of manufacture and industry of use is not as sharp as one might hope. Ideally, I would like to interpret manufacture patents as "product innovations" and use patents as "process innovations." However, conversations with Sam Kortum suggested that this interpretation is not entirely correct; for instance, process innovations often wind up being assigned the same industries of manufacture and use even if no new product is created, while new products with broad applicability often wind up being assigned no industry of use. My sense is that we can at least safely assume that manufacture patents contain a higher fraction of product innovations than do use patents, and that use patents contain a higher fraction of process innovations than do manufacture patents.

I present sample means for patent flows and patent stock growth in Table 1. The flows of both manufacture and use patents are highest in nonelectrical machinery and electronics, while patent stocks grow most rapidly in drugs and computers. Notice that manufacture patent flows exceed use patent flows in most industries, and for my sample as a whole; this reflects the fact that many product innovations originating in manufacturing are used in nonmanufacturing, while few innovations originate in nonmanufacturing. The table also documents the fact, discussed in Griliches (1989) and Kortum (1993), that patent stocks have grown more slowly in the postwar United States than R&D stocks, or equivalently that the amount of real R&D per patent has been steadily rising. Some observers assert that this trend is evidence of vanishing technological opportunities; others argue that the cost of patenting has risen secularly and that patenting has become more concentrated in high-value innovations. Recall that my VARs include time dummies, which will control for any economy-wide changes in the cost or benefits of patenting that have affected the ratio of inventive activity to patents.

In addition to examining the impact of own R&D and patents, I examine the impact of innovations in upstream industries. I construct these measures using data from the 1977 U.S. input–output study, following the methods used by Terleckyj (1975), Keller (1997), and others. I begin by constructing a 19-by-20 matrix whose (i, j) element shows the total flow of goods in 1977 from sample industry i to sample industry j, including both intermediate and capital flows; I describe the construction of total flow matrices from raw input–output data in Shea (1991, 1993). The 20th column combines flows to omitted manufacturing industries, nonmanufacturing industries, private consumption, and government. I set diagonal elements to zero, then divide by row sums to obtain the shares of external demand for each sample industry accounted for by each other sample industry. I then multiply these demand shares by each industry's R&D and patent flows, to obtain the implicit "flow" of R&D and patents to and from each sample industry. Taking column sums gives me an estimate of the flows of upstream R&D and upstream patent applications to each manufacturing industry in any year. I cumulate these flows into stocks using the methods described above. These measures exclude R&D or patents coming from omitted industries; as mentioned earlier, however, those industries account for little innovative activity for most of my sample period.

My measures of TFP and inputs for manufacturing industries come from the NBER productivity database, described in Bartlesman and Gray (1996). The NBER data include annual measures of gross output and capital, labor, and materials inputs for 450 four-digit manufacturing industries. I measure labor as total employment multiplied by hours worked per production worker, assuming that production and nonproduction hours per worker are perfectly correlated. I define total input growth as a Divisia index of capital, labor, and materials growth, weighting with factor shares in gross output and measuring the capital share as a residual. TFP growth is defined as output growth minus input growth. I measure input and TFP growth at the four-digit level, aggregate up to the 19 industries listed in Table 1 using shares in nominal gross output, then convert growth rates to level indices. Below, I examine the dynamic impact of technology shocks both on total input and on capital, labor, and materials separately, premultiplying log capital, labor, and materials by their shares in nominal gross output in order to avoid having to impose the condition that factor shares in production are identical across industries.

3. Preliminary Evidence

This section examines the univariate time-series properties of my data, and replicates previous work examining cross-section and contemporaneous time-series relationships between technology and TFP. My baseline data are annual observations for 19 manufacturing industries from 1959 to 1991 on TFP; total input and its share-weighted capital, labor, and materials components; stocks of own R&D, manufacture patents, and use patents; and stocks of upstream R&D, manufacture patents, and use patents.

Table 2   PANEL UNIT-ROOT TESTS

	Other Deterministic Terms	
X	Time Dummies	Time Dummies and Sectoral Trends
TFP	−0.003	−0.174
	(0.007)	**(0.022)
Total input	−0.024	−0.193
	(0.011)	**(0.026)
Capital	−0.014	−0.244
	(0.008)	*(0.034)
Labor	−0.107	−0.201
	(0.018)	**(0.028)
Materials	−0.038	−0.218
	(0.013)	**(0.029)
R&D	−0.017	−0.096
	(0.004)	**(0.011)
Manufacture patents	−0.009	−0.092
	(0.003)	**(0.011)
Use patents	−0.014	−0.058
	(0.004)	(0.010)

$\Delta \log X_{it} = \gamma_i +$ (other deterministic terms) $+ \beta \log(X_{it-1}) + \Sigma_{k=1}^{3} \alpha_k \Delta \log X_{it-k} + \epsilon_{it}$. This table presents estimates of β from Augmented Dickey–Fuller tests of the null hypothesis that log X contains a unit root, using annual panel data for 19 industries from 1959 to 1991. All regressions include sector-specific intercepts and time dummies; regressions in the right column also contain sector-specific linear time trends. Standard errors are in parentheses. * indicates that β is significant at 10%, while ** indicates significance at 5%. The critical values of 6.816 (10%) and 7.093 (5%) are taken from the asymptotic formula provided in Levin and Lin (1992).

Table 2 presents univariate time-series evidence. For each series, I perform an Augmented Dickey–Fuller test of the null hypothesis that the series has a unit root in log levels, including three lagged growth rates to correct for serially correlated errors. I include sector-specific intercepts and time dummies in each specification, and experiment with including sector-specific time trends; all other coefficients are constrained to be equal across sectors. Since these are panel data, I cannot apply the usual Dickey–Fuller critical values; I instead use the formula provided in Levin and Lin (1992), which with 19 industries implies a 5% critical value of −7.093 and a 10% critical value of −6.816. According to Table 2, I can never reject the null of a unit root when I include only sectoral intercepts and time dummies. However, I can reject a unit root in seven of eight cases when I include sector-specific trends. I conclude that my data are stationary around trends that differ across sectors.

Table 3 looks at the long-run relationship between technology and TFP growth. I estimate cross-section OLS regressions of mean TFP growth on a constant and the mean growth rates of my technology indicators, taken one at a time; the sample size for each regression is 19. The coefficients on own R&D and own manufacture patent growth are positive and significant at 10%, while the coefficients on own use patent growth as well as upstream use and manufacture patent growth are positive and significant at 5%. My sample is too small to allow for multivariate analysis, and the results are fragile; omitting computers, for instance, reduces the coefficient on technology in all cases, and renders the own R&D results insignificant. Still, these results suggest that my technology indicators capture something about technological progress. My findings are consistent with Griliches and Lichtenberg (1984), Scherer (1984, 1993), and Lichtenberg and Siegel (1991), who find that R&D and productivity growth are positively related across firms and industries, and with Terleckyj (1975), who reports a significant positive relationship across industries between TFP growth and upstream R&D. Notice that use patents are more strongly related to TFP growth than manufacture patents, suggesting that process innovations may be better captured by available TFP data than product innovations, a theme to which I return below.

Table 4 estimates contemporaneous time-series relationships between TFP and technology indicators in log levels, while Table 5 does the same in growth rates. I include sectoral intercepts and time dummies in the levels regressions, and experiment with sector-specific trends; I include a constant and time dummies in the growth-rate regressions, and experi-

Table 3   LONG-RUN EVIDENCE

X	γ Estimate	β Estimate
R&D	−0.005	0.328
	(0.009)	*(0.196)
Manufacture patents	0.006	0.426
	(0.004)	*(0.233)
Use patents	0.003	1.082
	(0.003)	**(0.275)
Upstream R&D	−0.023	0.752
	(0.021)	(0.483)
Upstream manuf. patents	−0.005	1.880
	(0.004)	**(0.768)
Upstream use patents	−0.006	2.345
	(0.006)	**(0.837)

$\Delta \log (\text{TFP}_i) = \gamma + \beta \Delta \log X_i + \epsilon$. This table presents estimates of cross-section relationships between long-run total factor productivity growth and long-run growth in technology indicators. Each variable is entered as a mean industry-level growth rate over 1960–1991; the sample size is 19. Standard errors are in parentheses. * denotes significance at 10%, while ** denotes significance at 5%.

Table 4 CONTEMPORANEOUS EVIDENCE: LOG LEVELS

	Other Deterministic Terms	
X	Time Dummies	Time Dummies and Sectoral Trends
R&D	0.334	0.056
	**(0.041)	*(0.035)
Manufacture patents	0.396	−0.300
	**(0.055)	**(0.063)
Use patents	1.102	0.121
	**(0.073)	(0.078)
Upstream R&D	0.773	−0.460
	**(0.095)	**(0.126)
Upstream manuf. patents	2.121	−0.441
	**(0.217)	**(0.149)
Upstream use patents	3.289	−0.784
	**(0.250)	**(0.263)

$\log (\text{TFP}_{it}) = \gamma_i +$ other deterministic terms $+ \beta \log X_{it} + \epsilon_{it}$. This table presents estimates of contemporaneous relationships between log levels of total factor productivity and technology indicators, using annual panel data on 19 industries from 1959 to 1991. All regressions include sector-specific intercepts and time dummies; regressions in the right column also contain sector-specific linear time trends. Standard errors are in parentheses. * indicates significance at 10%, ** indicates significance at 5%.

Table 5 CONTEMPORANEOUS EVIDENCE: GROWTH RATES

	Other Deterministic Terms	
X	Time Dummies	Time Dummies and Sectoral Trends
R&D	0.132	0.047
	**(0.049)	(0.050)
Manufacture patents	0.195	−0.070
	**(0.074)	(0.101)
Use patents	0.512	0.052
	**(0.099)	(0.124)
Upstream R&D	0.235	−0.058
	**(0.123)	(0.142)
Upstream manuf. patents	0.530	−0.291
	**(0.217)	(0.254)
Upstream use patents	1.140	−0.057
	**(0.280)	(0.367)

$\Delta \log (\text{TFP}_{it}) = \gamma +$ other deterministic terms $+ \beta \Delta \log X_{it} + \epsilon_{it}$. This table presents estimates of contemporaneous relationships between growth rates of total factor productivity and technology indicators, using annual panel data on 19 industries from 1960 to 1991. All regressions include a constant and time dummies; regressions in the right column also include sector-specific intercepts. Standard errors are in parentheses. * indicates significance at 10%, while ** indicates significance at 5%.

ment with sectoral intercepts. Results omitting sectoral trends in Table 4 suggest strong, positive contemporaneous relationships between TFP and all six technology indicators. However, including sectoral trends weakens the relationship substantially for own R&D and use patents, and reverses the sign in the other four cases. Similarly, in Table 5 there is a strong positive relationship between TFP growth and technology growth when I control only for time dummies, but this relationship vanishes when I add sectoral intercepts. I conclude that cross-industry differences in trend productivity growth are positively related to cross-industry differences in trend technology growth, but that once I control for these differences there is little correlation between TFP and technology. My results contradict Lach (1995), who reports a contemporaneous positive relationship between patent stock growth and TFP growth in a sample similar to mine, as well as Griliches and Lichtenberg (1984), who find no time-series relationship between TFP and R&D even when omitting sectoral trends.

Tables 4 and 5 suggest that there is no contemporaneous *within-industry* relationship between TFP and technology in annual data. Table 6 asks whether such a relationship exists over a longer horizon, by regressing *medium-run* TFP growth on technology growth measured over the sixteen-year intervals 1960–1975 and 1976–1991. There are two

Table 6   MEDIUM-HORIZON EVIDENCE: 16-YEAR GROWTH RATES

	Other Deterministic Terms	
X	Time Dummy	Time Dummy and Fixed Effect
R&D	0.285	0.140
	*(0.154)	(0.288)
Manufacture patents	0.297	−0.347
	(0.166)	(0.416)
Use patents	0.960	0.614
	**(0.233)	(0.451)
Upstream R&D	0.462	−1.206
	(0.406)	(0.872)
Upstream manuf. patents	1.209	0.149
	**(0.572)	(0.835)
Upstream use patents	2.348	2.371
	**(0.729)	(2.078)

$\Delta \log (\text{TFP}_{it}) = \gamma$ + other deterministic terms + $\beta \Delta\log X_{it} + \epsilon_{it}$. This table presents estimates of the relationship between medium-horizon growth rates of total factor productivity and technology indicators, using data on 19 industries for two 16-year periods, 1960–1975 and 1976–1991. All regressions include a constant and a dummy for the second period; regressions in the right column also include a sector-specific fixed effect. Standard errors are in parentheses. * indicates significance at 10%, while ** indicates significance at 5%.

observations per industry, implying a sample size of 38. In the first column, I control only for a constant and a dummy for the second period; these results suggest a positive and significant relationship between TFP and technology growth in the medium run. However, these results rely on both cross-industry and within-industry variation. Adding a sectoral fixed effect in the second column makes the relationship between TFP and technology insignificant, as standard errors rise substantially in all cases and point estimates fall substantially in five of six cases. These results suggest that most of the variation in medium-run technology growth is cross-industry rather than within-industry, and that within-industry medium-run variation in technology and TFP are only weakly related. I obtain similar results when I experiment with different starting and ending dates, as well as with four- and eight-year horizons.

One might wonder if Tables 4 through 6 obviate the need for any further investigation of time-series relationships between TFP and technology. The answer is no. Had I found a robust positive contemporaneous relationship between (say) R&D and TFP, I could not have concluded that R&D shocks cause TFP to rise, because of potential omitted-variables bias; shocks to industry output could raise measured TFP due to (say) cyclical utilization, while at the same time increasing R&D for accelerator reasons. Similarly, the absence of a contemporaneous relationship does not prove that R&D has no impact on TFP, since such an impact is likely to emerge only with a lag. Both of these problems can be addressed by using vector autoregressions.

4. *VAR* Evidence

In this section I present results from a series of vector autoregressions using annual industry panel data on inputs, TFP, and technological indicators from 1959 to 1991. All variables are in log levels, following the panel unit-root tests presented in Table 2, although the impulse response functions in log levels are broadly similar if I estimate using growth rates. All specifications include sector-specific intercepts, sector-specific time trends, and time dummies. The time dummies are intended to control for aggregate shocks that affect R&D and patenting intensity, but are unrelated to true technological progress, such as the changes in the U.S. Patent Office discussed in Griliches (1989). Of course, time dummies will also remove any variation due to aggregate technology shocks, which may bias my results against technology-shock models; fortunately, my results are broadly similar if I omit time dummies. I use four lags; experiments with other lag lengths yielded similar results.

Figures 2 through 4 present the complete set of estimated impulse response functions, along with 1.65 Monte Carlo standard error bands, for three-variable VARs estimated on the manufacturing sample. The VARs are ordered as total input, TFP, and either own R&D (Figure 2), own manufacture patents (Figure 3), or own use patents (Figure 4). I enter technology indicators one at a time for presentational simplicity; results are similar if I enter multiple indicators simultaneously. Placing technology last reflects my belief that shocks to R&D or patenting are likely to affect industry activity only with lags. Placing technology first would generate a significant but small expansionary initial impact of technology on inputs and TFP, but with otherwise similar impulse responses and variance decompositions. Figure 5 breaks the input responses to own technology into disaggregated components, taken from five-variable VARs ordered as capital, labor, materials, TFP, and technology. Figures 6 and 7 present the responses of input, TFP, capital, labor, and materials to upstream R&D and patents; these estimates are similar if I control for input–output weighted measures of upstream input demand, suggesting that upstream technology is not merely proxying for upstream activity. I summarize these impulse responses in Table 7, which lists the sign and horizon of every significant effect of technology shocks on nontechnology variables. Table 8 presents Granger causality evidence, and Table 9 presents variance decompositions.

While the results vary somewhat across specifications, some robust patterns emerge. First, the impulse responses of TFP to technology are not significantly positive at any horizon, and indeed are significantly negative in the long run for all three upstream technology measures. This result is reinforced in Table 8, which indicate that TFP is Granger-caused only by upstream R&D and upstream use patents (and in these cases with negative coefficients).

Second, the impulse responses of total input to technology tend, if anything, to be positive in the short run but negative in the long run. I find that technology shocks significantly raise input use in the short run for three of six technology indicators, while significantly decreasing long-run input use in four of six cases.

Third, the impulse responses of individual inputs (particularly labor and materials) to technology are stronger than the responses for total input, as the disaggregated impacts tend to wash out due to both staggering and conflicting signs. This pattern is mirrored in the Granger causality results, which show that technology shocks forecast total input for only three of six technology indicators, but forecast labor and materials in five of six cases. Favorable technology shocks increase short-run labor use significantly in five of six cases, while decreasing long-run materials

Figure 2 INPUTS, TFP, AND R&D

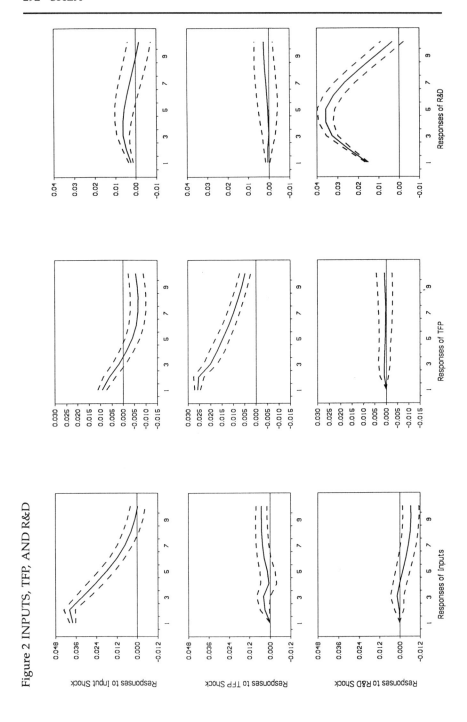

Figure 3 INPUTS, TFP, AND MANUFACTURE PATENTS

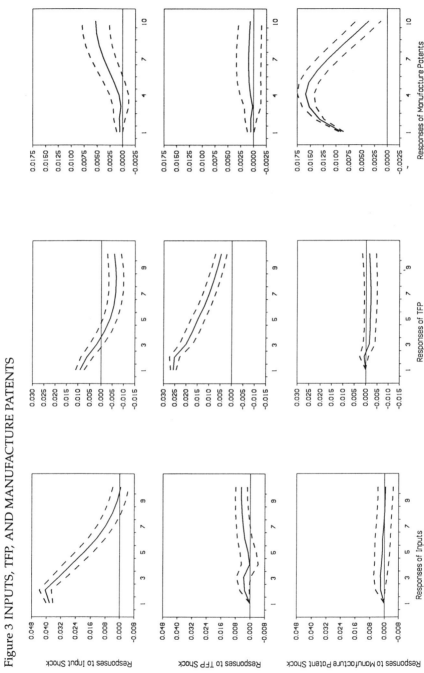

Figure 4 INPUTS, TFP, AND USE PATENTS

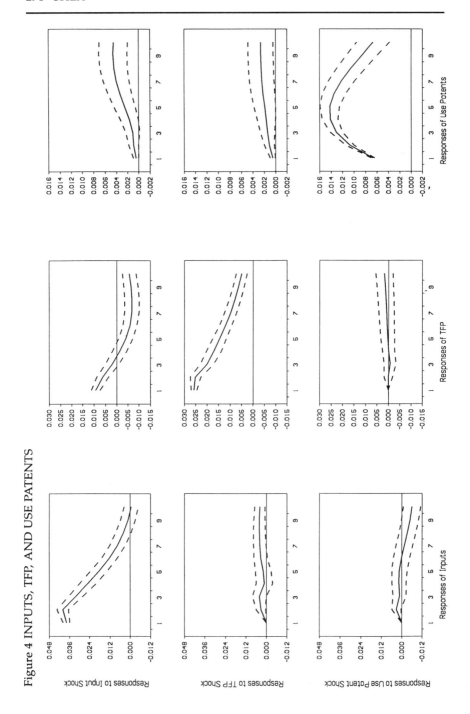

Figure 5 CAPITAL, LABOR, MATERIALS, AND OWN TECHNOLOGY SHOCKS

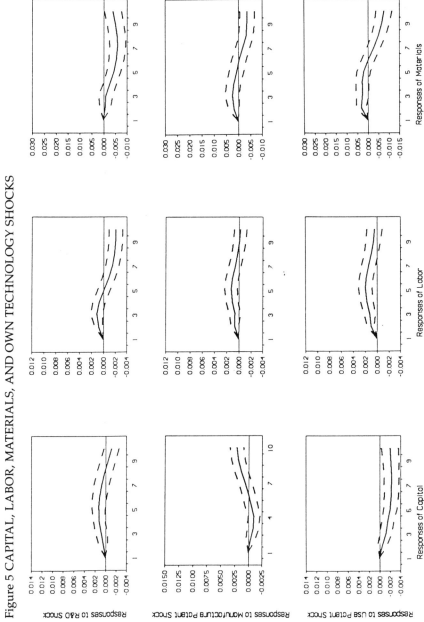

Figure 6 INPUTS, TFP, AND UPSTREAM TECHNOLOGY SHOCKS

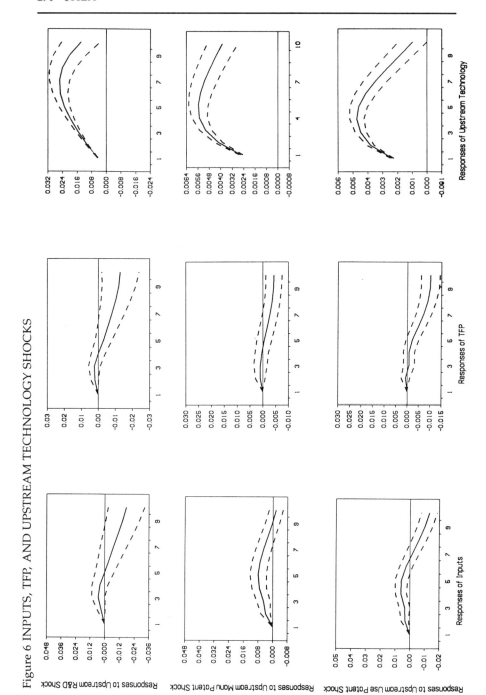

Figure 7 CAPITAL, LABOR, MATERIALS, AND UPSTREAM TECHNOLOGY SHOCKS

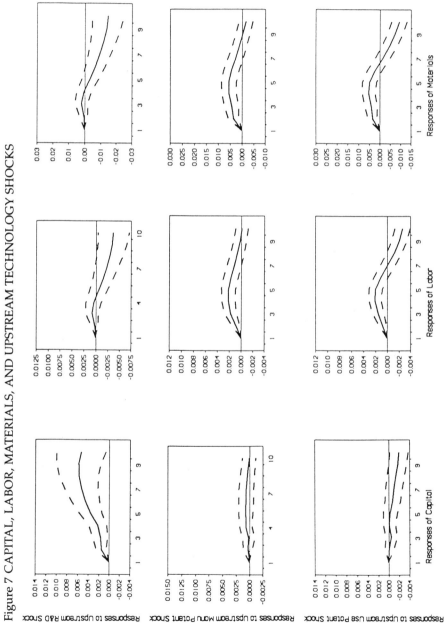

Table 7 IMPULSE RESPONSE FUNCTIONS: SUMMARY

Tech. Indicator	Three-Variable VAR		Five-Variable VAR		
	Total Input	TFP	Capital	Labor	Materials
R&D	↓ 7–10	—	↑ 4	↑ 2–3	↓ 4–10
				↓ 7–10	
Manufacture	—	—	↓ 4	↑ 4–5	↓ 8–10
patents			↑ 8–10		
Use	↑ 2	—	↓ 3–10	↑ 2–7	↑ 2
patents	↓ 9–10				↓ 8–10
Upstream	↓ 9–10	↓ 7–10	↑ 2–10	↓ 8–10	↓ 6–10
R&D					
Upstream	↑ 2–7	↓ 7–10	—	↑ 2–6	↑ 2–6
manuf. patents					
Upstream	↑ 2,4–5	↓ 6–10	↓ 9–10	↑ 2–5	↑ 2–5
use patents	↓ 8–10			↓ 8–10	↓ 8–10

This table summarizes the VAR impulse functions by reporting all cases of a significant (10%) impact of technology on industry variables, along with the relevant horizons in years. The impulse responses are calculated from VARs estimated using annual panel data for 19 industries from 1959 to 1991. The results in the first two columns are based on three-variable VARs ordered as total input, TFP, and technology, while the results in the last three columns are based on five-variable VARs ordered as capital, labor, materials, TFP, and technology. All VARs are estimated in log levels and include sector-specific intercepts and trends as well as time dummies. The standard errors are computed using Monte Carlo integration.

Table 8 GRANGER-CAUSALITY TESTS: P-VALUES

Technology Indicator	Three-Variable VAR		Five-Variable VAR		
	Total Input	TFP	Capital	Labor	Materials
Panel A: Does Technology Granger-Cause Inputs or TFP?					
R&D	0.21	0.95	0.42	0.01	0.02
Manufacture patents	0.85	0.51	0.04	0.05	0.13
Use patents	0.05	0.92	0.01	0.01	0.00
Upstream R&D	0.12	0.07	0.02	0.12	0.01
Upstream manuf. patents	0.01	0.46	0.47	0.03	0.01
Upstream use patents	0.00	0.01	0.15	0.00	0.00
Panel B: Do Inputs and TFP Granger-Cause Technology?					
R&D	0.38	0.62	0.34	0.95	0.63
Manufacture patents	0.05	0.41	0.58	0.14	0.21
Use patents	0.11	0.56	0.72	0.25	0.01
Upstream R&D	0.00	0.35	0.04	0.06	0.00
Upstream manuf. patents	0.06	0.48	0.08	0.03	0.51
Upstream use patents	0.00	0.32	0.01	0.02	0.16

This table presents P-values from Granger causality tests from technology to industry activity and vice versa. The tests are based on VARs estimated using annual panel data for 19 industries from 1959 to 1991.

Table 9   VARIANCE DECOMPOSITIONS

| Tech. Indicator | Years | Percentage of Variance Due to Technology | | | | |
| | | Three-Variable VAR | | Five-Variable VAR | | |
		Total Input	TFP	Capital	Labor	Materials
R&D	3	0.05	0.07	0.23	0.66	0.04
	6	0.38	0.06	1.08	0.95	2.06
	9	2.42	0.07	1.20	3.89	4.06
Manufacture	3	0.19	0.16	0.31	0.27	0.37
patents	6	0.22	0.60	0.53	1.22	0.42
	9	0.23	0.97	1.60	1.25	1.32
Use patents	3	0.26	0.04	0.54	0.87	0.70
	6	0.28	0.05	2.81	3.49	0.93
	9	0.98	0.19	5.22	4.13	3.49
Upstream R&D	3	0.76	0.44	1.47	0.22	0.16
	6	1.15	2.17	8.04	0.99	2.23
	9	8.21	12.51	20.33	8.01	14.10
Upstream	3	1.00	0.08	0.03	1.38	1.34
manuf. patents	6	3.98	0.25	0.28	4.65	3.94
	9	4.49	1.82	0.39	4.86	3.95
Upstream	3	0.60	0.08	0.09	1.09	1.19
use patents	6	2.11	1.48	0.23	3.69	2.97
	9	5.35	10.13	1.38	5.27	5.57

This table summarizes the VAR variance decompositions by reporting the share of variance of industry activity variables accounted for by shocks to technology at 3-, 6-, and 9-year horizons. The variance decompositions are calculated from VARs estimated using annual panel data for 19 industries from 1959 to 1991. The results in the first two columns are based on three-variable VARs ordered as total input, TFP, and technology, while the results in the last three columns are based on five-variable VARs ordered as capital, labor, materials, TFP, and technology. All VARs are estimated in log levels and include sector-specific intercepts and trends as well as time dummies.

use significantly in five of six cases. Note that shocks to both own and upstream R&D significantly increase capital accumulation in the short run. This result is consistent with Lach and Rob (1996), who find that R&D Granger-causes physical investment in industry panel data, and with Lach and Schankerman (1989), who find the same result in firm-level data. In my data, R&D does not Granger-cause capital, but it does Granger-cause investment.

Fourth, technology shocks explain only a small fraction of input and TFP variation at business-cycle horizons. Technology explains less than 2% of three-year volatility in all cases, and less than 5% of six-year volatility in all but one case. Technology has somewhat more explanatory power at longer horizons, particularly for upstream R&D and upstream use patents; recall, however, that the impulse responses for these cases suggest significant long-run *contractions* of inputs and TFP following favorable technology shocks. The fact that technology explains a larger share of variance at longer horizons is consistent with Jovanovic and Lach (1997), who model technology shocks as having long diffusion lags and find that technology shocks underexplain short-run volatility but overexplain long-run volatility.

Along with the results for technology shocks, two other features of my estimates are worth noting. First, own R&D and own patents respond positively and significantly to input shocks; moreover, R&D increases immediately, whereas patents increase only after five years. One possible interpretation is that industry expansions generate increased R&D immediately, and that this investment eventually leads to an increased flow of patentable inventions. Second, input shocks lead to short-run increases but long-run decreases in TFP. A possible interpretation is that industry expansions raise measured TFP in the short-run due to increasing returns or cyclical utilization, but reduce long-run productivity. An interesting question is how these two features of the data can coexist—if expansions increase R&D and patents, then why don't they increase productivity? One possibility is that expansions raise inventive activity but also allow lower-productivity firms to enter and survive, generating a net decline in productivity.

4.1 RESULTS FOR INPUT MIX, WORKER MIX, AND PRICES

While this paper is primarily concerned with the impact of technology shocks on total input and TFP, technology shocks are likely to affect other variables as well. Conventional models predict that favorable technology shocks reduce the relative price of industry output. Meanwhile, if technology shocks are permanent and the supply of capital is more elastic in the long run than the supply of labor or materials (as in the baseline RBC model), then favorable technology shocks increase the long-run ratio of capital to other inputs. Finally, some have hypothesized that technological advances have been biased towards skilled workers during the postwar period, either because skilled workers have an advantage in learning new technologies (Greenwood and Yorukoglu, 1997) or because technology shocks are investment-specific and capital is complementary with skill (Krusell *et al.* 1996).

In the working version of this paper (Shea, 1998), I present impulse response functions to own and upstream technology shocks for three variables: the *worker mix*, defined as the ratio of nonproduction to total employment; the *input mix*, defined as the log ratio of capital's product (capital raised to the power of capital's share of revenue) to labor and materials' product; and the industry's relative price, defined as the implicit gross output deflator divided by the GDP deflator. I assume that increases in nonproduction employment are positively correlated with changes in the ratio of skilled to unskilled employees, following Berman, Bound, and Griliches (1994). My input-mix variable is one of several ways I could quantify changes in capital relative to other variables; results are similar when I use more familiar measures such as the capital–labor ratio. The impulse responses are taken from four-variable VARs in which the new variables are ordered after inputs and TFP but before technology. Data for nonproduction employment, total employment and prices are taken from the NBER productivity database.

The results conform to prior intuition in two out of three cases. Favorable technology shocks cause significant long-run substitution towards capital for five of six technology indicators; technology improvements also significantly increase the ratio of nonproduction to total employment in five of six cases, although these increases often occur in the short run rather than the long run. However, the estimated impact of technology shocks on price is not robust; own R&D and own use patent shocks significantly reduce price in the long run, but manufacture patent shocks raise price in the medium run, while upstream use patent shocks raise price in the long run. The fact that own use patents (which should reflect process innovations) reduce prices while own manufacture patents (which should reflect product innovations) raise prices suggests that available price data might not accurately reflect product innovations, an idea to which I return below.

4.2 RESULTS FOR NONMANUFACTURING

My empirical results to this point have relied exclusively on manufacturing industries. However, technology shocks originating in manufacturing, such as the introduction of the jet engine in the late 1950s, often have important downstream impacts in nonmanufacturing. While disaggregated data on own R&D and own patenting in nonmanufacturing industries is not readily available—in part because virtually all R&D and patenting occurred in manufacturing until very recently—I can construct measures of upstream technology for nonmanufacturing using the techniques described in Section 2. Figure 8 presents impulse responses of inputs and TFP to upstream technology shocks for a panel of 10 nonmanufacturing industries: agriculture; mining; construction; transportation; communications; electric utilities; gas utilities; trade; finance, insurance and real estate (FIRE); and services. Data on inputs and TFP

Figure 8 INPUTS, TFP, AND UPSTREAM TECHNOLOGY IN NONMANUFACTURING

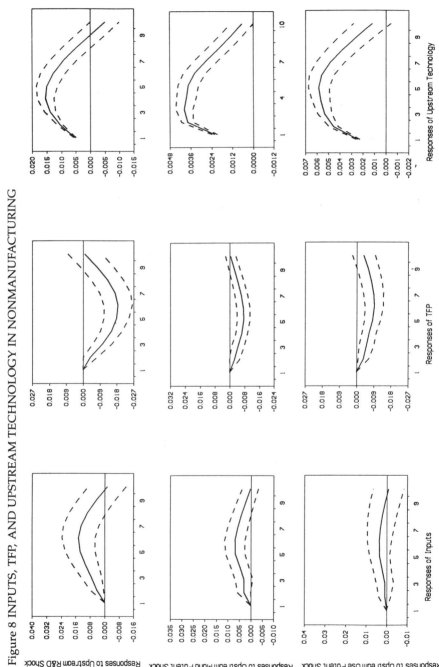

come from an updated version of the KLEM database described by Jorgenson, Gollop, and Fraumeni (1987), generously provided by Susanto Basu. Although their preferred measure of labor input corrects for variations in labor-force composition, I use man-hours to be consistent with the manufacturing data. The impulse responses for nonmanufacturing are striking and robust: favorable upstream technology shocks significantly increase total input in the short run, but reduce measured TFP in the short run; total input and TFP return to trend in the long run. In the working version of the paper, I show that results for capital, labor, and materials are similar to those for total input. The variance decompositions (available from the author) assign technology a substantial share of TFP and input volatility at six years, particularly for upstream R&D; however, technology has a much smaller role for output volatility, as the input and TFP effects cancel each other out.

4.3 MEASUREMENT ERROR IN PRICE INDICES

The fact that favorable technology shocks do not significantly increase measured TFP raises suspicions about the quality of the TFP data. Much recent research has criticized BLS price data for not registering implicit price changes due to quality improvements or new product introductions (e.g., Gordon, 1990), or, for sectors outside of manufacturing, for not registering price changes at all (e.g., Baily and Gordon 1988). If product innovations do not reduce measured prices, they are less likely to increase measured output or TFP; this is especially troublesome given that roughly 80% of U.S. R&D is devoted to product rather than process innovation (Scherer, 1984). Similarly, if nonmanufacturing prices are measured poorly, then upstream innovations that reduce true prices and increase true activity may not raise measured output; if measured inputs rise (perhaps because inputs are easier to measure than output), then measured TFP is likely to fall.

To examine whether measurement errors in prices are important for my results, I divide the 19 sample manufacturing industries into process-innovating vs. product-innovating sectors. Table 10 presents the average percentage of R&D spending in gross output over the period 1959–1991, as well as the percentage of process R&D in total R&D spending in 1974, as reported in Scherer (1984). The table indicates that there is a fairly sharp break between process- and product-innovating sectors, and that the most R&D-intensive industries are typically product-intensive. I assign food, textiles, lumber, paper, industrial chemicals, petroleum, rubber, stone, and primary metals to the process-innovating group, and the other ten industries to the product-innovating group. Figures 9 and 10 present the responses of total input, TFP, and price to

Table 10 PROCESS VS. PRODUCT R&D INTENSITY

Industry	R&D Intensity	Percentage of Process R&D
Food (SIC 20)	0.2	56.1
Textiles (SIC 22–23)	0.1	61.3
Lumber (SIC 24–25)	1.5	59.0
Paper (SIC 26)	0.7	33.1
Industrial chemicals (SIC 281–282, 286)	3.4	47.6
Drugs (SIC 28)	8.2	12.0
Other chemicals (other SIC 28)	1.4	14.6
Petroleum (SIC 29)	1.4	64.0
Rubber (SIC 30)	1.1	48.0
Stone (SIC 32)	0.9	52.5
Metals (SIC 33)	0.5	75.2
Metal prods. (SIC 34)	0.4	14.6
Computers (SIC 357)	12.5	5.5
Other nonelec. equip. (other SIC 35)	1.2	4.1
Electronics & commun. equip. (SIC 366–387)	5.4	21.2
Other electric equip. (other SIC 36)	2.3	11.5
Aerospace (SIC 372, 6)	4.4	21.7
Autos & other transp. equip. (SIC 37)	2.6	4.8
Instruments (SIC 38)	5.0	8.0

The first column reports the average value of R&D spending as a percentage of nominal gross output over the sample period 1959–1991. The second column reports the fraction of 1974 R&D spending devoted to process R&D, as reported in Scherer (1984).

technology shocks for the two groups. The results indicate a sharp distinction between process- and product-innovating industries: for process-innovating sectors, favorable technology shocks induce a significant long-run increase in TFP, a significant long-run decline in price, and a significant long-run decline in inputs; for product-innovating sectors, favorable technology shocks do not raise TFP in any instance, and reduce long-run inputs and prices in only one case. These results suggest that the failure of technology to increase TFP in my full sample may be due to the failure of available data to reflect price declines and productivity gains due to quality improvements and new-product introductions. Another interesting result is that process-industry TFP declines significantly in the short run in two of three cases. This result is consistent with models in which technological advances cause a short-run productivity decline as workers move down the new technology's learning curve (e.g., Greenwood and Yorukoglu, 1997; Hornstein and Krusell, 1996).

Figure 9 OWN TECHNOLOGY SHOCKS IN PROCESS-INNOVATING INDUSTRIES

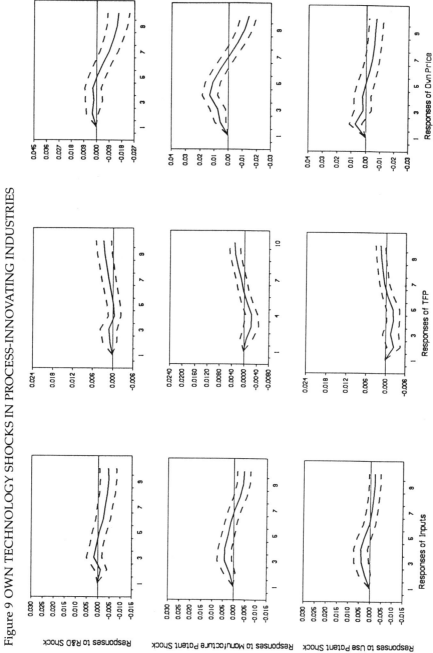

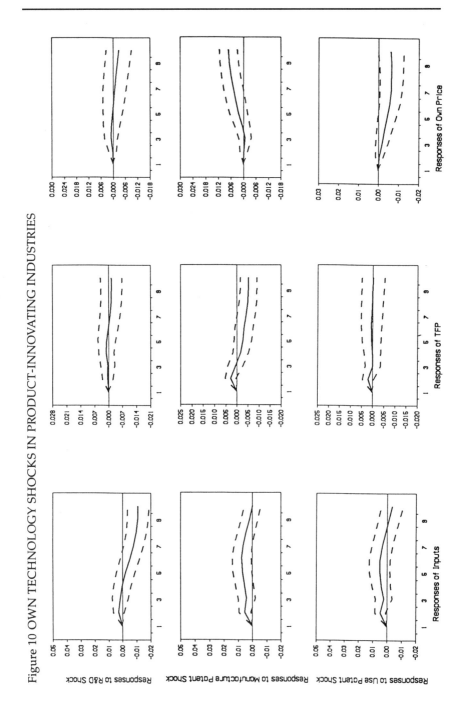

Figure 10 OWN TECHNOLOGY SHOCKS IN PRODUCT-INNOVATING INDUSTRIES

5. Conclusion

This paper's contribution is to estimate the impact of technology shocks on the economy using R&D spending and patent applications rather than observed total factor productivity to measure technology. The most surprising finding is that favorable technology shocks do not raise measured TFP at any horizon. Taken at face value, this suggests that observed procyclical variation in TFP is entirely due to factors such as increasing returns, cyclical utilization, and factor reallocation, and not at all due to procyclical technology. It also suggests that efforts to measure short-run changes in true technology by purging measured TFP of movements due to cyclical utilization and so on (e.g., Basu, Fernald, and Kimball, 1997; Burnside, Eichenbaum, and Rebelo, 1996) may be doomed from the start.

Of course, another interpretation of my results is that my R&D and patent data are riddled with measurement error that biases me against finding a significant impact of technology on TFP. While the R&D and patent data are certainly vulnerable to criticism, my results cannot be so easily dismissed. Measurement error should bias me against finding a significant impact of technology on anything. Yet I find that favorable technology shocks have a significant short-run expansionary impact on labor, a significant long-run contractionary impact on total input, and a significant positive impact on capital and nonproduction worker intensities. I also find that technology shocks raise long-run TFP and reduce long-run prices in a subsample of industries dominated by process R&D. These results suggest that the important measurement error is not in R&D or patents, but in output prices. Most R&D in the United States is devoted to product innovations, yet many observers believe that available price data systematically ignore real price declines due to quality improvements and new-product introductions. Similarly, a good deal of the impact of industrial R&D is felt in downstream nonmanufacturing sectors, yet many observers argue that price changes of all kinds in nonmanufacturing are poorly measured.

It is quite possible, then, that technology shocks are more important to actual output and TFP fluctuations than they are to observed fluctuations. To paraphrase Ed Prescott (1986), theory may be ahead of business-cycle measurement. If real-business-cycle enthusiasts want to convince the profession that technology shocks are genuinely important to business cycles, their first order of business should be to construct historical price series for manufacturing and nonmanufacturing sectors that correct for quality improvements and new product introductions, following the painstaking work of Gordon (1990) on durable goods.

Such a project will surely require many hours of research into the history of product innovations in particular sectors, but imagine how different the profession would be today had Friedman and Schwartz (1963) not devoted many hours of research to the history of monetary institutions and monetary shocks.

REFERENCES

Baily, M., and R. Gordon (1988). The productivity slowdown, measurement issues and the explosion of computer power. *Brookings Papers on Economic Activity* 2:347–431.
Bartlesman, E., and W. Gray. (1996). The NBER manufacturing productivity database. Cambridge, MA: National Bureau of Economic Research. NBER Technical Working Paper 205.
Basu, S., and J. Fernald. (1997). Returns to scale in US production: Estimates and implications. *Journal of Political Economy* 105:249–283.
———, ———, and M. Kimball. (1997). Are technology improvements contractionary? University of Michigan. Mimeo.
Berman, E., J. Bound, and Z. Griliches. (1994). Changes in the demand for skilled labor within U.S. manufacturing: Evidence from the Annual Survey of Manufactures. *Quarterly Journal of Economics* 109:367–397.
Burnside, C., M. Eichenbaum, and S. Rebelo. (1995). Capital utilization and returns to scale. In *NBER Macroeconomics Annual 1995*, B. Bernanke and J. Rotemberg (eds.). Cambridge, MA: The MIT Press, pp. 67–110.
———, ———, and ———. (1996). Sectoral Solow residuals. *European Economic Review* 40:861–869.
Caballero, R., and M. Hammour. (1994). The cleansing effect of recessions. *American Economic Review* 84:1350–1368.
———, and ———. (1996). On the timing and efficiency of creative destruction. *Quarterly Journal of Economics* 111:805–852.
Carlstrom, C., and T. Fuerst. (1997). Agency costs, net worth and business fluctuations: A computable general equilibrium analysis. *American Economic Review* 87:893–910.
Christiano, L., and M. Eichenbaum. (1992). Current real business cycle theory and aggregate labor market fluctuations. *American Economic Review* 82:430–450.
———, and ———. (1995). Liquidity effects, monetary policy and the business cycle. *Journal of Money, Credit and Banking* 27:1113–1136.
———, ———, and C. Evans. (1998). Monetary policy shocks: What have we learned and to what end? Cambridge, MA: National Bureau of Economic Research. NBER Working Paper 6400.
Cochrane, J. (1994). Shocks. *Carnegie-Rochester Conference Series on Public Policy* 41:296–364.
Cogley, T., and J. Nason (1995). Output dynamics in real business cycle models. *American Economic Review* 85:492–511.
DeLong, B., and L. Summers. (1991). Equipment investment and economic growth. *Quarterly Journal of Economics* 106:445–502.
Evans, C. (1992). Productivity shocks and real business cycles. *Journal of Monetary Economics* 29:191–208.

Farmer, R., and J.-T. Guo. (1994). Real business cycles and the animal spirits hypothesis. *Journal of Economic Theory* 63:42–72.

Friedman, M., and A. Schwartz. (1963). *A Monetary History of the United States, 1867–1960.* Princeton: Princeton University Press.

Galí, J. (1996). Technology, employment and the business cycle: Do technology shocks explain aggregate fluctuations? Cambridge, MA: National Bureau of Economic Research. NBER Working Paper 5721. *American Economic Review,* forthcoming.

———, and M. Hammour. (1992). Long run effects of business cycles. Mimeo.

Gordon, R. (1990). *The Measurement of Durable Goods Prices.* Chicago: University of Chicago Press.

Gort, M., and S. Klepper. (1982). Time paths in the diffusion of product innovations. *Economic Journal* 92:630–653.

Greenwood, J., and M. Yorukoglu. (1997). 1974. *Carnegie-Rochester Conference Series on Public Policy* 46:49–95.

Griliches, Z. (1973). Research expenditures and growth accounting. In *Science and Technology in Economic Growth,* B. R. Williams (ed.). New York: John Wiley and Sons, pp. 59–83.

———. (1989). Patents: Recent trends and puzzles. *Brookings Papers: Microeconomics,* 291–319.

———, and F. Lichtenberg. (1984). R&D and productivity growth at the industry level: Is there still a relationship? In *R&D, Patents and Productivity,* Zvi Griliches (ed.). Chicago: University of Chicago Press, pp. 465–501.

Hall, R. (1988). The relation between price and marginal cost in US industry. *Journal of Political Economy* 96:921–947.

Hornstein, A., and P. Krusell. (1996). Can technology improvements cause productivity slowdowns? In *NBER Macroeconomics Annual 1996,* B. Bernanke and J. Rotemberg (eds.). Cambridge: The MIT Press, pp. 209–259.

Horvath, M. (1997). Cyclicality and sectoral linkages: Aggregate fluctuations from independent sectoral shocks. Stanford University. Mimeo.

Jorgenson, D., F. Gollop, and B. Fraumeni. (1987). *Productivity and U.S. Economic Growth,* Cambridge: Harvard University Press.

Jovanovic, B., and S. Lach. (1997). Product innovation and the business cycle. *International Economic Review* 38:3–22.

Keller, W. (1997). Trade and the transmission of technology. Cambridge, MA: National Bureau of Economic Research. NBER Working Paper 6113.

Kimball, M. (1995). The quantitative analytics of the basic neomonetarist model. *Journal of Money, Credit and Banking* 27:1241–1289.

Kortum, S. (1993). Equilibrium R&D and the patent–R&D ratio: US evidence. *American Economic Review* 83(May):450–457.

———, and J. Putnam. (1997). Assigning patents to industries: Tests of the Yale Technology Concordance. *Economic Systems Research* 9:161–175.

Krusell, P., L. Ohanian, J. V. Rios-Rull, and G. Violante. (1996). Capital–skill complementarity and inequality. University of Rochester. Mimeo.

Kydland, F., and E. Prescott. (1982). Time to build and aggregate fluctuations. *Econometrica* 50:1345–1370.

Lach, S. (1995). Patents and productivity growth at the industry level: A first look. *Economics Letters* 49:101–108.

———, and R. Rob. (1996). R&D, investment and industry dynamics. *Journal of Economics and Management Strategy* 5:217–249.

——, and M. Schankerman. (1989). Dynamics of R&D and investment in the scientific sector. *Journal of Political Economy* 97:880–904.

Levin, A., and C.-F. Lin. (1992). Unit root tests in panel data: Asymptotic and finite-sample properties. University of California, San Diego. Mimeo.

Lichtenberg, F., and D. Siegel. (1991). The impact of R&D investment on productivity—new evidence using linked R&D–LRD data. *Economic Inquiry* 29:203–228.

Long, J., and C. Plosser. (1983). Real business cycles. *Journal of Political Economy* 91:39–69.

Prescott, E. (1986). Theory ahead of business cycle measurement. *Federal Reserve Bank of Minneapolis Quarterly Review* 10:9–22.

Quah, D. (1989). Permanent and transitory movements in labor income: An explanation for "excess smoothness" in consumption. *Journal of Political Economy* 98:449–475.

Rotemberg, J., and M. Woodford. (1995). Dynamic general equilibrium models with imperfectly competitive product markets. In *Frontiers of Business Cycle Research,* Thomas Cooley (ed.). Princeton, NJ: Princeton University Press, pp. 243–293.

Scherer, F. (1984). Using linked patent and R&D data to measure interindustry technology flows. In *R&D, Patents and Productivity,* Z. Griliches (ed.). Chicago: University of Chicago Press, pp. 417–464.

——. (1993). Lagging productivity growth: Measurement, technology and shock effects. *Empirica* 20:5–24.

Schmitt-Grohe, S. (1997). Comparing four models of aggregate fluctuations due to self-fulfilling expectations. *Journal of Economic Theory* 72:96–147.

Shea, J. (1991). The input–output approach to instrument selection: Technical appendix. University of Maryland. Mimeo.

——. (1993). The input–output approach to instrument selection. *Journal of Business and Economic Statistics* 11:145–154.

——. (1998). What do technology shocks do? Cambridge, MA: National Bureau of Economic Research. NBER Working Paper no. 6632, July.

Stadler, G. (1990). Business cycle models with endogenous technology. *American Economic Review* 80:763–778.

Terleckyj, N. (1975). Direct and indirect effects of industrial research and development on the productivity growth of industries. In *New Developments in Productivity Measurement,* J. Kendrick and B. Vaccara (eds.). Chicago: University of Chicago Press, pp. 359–386.

Comment

JORDI GALÍ
New York University and NBER

1. Technology and Business Cycles, in the Theory and in the Data

Under the world view advocated by real business cycle (RBC) economists, observed economic fluctuations can be interpreted, to a first approximation, as the result of agents' optimal responses to changes in aggregate technology, in an environment with perfect competition, market clearing, and flexible prices. The empirical basis for that claim lies in the ability of calibrated RBC models to match patterns of unconditional second moments of a number of macroeconomic time series.

Though that ability is largely acknowledged, some recent research has undertaken "more direct" assessments of RBC models—and of alternative business-cycle frameworks—by identifying the dynamic effects of variations in technology on different macroeconomic variables, and by evaluating quantitatively their role as a source of short-run economic fluctuations. Many interesting questions that may shed light on the nature of business cycles are addressed in that literature: What are the effects of technology shocks in actual economies? How do they differ from the predictions of standard RBC models? What is their contribution to business-cycle fluctuations? Shea's present paper fits squarely into that line of research.

The key challenge facing such an inquiry lies in the empirical identification of exogenous technology shocks, since it is generally accepted that conventional Solow residuals cannot be taken as reliable measures of "true" total factor productivity. Different approaches to identification have been pursued in the literature. Thus, Basu, Fernald, and Kimball (1997) identify technology shocks as the innovation in an "adjusted" Solow residual series, where the adjustment attempts to correct for the bias associated with the potential presence of increasing returns, imperfect competition, variable input utilization, and sectoral reallocation of inputs across heterogeneous sectors. In my own work (Galí, 1996) identification is achieved by restricting permanent technology shocks to be the only source of the unit root in labor productivity, i.e., the only shocks that may have a permanent effect on the level of that variable—a restriction that can be shown to hold under assumptions typically made in standard models.

Despite the different methodologies and data used, a number of common findings emerge in those papers, including a result that appears to be very robust: exogenous improvements in technology tend to reduce employment, at least in the short run.[1] That result is in stark contrast to the prediction of the standard RBC models, where a positive response of employment to an exogenous increase in TFP is at the center of the mechanism underlying business cycles. On the other hand, and as argued by the above-mentioned authors, the estimated effects of technol-

---

1. Basu, Fernald, and Kimball (1997) use postwar U.S. annual data. Galí (1996) uses quarterly data for the U.S. as well as the remaining G7 countries. Galí's methodology has been applied by Kiley (1997) to two-digit industry-level U.S. data.

ogy shocks are consistent with the prediction of New Keynesian models characterized by imperfect competition and sticky prices. The intuition underlying that prediction is straightforward: if nominal aggregate demand is predetermined and prices respond only sluggishly to shocks, real aggregate demand (and thus, the position of the demand schedule facing each firm) will change little in response to an increase in TFP. Accordingly, the quantity of goods each firm will wish to produce and sell will also remain largely unchanged (since, by assumption, adjusting prices downward is either unfeasible or too costly). Since firms now have access to a more efficient technology, that level of output can now be produced with less inputs, thus leading to a decline in employment (and, presumably, a lower capital utilization as well). Needless to say, such effects and the mechanism through which they are transmitted have little in common with those underlying RBC models.

2. Shea's Empirical Framework

Shea's "What Do Technology Shocks Do?" has a similar motivation to the papers by Basu, Fernald, and Kimball (1997) and Galí (1996), but uses a different strategy in order to identify exogenous technology shocks. Specifically, Shea's approach exploits the availability of data on "tangible" activities associated with technological innovation, and the fact that indicators of such activities display non-negligible short-run fluctuations.

Of course, the study of the empirical links between innovative activities and productivity measures has been the subject of a time-honored empirical literature.[2] Work in that tradition generally takes variations in technology (over time and/or across firms or industries) as the phenomenon to be explained, trying to detect and quantify the relationship between measures of technological change—typically, estimates of total factor productivity (TFP)—and indicators of innovative activity (R&D expenditures or patent applications). From the point of view of that literature, Shea's main contribution lies in the use of a structural VAR to model the connection between technological innovation and TFP growth, an approach which allows for largely unrestricted dynamics, including the possibility of an endogenous response of technological innovation to fluctuations in each industry's level of economic activity.

Shea uses two different variables as indicators of technological innovation: R&D (i.e., a measure of the input in the innovation process) and the number of patent applications (a measure of the output of that process). For each industry he estimates the responses of inputs and TFP to or-

2. See, e.g., the Griliches (1984) NBER volume devoted to the subject.

thogonalized shocks (1) to the industry's own technology indicators, and (2) to the technology indicators of upstream industries (constructed using input–output data).

It is important to distinguish between the two types of shocks, since the predicted responses are likely to be very different. In particular, technological innovation in upstream industries should not affect an industry's own TFP (unless technological spillovers are present), but only its marginal cost (to the extent that it is reflected in suppliers' prices). Thus, there is no reason why, in the presence of sticky prices, input use in an industry should decline in the face of a positive shock in upstream industries, as opposed to an analogous shock in the own industry. Hence, and for the sake of brevity and comparability with the existing literature, I will concentrate the remainder of my comments on the results based on own technological innovations.

Shea assumes that the level of R&D (or, alternatively, the number of patents) in industry i is determined by the equation

$$z_t^i = \sum_{j \geq 1} \alpha_j z_{t-j}^i + \sum_{j \geq 0} \beta_j y_{t-j}^i + \epsilon_t^i,$$

where z_t is the value taken by the industry technology indicator, y_t is a vector including industry TFP and inputs measures, and ϵ_t^i represents the "exogenous" technology shock. The key identifying assumption is that ϵ_t^i is orthogonal to y_t^i (as well as its lags), i.e., that a technology shock does *not* have a *contemporaneous* (within the year) impact on industry aggregates such as TFP or inputs.

The dynamic effects of technology on any industry variable y^i are then given by the sequence of coefficients $\{\phi_j\}$ of the regression equation

$$y_t^i = \sum_{j \geq 1} \phi_j \epsilon_{t-j}^i + u_t^i.$$

The structural VAR approach adopted by Shea seems, in principle, clearly suitable for the issue at hand, for it allows for an endogenous component in innovative activities, as well as rich, largely unrestricted dynamics. Furthermore, the recursive restriction used (namely, that shocks to R&D or patents cannot have a contemporaneous impact on industry aggregates such as TFP or inputs) seems reasonable when R&D data are used, given the likely lags between R&D expenditures and actual implementation of the resulting innovation (it may be more questionable when patent data are used).

Given the previous setup, Shea's question can be formulated as follows: what are the effects of exogenous variations in industry R&D or patents on the industry's TFP and its level of activity?

3. Shea's Main Results and their Interpretation

Let me focus on two of the results emphasized by Shea among those that are claimed to be reasonably robust across specifications:

RESULT 1   A positive own technology shock (i.e., one associated with an increase in R&D or the number of patents in the same industry) has no significant effect on industry TFP at any horizon.

RESULT 2   A positive own technology shock tends to increase inputs (especially labor), in the short run, but decrease them in the long run.

My main concern has to do with the economic interpretation of those results, i.e., what we learn from them regarding the merits of alternative business-cycle models. Standard business-cycle frameworks do not explicitly model the process of innovation in the R&D sector (or, for that matter, the process of patent application, grant, and diffusion of associated knowledge). Hence, Shea's technology shocks do not have an exact counterpart in those models, in which changes in TFP are taken to be exogenous (wisely or not). Given that the estimated response of TFP to a "Shea technology shock" is essentially flat, it is not clear what sort of prediction of those models could be refuted by looking at Results 1 and 2. In particular, models with imperfect competition and sticky prices predict a decline in employment in response to a technology shock *only if the latter is associated with an increase in TFP.* Since in Shea's evidence the level of TFP remains essentially unchanged in response to an orthogonalized innovation in own technology shocks (R&D or patents), the absence of a response of employment and other inputs to the same shock would seem to be consistent with the prediction of a conventional sticky price model. Thus, Results 1 and 2 can hardly be interpreted as providing evidence against New Keynesian models. Neither can they be seen as being in contradiction with the results reported in Galí (1996) and Basu, Fernald, and Kimball (1997), for those authors found evidence of a decline in employment after a technology shock that "succeeds" in raising productivity.

Most interestingly, in the only two VAR specifications for which Shea detects a significant short-run change in TFP in response to an (own) technology shock (namely, when the analysis is restricted to process-innovating industries and patents are used as a technology indicator), inputs are shown to respond in the direction opposite to the movement in TFP, i.e., in a way consistent with the predictions of sticky-price models!

In the remaining cases, the only hypothesis supported by the Shea's evidence is that innovations to industry R&D or patents have *no* significant dynamic effects on the same industry's TFP. That is an intriguing result, but not one with obvious implications for business-cycle theory.

4. Are All Industries Alike?

In spite of some of the rhetoric found both in the paper and in the present discussion, it is not completely true that the dynamics of the estimated model are "essentially unrestricted": Shea's methodology constrains the dynamic responses to shocks to be the same for all industries. Of course, if that restriction is satisfied in the population, its imposition in the estimation procedure can only increase the precision of the estimates. But a look at some simple statistics gives us a reason to be somewhat suspicious. Table 1 reports cross-correlations of R&D (or patents) and TFP, industry by industry, using Shea's data set. In addition to the contemporaneous correlation, the highest cross-correlation (in absolute

Table 1 INDUSTRY CROSS-CORRELATIONS

	R&D		Patents	
Industry	$\rho(A_t, Z_t)$	$\rho(A_{t+k}, Z_t)$	$\rho(A_t, Z_t)$	$\rho(A_{t+k}, Z_t)$
Food	0.61	0.65(−1)	−0.37	−0.49 (+4)
Textiles	0.05	−0.57 (+4)	0.11	0.51 (−2)
Lumber	−0.54	−0.54 (+0)	0.22	0.61 (−3)
Paper	−0.09	0.42 (+3)	−0.17	−0.17 (+0)
Ind. chem.	0.29	0.52 (+3)	0.53	0.58 (−1)
Drugs	−0.92	−0.92 (+0)	−0.85	−0.85 (+0)
Other chem.	−0.40	−0.58 (−4)	0.71	0.71 (+0)
Petroleum	0.29	0.73 (+3)	0.11	0.67 (+4)
Rubber	0.03	−0.38 (+4)	0.35	0.62 (−3)
Stone	0.39	0.62 (+2)	0.53	0.72 (−2)
Metals	−0.26	−0.34 (+2)	0.38	0.48 (−2)
Metal prod.	−0.05	−0.17 (−2)	0.43	0.49 (−2)
Computers	0.97	0.97 (+0)	−0.29	−0.72 (+4)
Other nonelec.	−0.41	−0.50 (+2)	0.74	0.74 (+0)
Elec. & Commun.	−0.20	0.42 (−4)	−0.18	−0.38 (+3)
Oth. elec. eq.	0.07	0.55 (−4)	0.58	0.58 (+0)
Autos & Trans.	0.05	−0.37 (−4)	0.54	0.64 (−1)
Aerospace	−0.51	−0.57 (+1)	−0.06	0.36 (+4)
Instruments	−0.72	−0.72 (+0)	0.32	0.57 (+3)

$\rho(A_t, Z_t)$ is the contemporaneous correlation between TFP and R&D (or patents). $\rho(A_{t+k}, Z_t)$ is the element of the cross-correlogram of the same variables with the highest (absolute) value, with the corresponding lead or lag being shown in brackets. Data are detrended.

value) and the lag or lead at which the latter is found are shown in parentheses. No clear common pattern emerges: values and signs are all over the place, pointing to substantial heterogeneity across industries (even across indicators) in the size and timing of the effects of technology shocks, and/or in the properties of the endogenous component of the innovation indicators. That result may not be surprising, since after all, industries as different in the nature of their production processes as lumber and aerospace are included in Shea's sample. But it clearly raises some doubts about the usefulness (and meaning) of any estimates that fail to take such heterogeneity into account.

5. Concluding Comments

John Shea has written a paper that addresses an issue at the center of some of the macroeconomic controversies of the past twenty years: the link between technological change and business cycles. In doing so he makes use of a data set as well as an empirical approach that seem very well suited to the issue at hand. Yet, many readers are likely to find some of the results somewhat disappointing, in the sense that they seem to raise more questions than they answer. The inability, for most specifications, to detect a significant effect of an industry's R&D expenditures or patent applications on its own TFP is worrisome, for it is hard to think of many other factors that may underlie variations in productivity measures at horizons other than the long run (though mismeasurement, cyclical or other, is always a likely candidate).

Most of the results also seem to fall short of yielding any obvious lessons that could further our understanding of business cycles and/or help evaluate the empirical merits of alternative models. Exceptions apply, however: as I have argued above, some of the few significant results seem to lend some additional support to the existing evidence that points to a short-run negative comovement between TFP and inputs in response to technology shocks, which is consistent with sticky-price models.

I am convinced that some of the interesting issues raised by Shea's approach and results will stimulate further work on the subject. We can only hope that, when alternative empirical models or data sets are used to ask the question that gives Shea's paper its title, the data choose to speak somewhat louder.

REFERENCES

Basu, S., J. Fernald, and M. Kimball. (1997). Are technology improvements contractionary? University of Michigan. Mimeo.

Galí, J. (1996). Technology, employment and the business cycle: Do technology shocks explain economic fluctuations? Cambridge, MA: National Bureau of Economic Research. NBER Working Paper 5721. Forthcoming in *American Economic Review*.

Griliches, Z. (1984). *R&D, Patents, and Productivity*. Chicago: University of Chicago Press.

Kiley, M. (1997). Labor productivity in U.S. manufacturing: Does sectoral comovement reflect technology shocks? Federal Reserve Board. Mimeo.

Comment

ADAM B. JAFFE
Brandeis University and NBER

This paper describes a valuable empirical exercise that was carried out with care and is presented with clarity. It provides a comprehensive summary of the empirical relationships, at the level of approximately two-digit SIC industries, among R&D, patents, other inputs, measured output, measured total factor productivity (TFP), and measured output prices. The results can be distilled into the following set of stylized facts:

1. There is a clear cross-sectional relationship across industries between indicators of technological activity and the growth rate of measured TFP.
2. For the set of industries taken as a whole, it is impossible to "find" this effect of technology on measured TFP in the form of significant impulse responses at any time horizon to technology shocks.
3. For a set of industries dominated by process rather than product innovation, there is a significant long-run positive response of measured TFP to technology shocks.
4. For all industries taken together, technology shocks have a significant short-run expansionary effect on labor input.
5. For all industries taken together, technology shocks have a significant long-run contractionary effect on total input, and induce significant long-run substitution of capital and nonproduction labor for production labor.

Shea concludes from these stylized facts that (1) technology shocks cannot be viewed as a significant driver of short-run movements in *measured* output or productivity for the economy as a whole; (2) technology shocks may be driving *actual* output and productivity even in the short run; and (3) macroeconomists should devote significant time and attention to the history of product innovation in particular sectors, in order to develop price series that would permit accurate measurement of output and productivity. While I am certainly not going to argue with the third conclusion, I believe that there is sufficient uncertainty about what is really going on in the data that the first conclusion must be somewhat qualified.

The separation of industries between those dominated by product innovations and those dominated by process innovations is a valuable and important improvement in the final version of the paper. I agree that the results for the process-innovation-dominated industries suggest that the absence of technology shock responses in the overall pooled sample is probably due, at least in part, to the failure of the output series to incorporate appropriately the effects of new products and quality improvements. I also agree that this partition confirms the results in the overall panel in which patents classified by industry of use typically have clearer effects on TFP than patents classified by industry of manufacture. Quite apart from its macro implications, this is a nice contribution to the industry-level literature on interindustry technology flows.

The only cloud over this otherwise sunny picture is that the greater effect of patents by industry of use relative to patents by industry of manufacture continues to hold when one looks at *upstream* patents. In principle, innovations "used" in my upstream industries should lower their costs and hence the prices of my inputs, but should not affect my measured productivity. In contrast, innovations "manufactured" in my upstream industries create precisely the kind of unmeasured product improvement that we are worried about; if my (actual) inputs are improving in quality but my (measured) inputs are not, then I should be having improvements in my (measured) TFP. In other words, the very story that explains the greater effect on "own" productivity of patents by industry of use relative to patents by industry of manufacture implies that this relationship ought to be reversed in the upstream patents. The fact that it is not suggests that some other factor may be at work. Econometrically, the pattern of results could be explained by inherently greater measurement error in the classification by industry of manufacture. But this doesn't seem very plausible; if anything, it is harder to figure out where something will be used than it is to figure out where it is made. This issue probably merits further exploration, looking in more detail at specific industries and examining how differences between the two patent totals drive the results.

The finding that the results differ significantly between product-innovating and process-innovating industries also confirms what one would suspect more broadly, which is that neither the magnitude nor the timing of technology responses is likely to be the same across such diverse industries. While it is perhaps possible to interpret the overall results as mean effects in a random-coefficients framework, the likely fragility of the results with respect to other partitions suggests that we should at least hesitate before concluding that technology shocks have no effect at the industry level.

More fundamentally, it remains quite plausible to me that, even at the level of individual industries (as defined here), one might find no effect of technology shocks at any specific time horizon, even if they did have real effects on measured TFP. The simplest way to view the above stylized facts about the relationship between technology and TFP is that technology does affect (measured) TFP, but it does so with lags that are so variable that it is impossible to pin down the timing of the effects. I am not a macroeconomist and do not know if a model in which technology shocks produce productivity and output impacts with highly variable lags will generate business cycles. If not, then these results may suggest that technology shocks are not a likely explanation for observed business cycles, but this is a little different from saying that they have no impact on measured TFP at the industry level.

Shea does a very good job of discussing the potential problems and limitations with the R&D and patent series as indicators of technological improvement. In addition to the problems that he discusses, I would emphasize the highly aggregated nature of the sectors that are the units of observation here, and the difficulty of R&D and patent series in measuring really big innovations. If one thinks of likely candidates for technology shocks, it is not hard to think of examples of innovations that have had perceptible effects on output or productivity, but would probably not be visible in the R&D or patents series for sectors as broad as those defined here. Consider Viagra relative to all prescription and nonprescription drugs; Aspartame relative to the entire food sector, or the electric-arc steel furnace relative to the entire metals sector. It is in some sense the essence of important shocks that their effects on productivity or output are highly disproportionate to the R&D or patents associated with them. For this reason, it is possible for the industry TFP series to be reflecting real technology shocks even if those shocks were not associated with R&D or patents.

Shea correctly points out that this kind of measurement error in the technology indicators ought to bias the results towards finding no effects of technology shocks, while he does find significant effects at some horizons on other inputs. He concludes from this that his negative conclusion about the effects of technology shocks on TFP and output should be taken at face value. While I agree that finding significant technology effects on inputs puts some qualitative limit on the amount of measurement error, it seems a bit of a jump to rule out its having a material impact on the TFP results.

My queasiness about using the significant effects of technology on inputs to conclude that the negative conclusion about technology and TFP is real is strengthened by the nature of these significant input effects. Specifically, the significantly negative long-run contractionary effect of technology shocks on total inputs seems inconsistent with the rest of the story. If inputs are falling because of process innovation, then there is no reason why this should not be seen in a long-run positive impact on measured TFP. On the other hand, if the story is that in the complete panel technology is largely producing product innovations that are not picked up in measured TFP, how can it be that technology shocks significantly reduce total input in the long run? If TFP is unchanged, than a significant decline in total inputs implies a significant decline in (measured) output. While we know that the *increase* in real output corresponding to improved products may not be reflected in measured output, it is hard for me to understand how product innovation would lead to a significant long-run *decline* in measured output. Overall, then, the significant pattern of effects of the technology indicators on inputs is not really consistent with the interpretation given to those indicators, so I cannot take much comfort from it.

It is the nature of a Comment to focus on criticisms and areas of disagreement. Despite my having done so, it is still true that I learned a lot from this paper, and believe that this kind of empirical analysis is crucial to a better understanding of the linkages between the macro economy and the microeconomic phenomena of innovation and technological change.

Discussion

The finding that the link between innovative activity and short-run output fluctuations is weak generated considerable discussion. Several participants, including David Backus, Susanto Basu, and Russell Cooper, stressed the point that, in the business-cycle literature, a "technology shock" occurs only at the time at which output is affected—not at the time that the inventive process begins or a technological innovation is patented. Various factors, including slow diffusion of knowledge, the need to work out details of implementation, and the time needed to adjust factors of production, can lead to long and varying lags between inventive activity and any effect on output.

The fact that measures of R&D fail even to affect total factor productivity (TFP) is a significant puzzle, as Basu noted. Julio Rotemberg pointed out that this result seems inconsistent with the finding that R&D activity and TFP growth are positively correlated across industries. Shea responded that the cross-sectional finding is not inconsistent with the conclusion that R&D activity has little effect on TFP or output in the short run. Michael Woodford added that the cross-sectional results may be spurious, in that R&D activity and TFP growth might be jointly determined across industries by some third factor. Henning Bohn suggested that as Shea's measures of R&D do not affect TFP, it is possible that there exist unmeasured sources of technical change which determine TFP; and therefore that we shouldn't necessarily conclude that TFP changes are irrelevant for business fluctuations. Backus noted that short-run output and TFP dynamics are more likely to reflect the underlying transmission mechanism than the nature of the shocks themselves, and that these shocks need not be technological to account for observed behavior.

A potentially important but hard-to-measure source of TFP growth is organizational change. As an illustration, Backus stressed the important effects on productivity of organizational changes in the airline industry. Shea and Rotemberg expressed skepticism that changes in organization were likely to have high-frequency effects.

John Cochrane questioned the implicit restriction that only unanticipated changes in research and development have real effects. Unlike anticipated changes in monetary policy, anticipated changes in R&D should have important effects on measured TFP and output. Shea defended his approach as an identification assumption; while anticipated R&D can have real effects, it is difficult to disentangle those effects from the effects of other shocks that change both R&D and output.

Simon Gilchrist pointed out that the effects of technology shocks on input use depends on auxiliary assumptions about the economy. For example, they will depend on the nature of the monetary authority's responses to various shocks. Jordi Galí cited results from his own work supporting the view that the Fed does not accommodate technology shocks sufficiently.

John H. Cochrane

University of Chicago, Federal Reserve Bank of Chicago, and NBER

A Frictionless View of U.S. Inflation

1. Introduction

The standard, quantity-theoretic approach to the price level is based on a transactions demand for money. Financial innovation challenges the foundations of this monetary theory: More and more transactions are handled electronically or via credit and debit cards, while ATMs, sweep accounts, and banking by computer have a major influence on cash management. Meanwhile, a wide array of privately provided, liquid, interest-paying, and often nonreservable assets have been created, leaving the supply of transaction-facilitating assets beyond the Fed's control. The quantity theory has also not had much success in describing the history of postwar U.S. inflation: Inflation seems to have very little to do with the history of monetary aggregates or interest rates. Money demand relations are dominated by *velocity shocks*, unrelated to changes in financial structure. Recent inflation has been remarkably stable despite continuing financial innovation.

Motivated by these observations, I ask: Can we understand the history of U.S. inflation using a framework that *ignores* monetary frictions? Until recently, there was no coherent way to think about this question: some friction seemed necessary to determine any value for unbacked fiat money. Recently, however, a series of authors including Leeper (1991), Sims (1994, 1997), and Woodford (1995, 1996, 1997) have advocated a *fiscal* theory of the price level. The analytical content of the fiscal theory is just the government's intertemporal budget constraint, versions of

I thank Henning Bohn, Eric Leeper, Julio Rotemberg, and Mike Woodford for many helpful comments, and I thank Andrea Eisfeldt for research assistance. My research is supported by the CRSP, Graduate School of Business, and by a grant from the National Science Foundation administered by the NBER. Data used in this paper can be found at **http://www-gsb.uchicago.edu/fac/john.cochrane/**.

$$\frac{\text{nominal debt}}{\text{price level}} = \text{present value of real surpluses.} \tag{1}$$

In a fiscal analysis, this equation determines the price level in much the same way that $Mv = py$ determines the price level in the quantity theory. However, since total government debt rather than the supply of transactions-facilitating assets appears on the left, fiscal price-level determination is immune to financial innovation, including elastically provided private media of exchange, and even a cashless or frictionless economy. More generally, as I will show below, the budget constraint provides an implicit backing or commodity standard for even apparently unbacked fiat money; equivalently, the fiscal theory regards money together with nominal debt as a (non-voting) equity claim on the flow of surpluses; these sources of value are transparently independent of financial structure or any special exchange or liquidity properties of money.

Since we see money and frictions, why abstract from them in studying the price level? First, monetary frictions have at best second-order effects on the price level in fiscal models, so why not start with the simple model? Second, a frictionless economy with lots of inside, privately provided media of exchange is, at the level of ingredients, a much more plausible abstraction for the U.S. economy than an economy with rigidly separate liquid "money" used for transactions and illiquid "bonds" used for saving. Now that we *can* determine the price level in a frictionless model, it seems sensible to do it. Third, though economic theorists have a great deal of experience with analytically convenient devices with which to introduce monetary frictions—cash-in-advance, money in the utility function, overlapping generations—none of these devices provides an *empirically* successful description of money demand or inflation. If we had a realistic and empirically successful monetary theory—a stable, exploitable, and well-understood money demand function, a well-defined and agreed-on monetary aggregate, and an empirically successful account of U.S. inflation—most of our interest in the fiscal theory would vanish. The fiscal theory would be a small dusty corner in which theorists battle over "foundations" of a successful empirical framework. Finally, the fiscal theory cannot hope to say much as an alternative solution concept for *given* models, especially models with strong enough monetary frictions to determine the price level. Its greatest promise is precisely that it allows us to determine the price level in *different* models, without monetary frictions.

In this paper, I first exposit a frictionless economy with fiscal price-level determination. Though the formal theory is well worked out by the above-cited authors, the interpretation, applicability, and plausibility of the fiscal theory are still disputed. I show how the fiscal theory describes a backed commodity standard and a tax-based theory of value. I clarify the vexing red herring of "Ricardian" and "non-Ricardian" regimes, and budget constraints that do or don't hold at off-equilibrium prices. I review the extension of the fiscal theory to long-term debt, which tells us when a shortfall in future surpluses can be met by a decline in long-term bond prices rather than an increase in the price level, and I show how explicit monetary frictions make small changes to the fiscal-theoretic description of the price level.

I then interpret the history of U.S. inflation with a fiscal-theory, frictionless view. This is potentially a tough assignment. The history of postwar U.S. inflation does not have obvious fiscal roots, nor does it offer the kind of clean exogenous movements in debt or surpluses that one hopes for in a test. Also, the fiscal theory (with short-term debt) relates the price level to the *present value* of future surpluses. In contrast, the quantity theory relates the price level to the *flow* of transactions or income. Present values are notoriously hard to measure. Most importantly, the correlations in the data seem wrong: The 1970s were a decade of low deficits and high inflation, while the 1980s saw a dramatic increase in government debt with low inflation. Large deficits also occur in the depths of recessions with low, not high inflation, and with rising, not declining, values of the debt. The centerpiece of the empirical work is to show how one can plausibly understand these correlations.

On the other hand, interpreting U.S. inflation history is potentially much too easy an assignment. One's first impulse is to *test* the fiscal theory; perhaps to run some vector autoregressions (VARs) to see whether surplus shocks rather than monetary shocks affect the price level. However, I show that the fiscal theory *per se* has no testable implications for the joint time series of prices, debt, and surpluses. Briefly, the identity (1) holds, in equilibrium, whether fiscal or monetary considerations determine the price level. Therefore, one can always rationalize the price level by reference to debt and subsequent surpluses. Additional identifying assumptions are not easy to find in U.S. experience. For this reason, the main focus of the empirical work is to construct a plausible story for the time series rather than pursue a test. The fiscal theory does predict that open market operations should have little effect on the price level, and this implication is fairly easy to see in the data.

I construct a detailed dataset on total outstanding federal debt, broken down by maturity on a zero-coupon basis. I infer the surplus from debt transactions, rather than use accounting data. I start by documenting the patterns of surpluses, debt, and inflation in the U.S. since 1960 (when useful data start). I find some surprises. For example, the biggest primary deficit occurs in 1975, along with the onset of serious inflation. The primary "Reagan deficits" are surprisingly small, and even those are largely accounted for by the dramatic recessions of 1980–1982. I also find that fluctuations in the rate of return of government bonds are as large as fluctuations in surpluses, so the rate at which future surpluses are discounted may be as important to the present value of the surplus as are changing expectations about future surpluses. I find interesting variations in maturity structure, correlated with inflation: maturities were very short in the 1970s, but have lengthened since long-term bond sales were reemphasized in 1975. Longer maturities have led to wider fluctuations in the rate of return on government debt, and they allow debt sales to immediately affect the price level.

The central issue is understanding fluctuations in the real value of the debt. The fiscal theory requires a forward-looking story: the value of the debt is determined by the present value of future surpluses. The standard story is backward-looking: the value of the debt is determined by the accumulation of past deficits and a money-determined price level. To tell the forward-looking story, I pursue models with exogenous surpluses that replicate important correlations in the data. The important ingredient of the models is that extra nominal debt sales in recessions must come with implicit promises to increase subsequent surpluses. Finally, I consider whether expected return variation and maturity structure are important elements of the story.

I ask what policies could have avoided postwar inflation. I find that fiscal policy already does a lot of price-level smoothing, and that variation in inflation comes from comparatively small failures to smooth. Even larger fluctuations in nominal debt would have been required to stabilize inflation; on the other hand, a $k\%$ rule would have resulted in disastrously fluctuating inflation.

2. The Fiscal Theory of the Price Level

2.1 A SIMPLE FRICTIONLESS ECONOMY

Start with a simple frictionless economy with one-period government debt. At the beginning of each period t, nominal bonds $B_{t-1}(t)$ are left outstanding from period $t - 1$ and will mature at t. Bondholders can use the maturing bonds to pay net real taxes (net of government spending and transfers) s_t or to acquire new bonds at price $Q_t(t + 1)$. (I use capital letters for nominal quantities and lowercase letters for real quantities.) Accounting for the flow of bonds, then, we have

$$B_{t-1}(t) - Q_t(t + 1)B_t(t + 1) = p_t s_t. \tag{2}$$

Fiscal price determination is easiest to see in a terminal period, or a period in which the government sells no new debt. Then, the budget constraint simplifies to

$$\frac{B_{t-1}(t)}{p_t} = s_t. \tag{3}$$

Nominal debt $B_{t-1}(t)$ is predetermined, so the price level must adjust to equate the real value of the debt to the real value of surpluses that will retire the debt.

To extend the analysis to infinite-period economies, define the ex post real return on government bonds

$$r^b_{t+1} \equiv \frac{1}{Q_t(t+1)} \frac{p_t}{p_{t+1}}. \tag{4}$$

Then we can write the accounting identity (2) as

$$\frac{B_{t-1}(t)}{p_t} - \frac{1}{r^b_{t+1}} \frac{B_t(t+1)}{p_{t+1}} = s_t. \tag{5}$$

Iterating forward and imposing the usual transversality condition or taking the limit of finitely lived economies with a terminal period described by (3), we obtain

$$\frac{B_{t-1}(t)}{p_t} = \sum_{j=0}^{\infty} \prod_{k=1}^{j} \frac{1}{r^b_{t+k}} s_{t+j}. \tag{6}$$

These accounting identities hold ex post for each realization, so they also hold ex ante, after taking time-t conditional expectations. We can write

$$\frac{B_{t-1}(t)}{p_t} = E_t \sum_{j=0}^{\infty} \prod_{k=1}^{j} \frac{1}{r^b_{t+k}} s_{t+j}. \tag{7}$$

Equation (7) is the multiperiod analogue of (3). The price level adjusts to equate the real value of nominal debt to the *present value* of the surpluses that will retire it.

It is often a convenient simplification to assume a constant expected real return r on government bonds. With this assumption, we can take expectations of (4) and find that the price of new debt is

$$Q_t(t + 1) = \frac{1}{r} E_t \left(\frac{1}{p_{t+1}} \right) p_t,$$

the flow budget constraint is

$$\frac{B_{t-1}(t)}{p_t} - \frac{1}{r} E_t \left(\frac{1}{p_{t+1}} \right) B_t(t + 1) = s_t, \tag{8}$$

and the present-value budget constraint is

$$\frac{B_{t-1}(t)}{p_t} = E_t \sum_{j=0}^{\infty} \frac{1}{r^j} s_{t+j}. \tag{9}$$

Equations (8) or (9) determine the *sequence* of prices $\{p_t\}$ given an exogenous sequence of surpluses $\{s_t\}$ and of nominal debt $\{B_{t-1}(t)\}$. I emphasize the determination of the *sequence* $\{p_t\}$ from the *sequences* $\{B_{t-1}(t), s_t\}$ to avoid an analysis that distinguishes between "date zero" events and subsequent history.

The reader may be uncomfortable that the rest of the economy is not specified—where are preferences, technology, and shocks? The answer is that a wide specification of models includes equations such as (8)–(9); those equations will determine the price level no matter what the rest of the economy looks like, so we don't have to spell it out.

"Budget constraint" is a poor term for equation (8) or (9). The whole point of the theory is that these equations are *not* constraints on the government's actions; instead they describe price-level determination. However, the form of these equations is so associated with the name "budget constraint" that I will continue to use this phrase to describe them.

The budget constraints become more complicated as one includes money (potentially held overnight despite an interest-rate penalty), long-term debt, and other realistic complications. In general, we add real or indexed assets and liabilities such as social security on the right-hand side, and other nominal claims including money and long-term debt to the left-hand side. Policy rules with feedback can be included, for example by writing $s_t(p_t, p_{t-1}, \ldots)$. Then one solves for the price-level sequence that solves the budget constraint at each date. In these more general situations, this *solution* for the price-level sequence will not be the same as the present-value budget constraint equation (9).

2.2 INTERPRETATIONS

The claim that fiscal considerations can determine the price level, even in a completely frictionless economy, is so strange at first that it merits closer examination. The fiscal mechanisms and equations apply to a wide variety of different institutional arrangements. Spelling out some of those arrangements makes fiscal price determination much more plausible and understandable, and makes it easier to apply the fiscal theory in practice.

2.2.1 Money in Frictionless Economies   A frictionless economy need not be a cashless economy. The budget constraints and hence the price level are completely unaffected if the government redeems some maturing bonds for cash during the period, and if this cash rather than maturing bonds is used for transactions, tax payments, and the purchase of new bonds. The split between cash and maturing bonds at any moment in time—a form of open-market operation—similarly has no effect at all on the budget constraint and hence on the price level.

Furthermore, the government can provide cash elastically with no effect on the price level. If the government prints a dollar and issues it as an interest-free intraday loan, that dollar is used for transactions, and then the loan is repaid by the end of the day, the budget constraints are again unaffected. Since Fedwire transactions are netted at the end of the day, this is in fact close to the current institutional arrangement. Unlimited inside moneys—private claims to reserves, cash, or maturing government bonds—can also be created and used to make transactions, with no effect on the budget constraint and hence on the price level.

The above timing and budget constraints are the same as those in a cash-in-advance economy in which the security market is always open. One can add a cash-in-advance constraint that bonds must be exchanged for cash in order to make purchases with no effect on the price level. "Frictionless" means the security market is always open; transactions may still require cash. The friction in typical cash-in-advance models is that the security market is only open part of the day, requiring people to hold some cash overnight to make transactions.

2.2.2 Commodity Standards   Credible commodity standards or exchange-rate pegs are intuitively transparent instances of the fiscal theory of the price level. The fiscal theory looks past the promised price level or exchange rate and past any official backing such as gold stocks or reserves to the overall real resources that in the end back the promises.

Suppose the government stands ready to exchange each dollar for a bushel of wheat, and that it maintains a warehouse with enough wheat to do so. The classical (100% backed) gold standard embodies this idea. Currency boards that peg exchange rates are more recently popular implementations.

This regime would seem to nail the price level at $1/bushel by arbitrage. Furthermore, the price level under a commodity standard is transparently immune to financial innovation. Any amount of privately issued, interest-paying, liquid assets or private banknotes can be created with no effect on the price level. Private banknotes are valued by their own fiscal theory, and may trade at a discount due to default risk. In a cashless economy, electronic claims to "dollars" are valued as claims to "one bushel wheat." Even monetary frictions are at most important for determining interest-rate spreads and quantities of liquid assets; they have no effect on the price level.

A commodity standard is an instance of the fiscal theory. Credibility is the crucial issue with a commodity standard or a peg. 100% backing regimes—warehouses full of wheat, a Ft. Knox full of gold, or a currency board holding foreign securities—are thought to provide such credibility, since the last dollar can be extinguished just as the backing vanishes. Such backing is an asset on the right-hand side of the budget identity, put there to guarantee that the budget constraint can always hold at the promised price level.

On closer inspection, however, we see that the overall government budget constraint is what really matters, not the backing, reserves, or the promised rate. For this reason, we write the fiscal theory with overall real resources on the right-hand side, not just whatever resources are explicitly devoted to backing. If a government is in financial trouble, it will try to appropriate the real assets or currency-board backing that is "uselessly" sitting in a warehouse, or (equivalently) it will devalue. On the other hand, a government with healthy finances can peg an exchange rate or commodity standard with no reserves—buying reserves on the spot market as needed, raising taxes, selling real assets, or borrowing against future surpluses to do so. Exchange-rate pegs do not fall to speculative attack when the government "runs out of reserves"; they fall apart when the government becomes unable or unwilling to *buy* reserves.

Furthermore, the government must back the entire stock of nominal debt, not just whatever currency is currently outstanding. For this reason, we write the fiscal theory with all government debt on the left-hand side, not just currency or the monetary base. If the currency outstanding is 100% backed, but there is a large stock of maturing nominal debt relative to real assets and current and future real surpluses, everyone can see that the backing promise or peg must soon be broken.

By pointing out that the overall budget matters and that all nominal debt must be backed, I do not mean to deny that 100% backing schemes, run by suitably independent agents with explicit rules and public accounting, are useful precommitment devices for government finance. These considerations do suggest however that their operation is really a matter of political economy or game theory, not, as is often argued, simple accounting.

2.2.3 Tax and Demand Interpretations The fiscal theory of the price level also formalizes an old view that fiat money is valued because the government requires its use for tax payments. Since the U.S. no longer follows an explicit commodity standard, a tax-based theory of value is a more plausible description of current institutions.

Consider a terminal period, or any period in which the government does not sell new debt. To tell the simplest story, suppose that the government redeems all the outstanding debt $B_{t-1}(t)$ for cash M_t at the beginning of the period, and that the government has no assets or explicit backing left. Now, the budget constraint simplifies to

$$\frac{M_t}{p_t} = s_t. \tag{10}$$

The government's surplus s_t is the private sector's net real tax liability, which must be paid with cash.

Suppose the price level is too high. There is too little cash around to pay taxes, so taxpayers try to sell goods for cash, which lowers the price level. Alternatively, suppose the price level is too low. Taxpayers have more cash than they need to pay taxes, so they try to buy more goods, driving up the price level. The same story applies to the multiperiod model, strung out through time.

These stories have a familiar feel: Inflation results from too much money chasing too few goods; money is a hot potato that individuals can try to get rid of, but in aggregate such actions only change the price level. Intuition and observations that inflation occurs in periods of high "aggregate demand" for goods and services are perfectly consistent with a fiscal theory. The crucial change, and one that would be easy to miss in analyzing the data, is that an excess of cash is measured relative to *tax liabilities* that soak it up, not relative to a transactions-based demand.

A tax-based theory of value is also transparently immune to financial innovation: the economy may operate cashlessly, and/or any amount of inside liquid assets may be created, with no change in the price level. To operate cashlessly, the government can simply accept maturing government bonds directly for tax liabilities, or may electronically convert them to dollars for a nanosecond before accepting them. (This is what happens now if you pay your tax bill with a check on a money-market mutual fund.) Tax liabilities define dollars as a unit of account, and taxes give meaning to a bond's promise to pay 100 "dollars" at maturity in a cashless economy. Inside moneys do not matter, for in the end taxes must be paid with government-issued nominal claims. Like the commodity standard, the tax-based story suggests that even monetary frictions will have at best second-order effects on the price level: The basic valuation story is not much affected if people obtain money to pay taxes a day or two in advance, suffering an interest penalty.

2.2.4 A Stylized History and Dramatic Implications   We started with a commodity standard. Then we realized that the overall real resources that back nominal debt matter in the end, not the promised redemption rate. Finally, when the resources are in place, the promise can vanish as well, as in the tax story.

This progression of ideas is also a useful stylized history. Early economies used raw metal or coins for transactions, and the price level was understood primarily in terms of the commodity content. Then, banknotes, checks, and government-issued paper claims to gold or silver were created. At first, people worried that these devices would not maintain their value relative to the commodity unit of account. However, 100% backed notes that explicitly promised redemption in commodity terms did in fact have stable values. Next, it was found that most of the backing was gathering dust in a warehouse. Why insist on 100% reserves? Despite reservations about price-level stability that remain to this day, it was gradually found that lower reserve ratios could be used and still maintain the value of the notes, *if* the issuing entity was in sound enough financial condition so that it could always purchase enough backing if required (and, often dramatically, not conversely). Eventually, the explicit promises in the form of the gold standard, also disappeared. Observers again worried (and still do) that removing the promise would lead to price-level explosion. But nothing worse than the slow postwar inflation has occurred in the United States.

The quantity theory offers an explanation for the last experience. In the quantity theory, an unbacked fiat money has value if and only if there is an inventory demand for it due to a special use in transactions, and if it and competing special assets are limited in supply. The price level did not explode when the gold standard was dropped, because its quantity-theoretic liquidity value already accounted for its value under the gold standard.

The fiscal theory offers an alternative explanation. In a fiscal theory, the backing is all that matters to a commodity standard in the first place. The price level did not explode when the gold standard was dropped, because it was already at its *fiscal* equilibrium level. A tax-based determination of value has the additional advantage over the gold standard that the implicit "commodity" is the full basket of government purchases, so changes in the relative price of gold do not disturb the price level.

As described above, we are in the midst of a new round of financial innovation. Quantity theorists are once again worried that this new set of financial innovations will destabilize the price level. This worry has even led to proposals to limit financial innovation in order to maintain price-level control. However, the price level has remained remarkably stable given the level of financial innovation. At best, a quantity theorist explains this fact by noting that the Fed follows an interest-rate policy, allowing money supply to accommodate shifts in velocity. However, the shifts in velocity are not traceable to financial innovation. A fiscal theorist is not surprised: financial innovations should have no effect at all on the price level.

This argument has dramatic implications. The fiscal theory is at heart a repudiation of (at least) 100 years of the quantity theory, and a return to backing theories of the value of money. It denies any sharp distinction between commodity backing regimes and unbacked fiat money. Apparently unbacked fiat money can be valued, and apparently was all along, through the implicit backing of overall government surpluses.

While a promised exchange rate or price level does not matter to the theory, the theory will be easiest to apply when there is an explicit promise. Then, we just have to evaluate whether the promise is credible given current and future government revenues. When promises are implicit, as in the case of the U.S. economy, we can only look at the actual history of overall surpluses to see if the price level does indeed correspond to its fundamental backing.

2.3 RICARDIAN AND NON-RICARDIAN REGIMES

2.3.1 *A Simple Example* In the one-period example,

$$\frac{B_{t-1}(t)}{p_t} = s_t, \tag{11}$$

we can see right away a special case in which the fiscal theory may not determine prices. If the government sets a *nominal* surplus S_t rather than a real surplus s_t, then the budget constraint is

$$B_{t-1}(t) = S_t.$$

Either the government commits to redeem the outstanding stock of nominal debt, $S_t = B_{t-1}(t)$, or it does not, $S_t \neq B_{t-1}(t)$. In the former case the price level is indeterminate, while in the latter case no value of the price level can eliminate the discrepancy.

In fact, the government determines *real* rather than nominal surpluses. Nominal tax liabilities are given by a rate θ times nominal income, $\theta p y$, and thus real tax liabilities θy are determined. If either the tax rate or the output is non-neutral, so that θy declines one for one with p, we could have a Ricardian regime. But if anything, nominal tax brackets mean that the real tax rate θ is higher with a higher price level, and nonneutralities are usually thought to give higher output with higher price level. Perhaps more importantly, the *limits* on tax collection are real; the top of the Laffer curve is real, and government can't tax more than 100% of real GDP, no matter what the price level.

2.3.2 Ricardian Regimes The above example with a fixed nominal surplus is a *Ricardian regime*. [This is Woodford's (1995) terminology. Canzoneri, Cumby, and Diba (1997) call the same thing a *money-determined* regime.] If we think of the two sides of (11) as two curves (functions of price) that determine the price level, a Ricardian regime is the special case in which the curves happen to fall right on top of each other. A Ricardian regime is the fiscal analogue to interest-rate targets or accommodative money-supply rules that can leave the price level indeterminate in the quantity theory. More generally, I use the following definition:

A *Ricardian regime* is any policy rule $\{B_t(t + j), s_t\}$ in which the sequence of government budget constraints holds for any sequence of price levels.

In an infinite-period context, when some new debt is sold every period, the present-value budget constraint is

$$\frac{B_{t-1}(t)}{p_t} = E_t \sum_{j=0}^{\infty} \frac{1}{r^j} s_{t+j}. \tag{12}$$

If the surplus $\{s_{t+j}\}$ reacts to p_t in such a way that (12) would hold for any p_t, then we have a Ricardian regime and (12) can no longer determine the price level. If the surplus does not react in just this way, then the price level must adjust to bring (12) into balance, and we have a fiscal regime.

2.3.3 The Quantity Theory as a Ricardian Regime The quantity theory is a particularly important case of a Ricardian regime. In the quantity theory, we add another equation, $Mv = py$. Fixing v and y, and with government control of M, the quantity equation now determines the price level. (I discuss more general cases with varying velocity and interest-rate policies below.)

However, the budget constraint (12) is still part of the system. (Strictly speaking, one must account for the interest advantage to the government of money held overnight; I do so below, and the difference is not important to the current discussion.) Since nominal debt $B_{t-1}(t)$ and p_t are now determined, the budget constraint is interpreted as a constraint on fiscal policy $\{s_{t+j}\}$. If the right-hand side of (12) is insufficient for a given real value of the debt, the government must raise future surpluses, by seignorage if explicit taxation is insufficient. Thus, the quantity theory is a Ricardian regime.

Quantity theorists have long recognized the tension between two equations, $Mv = py$ and the budget constraint, each of which seems to determine the price level. Therefore, fiscal considerations have long been important in the quantity theory. Sargent (1986) interprets Friedman's $k\%$ rules in part as a way of precommitting the monetary authority in a game of chicken with the Treasury over whether surpluses would be met by taxes or seignorage. Cash-in-advance models following Lucas (1980) (or see Sargent 1987, p. 162) explicitly rebate seignorage revenues. These models assume fiscal policies in which the government follows a Ricardian regime *by choice*, so that the budget constraint will not fight with the quantity theory for price-level determination.

In fact, the intellectual history of the fiscal theory comes precisely from thinking hard about the government budget constraint in the quantity theory. Leeper (1991), Sims (1994), and Woodford (1994) asked: what happens to a cash-in-advance model if the government does *not* choose to follow a fiscal policy that renders the budget constraint vacuous? As the above analysis shows, the budget constraint and a non-Ricardian regime can determine the price level in a cash-in-advance model, even if the security market is always open.

2.3.4 Equilibrium and Off-Equilibrium: Is a Fiscal Regime Possible? A long and rather confusing debate pervades the fiscal theory over whether the government *must* follow a Ricardian regime. We usually derive demand curves by having the auctioneer announce a price vector, and then finding utility- or profit-maximizing quantities that satisfy the budget constraint at those prices. Demands satisfy budget constraints, even at off-equilibrium prices. This logic suggests that the government *must* adjust. future surpluses in response to an off-equilibrium price level, so there is a fundamental mistake in using the budget constraint as we do to determine the price level given surpluses.

There must be a flaw in the reasoning: what happens if the auctioneer calls out such a low price level that the required surpluses are *impossible*, for example twice real GDP, forever? To think about this issue, return to a 100%-backed commodity standard as an instance of a fiscal regime. One dollar equals one bushel of wheat. The government keeps a warehouse with enough wheat to back the entire nominal debt open 24 hours a day. Institutional arrangements are strong enough that the government can never raid the warehouse. This arrangement would seem to decisively nail the price level at $1/bushel. Yet a Ricardian regime advocate would argue that it does *nothing* to determine the price level. He would argue that if the Walrasian auctioneer were to announce a price of $0.50 per bushel, the government would not have enough wheat to back the debt. It would then be forced to raise taxes to obtain more wheat, selling it at and validating the lower price.

In the example, it's easy to see that the argument is false. There is nothing that prevents the government from sticking to a $1/bushel redemption rate no matter what the auctioneer or secondary market announces. If the secondary market price is $0.50, the government will buy lots of wheat; but there is no limit to the amount of nominal bonds or cash it can create in exchange for wheat. On the other hand, if the secondary-market price is $2, the government will sell lots of wheat at $1. The last ounce of wheat leaves the warehouse just as the last cent of nominal government debt is redeemed. The policy might seem foolish: the government wastes resources by selling wheat at $1 when the secondary market price is $2, or by buying it at $1 when the secondary market price is $0.50. But the argument is about constraints, not objectives; if the government wants to freely buy and sell at $1/bushel, there is no constraint that stops it from doing so.

The argument does not hinge on the commodity standard or promised redemption rate. Suppose there are 100 bushels of wheat in the warehouse, $100 in notes outstanding, and no further taxes or assets on the last day of an economy, but the government will accept its notes for wheat at the market (auctioneer) price rather than posting a price. If the market price is $2/bushel, the government will wind up with unsold wheat at the end of the day. If the price is $0.50/bushel, the government may run out of wheat before consumers have redeemed all the money. There is nothing wrong with either outcome. The government can certainly waste or consume wheat at the end of the period. Similarly, the budget constraint must allow consumers to keep some money. The facts that money is not intrinsically valuable to consumers and that wheat is not valuable to the government must be reflected in preferences, not constraints.

The mistake, from a Walrasian view, is in insisting that government debt must be paid off because of budget constraints. The government starts with an endowment of wheat, and consumers start with an endowment of money. The budget constraint says that *trades* away from the endowment points must take place at or at worse than market (auctioneer) prices. This constraint is satisfied in both of the above examples.

What about previous dates, at which the money is issued or bonds are sold? The same points extend to multiperiod models. Though money and bonds at each date are the result of previous period's trades, we always come down to an initial period with endowments outstanding, and then each period markets reopen as if the previous period's outcomes were endowments.

Similarly, there is a longstanding suspicion that one must assume something special about a government in a fiscal theory; that the government is a special agent that can announce demands that do not satisfy budget constraints or repay debts at off-equilibrium prices; that it enjoys a special first-mover status in some game with the private sector. As the examples make clear, there is nothing special about the government. If I give away 100 IOUs saying "John Cochrane will pay the bearer $1 on demand," I have $100 in my wallet that I will only use for repaying IOUs, and all this is perfectly credible, visible, etc., I can nail the price of my IOUs at $1 each. If for some reason they become worth more (if the auctioneer announces a different price), I can (and will!) print up IOUs like mad; if they become worth less I can redeem them all. I may not *choose* to, but I *can*. I can also issue "equity claims on John Cochrane's wallet," and then repurchase them via auction. If the auctioneer announces the wrong price, I can leave the room when IOUs or dollars in my wallet run out.

In the same way, private entities as well as multiple governments can create nominal claims, with or without explicit promises about redemption in dollars or real baskets of goods. The only special thing about the government is the convention or legal restriction that the rest of the economy uses its IOUs as numeraire.

This is reassuring. If we relied on the government being able to violate budget constraints, nonsensical conclusions would follow. The government could announce lots of spending and zero taxes,[1] the budget constraint be damned.

---

1. I thank Larry Christiano and Martin Eichenbaum for repeatedly stressing this point, when I thought one *did* have to assume something special about the government.

2.4 TESTING FOR FISCAL DETERMINATION

Even though governments *can* follow non-Ricardian regimes in which fiscal theory determines the price level, they may not *choose* to do so. Looking forward to our task of bringing a fiscal theory to data, one's natural impulse is to "test" the fiscal theory, and the natural "test" is whether the government has chosen to follow a Ricardian or a non-Ricardian policy regime.

Unfortunately, the fiscal theory of the price level per se has no testable implications for the time series of debt, surplus, and price level.

The budget constraint (12) holds in equilibrium for both fiscal and Ricardian regimes. The issue is whether, in determining or adjusting towards equilibrium, the price level adjusts to expected future surpluses, or whether the path of surpluses adjusts in response to the price level. All we ever observe is an equilibrium; we do not observe who adjusted to bring about that equilibrium, or what off-equilibrium behavior looks like. Analogously, if one observes a market, one sees the transactions price and quantity, but not the slopes of the underlying supply and demand curves.

It is tempting to test "who adjusted" by looking at dynamic responses to shocks as in a VAR. But the (state-contingent) *sequence* of price levels, surplus, and debt $\{p_t, s_t, B_{t-1}(t + j)\}$ is a *single* equilibrium. It is not a sequence of equilibria, and even less a tatônnement process for the formation of an equilibrium. The issue is which sequence, $\{p_t\}$ or $\{s_t\}$, adjusts to the other sequence, not whether shocks to p_t precede those to s_t in an equilibrium sequence.

Woodford's (1995) analysis argues even more strongly that a test for fiscal determination is meaningless. As I will review below, Woodford argues that all monetary regimes (money demand specification and monetary policy rule) that are vaguely plausible descriptions of the U.S. economy leave the price level indeterminate. Therefore, Woodford's analysis implies that if the price level is determined at all it must be determined by fiscal means. There is no coherent alternative.

Clear as these points are in the abstract, it is helpful to apply them to empirical approaches one might attempt and see how those approaches break down.

2.4.1 Feedback Rules?

FEEDBACK RULES TO GENERATE RICARDIAN REGIMES   We often think of policy in terms of rules plus innovations. Fixing a nominal surplus is equivalent to a feedback rule $s_t(p_t) = S_t/p_t$ that increases the real surplus

1% for every 1% decrease in the price level. The budget constraint in the one-period case now reads

$$\frac{B_{t-1}(t)}{p_t} = s_t(p_t) = \frac{S_t}{p_t},$$

and the price level drops out as before. We can also think of this case as a commitment to adjust the *real* surplus to soak up the *real* value of outstanding debt, a rule $s_t = B_{t-1}(t)/p_t$.

We retain fiscal price-level determination if the government follows a policy rule with some feedback, so long as the feedback is not exactly one-for-one. If the government responds linearly to real debt,

$$s_t = \bar{s} + \alpha \frac{B_{t-1}(t)}{p_t}, \tag{13}$$

only the case $\bar{s} = 0$, $\alpha = 1$ implies that the budget constraint is vacuous.

In an infinite-period context with one-period debt, the constraint is

$$\frac{B_{t-1}(t)}{p_t} = E_t \sum_{j=0}^{\infty} \frac{1}{r^j} s_{t+j}.$$

The constraint holds for any price level and the regime is Ricardian if $\left\{ \sum_{j=0}^{\infty} (1/r^j) s_{t+j} \right\}$ reacts to p_t in a one-for-one manner.

It is more common to think about feedback rules for the one-period surplus than rules for the discounted value of future surpluses. Generally speaking, policies in which surpluses adjust to the price level in such a way that real debt does not grow faster than the real interest rate generate a Ricardian regime. The constraint

$$\frac{B_{t-1}(t)}{p_t} = \sum_{j=0}^{k} \prod_{l=1}^{j} \frac{1}{r_{t+l}^b} s_{t+j} + \prod_{l=1}^{k} \frac{1}{r_{t+l}^b} \frac{B_{t+k}(t+k+1)}{p_{t+k}}$$

holds as an accounting identity, and if the last term or its expectation converges to zero for any p_t, the budget constraint holds for any p_t. This statement is the natural infinite-period counterpart to the one-period example in which real surpluses adjust to soak up the real value of the debt.

As a specific example, consider linear feedback rules that raise the surplus in response to increases in real debt:

$$s_t = \alpha \frac{B_{t-1}(t)}{p_t} + \epsilon_t. \tag{14}$$

The one-period identity is then

$$\frac{B_t(t+1)}{p_{t+1}} = r^b_{t+1}\left(\frac{B_{t-1}(t)}{p_t} - s_t\right) = r^b_{t+1}(1 - \alpha)\frac{B_{t-1}(t)}{p_t} + r^b_{t+1}\epsilon_t.$$

Thus, any $\alpha > 0$ implies real debt that grows at a rate less than the interest rate and so a Ricardian regime.

One may wish to be a bit more restrictive, if one wants to consider only infinite-period results that are the limits of finite-lived economies. If $0 < \alpha < r - 1$, real debt still explodes, though at a rate less than the interest rate. Feedback $\alpha \geq r - 1$ is necessary to keep real debt bounded, and $\alpha \geq r -$ (GDP growth) is necessary to keep the debt/GDP ratio bounded. Canzoneri, Cumby, and Diba (1997) derive these results as special cases of considerably more general feedback rules.

TESTING FEEDBACK RULES?   Given these feedback restrictions, it is natural to test for a Ricardian regime by running regressions of surpluses on real debt to see if surpluses do adjust enough in response to real debt. The trouble is, this is always true in the data. In the one-period context, the constraint

$$s_t = \frac{B_{t-1}(t)}{p_t}$$

does hold, in equilibrium. We cannot tell which variable—p or s—adjusted to the other in order to produce the equilibrium. We could run the regression with s on the left and interpret the results as an estimation of (13), giving the Ricardian result, or we could put p on the left and interpret the result as confirmation of fiscal price determination from B and s.

Similarly, it is tempting in an infinite-period context to run a regression of (14), and test whether surpluses adjust to the value of debt, $\alpha > 0$ (or $\alpha > r - 1$). Alas, this coefficient again tells us nothing about the regime. For example, suppose the surplus is completely exogenous, $s_t = \rho s_{t-1} + \epsilon_t$, and B is constant. In a "fiscal" regime, prices are then

$$p_t = \frac{B_{t-1}(t)}{E_t \sum (1/r^j)s_{t+j}} = \frac{B}{s_t}\left(1 - \frac{\rho}{r}\right).$$

In this example, a low surplus leads to a low real value of the debt,

$$\frac{B}{p_t} = \frac{1}{1 - \rho/r} s_t.$$

But one could easily put s on the left and, mistakenly, find a surplus feedback rule that generates a Ricardian regime. I give an explicit example below in which an exogenous surplus process generates a VAR in which debt forecasts future surpluses.

FEEDBACK ON EQUILIBRIUM VS. OFF-EQUILIBRIUM PRICE LEVELS   Even more fundamentally, the government *can* distinguish the nominal quantity of debt from the price level. Therefore, it can follow a policy which systematically responds to the real value of debt for the equilibrium price level while refusing to validate out-of-equilibrium price levels.

To give a precise example, suppose the government wants to attain a price level p^*. It may follow a one-for-one feedback rule, promising to change taxes so as to soak up the real value of any debt $B_{t-1}(t)$ that happens to be outstanding due to stochastic variation in debt or surplus along the way—it may follow the feedback rule $s_t = B_{t-1}(t)/p^*$. However, it does *not* promise to validate an out-of-equilibrium price $p_t \neq p^*$; it will *not* change taxes to $s_t = B_{t-1}(t)/p_t$ for $p_t \neq p^*$. We observe a one-for-one feedback rule, over time and across states of nature, but the price level *is* determinate at p^*.

2.4.2 A VAR?   With words like "exogeneity" and "causality" around, it is tempting to examine "who adjusts" in the context of a VAR, watching the response of variables to innovations. But again, since we are watching the evolution over time of one equilibrium, a fiscal regime poses no restrictions on such VARs.

A SUGGESTION BASED ON THE SURPLUS→DEBT RESPONSE FUNCTION   Canzoneri, Cumby, and Diba (1997) propose the following test for a fiscal regime. If a positive surplus shock leads to higher surpluses but lower real value of the debt, they find a Ricardian or "money-determined" regime. If it leads to higher real value of the debt, they find a non-Ricardian or "fiscal-determined" regime. Not surprisingly, they find that positive shocks to surpluses reduce the real value of debt, and hence a "money-determined" regime.

These restrictions flow from the central idea that the value of the debt is forward-looking in the fiscal theory (debt is the present value of future surpluses) and backward-looking in a Ricardian or monetary regime (debt is the accumulation of past surpluses). Denote the real value of debt by $v_{t+1} = B_t(t + 1)/p_{t+1}$. Then, the identity

$$v_{t+1} = r^b_{t+1}(v_t - s_t) \tag{15}$$

motivates the idea that a positive surplus shock should lower next period's real debt. The time-$(t + 1)$ present-value constraint

$$v_{t+1} = E_{t+1} \sum_{j=0}^{\infty} \frac{1}{r^j} s_{t+1+j}$$

motivates the idea that a positively autocorrelated surplus shock should raise the real value of the debt.

One should of course be suspicious, since both equations hold in both regimes. In fact, the response-function sign prediction requires a different surplus driving process, not a difference in regime. The time-t present-value constraint is

$$v_t = \frac{B_t(t)}{p_t} = E_t \sum_{j=0}^{\infty} \frac{1}{r^j} s_{t+j}.$$

$B_t(t)$ is predetermined. In a money-determined regime, the price level is set by $p_t = M_t v/y$ and therefore does not change. If s_t rises and $\{E_t s_{t+j}\}$ do not decline, the budget constraint no longer holds. The only way to salvage the budget constraint is if the Fed agrees to monetize—if M moves with the innovation in s—producing exactly the price-level rise that would be predicted by the fiscal theory. Then, the ex post real interest rate in (15) adjusts so that the real value of the debt can rise next period. If the Fed does not monetize the deficit, future surpluses *must* decline.

2.4.3 Budget Explosions?

2.4.3 *Budget Explosions?*   Hamilton and Flavin (1986) pursue interesting tests for present-value budget balance. Essentially, they test whether the debt or debt/GDP ratio is explosive. This seems a natural test for a non-Ricardian regime. But the non-Ricardian regime only specifies explosive paths for real debt (the infinite-period counterpart to resources or money left at the end of single period economies) in response to never observed, off-equilibrium prices. In equilibrium, the budget constraint holds, and we do not observe explosive debt.

2.4.4 Identification and Nontestability It may seem that I have made too much of the lack of testable restrictions. The pure quantity theory does not have testable implications either: $Mv = py$ is also an accounting identity—a definition of velocity. It too requires additional assumptions; that velocity is not affected by some variable or shock; that some monetary or income shocks are exogenous, etc. Every economic theory requires some extra assumptions; why pick on the fiscal theory?[2]

With identifying assumptions, the fiscal theory does make predictions. Again, look at the budget constraint,

$$\frac{B_{t-1}(t)}{p_t} = E_t \sum_{j=0}^{\infty} \frac{1}{r^j} s_{t+j}. \tag{16}$$

If we could find a shock to nominal debt that leaves future surpluses unchanged, the fiscal theory does predict that the price level should rise. If we find a shock to surpluses with no effect on nominal debt, the price level should decline. Shocks to the composition of nominal debt that leave its value the same, such as open-market operations, should have no effect on the price level if they are not associated with changes in future surpluses.

All of these are valid predictions of the theory. The trouble is that the constraint (16) holds under all of the alternatives as well. For example, the quantity theory includes $Mv = py$ and the constraint (16). A shock to nominal debt with no change in future surpluses must come with just enough increase in M to give the same price-level prediction as the fiscal theory; if not, the shock *must* lead to a change in future surpluses. If one showed that neither happened, then one could reject the $Mv = py$ part of the quantity theory. But there is no way to reject the *fiscal* part of the theory.

2.5 UNCERTAINTY AND LONGER-MATURITY DEBT

So far, I have simplified the analysis by assuming one-period debt. In addressing the data, it is important to consider longer-maturity debt as well. In perfect-foresight models, the addition of long-term debt makes no difference, but with uncertainty, long-term debt changes the fiscal theory in some crucial ways. For example, news of future deficits can be met by a decline in long-term bond prices rather than by a rise in the price level.

2. I thank Benjamin Friedman for raising this point emphatically at the conference.

2.5.1 *Statement of the Budget Constraints* Suppose a full spectrum of bonds is outstanding at the beginning of period t, and let

$B_{t-1}(t + j)$ = bonds outstanding at the beginning of t that mature at $t + j$,
$Q_t(t + j)$ = price at t of bonds that mature at $t + j$.

Again, we start from the accounting identity that just-maturing bonds plus net revenue from the purchase or sale of long-term bonds must add up to the nominal net-of-interest surplus,

$$B_{t-1}(t) - \sum_{j=1}^{\infty} Q_t(t + j)[B_t(t + j) - B_{t-1}(t + j)] = p_t s_t.$$

We can express the ex post real rate of return on government bonds equivalently as (value at tomorrow's prices) /(value today) or as a weighted sum of individual bond returns. The generalization of (4) is thus

$$r_{t+1}^b \equiv \frac{p_t \sum_{j=1}^{\infty} Q_{t+1}(t + j)B_t(t + j)}{p_{t+1} \sum_{j=1}^{\infty} Q_t(t + j)B_t(t + j)}$$

$$= \frac{p_t}{p_{t+1}} \sum_{j=1}^{\infty} \frac{Q_{t+1}(t + j)}{Q_t(t + j)} \times \frac{Q_t(t + j)B_t(t + j)}{\sum_{k=1}^{\infty} Q_t(t + k)B_t(t + k)}.$$

If we write the real value of the debt

$$v_t = \frac{\sum_{j=0}^{\infty} Q_t(t + j)B_{t-1}(t + j)}{p_t},$$

then our earlier identities (5) and (6) still hold:

$$v_t = \frac{1}{r_{t+1}^b} v_{t+1} + s_t, \tag{17}$$

$$v_t = \sum_{j=0}^{\infty} \left(\prod_{k=1}^{j} \frac{1}{r_{t+k}^b} \right) s_{t+j}. \tag{18}$$

It is again often convenient to assume that the real rate of interest is a constant r both across time and bonds. Then, again using $Q_t(t + j) = 1/r^j \times E_t[p_t/p_{t+j}]$, the identities simplify to, first, (value of maturing bonds) − (revenue from new bond sales) = surplus,

$$\frac{B_{t-1}(t)}{p_t} - \sum_{j=1}^{\infty} \frac{1}{r^j} E_t \left(\frac{1}{p_{t+j}} \right) [B_t(t+j) - B_{t-1}(t+j)] = s_t, \tag{19}$$

and second, (value of outstanding debt) = (present value of surpluses),

$$v_t = \frac{B_{t-1}(t)}{p_t} + \sum_{j=1}^{\infty} \frac{1}{r^j} E_t \left(\frac{1}{p_{t+j}} \right) B_{t-1}(t+j) = E_t \sum_{j=0}^{\infty} \frac{1}{r^j} s_{t+j}. \tag{20}$$

2.5.2 Solving for Prices in Terms of Debt Policy and Surplus With only one-period debt, equation (20) expressed the price level at t in terms of the present value of future surpluses. It was also a *solution* for the equilibrium price-level sequence $\{p_t\}$ in terms of exogenous debt and surplus paths $\{B_t(t+j), s_t\}$. With long-term debt, future p_{t+j} enter into the equation on the left-hand side, not just p_t. Therefore, we have to work more to get an expression with p_t on the left and other variables on the right.

Cochrane (1998) derives the general solution for the price-level sequence $\{p_t\}$ given any surplus and debt path. The general formula is rather cumbersome. To get a flavor of some of the possibilities, we can directly solve three special cases, generated by three special types of debt policy:

1. *One-period debt.* If the government follows a policy of always rolling over one-period debt, $B_t(t+j) = 0$ for $j > 1$, then equation (20) reduces to

$$\frac{B_{t-1}(t)}{p_t} = E_t \sum_{j=0}^{\infty} \frac{1}{r^j} s_{t+j}. \tag{21}$$

2. *No new debt.* Suppose the government does not issue new debt, but pays off existing debt (perhaps a perpetuity) as it matures. Then we have $B_t(t+j) - B_{t-1}(t+j) = 0$, and equation (19) becomes

$$\frac{B_{t-1}(t)}{p_t} = s_t. \tag{22}$$

The price level is now set only by debt that comes due each day and that day's surplus.

3. *Geometric maturity structure.* Suppose the government commits to a maturity structure

$$B_{t-1}(t+j) = \phi^j B_{t+j-1}(t+j).$$

Then (19) or (20) implies

$$\frac{B_{t-1}(t)}{p_t} = s_t + (1 - \phi)\sum_{j=1}^{\infty}\frac{1}{r^j}E_t(s_{t+j}),$$

which nicely nests (21) and (22).

We have spent so much time looking at equations like (21) that these examples are worth examining closely: *It is not generally true that each period's price level is determined by the value of all debt relative to the present value of surpluses.* The latter conclusion is a very special case that comes entirely from the restriction that short-term debt is continuously rolled over.

2.5.3 Reaction to News of Surpluses To understand the effects of long-term debt, let us ask how the price level reacts if there is bad news about future surpluses. With one-period debt, the answer is simple: the price level must rise today, and we have

$$\frac{B_{t-1}(t)}{p_t} = E_t\sum_{j=1}^{\infty}\frac{1}{r^j}s_{t+j}, \tag{23}$$

so if $E_t s_{t+j}$ declines, p_t must rise.

With long-term debt, the equation (value of debt) = (present value of surpluses) is instead, from (20),

$$\frac{B_{t-1}(t)}{p_t} + \sum_{j=1}^{\infty}\frac{1}{r^j}E_t\left(\frac{1}{p_{t+j}}\right)B_{t-1}(t+j) = \sum_{j=0}^{\infty}\frac{1}{r^j}E_t s_{t+j}. \tag{24}$$

Now when expected future surpluses decline, expected *future* prices p_{t+j} can rise to reestablish the budget constraint. Equivalently, the real or relative price of long-term debt, $q_t(t+j) = (1/r^j)E_t(1/p_{t+j})$, can decline.

Which of these possibilities happens? The answer depends on debt policy, $\{B_{t-1}(t+j)\}$. For example, in the extreme case that the government sells no new debt, equation (22) shows that a decline in surpluses at date $t+j$ has no effect on the price level at time t. It affects only the price level at $t+j$, and hence only the price of outstanding $t+j$ bonds at time t. The geometric case gives an intermediate result.

2.5.4 Reaction to Debt Sales   What happens if at period t, the government issues more debt, with no change in surpluses? If no long-term debt is outstanding, again, the price level at t is set by

$$\frac{B_{t-1}(t)}{p_t} = E_t \sum_{j=1}^{\infty} \frac{1}{r^j} s_{t+j}.$$ (25)

Hence, a change in $B_t(t+1)$ has no effect on the price level at period t. It does affect the price level at $t + 1$:

$$\frac{B_t(t+1)}{p_{t+1}} = E_{t+1} \sum_{j=1}^{\infty} \frac{1}{r^j} s_{t+1+j},$$ (26)

so every 1% increase in debt sold at t translates into a 1% increase in the price level at $t + 1$.

We can describe this result as a unit-elastic demand curve for nominal debt at each date: extra debt sales simply drive down the price of debt, and the real revenue raised by bond sales is independent of the number sold. To see this, write the real value of debt at the end of time t as

$$q_t(t+1)B_t(t+1) = \frac{1}{r} E_t \left(\frac{1}{p_{t+1}} \right) B_t(t+1).$$

From (26), the quantity $B_t(t+1)/p_{t+1}$ is the same no matter what the level of debt sales $B_t(t+1)$, if surpluses do not change.

With long-term debt outstanding, unexpected long-term bond sales with constant surpluses can raise revenue and thus lower the price level. Unexpected debt sales dilute the claims of existing long-term debt to the real resources that will be available to redeem debt on the maturity date. This is an attractive story for the association of declining inflation and rising long-term debt in the early 1980s, or for the fact that inflation often moderates in recessions when long-term debt sales are particularly high.

2.6 MONETARY FRICTIONS

2.6.1 Money Demand in the Fiscal Theory   The essence of the fiscal theory does not involve money or monetary frictions. Since we have spent so much time thinking about money, however, it is important to verify that adding money back in to a fiscal regime does not alter the basic story of price-level determination.

We have already considered how *money* can be added to a fiscal and frictionless regime. Here, we consider how monetary *frictions* affect a fiscal regime. Above, people could use money for transactions during the day, but nobody held non-interest-paying money overnight. Now assume they may; the security market may not always be open, so money for the next day's purchases must be held overnight, or real (overnight) money balances may enter the utility function.

The summary is simple: If monetary considerations can determine the price level, they do. If $Mv = py$ holds, with constant v and well-controlled M, and if the Treasury adapts fiscal policy to the money-determined price level, the fiscal theory has little to say. However, in most monetary models that describe anything like modern institutions, monetary considerations alone do *not* determine the price level. In this case, the fiscal theory determines the price level, leaving monetary frictions at best to determine quantities or interest-rate spreads for liquid assets. As monetary considerations get weaker, fiscal considerations get stronger. This is the central point of Woodford (1995), and much of this section is a simplified version of Woodford's analysis.

Introduce money, and let M_t denote money balances held overnight from time t to time $t + 1$. For simplicity, revert to one-period debt. The flow budget constraint now reads

$$B_{t-1}(t) - \frac{B_t(t + 1)}{R_t} + M_{t-1} - M_t = p_t s_t, \tag{27}$$

where $R_t = 1/Q_t(t + 1)$ denotes the nominal interest rate. A useful form of the present-value budget constraint is

$$\frac{B_{t-1}(t)}{p_t} = E_t \sum_{j=0}^{\infty} \frac{1}{r^j} \left(s_{t+j} + \frac{M_{t+j} - M_{t+j-1}}{p_{t+j}} \right). \tag{28}$$

In this form we see how money can introduce potential seignorage revenues. Consider a simple money demand function,

$$M_t v(R_t) = p_t y_t. \tag{29}$$

Now, why doesn't control of the money supply, plus the money demand equation (29), determine the price level?

CONSTANT VELOCITY   In the most simplified quantity-theoretic tradition, it does. If the money supply is controlled, and if velocity is independent of interest rates, $Mv = py$ determines the price level p. If this price level agrees with the government budget constraint, fine. If it does not, one of the two determinants of the price level must give way. As we have seen, most users of this model specify that the government chooses a Ricardian fiscal policy in which the budget adapts.

VARYING VELOCITY   Truly constant velocity, in the face of arbitrarily large interest differentials, is an extreme and unlikely assumption. With an interest-elastic demand and fixed supply, money demand can still determine the expected rate of inflation or expected price level, but it does not determine the (ex post) price level. The government budget constraint then determines the price level.

For example, write money demand

$$\ln M_t = \ln p_t + \ln y - b(\ln r + E_t \ln p_{t+1} - \ln p_t). \tag{30}$$

Assume constant output and real interest rate, and fixed money supply. Now, (money demand) = (money supply) gives a log-linear difference equation for the price level, and hence pins down the rate of inflation at each date,

$$E_t \ln p_{t+1} = \frac{1+b}{b} \ln p_t + \frac{1}{b}(\ln y - \ln M_t) - \ln r. \tag{31}$$

Depending on the initial price level p_t, there are an infinite number of paths that satisfy this difference equation. It is conventional to pin down the price level as the nonexplosive solution,

$$\ln p_t = \sum_{j=0}^{\infty} \left(\frac{b}{1+b} \right)^j \frac{1}{1+b} (E_t \ln M_{t+j} - \ln y - b \ln r). \tag{32}$$

But this choice is an extra condition, not derived from money demand, optimization, or any other principle. We may be able to rule out *real* quantities that grow faster than the real rate of interest, but nominal quantities may happily explode.

With a non-Ricardian fiscal regime, the budget constraint pins down the (ex post) price *level* at each date. If that choice implies an explosive expected future price level despite constant money supply, so be it. As Woodford (1995) notes, if we do not observe exploding price levels with constant money supply, that just means that governments do not follow constant-money-supply policies in the face of exploding price levels.

VARYING VELOCITY; MONEY PAYS INTEREST   (Money demand) = (money supply) really determines the interest *differential* between monetary and nonmonetary assets. In the above example, the convention that money pays no interest then means that (money demand) = (money supply) must determine the inflation rate. If monetary assets pay interest R_t^m, however, as more and more monetary assets do, then the money demand equation becomes

$$M_t v(R_t - R_t^m) = p_t y_t.$$

Now the price level at each date can be entirely determined by the fiscal condition (28). (Money demand) = (money supply) only affects the interest differential between money and other assets.

INTEREST-RATE TARGETS   The money-supply regime matters as well as money demand. For example, even with $Mv = py$, monetary considerations alone do not determine the price level if money supply is sufficiently accommodative. Then, the government budget constraint can do so. A nominal-interest-rate target is the classic example. If the government provides whatever quantity of money is necessary for the nominal interest rate to equal R, then $Mv(R) = py$ determines M/p but not the level of either M or p.

2.6.2 Why Abandon Frictions for Studying Inflation?   I use the fiscal theory to avoid monetary frictions altogether in the study of the price level, rather than follow the above style of analysis and the bulk of the fiscal-theory literature including Woodford (1995, 1996, 1997), Leeper (1991), Sims (1994), Dupour (1997), and Schmitt-Grohé and Uribe (1997), by including standard theoretical devices for generating monetary frictions. I argued in the introduction that these frictions have at best second-order implications for the price level, as we have seen, and that they are not a realistic or empirically successful description of the U.S. economy. Here, I document the latter claims. Of course, monetary and other frictions will be important to financial economists and practitioners who want to study interest-rate spreads among liquid assets. Similarly, one will have to specify some frictions in order to be precise about why we *care* about inflation.

NO EXPLANATION FOR INFLATION   Figure 1 presents the history of CPI inflation together with growth in the popular monetary aggregates. The history of business-cycle and even decade-long variation in inflation has essentially nothing to do with the history of monetary aggregates. The swings of inflation in the 1970s and especially the dramatic end of inflation in the early 1980s occurred without any obvious corresponding changes in monetary growth. If anything, M1 and M2 growth are *negatively* correlated with inflation in the 1970s, requiring artfully specified

Figure 1 INFLATION AND GROWTH IN MONETARY AGGREGATES

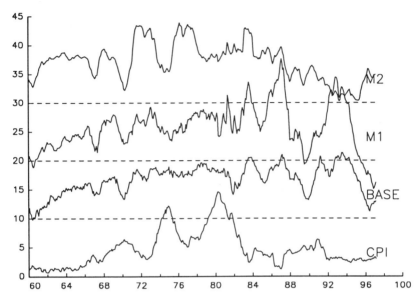

All series are monthly observations of annual growth rates. Base, M1, M2 are shifted up for clarity.

long and variable lags if one is going to insist that money growth caused the inflation. Base and M1 growth were much more volatile in the 1980s and 1990s with stable inflation than they were when inflation was more volatile in the 1970s.

Monetary VARs provide a more formal accounting of variation. Despite a wide range of monetary policy indicators, identification schemes, and specifications, such VARs regularly assign trivial fractions of price-level variance to monetary shocks, and almost all to "price shocks." Cochrane (1994b) surveys this literature. As a specific example, Table 1 is an abridged version of Tables 3 and 4 from Christiano, Eichenbaum, and Evans's (1998) survey. Note in particular that federal-funds-rate shocks in the top left quadrant explain essentially no price variation. Therefore, the VARs refute the standard analysis that price variation results from unusually "tight" or "loose" interest-rate policy.

Since the total quantity of nominal debt appears on the left-hand side of the budget constraint, the irrelevance of open-market operations to the price level is an obvious fiscal proposition. Of course, exact irrelevance is a special case. Open-market operations do slightly alter the maturity structure of the debt, which can affect the timing of inflation;

open-market operations can change the rate of return on government debt; open-market operations result in tiny but nonzero seignorage; and open-market operations may forecast changes in surpluses and so inherit a noncausal association with inflation.

To check whether monetary shocks forecast surpluses, Table 2 presents regressions of the surplus data described below on Christiano, Eichenbaum, and Evans's federal funds shock. With negative $\bar{R}^2$ and most t-statistics below one, there is not a shred of statistical evidence that federal-funds shocks forecast surpluses. The point estimates in the first three rows are large: a 1-percentage-point federal-funds shock results in a roughly 1-percentage-point rise in the surplus/consumption ratio for as much as 2 years. Since the real debt/consumption ratio is about 0.5, such an estimate implies as much as a 4% decline in the price level, roughly consistent with the VAR point estimates. However, as one expects from the t-values and $\bar{R}^2$, the coefficients are driven by two outliers (1969,1975) in an otherwise symmetrical scatterplot. The negative point estimates in the last row add up to an economically as well as statistically insignificant effect.

MONEY DEMAND AND VELOCITY SHOCKS   Money demand functions explain some of the fluctuations in money growth rates documented in Figure 1 via income and interest elasticities (endogenous velocity), but not

Table 1   PERCENTAGE OF k-QUARTER-AHEAD FORECAST ERROR VARIANCE DUE TO POLICY SHOCKS

Policy Shock	k	Y	P	Policy Shock	k	Y	P
FF	2	0.4	0.5	MB	2	0	0
	4	21	0.3		4	5	3
	8	44	0.4		8	5	4
	12	38	2.5		12	3	2
NBR	2	0	0	M1	2	0	0
	4	7	0		4	0	0
	8	10	1		8	3	0
	12	8	1		12	6	0
NBR/TR	2	0	0	M2	2	2	0
	4	17	0		4	14	1
	8	30	0		8	29	6
	12	22	1		12	24	15

Source: Christiano, Eichenbaum, and Evans (1998). Y = industrial production; P = price level; k = horizon; FF = federal funds rate; MB = monetary base; NBR = nonborrowed reserves; TR = total reserves.

Table 2 REGRESSIONS OF ANNUAL SURPLUS/CONSUMPTION RATIO
ON ANNUAL AVERAGES OF CHRISTIANO, EICHENBAUM, AND
EVANS'S (1998) FEDERAL-FUNDS SHOCKS.

Coefficient (t-statistic)							
ϵ_t^{ff}	ϵ_{t-1}^{ff}	ϵ_{t-2}^{ff}	ϵ_{t-3}^{ff}	ϵ_{t-4}^{ff}	ϵ_{t-5}^{ff}	$\bar{R}^2$	p-Value
	1.11					−0.00	0.40
	(0.86)						
1.52	0.59					−0.006	0.41
(1.06)	(0.42)						
1.56	0.58	−0.33				−0.07	0.69
(1.01)	(1.55)	(−0.23)					
1.23	0.14	−1.52	0.09	−0.10	0.85	−0.26	0.96
(0.69)	(0.08)	(−0.82)	(0.05)	(−0.06)	(0.05)		

p = value for test that all coefficients are zero.

much. To quote a recent review by Baba, Hendry, and Starr (1992), "Estimated U.S. M1 demand functions appear unstable, regularly breaking down . . . (e.g., missing money, great velocity decline, M1-explosion)." Even the staunchest defenders of empirical money demand relations, such as Lucas (1988), can at best point to a stable income and interest elasticity over very long time scales, 50 years or more.

Suspiciously, "velocity shocks" are not traceable to changes in financial structure, and changes in financial structure do not seem to lead to velocity shocks. Velocity shocks also do not appear to be exogenous: Times such as 1980–1982 when the Fed pushes hard on the monetary lever are precisely the times when velocity becomes least predictable.

The following conceptual experiment offers one interpretation of elusive elasticities and velocity shocks. It is not surprising that the short-run interest elasticity of money demand is low, since changes in interest costs are trivially small. If you keep $1,000 in cash and a non-interest-bearing-checking account, a change from 5% to 6% in annual interest rates increases monthly interest costs by $0.83. And since holding extra cash has benefits that at the margin are equal to marginal costs, the utility cost is another order of magnitude smaller than $0.83, say $0.08 per month. Consumers can be forgiven if they don't immediately change their cash management habits for 8 cents in monthly utility gains.

But suppose instead that the government moved $100 from each person's savings account or mutual fund to their checking account overnight. A small interest elasticity implies that interest rates must jump dramatically in response to this change. For now, instead of looking at

$$\ln M = \ln P + a \ln y - br$$

and noticing b is small, we are looking at

$$r = \frac{1}{b}(-\ln M + \ln P + a \ln y)$$

and noticing that $1/b$ is very large.

Intuition suggests the opposite reaction, however: people would just tolerate the suboptimal allocation of $100, because, again, fine details of cash management don't matter that much. At a 5% interest spread, an extra $100 implies $0.42 per month interest cost and an order of magnitude smaller utility cost, say $0.04 per month. If consumers do not adjust immediately to gain the extra 4 cents, we see an endogenous velocity shock, associated with the open-market operation.

Obviously, if the elasticity depends on which variable is pushed, one would not want to impose a rigid money demand curve on any model. [This analysis owes a strong debt to Akerlof (1979) and Akerlof and Milbourne (1980). They show that s–S money demand policies have similar mushy implications, since people must change the s–S bounds before interest rates have any effect.]

THEORETICAL OBJECTIONS   A generation of theorists have argued that the quantity theory is an increasingly implausible description of modern economies with competitive banking systems, including Black (1970), Fama (1980, 1983, 1985), Hall (1983), King (1983), White (1984), and Cowen and Kroszner (1994). Considering the vast number of liquid, nonreservable inside assets, as well as trade credit, credit cards, debit cards, and other means of financing transactions, and considering the flexibility and competitiveness of financial institutions, it is difficult to believe that an artificial scarcity of one liquid asset can have any systematic effect.

As these authors recognized, some sort of perfectly competitive, frictionless model is a more sensible first-order approximation to the U.S. financial system than is a rigid separation of assets into liquid "money" or "transactions-facilitating assets" and illiquid "investment assets." However, these authors could not get around the view that the price level had to be determined by an explicit commodity-based unit of account, or a special transactions demand for the monetary base together with a limited supply. The fiscal theory gives us a structure that can determine the price level within the natural perfectly competitive or frictionless approximation, while preserving the fact of apparently unbacked fiat money.

One can of course study an infinite-velocity limit of the quantity theory, as advocated by Woodford (1997) and the "currency ghost" view of Cowen and Kroszner (1994). However, it does not seem productive to hinge the price level on whether U.S. transactions can be accomplished with fast-moving claims to one dollar bill, or whether two will be required. At some point, and especially as the interest costs of holding the remaining money become vanishingly small, velocity must become endogenous rather than rigidly linking money to transactions via an ever-longer lever.

WHAT ABOUT OPEN MARKET OPERATIONS AND MONEY DEMAND?   What about the common view and empirical evidence that monetary policy affects output? For example, Table 1 shows that federal-funds-rate shocks explain up to 40% of the variance of output, while explaining none of the variance of prices.

Choosing a fiscal and even frictionless description of the *price* level does not require that open-market operations have *output*-neutral effects. Open-market operations can still affect the interest-rate spreads of monetary assets, and interest-rate spreads can affect output. For example, Bernanke's (1983) nonmonetary view of the Great Depression stresses the disruption of credit arrangements following open-market operations. These output effects can occur while the fiscal constraint alone determines the price level. As Goodfriend (1988) reminds us, central banks pursued active interest-rate policy, with visible output effects, even under the classical gold standard. One *can* add sticky prices to a fiscal model with monetary frictions, as in Woodford (1997), to generate output variation related to inflation, but one need not tie output to inflation (counterfactually, I might add) in order to explain output effects of open-market operations.

Similarly, a fiscal theory of the price level is not inconsistent with the observation that money and nominal income often move together. Money *is* useful for transactions, and governments typically provide it elastically as needed, for example by following interest-rate policies. It does not follow from this observation that if the government exchanged bonds for money, there would be any effect on the price level.

2.7 EPISODES

Dramatic episodes of hyperinflation, stabilization, currency collapse, and so forth are perhaps the most natural place to start evaluating the fiscal theory. I focus instead on U.S. data below, in part because theories that are only good for extreme events in the unstable monetary arrangements of far-away (to admittedly parochial U.S. observers) lands will not in the end influence monetary analysis of the U.S. economy. However, a quick look at such episodes helps to illustrate the fiscal theory and make it plausible.

There is no tight relation between debt and the price level in many historical episodes. Wars offer the most dramatic example. Nominal debt increases substantially, often with relatively little change in the price level. Of course, such nominal-debt increases also come with the explicit or implicit promise that future taxes will be raised to retire the debt after the war. Hence both sides of the budget identity change, and the price level need not be affected. In fact, recall that (short-term) debt sales with no change in future surpluses produce no extra revenue. The whole point of selling extra nominal debt in a war is to raise revenue. If they raise revenue, such sales *must* have come with an implicit promise to raise future taxes.

The same lesson applies in peacetime: If the government raises revenue by selling additional (short-term) bonds, the debt sale must have come with an explicit or implicit promise to raise future surpluses. Both sides of the identity move at the same time, so we should not expect a tight relation between total nominal debt and the price level.

Hyperinflations are classic pieces of evidence for the quantity theory, since money and the price level both grow very quickly. However, hyperinflating countries issue little nominal debt other than money, so money and nominal debt are the same thing and the fiscal theory predicts the same hyperinflation as the quantity theory.

Hyperinflations are of course linked to government finances. In the standard quantity-theoretic analysis, an intractable budget shortfall forces the government to print money to pay its bills, and the money causes inflation. If a country tried to finance an intractable budget shortfall by rolling over explosive quantities of one-week interest-paying debt, while rigidly controlling the money stock, this would provide a nice experiment: the quantity theory predicts no inflation while the fiscal theory predicts hyperinflation. Alas, it hasn't happened. A country that had explosive *inside* money growth with no government budget problems would provide another nice experiment: The fiscal theory predicts no inflation and the quantity theory predicts hyperinflation. Unfortunately for economists, all the recorded hyperinflations resulted from explosive growth in nominal government debt.

Sargent's (1986) classic study of the ends of hyperinflations again points to a fiscal link, though his analysis is quantity-theoretic and Ricardian. The budget problem is solved; seignorage stops, so inflation stops. Again, the fiscal theory makes the identical prediction that inflation will stop once the budget problem is solved, though directly rather than via its inducements to seignorage. In fact, the fiscal theory nicely accommodates a troubling fact: money growth usually does not stop at the time of the fiscal announcement that ends the hyperinflation. This fact usually has to be explained by an increase in money demand at lower nominal interest rates.

Sargent's analysis and a fiscal theory can differ substantially over the effects of news about *future* surpluses or deficits. In a quantity-theoretic analysis, news about future deficits that will result in future seignorage primarily affects only future inflation. Cagan-style hyperinflation dynamics are the only way that future seignorage can affect today's price level, but such effects are weak, since future money growth is discounted at the interest elasticity of money demand [see equation (32)], which is on the order of 0.15. In a fiscal model with short-term debt, future deficits are discounted at the much higher gross interest rate, producing discount factors on the order of 0.95. Thus, the fiscal theory can predict a much stronger reaction of current prices to news of far-off deficits. This prediction depends on details in both cases: if news of future deficits causes the government to start printing money now, the quantity theory can also predict current inflation, and if there is a lot of long-term debt, the fiscal theory can predict no current inflation but instead a fall in long-term bond prices reflecting expected future inflation.

Along this line, the Asian currency plunges of late 1997 cry for a fiscal analysis. It seems much more plausible that the currencies plunged on bad fiscal news, induced by a wave of bank insolvencies, than on news that open-market purchases or seignorage would soon double the money supply. Bad fiscal news lowers the price—raises the interest rate—of longer-term debt, and high interest rates are characteristic of these crises. The fiscal story also makes sense of the fact, surprising to a standard analysis, that many governments had ample foreign exchange reserves (Burnside, Eichenbaum, and Rebelo 1998).

Similarly, Argentina suffered great stress on its currency board during the Mexican peso crisis, including very high interest rates. Reserves were high in this case as well—the currency was 100% backed. Again, this was a time of great fiscal stress for the government. The temptation to abrogate the board and devalue might well have turned into necessity. The high interest rates make sense again as high nominal rates that include this probability.

Brash (1996) unwittingly offers an essentially fiscal view of New Zealand's celebrated monetary reforms. Though he is the governor of the Reserve Bank of New Zealand, his description of that country's disinflation spends 40 pages on microeconomic reforms, tax reforms, and large and successful fiscal policy reforms before even talking about monetary policy. Then he describes only the political economy of an inflation contract, without once mentioning monetary restriction or open-market operations by which this contract is supposed to be implemented. A fiscal theorist sees direct causality from dramatically good fiscal news to the price level, with the actions of the central bank largely irrelevant.

As Woodford (1996) emphasizes, a fiscal analysis makes sense of the otherwise pointless deficit targets for entry into the European Monetary Union. If (say) Italian debt is to trade at par with (say) German debt, then either Italian surpluses must be sufficient to value that debt, or Germany must implicitly or explicitly stand ready to bail out the Italian budget. Of course, Italian debt may instead trade at a discount, reflecting a possibility of explicit default. Therefore, one must read the deficit targets as an attempt to avoid explicit default as well as subsidy.

3 U.S. Debt and Inflation

3.1 DATA

Easily available U.S. government deficit and debt data are potentially poor approximations to the economic concepts one wants. Above all, it is important to create a surplus series that corresponds to the revenue from debt operations. [Auerbach, Gokhale, and Kotlikoff (1994) stress the larger difficulties of deficit measurement.]

To produce more accurate data, I created annual data on privately held U.S. government debt from the CRSP government bond files, which in turn record data from the *Treasury Bulletin*. From these data, I created an annual series on the total real value of the debt, v_t^a, as the sum of December 31 price times quantity of all bonds outstanding, divided by the December CPI. I estimated the annual rate of return r_{t+1}^a on the government bond portfolio from the Fama–Bliss (1987) zero-coupon bond return series multiplied by December 31 (year t) portfolio weights. Then, I estimated the annual surplus from the identity $s_{t+1}^a = v_t^a r_{t+1}^a - v_{t+1}^a$. (It is more natural in annual data to date December 31 year-t debt as v_t^a rather than v_{t+1}^a, so this identity has slightly different timing than the discrete-time identities studied above, in which v_t denotes the beginning of period debt.) I also created a zero-coupon equivalent maturity structure $B_t(t + j)$ by adding up the principal and all coupons of all bonds outstanding at December 31, year t, that come due in year $t + j$. I count the monetary base as zero-maturity debt. The data are described in detail in an appendix available on the author's Web site listed in the first footnote.

3.2 SURPLUS, DEBT, AND RETURNS

Before addressing the fiscal theory directly, I characterize the new data on surplus, debt, and returns. I also develop the central patterns that we must try to match.

3.2.1 Surplus Figure 2 presents the primary surplus inferred from bond data described above, together with the conventionally measured surplus or deficit. The two series correlate well through the 1970s, when interest payments on the debt were small. In the 1980s, however, the primary surplus does become positive, while the deficit remains large, reflecting large interest payments on the outstanding debt.

One's first reaction to a view that the price level is set by the interaction of nominal debt and real surpluses might be to ask: what surpluses? Has not the federal government been in deficit continuously for the last 30 years? Of course, the theory refers to the *primary* surplus, correctly measured; the graph offers hope for the view that debt is eventually repaid with primary surpluses.

The surplus shows a clear cyclical pattern, dipping in the recessions of 1975, 1982, and 1990. Interestingly, the primary surplus suffers its big-

Figure 2 REAL PRIMARY SURPLUS INFERRED FROM BOND DATA AND
FEDERAL SURPLUS OR DEFICIT

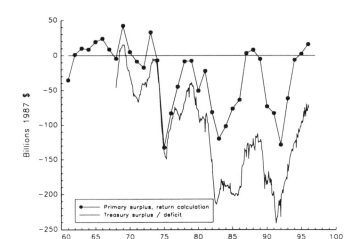

All series deflated by the consumer price index. The federal surplus or deficit is monthly observations of annual averages.

Figure 3 REAL SURPLUS INFERRED FROM BOND DATA AND NET-OF-
INTEREST SURPLUS REPORTED BY THE TREASURY

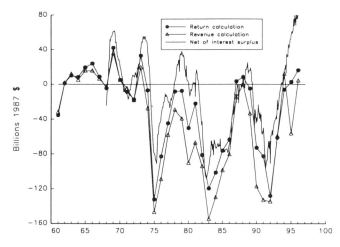

The return calculation starts by estimating the rate of return on government bonds, and then imputes the surplus from the rate of return and growth in total value. The revenue calculation is based on a direct estimate of revenue from debt transactions.

gest negative shock in 1975, with the onset of severe inflation, not during the Reagan deficits of the 1980s.

Figure 3 contrasts three measures of the primary surplus. The preferred *return calculation* infers the surplus from growth in total debt and the estimated rate of return on government bonds, while the *revenue calculation* sums up revenue from bond transactions during the year, as described in the Appendix. The net-of-interest surplus is reported by the Treasury, and consists of the total surplus or deficit less interest payments, but not gains and losses incurred from bond sales or purchases.

The three series correlate well, but not perfectly. Unusually active debt policy in 1990–1991 and 1995 drove a wedge between the revenue and return calculations. Both measures are somewhat more pessimistic than the net-of-interest surplus series. The difference is substantial most recently: rather than a $80 billion primary surplus, the bond data show almost no primary surplus or deficit.

Figure 4 presents the components of the revenue-based real surplus series. One can see that the cyclical variation in surplus (the negative of revenue) is driven by variation in new bond and bill sales. However, the need to pay coupons and redeem maturing bonds soon catches up with new sales. From 1983 to 1987, for example, new sales continue to rise, but revenue declines. Bond sales are spread over maturities, and thus the maturing bonds are much smoother than the bond sales. For example, with only one-period debt, maturing bonds would equal the previous period's sales. Lately, the Treasury has started to sell more of existing issues. Seignorage—change in the monetary base—is an insignificant fraction of government revenue.

3.2.2 Surplus and Output   In order to focus on the cyclical properties of the surplus, Figure 5 contrasts the surplus/consumption ratio with the output/consumption ratio. Dividing by consumption allows us to scale variables with growth, producing plausibly stationary series. I divide the surplus by consumption rather than output to avoid putting business-cycle output variation in the surplus measure. The output/consumption ratio exploits the relative stability of consumption (permanent income) to produce a business-cycle indicator (see Cochrane, 1994a).

The graph emphasizes that most variation in the surplus is the predictable result of output variation. The dramatic deficit of 1975 is associated with a severe drop in output. The initial Reagan deficits also line up nicely with output. Only 1984 and 1985 are years with somewhat larger deficits than would be expected. The Reagan deficits resulted from large interest costs on a stock of debt built up over several recessions, not, as is

Figure 4 COMPONENTS OF REAL REVENUE FROM BOND SALES

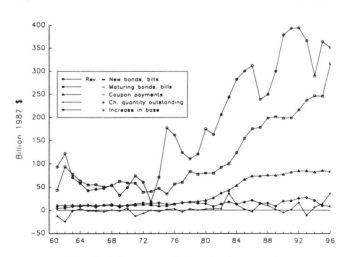

Revenue (negative surplus) is, by definition, equal to (new bond sales) + (change in quantity outstanding) + (change in base) − (maturing bonds) − (coupon payments).

Figure 5 SURPLUS/CONSUMPTION AND OUTPUT/CONSUMPTION RATIO

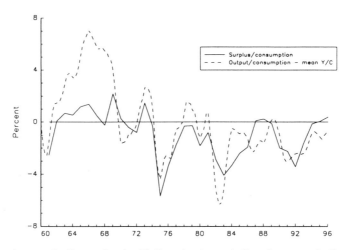

The output/consumption line graphs $y/c - E(y/c)$, so that the graphs fit on the same scale. Consumption is nondurable plus services consumption; output is GDP.

Figure 6 REAL PRIMARY SURPLUS DIVIDED BY NONDURABLES AND
SERVICES CONSUMPTION, AND ANNUAL CPI INFLATION

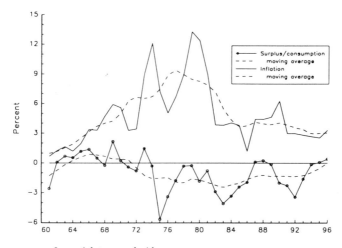

Moving averages use 3 years' data on each side.

often claimed, from an unusually loose primary fiscal policy. The graph also points to a secular relation between surpluses and output. The output slowdown that started in about 1973, even relative to consumption, is associated with a similar secular decline in the surplus.

3.2.3 Surplus and Inflation   Figure 6 presents the surplus/consumption ratio together with annual CPI inflation. Since inflation and the surplus are both procyclical, it is little surprise that business-cycle movements in the surplus are positively correlated with business-cycle movements in inflation through the 1970s. On the other hand, the longer-term variation in the surplus and inflation are negatively correlated, as shown by the moving averages.

3.2.4 Bond Returns and Debt Growth   Figure 7 presents the real rate of return on the government bond portfolio, together with the three-month and five-year real rates of return which, along with other returns, are used to construct it.

Before about 1980, the average maturity structure is still quite short. Therefore, the government bond portfolio return tracks the three-month rate pretty well. In fact, since the monetary base, which pays no interest,

Figure 7 RETURN ON GOVERNMENT BOND PORTFOLIO, AND
THREE-MONTH AND FIVE-YEAR ZERO-COUPON RETURNS

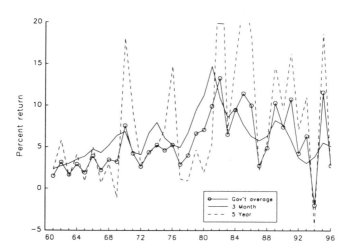

The government bond portfolio return is estimated as the average of all zero-coupon returns weighted by the zero-coupon maturity structure at the beginning of the year.

Figure 8 REAL RETURN ON GOVERNMENT BOND PORTFOLIO, REAL
DEBT GROWTH, AND SURPLUS/DEBT RATIO

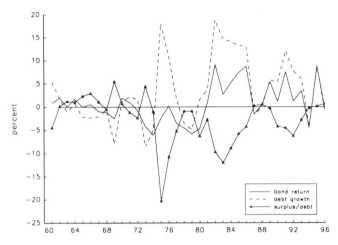

The real bond return is estimated from the returns on zero-coupon bonds weighted by the beginning-of-year maturity structure. Real debt growth is the growth in total market value of the debt. The three series are related by the accounting identity $v_t/v_{t-1} = r_t^b - s_t/v_{t-1}$.

is such a large fraction of government debt in this period, the rate of return on government bonds is typically a few points *less* than the three-month rate. In the 1980s and 1990s, the maturity structure lengthens. During this period the return on government debt behaves much more like a long-term rate, subject to large swings as long-term bond prices move around.

Figure 8 presents the real rate of return on government bonds and the real percentage increase in the value of the debt. The surplus (as a fraction of value) is the difference between the growth in total debt and the return on the government bond portfolio,

$$\frac{s_{t+1}^a}{v_t^a} = r_{t+1}^a - \frac{v_{t+1}^a}{v_t^a},$$

so this graph documents the sources of surplus variation.

In 1975 there was a large (25%) increase in the total value of government debt. However, the rate of return on government bonds was not large at all, so we estimate a large primary deficit, as shown. Debt also grew very quickly in the early 1980s, but around half of that growth was due to very high real returns on outstanding debt. This is why the

Table 3   CORRELATION MATRIX OF
GOVERNMENT BOND RETURN,
REAL DEBT GROWTH, AND
SURPLUS/DEBT RATIO

	r^a_{t+1}	v^a_{t+1}/v^a_t	s^a_{t+1}/v^a_t
r^a_{t+1}	1	0.70	−0.16
v^a_{t+1}/v^a_t		1	−0.82
s^a_{t+1}/v^a_t			1

surplus measure above did not find extreme primary deficits, as one might have expected.

The graph also reminds us that the real rate of return on government debt increased dramatically in the early 1980s and has stayed high and variable since. This is in part due to higher real returns on government bonds and in part due to the smaller proportion of monetary base in the debt.

Finally, the graph documents an important and interesting correlation pattern. The surplus is very well negatively correlated with debt growth; returns are positively correlated with debt growth, and the surplus is negatively, though weakly, correlated with returns. (See Table 3.)

3.2.5 Surplus, Value, and Inflation   Figure 9 presents the real value of the debt value and the surplus, each scaled by consumption, and inflation. The surplus is positively associated with inflation, and negatively associated with changes in value; we will work hard to understand these correlations.

3.3 EXPLAINING THE CORRELATIONS

Our task is now to understand the pattern of correlations documented above. I start by viewing the surplus and nominal debt as policy choices. The price level is then determined by the government budget constraint. The central issue in matching the data this way is understanding the real value of the debt. If the government controls the nominal value, then the price level is trivially the ratio of nominal to real value of the debt.

A Ricardian or monetary story is *backward-looking*: the nominal value of the debt is determined by the accumulation of past deficits, the price level is determined by $Mv = py$, and these two variables determine the real value of the debt. Future surpluses must then adjust to pay off this debt. A fiscal story is *forward-looking*. The real value of the debt is determined by the present value of expected future surpluses, and the price

Figure 9 VALUE/CONSUMPTION, SURPLUS/CONSUMPTION,
AND INFLATION

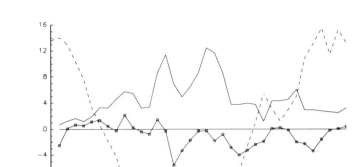

Value/consumption is shifted down by 45 percentage points to fit on the graph with the other two series.

level (and/or long-term bond prices) adjusts to equate that real value to the nominal value. Equivalently, the monetary and fiscal analyses tell different stories about *growth* in value. In either case, the accounting identity

$$\frac{v_{t+1}^a}{v_t^a} = r_{t+1}^a - \frac{s_{t+1}^a}{v_t^a}$$

holds. In a monetary story, the ex post real rate of return on government bonds is the predetermined nominal rate deflated by the monetarily determined price level. Therefore, this identity determines the new real value v_{t+1}^a of the debt from current and past information. In a fiscal story, the value v_{t+1}^a of the debt is determined first; this identity then determines the ex post rate of return on government bonds, r_{t+1}^a ; the price level (or the prices of long-term bonds) adjust $r_{t+1}^a = rp_t/p_{t+1}$ so that the identity holds.

From this perspective, the central puzzles are that the level of the real value of the debt seems to have very little to do with surpluses, and, worse, high surpluses are associated with declines in the value of the debt. This pattern of correlations is what a backward-looking view with relatively stable money and hence prices might expect: high deficits mean growing real debt, and the current value of the debt is just cumulated past surpluses.

To see the puzzle from the perspective of a forward-looking view, consider an AR(1) model for the surplus, which the graphs suggest is reasonable. If we write $s_t^a = \rho s_{t-1}^a + \epsilon_t$ with constant expected returns, we obtain a perfect *positive* correlation between surpluses and debt:

$$v_t^a = E_t \sum_{j=1}^{\infty} \beta^j s_{t+j}^a = \frac{\beta\rho}{1 - \beta\rho} s_t.$$

Currently high surpluses indicate high surpluses in the future, and thus should indicate a *high* real value of the debt. But this positive correlation between surpluses and the value of the debt is completely counterfactual; the value of the debt declines when surpluses are high. This is the basic idea of Canzoneri, Cumby, and Diba's (1997) rejection.

Of course, an AR(1) surplus process is obvious but perhaps too simple. If we model the surplus as an AR(2) or higher process, low current surpluses can come with news of higher future surpluses, so that the value of the debt rises. While appeal to such a model may seem contrived at first, on second thought it is in fact the most plausible view. Deficits go up—surpluses decline—when taxes decrease and spending increases in a recession. In this situation, the government sells more nominal debt precisely to raise revenue. As we have seen, the only way extra nominal debt sales can raise revenue is if they come with a promise to raise surpluses in the future. If a low surplus did not come with promises of increased surpluses in the future, the government would not raise any extra revenue with extra nominal debt sales.

To understand the issue, it is worth thinking about alternative policies that the government might follow. The extra revenue to cover the declining surplus must come from somewhere. If current surpluses decline in a recession and the government holds future surpluses constant, the price level must increase. This implies a low or negative (net) real return on government bonds; the "extra revenue" comes by inflating away the real value of outstanding debt. This policy—financing cyclical deficits by inflating away outstanding debt—would obviously lead to much more volatile and countercyclical inflation. Thus, the fact that the government follows the current policy, selling more debt in recessions while promising to raise surpluses in the following booms, smooths inflation and the value of government bonds, at least to some extent.

3.3.1 An Exogenous-Surplus Model with Short-Term Debt To tell a quantitative version of this story, I specify an exogenous path for the surplus and debt. I find the real value of the debt as the present value of the surplus, and the price level as the ratio of real to nominal debt. I specify the processes to deliver the correlations in the data; surpluses are correlated with declining values of the debt, the debt moves much more slowly than the surplus, and its level is poorly correlated with the surplus; real and nominal debt growth track closely, and the surplus is negatively correlated with inflation.

MODELING SURPLUS AND VALUE   To match the model with stationary time series, I examine the (real value)/consumption and surplus/consumption ratios and the inflation rate (rather than price level). As an accounting identity, the value/consumption and surplus/consumption ratios obey

$$\frac{v_t^a}{c_t} = \frac{1}{r_{t+1}^a} \frac{c_{t+1}}{c_t} \left(\frac{s_{t+1}^a}{c_{t+1}} + \frac{v_{t+1}^a}{c_{t+1}} \right). \tag{33}$$

Define $\beta = E[c_{t+1}/(c_t r_{t+1}^a)]$. I start by assuming this discount factor is constant over time. Then, we can iterate (33) forward, take expectations, and write the value/consumption ratio as the present value of the surplus/consumption ratio. Denote $vc_t \equiv v_t^a/c_t - E(v_t^a/c_t)$, $sc_t \equiv s_t^a/c_t - E(s_t^a/c_t)$. Then the value/consumption ratio also obeys the familiar identity,

$$vc_t = E_t \sum_{j=1}^{\infty} \beta^j sc_{t+j}.$$

I model the surplus as the sum of a business-cycle component a_t and a long-run component z_t:

$$\begin{aligned} sc_t &= z_t + a_t, \\ z_t &= \eta_z z_{t-1} + \epsilon_{zt}, \\ a_t &= \eta_a a_{t-1} + \epsilon_{at}. \end{aligned} \tag{34}$$

We saw above how the surplus is highly correlated with output. Therefore, think of the business-cycle component a_t as driven by varying output at constant tax and spending policies, and not controlled by the government. Think of the long-term component z_t as reflecting tax rates, spending policies, and so forth, which the government does control. However, for optimal-taxation reasons, the government does not want to vary z_t period by period to offset a_t, for example increasing tax rates in recessions in order to offset the loss of tax revenue. Thus, as in much of the tax-smoothing literature, write z_t as a very persistent process, almost if not exactly a random walk, and assume that the government chooses ϵ_{zt} each period.

Given this surplus process, the real value of the debt is

$$vc_t = E_t \sum_{j=1}^{\infty} \beta^j sc_{t+j} = \frac{\beta\eta_z}{1 - \beta\eta_z} z_t + \frac{\beta\eta_a}{1 - \beta\eta_a} a_t. \tag{35}$$

Putting together (34) and (35), we can write the observable series s, v in terms of the unobservable surplus components z, a as

$$\begin{bmatrix} sc_t \\ vc_t \end{bmatrix} = \begin{bmatrix} 1 & 1 \\ \dfrac{\beta\eta_z}{1-\beta\eta_z} & \dfrac{\beta\eta_a}{1-\beta\eta_a} \end{bmatrix} \begin{bmatrix} z_t \\ a_t \end{bmatrix} = B \begin{bmatrix} z_t \\ a_t \end{bmatrix}. \tag{36}$$

PARAMETERS   I pick parameters so that sc, vc follow

$$\begin{bmatrix} sc_t \\ vc_t \end{bmatrix} = \begin{bmatrix} 0.55 & 0.06 \\ -0.55 & 0.96 \end{bmatrix} \begin{bmatrix} sc_{t-1} \\ vc_{t-1} \end{bmatrix} + \delta_t, \tag{37}$$

$$\begin{bmatrix} \sigma(\delta_s) & \rho_{sv} \\ & \sigma(\delta_v) \end{bmatrix} = \begin{bmatrix} 0.013 & -0.55 \\ & 0.035 \end{bmatrix}$$

This is the OLS estimate, except for the lower left coefficient -0.55 of vc_t on sc_{t-1}. The OLS estimate is -0.75 (s.e. $= 0.26$); I use -0.55 instead in order to satisfy the constraint that this coefficient must equal the negative of the coefficient of sc_t on vc_{t-1} implied by the structural model, or more generally by the fact that vc is the present value of sc. The corresponding *structural parameters* are

$$\begin{bmatrix} a_t \\ z_t \end{bmatrix} = \begin{bmatrix} 0.64 & 0 \\ 0 & 0.87 \end{bmatrix} \begin{bmatrix} a_{t-1} \\ z_{t-1} \end{bmatrix} + \epsilon_t, \tag{38}$$

$$\begin{bmatrix} \sigma(\epsilon_z) & \rho_{az} \\ & \sigma(\epsilon_a) \end{bmatrix} = \begin{bmatrix} 0.023 & -0.95 \\ & 0.011 \end{bmatrix}, \quad \beta = 0.988.$$

The difference between the *structural* representation (38) and the surplus value VAR (37) is very important. The surplus $s = a + z$ is exogenous; it does not respond to the real value of the debt or to prices. Yet the surplus seems to respond to the debt in the VAR representation, what Bohn (1998) interprets as "corrective action." In this case, the value of the debt reveals changing surplus forecasts.

As expected, the structural representation has one business-cycle component, $\eta_a = 0.64$, and one slow-moving component with $\eta_z = 0.87$.

The negative correlation between surplus and value innovations in the data, -0.55, induces an even stronger negative correlation between business-cycle and long-run surplus innovations in the structural model, -0.95. As above, this is a central part of the story: when there is a negative business-cycle surplus shock, the government wants to raise revenue by nominal debt sales; to do so it must increase the present value of future surpluses by increasing the long-run component of the deficit.

INFLATION AND NOMINAL DEBT   I consider only one-period debt, whose nominal value is V_t^a. Real and nominal debt are of course related by

$$\frac{V_t^a}{p_t} = v_t^a \tag{39}$$

In this simple model, inflation is controlled by the government via the decision of how much nominal debt to issue for a given real value of the surplus. Therefore, we can model either inflation or nominal debt and find the value of the other. I model inflation, and then calculate the supporting nominal debt policy later. (There is a small approximation in this procedure: The government can only affect next period's price level by changing nominal debt. If we think of the model operating at monthly or daily frequency, however, the government can control almost all of this year's price level with this year's debt.)

The government chooses debt so that inflation is a function of the two state variables z, a:

$$dp_t \equiv \Delta \ln p_t - \Delta \ln p = \begin{bmatrix} \alpha_z & \alpha_a \end{bmatrix} \begin{bmatrix} z_t \\ a_t \end{bmatrix}$$

where $\Delta \ln p = E(\Delta \ln p_t)$ is the steady state. I chose the parameters α so that

$$dp_t = \begin{bmatrix} 1 & -0.21 \end{bmatrix} \begin{bmatrix} sc_t \\ vc_t \end{bmatrix}. \tag{40}$$

One can recover the underlying nominal debt policy by differencing (39).

Clearly, this model will only capture the parts of inflation that are correlated with surplus and value. This is in some sense the interesting part: we want to understand the puzzling positive correlation of surplus and inflation. To fully capture the inflation time series, we can add an additional inflation or nominal debt shock.

Figure 10 ARTIFICIAL DATA ON SURPLUS/CONSUMPTION,
VALUE/CONSUMPTION, AND INFLATION.

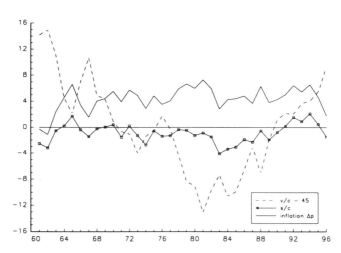

Shocks are drawn from a random number generator.

ARTIFICIAL TIME SERIES   Figure 10 presents artificial time series from this system. The shocks are generated by a random number generator. Comparing artificial to actual data on the same series in Figure 9, we see that the system replicates the initially puzzling features of the data: The value of the debt is poorly correlated with the surplus and moves more slowly than the surplus; the short-run correlations between value and surplus are negative—the surplus is highly negatively correlated with *growth* in the value of the debt, and business-cycle movements in inflation are positively correlated with the surplus.

If we use the sample residuals from the *sc, vc* VAR representation rather than draw residuals from a random number generator, the sample and artificial *sc, vc* series match by construction. However, since we do not have an inflation shock, inflation does not match exactly. Figure 11 shows actual and simulated inflation, using the parameters (40). The figure shows that the model does a good job of matching both the secular and cyclical fluctuations in inflation.

The parameters relating inflation to *sc, vc* are ad hoc. I tried picking parameters to replicate the OLS regression $dp_t = 0.08\ sc_t - 0.21\ vc_t + \epsilon_t$. This simulation tracks the level of inflation more closely but misses the cyclical fluctuations. Since we cannot statistically fit a three-series model with two shocks, one cannot argue between the two parametrizations on statistical grounds; I stick with the former parametrization, since it produces a subjectively more convincing story at the business-cycle frequencies.

DEBT POLICY AND INFLATION SMOOTHING   We think of the government as picking the nominal debt V_t along with the long-run surplus shock ϵ_{zt} each period. For convenience, I have characterized this policy by its inflation outcome, but we should look at the actual nominal debt policy. The actual and simulated *real* debt growth (vc_{t+1}/vc_t) are exactly the same. Hence, I calculate the nominal debt growth that generates simulated price level p^{sim} by $V_t = p_t^{\text{sim}}v_t^a$. Actual nominal debt growth similarly generates actual inflation. Figure 12 presents real and nominal debt growth; inflation is of course the difference between them.

Figure 12 emphasizes that *fluctuations in debt growth are far larger than fluctuations of inflation.* Furthermore, *fluctuations in nominal debt growth closely mirror fluctuations in real debt growth.*

What policy for nominal debt growth would have resulted in *zero* inflation? The answer is one way of getting at the question, what *caused* inflation? One answer in this case is easy: if nominal debt growth had been the same as real debt growth, inflation would have been zero. However, the *character* of such a policy is quite surprising, since real debt growth and inflation are so strongly negatively correlated. Nominal debt growth should have been *more* volatile. It should have declined even more sharply than it already did in 1973 and 1979, for example.

Figure 11 ACTUAL AND SIMULATED INFLATION

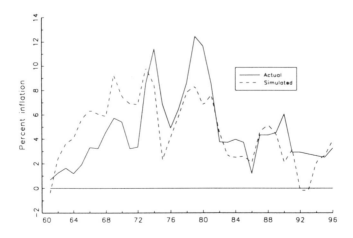

Figure 12 REAL AND NOMINAL DEBT GROWTH, AND SIMULATED
NOMINAL DEBT GROWTH = (REAL DEBT GROWTH) ×
(SIMULATED INFLATION)

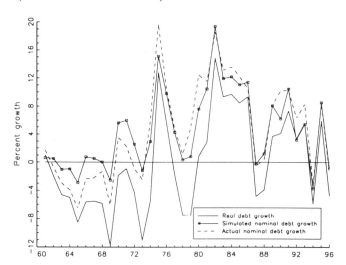

We are used to the monetarist claim that bad inflation outcomes have
come from excessively volatile monetary policy; that stable ($k\%$) money
growth rules would have led to stable inflation. The exact opposite is the
case here. Growth in the *real* value of the debt is so volatile that steady
($k\%$) nominal debt growth would have resulted in wildly fluctuating
inflation. Wild swings in nominal debt growth in fact did a great deal to
stabilize inflation.

Real debt growth could also have been different. Of course, constant
surplus along with constant nominal debt would have given a constant
price level, but it is more convincing to think about alternative surplus
policies within the constraint that the cyclical component a_t is beyond the
government's control, and that the persistence of the long-run component z_t must be respected, leaving the government only the choice of its
innovation ϵ_{zt}. To have a constant price level in this way, the government
must choose positive long-run shocks to exactly offset bad cyclical
shocks. From the identity (33), with $\Delta \equiv E_t - E_{t-1}$, no innovation in the
rate of return implies

$$-\Delta\, sc_t = \Delta\, vc_t = \Delta\sum \beta^j\, sc_{t+j}.$$

The model implies

$$\Delta \sum \beta^j sc_{t+j} = \frac{1}{1 - \beta \eta_z} \epsilon_{zt} + \frac{1}{1 - \beta \eta_a} \epsilon_{at},$$

$$\Delta sc_t = \epsilon_{zt} + \epsilon_{at}.$$

Solving for ϵ_{zt}, we have

$$\epsilon_{zt} = -\frac{1 + \dfrac{1}{1 - \eta a \beta}}{1 + \dfrac{1}{1 - \eta z \beta}} \epsilon_{at}.$$

Only this choice for ϵ_{zt} will leave no innovation in the price level.

Evaluating this expression using the above persistence parameters η_a, η_z, the government could have eliminated inflation with a z-process that had -1.00 correlation with the a-process, rather than the actual -0.95 correlation, and with a standard deviation of 0.105 rather than 0.11. Again, we see how much inflation smoothing is already in debt policy. The orthogonal component of the surplus process that "caused" inflation is quite small.

This example also shows quantitatively how the initially puzzling features of the data flow naturally from a government that is trying to smooth inflation despite large cyclical surplus shocks. In order to smooth inflation, long-term surpluses must rise when short-term surpluses decline, and low surpluses must be associated with declining value of the debt.

This logic and Figure 12 also suggest how we could have missed a fiscal determination of inflation all along. If we had lived in an economy with stable nominal debt, fluctuating real values, and correspondingly fluctuating inflation, or if we had lived in an economy with stable real values of the debt but fluctuating nominal values causing inflation, we would have noticed. In fact, we lived in an economy with wildly fluctuating real values of the debt, and with nominal values that almost—but not quite—smoothed inflation. Equivalently, there is so little independent variation in real and nominal values of the debt that we never see time series corresponding to classic experiments, in which one of surplus and debt is varied and the other is held constant.

The idea that the government can separately determine nominal debt and surpluses is strained, however. In fact, nominal debt sales are the most likely signal of future surpluses. If the government simply sold less debt in the late 70s, consumers may have misread this to mean that future surpluses were also going to be lower, so revenue from bond sales would have been less. The next step in this kind of modeling therefore should be to recognize a *regime*. Consumers rationally infer expected future surpluses from nominal debt sales. Then, the government can really only choose one quantity at each date. To change inflation, the government must change regimes to one in which nominal debt sales do and are understood to carry larger changes in future real surpluses.

Over the long run of decades, nominal debt growth and inflation are positively rather than negatively correlated. Hence, at very low frequencies we can understand inflation as the consequence of excessive nominal debt growth with relatively constant surpluses rather than require changing expectations of future surpluses to do the work.

3.4 BOND RETURNS

So far, I have assumed that the expected government bond return is constant. Variation in the expected rate of return at which future surpluses are discounted may account for substantial variation in the real value of the debt. Suggestively, the government-bond return varies by about as much as the surplus/consumption ratio, so variation in bond returns is at least a plausibly important source of variation in the real value of the debt. Also, fluctuations in government bond returns are clearly associated with cyclical movements in inflation, and the disinflation of the early 1980s was associated with a large increase in bond returns.

In this section, I give a preliminary assessment of whether expected return variation is an important part of the story. I apply the methodology used by Campbell and Shiller (1988) and Cochrane (1992) to decompose the variation in stock-market prices into expected dividend growth, expected return, and bubble components. They find that almost all variation in stock-market values is due to varying expected returns and almost none due to variation in expected future dividend growth, so perhaps the same is true here.

LINEARIZING THE PRESENT-VALUE RELATION   To separate the present-value identity into additive return and surplus components, I Taylor-approximate the one-period identity (33) around its steady state and iterate forward, following Campbell and Shiller (1988). Table 4 summarizes steady-state values and deviations from steady state.

The linearized version of the iterated identity is

$$vc_t \approx -\sum_{j=1}^{k} \rho^{j-1}\tilde{r}_{t+j}^a + \sum_{j=1}^{k} \rho^{j-1}dc_{t+j} + \frac{1}{vc}\sum_{j=1}^{k} \rho^j\, sc_{t+j} + \rho^k\, vc_{t+k}. \tag{41}$$

s_t^a/c_t can be negative, so I do not approximate it in logs. I verified the accuracy of the approximation by graphing vc_t constructed back from the last date in the sample according to (41) against the actual value, and it is

Table 4   VARIABLE DEFINITIONS AND VALUES FOR APPROXIMATE
PRESENT-VALUE IDENTITY

| | Notation | | | Steady-State |
Variable	Steady State	Deviation from Steady State	Sample Mean[a]	Value in Calculation
v_t^a/c_t	vc	$vc_t = \ln(v_t^a/c_t) - vc$	43%	43%
s_t^a/c_t	sc	$sc_t = s_t^a/c_t - sc$	−0.9%	+0.4%
c_{t+1}/c_t	Δc	$dc_t = \ln(c_{t+1}/c_t) - \Delta c$	3.2%	
r_{t+1}^a	r^a	$\tilde{r}_{t+1}^a = \ln(r_{t+1}^a) - \ln(r^a)$	0.64%	
$(1/r_{t+1}^a)c_{t+1}/c_t$	ρ		1.025	0.99

[a] Geometric mean where appropriate, e.g. $vc = \exp\{E[\ln(v_t/c_t)]\}$.

quite accurate. Letting the horizon go to infinity and taking expectations yields a linearized version of the present-value formula:

$$vc_t \approx -E_t \sum_{j=1}^{\infty} \rho^{j-1}\tilde{r}_{t+j}^a + E_t \sum_{j=1}^{\infty} \rho^{j-1}\, dc_{t+j} + \frac{1}{vc}E_t \sum_{j=1}^{\infty} \rho^j\, sc_{t+j} \qquad (42)$$

Real debt/consumption is high if the effective discount rate is low, or if future surpluses are high. This identity holds for any information set that includes v_t^a/c_t.

The steady state is defined by $(1 - \rho)\, vc = \rho\, sc$ and $\rho \equiv dc/r^a$. We may rightly worry that the steady state and the fiscal theory in general require consistently positive and high surpluses. However, since ρ is quite near one—the average real bond return is close to the average consumption growth rate—a very small steady-state surplus can service a large real debt.

The sample mean surplus/consumption ratio is in fact negative, and the sample mean real bond return in Table 4 is less than the sample mean consumption growth, implying that $\rho > 1$ and that all the sums explode. However, as Figure 8 shows, the low returns are driven by the 1970s and the low average surplus is driven by the 1980s. One might reasonably regard these experiences as unusual. For this reason I impose $\rho = 0.99$ rather than use sample means. The implied steady-state surplus/consumption ratio is 0.4%, which is positive but not unbelievably high, given the sample experience that has ranged from +2% to −6% (see Figure 5).

PERFECT FORESIGHT   The next question is, how much information should we consider when evaluating the identity? First, let us assume perfect foresight. Suppose people knew exactly what the path of future real gov-

ernment bond returns and future surpluses was going to be. Does variation in surpluses or variation in ex-post returns account for variation in the
real value of the debt?

To answer this question, I calculate at each date t the terms in (41),
iterated to the end of the sample. For example, at date t, the component
due to future returns is

$$\text{return component}_t = -\sum_{j=t+1}^{T} \rho^{j-t-1} \tilde{r}_j^a .$$

Figure 13 presents the results. The sloping dashed line is the mean or
steady state plus the present value of the endpoint, $\rho^{T-t} v_T^\alpha / c_T$. The solid
and dashed variable lines add the return component and the return plus
surplus components to the endpoint component. As we move back
through time, these variable components explain variation of the v^a/c
ratio through time. The difference between end + return + surplus and
the actual v^a/c ratio is due to the consumption component and approximation error, both of which are small.

Starting in the mid-1960s, the value of the debt falls dramatically. Since
the end+return line is fairly steady but the end+return+surplus line
tracks the decline, the decline is attributed to changing surpluses: The
large deficits of 1975 and the early 1980s were starting to appear on the
horizon, driving down the value of the debt. Starting in 1972, however,
the end+return+surplus line is fairly steady, while the end+return line
drops rapidly. Now the high returns of the 1980s are starting to matter.
By 1980, future budgets moved back into surplus, but the value of the

Figure 13 COMPONENTS OF VALUE/CONSUMPTION RATIO

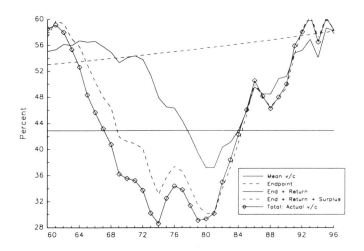

debt is still low because interest (discount) rates are so high. As we move to the present, good surpluses are discounted with fewer and fewer high interest rates, raising the value of the debt.

With perfect foresight, then, both surplus and return variation are important in understanding the real value of the debt.

A SIMPLE VAR   Perfect foresight is of course an extreme assumption. What story can we tell based on documentable patterns of forecastability in the variables? To address this question, I form the expectations in (42) with simple VARs. Denoting the VAR by

$$x_t = A x_{t-1} + \epsilon_t,$$

we measure terms in (42) by, for example,

$$E\left[\sum_{j=1}^{\infty} \rho^{j-1} \Delta \ln r_{t+j}^a \,\Big|\, x_t\right] = e_r'\,[A(I - \rho A)^{-1} x_t],$$

where e_r is a vector of zeros and ones that picks off the return element of the VAR.

I form the VAR with a single lag of the debt/consumption ratio, real bond return, surplus/consumption ratio, and consumption growth. Table 5 presents the estimated VAR equations. The important points: The real debt/consumption ratio is very persistent (0.96), as we expect. Higher surpluses forecast lower debt (-0.73). Again, we must think that high surpluses forecast low future surpluses to account for this fact. The

Table 5   OLS REGRESSIONS, 1960–1996

Left-hand variable	Right-hand variable				
	$\ln\left(\dfrac{v}{c}\right)_{t-1}$	$\left(\dfrac{1}{vc}\dfrac{s}{c}\right)_{t-1}$	$\ln r_{t-1}^b$	$\ln\dfrac{c_{t-1}}{c_{t-2}}$	R^2
$\ln\left(\dfrac{v}{c}\right)_t$	0.96 (21)	-0.73 (-3.1)	0.18 (0.6)	-2.31 (-3.7)	0.95
$\left(\dfrac{1}{vc}\dfrac{s}{c}\right)_t$	0.067 (2.9)	0.46 (3.9)	-0.19 (-1.4)	1.23 (4.0)	0.58
$\ln r_t^b$	0.046 (1.3)	-0.23 (-1.3)	0.13 (0.7)	-0.46 (-1.0)	0.20
$\ln\dfrac{c_t}{c_{t-1}}$	0.00 (0.00)	0.001 (0.02)	0.06 (0.8)	0.37 (2.2)	0.05

t-statistics in parentheses.

surplus is also persistent (0.46). Higher debt forecasts slightly higher (0.067) surpluses. The last is a key coefficient, and its statistical significance is encouraging. Higher debt also forecasts higher bond returns (0.046), though this is less significant. Overall, bond returns and consumption growth seem nearly unforecastable.

Figure 14 presents the contributions of return, surplus, and consumption growth terms to explaining the debt/consumption ratio, along with the actual ratio. For example, the line marked Return graphs the time series $e'_r A(I - \rho A)^{-1} x_t$.

In contrast to the ex post decomposition, *the forecastable components of the surplus now almost exactly account for all variation in the value of the debt.* The central facts behind this result is that higher value forecasts higher future surpluses, as seen in the coefficient of surplus on value in the VAR, and surpluses are persistent. Though a higher value also forecasts a lower bond return, bond returns are much less persistent.

We can make the same point quantitatively with a variance decomposition. From (42),

$$\text{var}\,[vc_t] \approx -\sum_{j=1}^{\infty} \rho^{j-1} \text{cov}\,(vc_t, \tilde{r}^a_{t+j}) + \sum_{j=1}^{\infty} \rho^{j-1} \text{cov}(vc_t, dc_{t+j})$$
$$+ \frac{1}{vc} \sum_{j=1}^{\infty} \rho^j \text{cov}(vc_t, sc_{t+j}).$$

The debt/consumption ratio can vary *only* if it forecasts returns, surpluses, or consumption growth. The question is, which components account for fluctuations in value? To answer this question, I estimate the above moments from the VAR representation. For example,

$$\sum_{j=1}^{\infty} \rho^j \text{cov}(vc_t, sc_{t+j}) = e'_v E(xx')\rho A(I - \rho A)^{-1} e_s, \qquad E(xx') = \sum_{j=0}^{\infty} A^j \Sigma A^{j\prime}$$

Table 6 presents the fractions of debt value variance so explained. Again, we see that forecasts of future surpluses account for the vast majority of

Table 6 FRACTIONS OF (DEBT VALUE)/CONSUMPTION EXPLAINED BY VAR FORECASTS OF SURPLUS/ CONSUMPTION, GOVERNMENT BOND RETURNS, AND CONSUMPTION GROWTH

Surplus	*Return*	*Consumption*
84.7%	13.6%	2.6%

Each term is $100 \times \text{cov}(vc_t, \Sigma_j \rho^j x_{t+j})/\text{var}(vc_t)$, as estimated from the VAR representation.

fluctuations in debt value. Furthermore, almost all variation is accounted for; we do not have to rely on bubble terms.

We are left with an unsettling picture. Based on perfect foresight, expected return variation is an important determinant of the value of the debt. Based on a simple VAR, expected return variation is unimportant. The latter result depends on the VAR: Variables such as yield spreads that forecast more long-run interest-rate variation could raise the contribution of bond returns.

3.5 MATURITY

The maturity structure is also potentially significant in our attempt to make sense of fiscal price determination. Bad fiscal news might be met by declines in long-term bond prices rather than a rise in the price level. Long-term debt sales can raise revenue with no change in future surpluses, by diluting the claims of existing long-term bonds. The inflation of the 1970s came down sharply along with large sales of long-term debt in the early 1980s, and inflation comes down with large debt sales in recessions. This mechanism may provide part of the explanation. Here I present some facts about the maturity structure that help us to see whether this is an important route to follow.

Figure 15 presents measures of the maturity structure, on a zero-coupon-equivalent basis as always. Overall, the maturity structure is surprisingly short: 40 to 70% of the debt has maturity one year or less,

Figure 14 COMPONENTS OF VALUE, AS MEASURED BY VAR

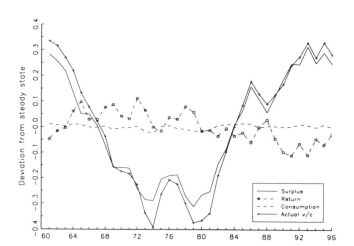

Figure 15 MATURITY STRUCTURE OF DEBT, ON A ZERO-COUPON
EQUIVALENT BASIS

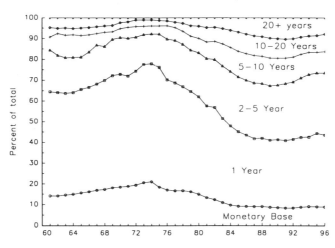

For example, debt between one and two years includes debt with one- and two-year maturity, plus all coupon payments that come due between one and two years.

Figure 16 MATURITY STRUCTURE OF DEBT, ON A ZERO-COUPON BASIS

Maturity structure, debt greater than 1 year maturity

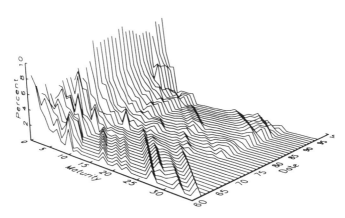

Each curve is the face value of outstanding debt divided by the face value of all debt.

and is rolled over every year. These are *face* values; the market values of long-term debt are even smaller. As is well known from simpler measures, the maturity structure was quite short until about 1975. Then longer-term debt gradually became more and more important. The buildup in long-term debt has been gradual, peaking about 1988.

Figure 16 presents the maturity structure of debt with more than one-year maturity. (One-year and less maturity is such a large fraction of the debt that one cannot see the rest if it is included.) Starting in 1960, a few very long-term, low-coupon bonds are outstanding. The spikes in the maturity structure are the principal amounts of these bonds. As the bonds age, the spikes move in towards the zero-maturity point. The government sold very little long-term debt, so the major feature of the term structure, and the root cause of the shortening maturity structure seen in Figure 15, is the aging of this long-term debt.

Starting about 1975, along with the first big primary deficit, we can see the effect of new, regular long-term debt sales. Initially, these sales also leave lumps in the maturity structure, but soon the coupons of the accumulated long-term bonds smooth the maturity structure. A few large sales in the mid-1980s show up as lumps that then age. One can also see increased sales of 10-year debt and 2-year debt in the eventual height of the lines on the left-hand side.

4. Conclusion

Two main themes recur through this article. First, one can use the fiscal theory to understand why money is valued in modern economies with apparently unbacked fiat money. In systems in which money is explicitly backed, such as a gold standard or currency board, it turns out that the backing in terms of overall government resources is all that really matters: The fiscal theory points out that this backing continues to matter when explicit backing disappears. When money is valued because it is backed, the fact that certain assets have a liquidity value in exchange has at best second-order effects on the price level, and the value of money will therefore not be affected by financial innovation.

Second, in order to understand U.S. data from this fiscal perspective, we must view the primary surplus as following a process in which a negative shock today induces a positive change in the long run. While not immediately obvious, this is a natural specification. The government is faced with cyclical surplus shocks about which it can do little, yet it does not want wildly fluctuating and countercyclical inflation. Therefore, it sells extra debt in recessions, raising revenue by so doing because it implicitly promises to raise subsequent surpluses.

REFERENCES

Akerlof, G. A. (1979). Irving Fisher on his head: The consequences of constant threshold-target monitoring of money holdings. *Quarterly Journal of Economics* 93:169–189.
———, and R. D. Milbourne. (1980). Irving Fisher on his head II: The consequences of the timing of payments for the demand for money. *Quarterly Journal of Economics* 95:145–157.
Auerbach, A. J., J. Gokhale, and L. J. Kotlikoff. (1994). Generational accounting: A meaningful way to evaluate fiscal policy. *Journal of Economic Perspectives* 8:73–94.
Baba, Y., Hendry, D. F., and Starr, R. M. (1992). The demand for M1 in the U.S.A., 1960–1988. *Review of Economic Studies* 59:25–61.
Bernanke, B. S. (1983). Nonmonetary effects of the financial crisis in the propagation of the Great Depression. *American Economic Review* 73:257–276.
Black, F. (1970). Banking and interest rates in a world without money. *Journal of Bank Research*, Autumn, 9–20.
Bohn, H. (1998). The behavior of U.S. public debt and deficits. University of California at Santa Barbara. Working Paper.
Brash, D. T. (1996). New Zealand's remarkable reforms. Institute for Economic Affairs. Fifth IEA Annual Hayek Memorial Lecture, Occasional Paper 100.
Burnside, C., M. Eichenbaum, and S. Rebelo. (1998). Prospective deficits and the Asian currency crisis. Northwestern University. Working paper.
Campbell, J. Y., and R. J. Shiller. (1988). Stock prices, earnings, and expected dividends. *Journal of Finance* 43:661–676.
Canzoneri, M. B., R. E. Cumby, and B. T. Diba. (1997). Is the price level determined by the needs of fiscal solvency? Georgetown University. Working Paper.
Christiano, L. J., M. Eichenbaum, and C. L. Evans. (1998). Monetary policy shocks: What have we learned and to what end? Northwestern University and Federal Reserve Bank of Chicago. Manuscript.
Cochrane, J. H. (1992). Explaining the variance of price-dividend ratios. *Review of Financial Studies* 5, 243–280.
———. (1994a). Permanent and transitory components of GNP and stock prices. *Quarterly Journal of Economics* CIX:241–266.
———. (1994b). Shocks. *Carnegie-Rochester Conference Series on Public Policy* 41:295–364.
———. (1998). Long-term debt and optimal policy in the fiscal theory of the price level. Cambridge, MA: National Bureau of Economic Research. NBER Working Paper.
Cowen, T., and R. Kroszner. (1994). *Explorations in the New Monetary Economics.* Cambridge, MA: Blackwell.
Dupor, B. (1997). Exchange rates and bank notes: The fiscal theory of the price level. University of Pennsylvania. Manuscript.
Fama, E. F. (1980). Banking in a theory of finance. *Journal of Monetary Economics* 6:39–57.
———. (1983). Financial intermediation and price level control. *Journal of Monetary Economics* 12:7–28.
———. (1985). What's different about banks? *Journal of Monetary Economics* 15:29–39.
———, and R. R. Bliss. (1987). The information in long-maturity forward rates. *American Economic Review* 77:680–692.

Goodfriend, M. (1998). Central banking under the gold standard. *Carnegie-Rochester Conference Series on Public Policy* 29:85–124.

Hall, R. E. (1983). Optimal fiduciary monetary systems. *Journal of Monetary Economics* 12:33–50.

Hamilton, J. D., and M. A. Flavin. (1986). On the limitations of government borrowing: A framework for empirical testing. *American Economic Review* 76:808–819.

King, R. G. (1983). On the economics of private money. *Journal of Monetary Economics* 12:127–158.

Leeper, E. (1991). Equilibria under "active" and "passive" monetary policies. *Journal of Monetary Economics* 27:129–147.

Lucas, R. E., Jr. (1980). Equilibrium in a pure currency economy. *Economic Inquiry* 18:203–220.

———. (1988). Money demand in the United States: A quantitative review. *Carnegie-Rochester Conference Series on Public Policy* 29:137–167.

Sargent, T. J. (1986). *Rational Expectations and Inflation.* New York: Harper & Row.

———. (1987). *Dynamic Macroeconomic Theory.* Cambridge, MA: Harvard University Press.

Schmitt-Grohé, S., and M. Uribe. (1997). Price level determinacy and monetary policy under a balanced-budget requirement. Federal Reserve Board. Manuscript.

Sims, C. A. (1994). A simple model for the determination of the price level and the interaction of monetary and fiscal policy. *Economic Theory* 4:381–399.

———. (1997). Fiscal foundations of price stability in open economies. Yale University. Working Paper.

White, L. H. (1984). Competitive payments systems and the unit of account. *American Economic Review* 74:699–712.

Woodford, M. (1994). Monetary policy and price level determinacy in a cash-in-advance economy. *Economic Theory* 4:345–389.

———. (1995). Price level determinacy without control of a monetary aggregate. *Carnegie-Rochester Conference Series on Public Policy* 43:1–46.

———. (1996). Control of the public debt: A requirement for price stability? Cambridge, MA: National Bureau of Economic Research. NBER Working Paper 5684.

———. (1997). Doing without money: Controlling inflation in a post-monetary world. Cambridge, MA: National Bureau of Economic Research. NBER Working Paper 6188.

Comment

HENNING BOHN
University of California, Santa Barbara

1. Introduction

John Cochrane provides a provocative and quite radical perspective on U.S. inflation: Money and monetary frictions are irrelevant. Money need not even exist for the price level to be determinate, but nominal bonds are essential. The price level is obtained by equating the present value of exogenous budget surpluses with the real value of nominal debt. After explaining the general idea of the fiscal theory and acknowledging that the basic model has problems explaining U.S. data, the paper offers a more complicated model with long-term bonds and goes on to attack competing theories.

The paper's scathing critique of traditional monetary theory invites a somewhat critical response. Since my comments will indeed be mostly critical, let me emphasize that I am quite sympathetic towards fiscal theory in principle, e.g., towards Woodford's (1997) cashless limit version. Cochrane's version is more extreme, however, in abstracting from all monetary frictions; and he claims to explain U.S. history.

My comments will focus on three questions. How promising is the cashless view of U.S. history? Is it theoretically coherent? And how can we distinguish empirically between a fiscal and a monetary price determination?

2. How Promising Is the Cashless View of U.S. History?

John's attacks on the quantity theory should not distract from the real question: Does the cashless view provide a good (better?) explanation of postwar U.S. inflation? There are good reasons to be skeptical.

First, the basic model is counterfactual. In Cochrane's words: "The 1970s were a decade of low deficits and high inflation, while the 1980s saw a dramatic increase in government debt with low inflation." In the model, high deficits should be inflationary. Should we really credit Ronald Reagan with defeating inflation? Because his actions signaled future budget surpluses? And Paul Volcker had nothing to do with it? At the end, Cochrane hints that adding long-term bonds (adding degrees of freedom?) might improve the model's fit, but that remains a conjecture.

Second, Cochrane applies a rather low plausibility standard. The best evidence in favor is a graph showing roughly parallel movements of actual and simulated inflation (Figure 11). The simulated inflation is, however, based on parameters chosen ad hoc to produce a "subjectively . . . convincing story." Moreover, "the model will only capture the parts of inflation that are correlated with surplus and value." How much is that? Since Cochrane criticizes quantity theory for not explaining *all* of inflation within a simple model, his model should be held to the same standard.

Finally, note that transactions balances show no signs of decline. Since 1980, the downward drift in the M1/GDP ratio has stopped. The currency/GDP ratio has actually risen by about 25%. Though financial innovation has produced new means of payment and plausibly destabilized the demand for specific monetary aggregates, the U.S. economy is not moving in a cashless direction.

3. Is the Cashless View Theoretically Coherent?

My most serious concerns are about the political economy of John's model. The notion that bondholders are residual claimants on the government is a dangerous and misguided idea. Over the past 20 years, economists have tried hard to convince politicians that money and nominal bonds raise serious time-consistency problems and that politicians should commit to a noninflationary policy. This policy advice presumes—correctly I believe—that inflation and inflation uncertainty have some real cost. The entire literature on central-bank independence is, for example, based on this presumption.

In a frictionless economy, why should we advise politicians to maintain stable prices? Why should we expect a politician ever to enact a budget surplus? Nominal debt could be inflated away instantly and painlessly. If inflation has no cost while other taxes are distortionary, this would be efficient. In the time-consistency literature, it is well established that monetary frictions are essential to explain why a government can issue nominal bonds in the first place (Calvo, 1978; Bohn, 1988). Cochrane avoids this issue by assuming that nominal bonds are outstanding from the start. When it comes to new debt issues, he mentions "implicit promises to increase subsequent surpluses." It is unclear how and by whom these "promises" are made and how they are enforced. Moreover, if debt sales require a promise of future surpluses, isn't that making future surpluses endogenous, a function of debt? In Section 3.3.1, the z_t-component of the primary surplus is described as an exogenous stochastic process on one page and as being controlled by the government on another page. Overall, there is no coherent story of how budget surpluses are determined.

A nonmonetary example (to avoid misleading monetary intuition) may help to clarify why nominal debt is difficult to imagine in a frictionless economy. Consider a real economy with a homogeneous good, say, apples. The harvest is 100 apples. The government has 10 employees that each need to consume 1 apple. One feasible policy is to impose a tax of 10 apples. Alternatively, the government may try to borrow 1 apple and impose a tax of 9 apples. If individuals have a 100% time preference, the government can borrow 1 apple in period 1 if and only if it can credibly promise to repay 2 apples in period 2, i.e., it promises to impose a tax of 12 apples.

Now suppose the government decides to offer bonds denominated in "widgets." What's a widget? No one knows, but fortunately, no one cares. Individuals will trade 1 apple for a 1-widget government bond if and only if the government can credibly promise that a widget will be worth 2 apples in period 2. Uncertainty could be added easily, say, a value of 1 or 3 apples conditional on a coin toss. The key point is that a credible commitment about the value of widgets is required before any borrowing can take place. The same logic applies to dollar-denominated debt. In Cochrane's frictionless model, a dollar is just a label like "widget." The government must make promises about the future purchasing power of dollars before it can issue dollar-denominated bonds. When the repayment period arrives, the budget surplus is constrained by these prior commitments. Since John's model is silent about such commitments, it is an incomplete theory. Either the government is constrained or there is a time-consistency problem.

The widgets story highlights another issue, the difference between default and inflation. Suppose the government reneges on its promises and declares a widget to be worth 1 apple instead of 2. If only the government issues widget-denominated bonds, a cut in the purchasing power of widgets (inflation) is equivalent to a partial default. If widgets are used as unit of account by the private sector, however, an outright default leaves private claims unaffected while inflation devalues private loans, too. To persuade individuals to use widgets (dollars) as numeraire, the government will have to make credible promises about their value.

The private use of dollars raises further questions about the dynamics of consumer prices. Empirically, consumer prices move quite sluggishly as compared to speculative asset prices. This is a long-standing puzzle, e.g., in the purchasing-power parity literature. The frictionless view treats $1/p_t$ as the price of a speculative asset, as a claim on stochastic future budget surpluses. This does not look promising. For example, suppose there is a news announcement that all future primary budget surpluses are cut in half: Do we really expect all stores to immediately change their price tags to double all nominal prices?

This question is analogous to the old question of what would happen if the Fed doubled the money supply. Realistically, prices would rise, but much more slowly than the quantity theory predicts. The question about halving the budget surplus should have the same answer. The failure to account for sluggish price adjustment is a major reason for the quantity theory's empirical problems. It seems unfair to denounce the quantity theory without acknowledging that the fiscal theory faces similar problems. Basic versions of both theories falsely predict that consumer prices should jump around in response to news announcements.

Overall, Cochrane is creating unnecessary controversy by assuming away monetary frictions. Monetary and fiscal theories of inflation have actually much in common. Monetary theorists have long accepted that the government budget constraint matters for inflation because budget deficits can be monetized. When fiat money is held as medium of exchange, nominal bonds are not required in the basic monetization story (e.g., in Sargent, 1986). Nominal bonds are quantitatively important, however, because they magnify the government's financial gains from inflation. On the fiscal side, Woodford (1997) has shown that the fiscal theory can be derived as a "cashless limit" within the same conceptual framework. The more relevant question is which theory fits better for a certain country over a certain period.

4. How Can We Identity an Economy with Fiscal Price Determination?

The question if inflation is better explained by monetary ("Ricardian") or by fiscal ("non-Ricardian") considerations is at heart a political-economy question. If fiscal policymakers control the central bank, budget deficits are likely important for inflation. If the money supply is determined independently, fiscal authorities must either satisfy the intertemporal budget constraint or face default. Cochrane stacks the deck against the Ricardian case by ignoring the possibility of outright defaults, making the Ricardian case look special.

The political-economy perspective provides considerable guidance for empirical analysis. Of course, nothing is testable without auxiliary assumptions, which Cochrane refuses to make. Common sense suggests, however, that a positive regression response of the money supply to budget deficits would provide prima facie evidence for monetization. Similarly, a positive regression response of budget surpluses to debt accumulation provides prima facie evidence for fiscal adjustment. For the U.S., there is no convincing evidence for monetization, but Bohn (1998) and Canzoneri, Cumby, and Diba (1997) have found clear evidence for a surplus-to-debt linkage.

Cochrane's rebuttal is that one can create an observationally equivalent *statistical* model that interprets this linkage as a signaling effect. This is unconvincing, however, because the statistical model is ad hoc, whereas the evidence for fiscal adjustment is based on a coherent *economic* model. [Bohn (1998) examines an optimizing, tax-smoothing government.] The challenge for fiscal theory is to explain the data within a convincing model of government behavior. Exogenous policy rules don't qualify in this context, because they beg the question of who makes and enforces them.

Alternatively, one may try to find other statistical tests, though that seems easier in principle than in practice. For example, suppose there are shocks to the real interest rate. In a Ricardian model, increased debt service will force the fiscal authority to raise the primary surplus or face a default. In a fiscal-theory model, a higher discount rate on future real surpluses should trigger an immediate increase in prices. Thus, the fiscal theory has testable implications. Real interest rates are unfortunately difficult to measure, so that this particular test is likely inconclusive. A search for a better test is an important issue for future research. For now, an insistence on theory-based regressions is perhaps the best defense against arbitrary statistical modeling.

5. A Technical Complaint

Finally, in a paper about budget constraints, an incorrect intertemporal budget constraint should not be left unchallenged. Equation (7) is wrong. In a stochastic economy, budget surpluses must be discounted at a risk-adjusted interest rate that depends on the stochastic process for the primary surplus and on the economy's pricing kernel (Bohn, 1995). Except in special cases, the discount rate differs from the ex post return on government debt. Contrary to Cochrane's claims, assumptions about the rest of the economy do matter in this context.

REFERENCES

Bohn, H. 1988, Why do we have nominal government debt? *Journal of Monetary Economics* 21:127–140.
———. (1995). The sustainability of budget deficits in a stochastic economy. *Journal of Money, Credit, and Banking* 27:257–271.
———. (1998). The behavior of U.S. public debt and deficits. *Quarterly Journal of Economics* 113:949–964.
Calvo, G. A. (1978). On the dynamic consistency of optimal policy in a monetary economy. *Econometrica* 46:1411–1428.
Canzoneri, M., R. Cumby, and B. Diba. (1997). Is the price level determined by the needs of fiscal solvency? Georgetown University. Working Paper.
Sargent, T. (1986). *Rational Expectations and Inflation*. New York: Harper & Row.
Woodford, M. (1997). Doing without money: Controlling inflation in a post-monetary world. Cambridge, MA: National Bureau of Economic Research. NBER Working Paper 6188.

Comment

MICHAEL WOODFORD
Princeton University

1. Introduction

John Cochrane has written a fascinating and provocative paper that is certain to stimulate a great deal of further discussion and research. The paper ranges over quite a broad territory and throws out far too many new ideas for me to comment on all of them here. I do think, however, that it is important to mention several of the paper's broad themes, in order to distinguish among them. This is necessary in order for my subsequent remarks, which mainly concern one particular strand in the paper's analysis, to be properly understood.

2. Broad Themes of the Paper

The paper argues for (and illustrates) several heterodox views about the explanation of inflation. Each is interesting and worth discussion, but I think it is important to realize that they are distinct theses, and need not be accepted or rejected as a package. I would distinguish at least three distinct themes, each of which would be quite controversial in many quarters:

1. Abstraction from *monetary frictions*, even when modeling inflation.
2. A *fiscal* theory of price-level determination.
3. Monetary-policy *ineffectiveness*, especially in the sense of having no effect upon inflation.

None of these provocative theses necessarily implies the others. For example, a "cashless" account of U.S. inflation [in the sense defined in Woodford (1998a)] may nonetheless (a) ascribe no role to fiscal policy, and (b) imply that monetary policy matters a great deal, for the evolution of inflation among other things. An example is the model of post-1979 U.S. monetary policy presented in Rotemberg and Woodford (1997). The theoretical model underlying that work is a neo-Wicksellian model of inflation determination, in which the key elements are a specification of monetary policy in terms of an interest-rate feedback rule (which links *nominal* interest rates to the behavior of inflation), and a theory of the

I would like to thank Michael Bordo, Matt Canzoneri, and Eduardo Loyo for helpful discussions, and Loyo for collaboration on the empirical work reported here.

determinants of the equilibrium *real* rate of interest (which is affected by inflation as a result of nominal rigidities). The model abstracts entirely from monetary frictions in its account of the economic determinants of the equilibrium real rate of return, and since monetary policy is formulated directly in terms of an interest-rate rule, it is not necessary to explicitly model the sources of the demand for the monetary base that allow the central bank to achieve the interest-rate changes that it seeks. In such a model it is not essential that one abstract from the existence of monetary frictions, but it is possible to do so, and since they are not central to the model, and likely to be quantitatively small in any event, exposition and analysis of the model is simpler when they are dispensed with.

But the price level may be determined in such a model without any reference to the government's budget or to the size of the public debt. [See the discussion in Woodford (1998a) of "Wicksellian" policy regimes.] In Rotemberg and Woodford (1997), fiscal policy is assumed to be Ricardian, in the sense discussed by Cochrane. This implies that Ricardian equivalence obtains in that model, and fiscal variables are irrelevant to the determination of both output and inflation.

Furthermore, monetary policy matters in that model, for the equilibrium behavior of both inflation and output. Here it is important to distinguish between "cashless" models in the sense of Woodford (1998a)—in which the *money supply* is not an important state variable, because the amount of cash needed for transactions is small enough to result in only negligible distortions—and models in which the central bank has *no lever* with which to affect equilibrium, because it is too small a player in financial markets, and government-supplied financial claims have no special features. In the *cashless limit* as I define it, the central bank *can* still control nominal interest rates through open-market operations between money and bonds, due to the existence of a residual demand for the government-monopolized monetary base. But once one models the way in which the bank sets its interest-rate instrument, the details of the associated changes in the money supply are unimportant; and even the level of nominal interest rates only matters through its implication for the level of short-term *real* interest rates, given inflation expectations. The Fed's assumed control of the federal funds rate is an important element of the reconstruction of U.S. time series given in Rotemberg and Woodford (1997), as is the assumption that other short-term nominal rates move with it in equilibrium; and the model used there implies that alternative monetary policy regimes would lead to very different inflation performance, as shown by the counterfactual policy simulations reported in the paper.

Similarly, a "fiscal theory of the price level" of the kind proposed in Woodford (1995) need not abstract from monetary frictions, and may well assign an important role to monetary policy. As Cochrane notes, many previous presentations of fiscalist models incorporate a conventional specification of money demand.[1] Cochrane is right that liquidity preference plays no central role in a fiscalist account of price-level determination, and so there are expository advantages to dispensing with it [as I do in much of the analysis in Woodford (1998b)]. But it is also useful to remember that the fiscalist view does not depend upon any unconventional view about the substitutability of money and other assets—a point that I was concerned to make in discussions such as Woodford (1995), exactly because of the importance of questions about the existence of a clear distinction between monetary and nonmonetary assets in previous (but very different) criticisms of the quantity theory of money.

And whether one assumes a cashless limiting economy or not, fiscalist accounts of inflation determination generally imply that the specification of both monetary and fiscal policy matters. For central-bank interest-rate policy will affect the evolution of nominal government liabilities, a crucial state variable in a fiscal theory of the price level, even if one ignores the effects of monetary distortions in private-sector behavioral relations. For example, in Loyo's (1997) explanation of Brazilian inflation in the early 1980s, the crucial event that triggers the inflationary spiral is a change in the *monetary policy* rule, from a "passive" rule to an "active" one in Leeper's (1991) sense. Loyo expounds his theory in a cashless model, and assumes a non-Ricardian fiscal policy (that does not substantially change between the late 1970s and early 1980s); equilibrium inflation is then determined by price-level adjustment at each date to equate the value of existing public debt with the present value of expected future budget surpluses. Still, the specification of monetary policy matters for his model, and indeed the change in monetary policy is crucial to his story.

Thus Cochrane's three themes deserve separate consideration. My own view is that the consideration of "cashless" models is quite appropriate and often useful, at least as a first approximation; there are surely some economies and some issues for which modeling the demand for monetary assets does matter, but it is often a second-order issue, even when analyzing monetary policy and the determinants of inflation.

The fiscalist view of price-level determination is probably of more restricted applicability, for its application depends upon *what kind* of fiscal policy, Ricardian or non-Ricardian, a government is expected to

---

1. See, e.g., Leeper (1991), Sims (1994), or Woodford (1995, 1996).

follow. The non-Ricardian alternative seems to me a perfectly logical possibility [and one can even think of reasons for a non-Ricardian regime to be deliberately chosen, as part of an optimal policy regime, as discussed in Woodford (1998b)], but the frequency with which actual fiscal policies are or have been of that kind remains an open question at present. The interest of the theory does not require an assertion that all or even most policy regimes are of that kind; it would still be of interest to consider its *normative* properties even if no actual governments had ever behaved in such a way. And as I discuss below, there are certainly reasons to doubt that U.S. fiscal policy is non-Ricardian, at least as things stand at present. But I am less sure about U.S. policy during the late 1960s and in the 1970s, as discussed below. And I find it quite plausible that the regime in effect prior to the 1951 Federal Reserve–Treasury accord should be described as non-Ricardian. [That period would represent a historical example of the kind of interest-rate pegging regime for which the theory was developed, in Woodford (1995).]

The thesis of Cochrane's which I find least plausible is the last one: his assertions that open-market operations have actually been ineffective in the U.S. over the period that he studies, and that monetary policy is unimportant for an explanation of inflation history. As noted above, the assumption that the Fed can control short-term nominal interest rates is central to the account of recent U.S. time series given in Rotemberg and Woodford (1997). I also believe that an attempt to interpret recent U.S. inflation history along fiscalist lines would be most plausible if it incorporated such a view, and allowed for feedback from inflation to the level of nominal interest rates as a result of Fed policy. (I illustrate how such an account might proceed below.)

The VAR evidence discussed in Section 2.6.2 is no real reason to doubt the importance of monetary policy. It simply implies that the *unsystematic* component of monetary policy has not been a very important source of disturbances to the economy. That finding might be disquieting to some monetarists, though I actually suspect that it would be cheerfully accepted by Friedman and Schwartz. It in no way implies that the nature of *systematic* monetary policy does not greatly matter for the effects (upon both inflation and output) of *other* kinds of economic disturbances. For example, the Rotemberg–Woodford (1997) reconstruction of the U.S. data attributes less than 2% of inflation variation since 1979 to the effects of exogenous monetary policy shocks (see Figure 3 of that paper), while at the same time implying that alternative coefficients in the interest-rate rule followed by the Fed should lead to radically different inflation outcomes (see Table 2 of that paper).

It is not entirely clear which of these themes Cochrane means to emphasize more. The paper's title stresses the "frictionless" aspect of his account, which might be a reference either to his neglect of monetary frictions, or to his view that monetary policy has been irrelevant. In fact, it seems to me that the paper spends the most time on, and has the greatest number of new results about, the second thesis—the fiscal theory of the price level. Accordingly, I shall direct my remaining remarks solely to that aspect of the paper. And since the most ambitious aspect of Cochrane's discussion of the fiscal theory is his discussion of its empirical implications, I shall direct my attention there.[2]

3. Can One Distinguish Ricardian from Non-Ricardian Policy Regimes?

The most important contribution of the paper is surely its discussion of whether the record of U.S. fiscal policy and inflation since 1960 can be squared with a fiscalist view of inflation determination.[3] Probably few readers will feel that Cochrane's proposed interpretation of the U.S. data conclusively settles this issue. However, his illustration of how a fiscalist interpretation of those data is possible makes an important advance, in that it shows that it is not nearly so easy to reject the fiscalist view out of hand as might have been supposed. Many have supposed that the simple fact that U.S. deficits (and the size of the public debt) increased in the early 1980s, while inflation dramatically declined at almost the same time, was in itself a clear demonstration that the variations in U.S. inflation in this period could not be explained in fiscalist terms. Cochrane shows that this is not so. The data can be reconciled with a fiscalist account, in which U.S. real primary deficits have evolved exogenously and in turn determined the inflation rate; and this is because they can be reconciled with a statistical model of the deficit process according to which expectations of future fiscal surpluses *improved* sharply over the first half of the 1980s. This demonstration will surely spark further discussion of the merits of alternative possible interpretations. Cochrane's construction of a useful annual data set for the changing value of U.S. public debt and for the associated primary deficits should also help to stimulate further work of this kind.

2. For a recent attempt of my own to clarify some of the theoretical issues, see Woodford (1998b).
3. Despite the amount of recent theoretical analysis in this vein, few attempts at empirical applications have yet been made. Two noteworthy early efforts were Shim (1984) and Leeper (1989). Leeper stresses the importance for empirical testing of recognition that the private sector is likely to have information about future government budgets that is not revealed by the recent evolution of the government budget itself, an important theme of Cochrane's work here as well.

Cochrane resists the idea that one should try to "test" the validity of a fiscalist interpretation by seeking to test whether or not U.S. fiscal policy has been Ricardian; instead, he simply proposes to construct a fiscalist interpretation of the data, to see if one can, and to see how implausibly complicated such an interpretation of the data would have to be. He is right, I think, not to organize his investigation around a formal hypothesis test. This is not because the hypothesis of a non-Ricardian fiscal regime has no testable implications. The problem is simply that it is a hypothesis not about what has happened (say, whether inflation has been correlated with changes in the value of the public debt) but about *why* it has happened, about the *causal* connections between the changes in various variables. Such hypotheses about causality can never be confirmed or rejected on the basis of a series of observations without the help of identifying assumptions of one sort or another, and these identifying assumptions are seldom implied by the hypothesis itself, in its most general form. Thus it is often not possible to test a hypothesis (which is nonetheless of considerable import) except jointly with a number of other maintained assumptions, the validity of which may be debatable to a greater or lesser extent. Careful thought about the source of convincing identifying assumptions is always crucial in applied work, and in the absence of them, it is better to admit that one is not engaged in hypothesis testing.

It does not seem easy to test in a convincing way for the existence of a Ricardian or non-Ricardian fiscal regime simply on the basis of the observed evolution of government budget deficits and the value of the public debt. For example, it is a mistake to suppose that tests of the "sustainability" of fiscal policy, in the sense of asking whether the value of the public debt would satisfy a transversality condition of the form

$$\lim_{j \to \infty} E_t \frac{1}{r^j} v_{t+j} = 0 \tag{1}$$

in the absence of a change in the law of motion associated with current policy, show whether current fiscal policy is Ricardian or not. The reason, as Cochrane notes, is that under a non-Ricardian regime, (1) is predicted to hold in *equilibrium*. It is simply not guaranteed to hold as a result of the way that government budgets are determined, regardless of the path of goods and asset prices, and as a result it can help to determine equilibrium prices.

In fact, if anything, it is under a regime of fiscal determination of the price level that one should *least* expect to see, in a finite sample, a path of the public debt apparently inconsistent with the transversality condition. The reason is that the fiscal theory of the price level implies that even if government fiscal policy does *not* guarantee a bounded debt/GDP ratio, any disturbances (fiscal or otherwise) that lead to an expectation of an explosive public debt, in the absence of any change in the price level, will stimulate aggregate demand and so drive up prices enough to restore the expectation that (1) will be satisfied. In a Ricardian world, by contrast, where people do not regard government debt as net wealth because they are confident that fiscal policy will eventually have to adjust to satisfy (1), a transitory period of failure of government budgets to adjust so as to maintain the debt/GDP within normal bounds might well result in explosive debt growth for a time—exactly because the private sector's confidence that fiscal policy will eventually adjust would prevent adjustment from occurring through inflation.[4] Thus evidence of the stationarity of the U.S. debt/GDP ratio is actually more compatible with a fiscalist account of U.S. inflation determination than a contrary finding would be.

Tests based upon estimation of specific feedback rules for the determination of government budget surpluses, as in Bohn (1998), are more to the point. In principle, estimation of such a fiscal policy rule is exactly what should determine whether policy is Ricardian or not. However, it is important to realize that valid inference depends upon being able to treat the estimated relation as truly structural; hence the usual problems with simultaneous-equations bias and other sorts of potential specification error must be attended to. For example, if fiscal policy were known to be described by a linear feedback rule like

$$s_t = \alpha \frac{B_{t-1}(t)}{p_t} + \epsilon_t,$$ (2)

where ϵ_t is an exogenous fiscal policy disturbance, then estimation of the coefficient α would indeed settle the question of whether policy is

4. Woodford (1998b) analyzes the possible equilibria under a fiscal regime in which the real primary surplus is exogenously fixed unless the real public debt reaches the government's "debt limit," at which point financial markets force the government's budget to adjust due to inability to borrow more. If the private sector has Ricardian expectations, the resulting equilibrium is one in which a shock can give rise to a debt explosion which eventually results in the debt limit being reached and a forced adjustment of the government's budget, confirming the Ricardian expectations. An econometrician observing such an equilibrium prior to the debt crisis would correctly infer that fiscal policy was "unsustainable." On the other hand, under the same government policy, if the private sector has fiscalist expectations, the same sort of shock results in a price-level adjustment, as a result of which the debt limit is never hit, and the government never deviates from its desired exogenous path for the real primary surplus, confirming these expectations as well.

Ricardian. On the other hand, even granting the correctness of this specification, an OLS estimate of α could be expected to be unbiased only if one were sure that the disturbance ϵ_t should be uncorrelated with the regressor $B_{t-1}(t)/p_t$. In the case of a fiscalist equilibrium, one would not expect this to be true, and indeed the likely bias in the estimate of α would be positive. The same kind of fiscal disturbances that would increase the current surplus (in the absence of any change in the market value of the public debt) would also be likely to cause an endogenous increase in the market value of existing government debt, as Cochrane discusses.

The obvious way to deal with this problem is by looking for instrumental variables that are associated with some nontrivial degree of variation in the market value of the public debt, but are believed to be uncorrelated with exogenous fiscal policy shifts. The most likely source of such variables would involve identifying one or more structural disturbances *not* related to fiscal policy. Of course, even if one could agree upon those, there would remain the question of the correctness of the specification of the fiscal rule (2). If ϵ_t actually includes omitted endogenous variables to which fiscal policy responds, and the nonfiscal shock affects those variables, the assumption that ϵ_t should be uncorrelated with the identified nonfiscal shock might well be wrong. Still, future work along these lines is likely to be fruitful. But it is important to realize that it will have to involve looking at more than just the evolution of the budget surplus and the market value of the debt alone. Not only would such estimation require the use of one or more other instruments, but the construction of the instrumental variables is likely to require the specification and estimation of additional structural equations, such as a feedback rule for monetary policy that would allow identification of a monetary policy shock, that could then be used as an instrument in the estimation of the fiscal policy rule.

In fact, the most fruitful approach to the problem may well involve estimation of joint specifications of monetary and fiscal policy. For the predicted consequences of alternative monetary policy rules depend a great deal on whether fiscal policy is Ricardian or not; this is one of the main reasons why the question of whether a given country's fiscal regime should be modeled as Ricardian is of such importance. Exactly because the predictions are dramatic, they are an appealing basis for inference about the character of fiscal policy (and of private-sector expectations regarding it). For example, Leeper (1991) shows, in the context of parametric families of monetary and fiscal policy rules, that a certain type of monetary policy rule (his "active" monetary policy) implies a unique stationary rational expectations equilibrium, associated with stationary fluctuations in both inflation and the real public debt, in the case of a (locally) Ricardian fiscal policy[5]; but the same kind of monetary policy is inconsistent with the existence of a stationary equilibrium in the case of (locally) non-Ricardian fiscal policy. [In the case of the latter policy configuration, the only possible equilibrium may involve explosive inflation dynamics, as in Loyo's (1997) analysis of Brazilian inflation in the early 1980s.] Similarly, an alternative type of monetary policy rule (Leeper's "passive" monetary policy) implies a unique stationary equilibrium in the case of a (locally) non-Ricardian fiscal policy, but makes rational expectations equilibrium indeterminate in the case of a (locally) Ricardian policy, so that the economy might in the latter case be subject to inflation variations due purely to self-fulfilling expectations.[6]

Results of this kind make possible inferences about the nature of fiscal policy on the basis of estimates of *monetary* policy rules. Thus, for example, Loyo (1997) argues that Brazilian fiscal policy in the late 1970s and early 1980s was non-Ricardian, not on the basis of an estimated feedback rule for fiscal policy, but on the ground that the shift around 1980 from "passive" to "active" monetary policy (according to his estimated monetary policy rules) coincided with a transition from a period of stable inflation to one of ever-accelerating inflation. Similarly, given the stability of U.S. inflation, and assuming that one prefers an explanation under which this represents a determinate equilibrium prediction rather than simply one among a vast set of possible outcomes, one might suppose that recent U.S. experience could only plausibly be attributed to a combination of "active" monetary policy and Ricardian fiscal policy, *or* to a combination of "passive" monetary policy and non-Ricardian fiscal policy. Under such reasoning, convincing estimates of the U.S. monetary policy rule would tell one a great deal about this aspect of fiscal policy.

In fact, much recent literature follows Taylor (1993) in characterizing recent U.S. monetary policy by an interest-rate feedback rule of the form

$$R_t = R^* + \phi_p(\pi_t - \pi^*) + \phi_y y_t, \tag{3}$$

5. Technically, Leeper's distinction between "passive" and "active" fiscal policies—α greater or less than $r-1$ in (2)—corresponds to policies that are "locally Ricardian" and "locally non-Ricardian," respectively, in the sense defined in Woodford (1998b). A locally non-Ricardian rule may nonetheless be globally Ricardian, and in fact, when $0 < \alpha < r-1$, the fiscal policy rule allows the value of the public debt to explode, though not at a rate as high as the interest rate. The local criterion is the relevant one if, as Leeper is, one is interested in equilibria in which fluctuations in inflation and in the debt/GDP ratio are stationary.

6. For further discussion of how the determinacy of equilibrium is affected by the joint properties of monetary and fiscal policy rules, see Benhabib, Schmitt-Grohé, and Uribe (1998).

or a generalization of this allowing for lags, forecasts, and a stochastic disturbance term. Here R_t represents the federal funds rate, π_t the inflation rate, π^* the implicit inflation target, R^* the steady-state funds rate consistent with stationary inflation at the target rate, and y_t the log of real GDP relative to trend; Taylor argues that desirable coefficients, and empirically realistic ones for the U.S., at least since the late 1980s, involve $\phi_p > 1$, $\phi_y > 0$.[7] In the context of Leeper's model, which assumes an exogenous level of real GDP (because prices are flexible), the coefficient ϕ_y is irrelevant to the issue of stability and determinacy of equilibrium, and a policy of the form (3) corresponds to what he calls "active" monetary policy if and only if $\phi_p > 0$. Thus if Taylor's characterization of U.S. monetary policy is correct, it suggests that U.S. fiscal policy must be expected to be Ricardian, given that we do not observe signs either of a Brazilian-style debt explosion and inflationary spiral, or of a Japanese-style deflationary trap.

Of course, the conditions for stability and determinacy of equilibrium depend upon the specification of one's model's other structural equations, and not simply upon the form of the monetary policy rule, and so a conclusive judgment cannot be reached without consideration of alternative, more realistic specifications—both of the monetary policy rule (3) and of the model's structural equations. Still, such alternative analyses as have been undertaken to date tend to confirm that $\phi_p > 1$, $\phi_y > 0$ are sufficient conditions for determinacy under a Ricardian fiscal policy and instability under a non-Ricardian policy,[8] and also to confirm that U.S. monetary policy since the 1980s is of a form that implies these results, even when the specification (3) is generalized.[9] This is why the account given in Rotemberg and Woodford (1997) of U.S. inflation since 1980 assumes a Ricardian fiscal policy—not because of any evidence about the nature of fiscal policy, but because our estimated monetary policy rule is only consistent with a stationary equilibrium (given our structural equations) under that hypothesis. Furthermore, our model is able to account quite well for the estimated effects of monetary policy shocks during this period under the hypothesis of Ricardian fiscal policy,

---

7. Taylor's (1993) description of recent U.S. monetary policy assumes $\pi^* = 0.02$ per year, $R^* = 0.04$ per year, $\phi_p = 1.5$, and $\phi_y = 0.5$.
8. For example, Woodford (1996) generalizes Leeper's model to allow for sticky prices and endogenous supply, and finds that in that case $\phi_y > 0$ only lowers the threshold value of ϕ_p needed to get Leeper's results. Rotemberg and Woodford (1998) demonstrate this as well, in the context of a more complicated sticky-price model, and also show that partial adjustment of the funds rate toward a time-varying target defined by (3) does not change this threshold. See, however, Benhabib, Schmitt-Grohé, and Uribe (1998) for results with a contrary flavor.
9. See, e.g., Clarida, Galí, and Gertler (1998).

whereas the predicted effects would be different in the case of a different type of fiscal policy, such as the exogenous process for the real primary surplus assumed by Cochrane in his account of U.S. inflation here.

On the other hand, these results, even if taken to imply that current U.S. fiscal policy is best modeled as Ricardian, do not imply that all government policies are always best modeled that way, or even that U.S. policy has always been of that kind. Indeed, attempts to extend the characterization of U.S. monetary policy in terms of a "Taylor rule" to the period prior to 1979 have typically estimated a coefficient ϕ_p well *below* one for the earlier period.[10] In the context of Leeper's model, and other simple models with a similar structure, this would imply that inflation should have been subject to fluctuations due purely to self-fulfilling expectations in this period, and that is indeed the interpretation suggested by Clarida, Galí, and Gertler (1998). That is perhaps one possible interpretation of the instability of the 1970s. But such estimates of the monetary policy rule are also quite consistent with the view that fiscal policy was non-Ricardian during that period, and that there was a determinate stationary equilibrium inflation process—determined by variations in fiscal expectations. Indeed, the latter interpretation would have the advantage (apart from explaining how equilibrium is determined) of offering a potential explanation of *why* monetary policy was conducted in the way that it was in that period, namely, that "passive" monetary policy was made necessary by the determination of the fiscal authorities to follow a non-Ricardian policy. Similarly, attempts to estimate "Taylor rules" for other countries sometimes result in estimated rules that would imply indeterminacy of equilibrium in the case of a Ricardian fiscal policy.[11] Possibly these results imply that the assumed form of feedback rule for monetary policy is mis-specified, but an interpretation in terms of a non-Ricardian policy regime would also seem to be worth pursuing.

4. A Fiscalist Interpretation of U.S. Inflation History

I turn now to Cochrane's proposed interpretation of U.S. time series in terms of a fiscal regime under which the evolution of the real primary budget surplus has been completely exogenous. Such a characterization, if correct, would represent a classic example of a non-Ricardian fiscal policy rule. If the policy were correctly understood by the private sector, fiscal shocks ought to have wealth effects and affect aggregate demand, and, in the simple model assumed here (in which prices are perfectly

10. See, e.g., Clarida, Galí, and Gertler (1998) and Taylor (1998).
11. See, e.g., Kutter (1998).

flexible and equilibrium real activity and real rates of return accordingly exogenous), equilibrium would have to be restored by price-level adjustments. The primary achievement of this analysis is to show that the fiscal series themselves are not inconsistent with the non-Ricardian hypothesis. In particular, a model of the debt and surplus series is presented that is fully consistent with the evidence that Bohn (1998) and Canzoneri, Cumby, and Diba (1998) offer as support for Ricardian policy in the U.S., but that contradicts their Ricardian interpretations of these facts. This illustrates concretely how difficult it is to distinguish between Ricardian and non-Ricardian regimes on the basis of these series alone.

The explanation of inflation variations under such a regime is given somewhat less thorough attention, although an illustration is given (in his Figure 11) of the extent to which the assumption that inflation is a linear function of the current surplus and the current value of the public debt (each deflated by a consumption-based measure of "permanent income") with suitable coefficients could account for both low-frequency and cyclical fluctuations in inflation over the period. This does not seem to quite represent a complete model of how inflation is determined.[12] In particular, there is no discussion of how the particular coefficients in his equation (40) relate to the mechanism stressed in the fiscal theory of the price level, according to which inflation variations occur insofar as they are necessary to make the real value of the public debt consistent with expectations regarding future surpluses. The results of the exercise do show that an explanation of inflation variations as largely due to exogenous fiscal developments is not absurd on its face, as would be the case if the inflation series were completely independent of the fiscal series. Instead, Figure 11 shows that *if* one could explain why variations in the fiscal series should affect inflation in the hypothesized way, one might potentially explain a good bit of the variation in annual inflation rates along such lines.

A more interesting version of such an exercise, in my view, would

12. The inflation equation (40) is described as resulting from rules by which the government picks the long-run surplus shock ϵ_{zt} and the nominal government debt V_t each period. But this seems to allow *too many* independent dimensions of variation in fiscal policy. The government can control the growth of the public debt by varying the size of its budget surplus, and it has many instruments through which it can affect the size of the surplus. But it can't use its control of its budget to *simultaneously* achieve target levels of the *real* public debt and of the *nominal* public debt, which is essentially what this discussion assumes. What is missing is the specification of a *monetary* policy rule. This is presumably left out because, under Cochrane's view that open-market operations are irrelevant, monetary policy should not be able to affect market rates of return. But in that case, the missing equation would still be a specification of the short-term nominal interest rate—as an exogenous process, if monetary policy cannot affect it. See the treatment of a regime with elastic supply of private money in Woodford (1995).

involve specifying a monetary policy rule as well as the stochastic process for the primary budget surplus, and then asking what endogenous inflation variations would be implied by the fiscal theory of the price level. Such a variation is interesting for several reasons. First, it allows us to ask whether we can account for the history of U.S. inflation in terms of the variations required to ensure a value for the U.S. public debt commensurate with expected future budget surpluses. I shall not claim that the possibility of such a reconstruction of the data proves that the explanation is correct; but, in the spirit of Cochrane's exercise, it is certainly worth seeing if any story of that kind can be told at all, and what it would involve.

Second, an estimated monetary policy rule may or may not even be consistent with the existence of a stationary equilibrium under the proposed model of fiscal policy, as discussed above. This means that we can go beyond simply saying that Cochrane's structural interpretation of his VAR model of the debt and surplus series is another possible structural interpretation, no better and no worse than the Ricardian interpretation favored by Bohn (1998) and by Canzoneri, Cumby, and Diba (1998); we can instead test the consistency of this interpretation with an estimated monetary policy rule, and one of the interpretations of the fiscal VAR will necessarily fit better with that rule. And finally, given an estimated monetary policy rule, we can ask not only about the conformity of overall inflation variations predicted by the model with those observed, but about how the model predicts inflation should respond to *each* of the different shocks in the VAR model of fiscal policy; for example, we can ask how inflation should respond both to Cochrane's "cyclical" surplus innovation and to his "long-run" surplus innovation, and compare these predictions with historical experience, given the identification of those shocks under his interpretation of the VAR.

I shall illustrate how this could be done without pretending to have carried out a complete or conclusive analysis, which would be beyond the scope of this discussion. I first estimate a VAR model of the debt and surplus processes, intermediate in size between the VARs reported by Cochrane in his equations (37) and his Table 5. My VAR is of the form

$$x_t = Ax_{t-1} + \epsilon_t, \qquad (4)$$

where x_t is the transpose of the vector $[vc_t \ sc_t \ dc_t]$.[13] Under the proposed non-Ricardian interpretation, these three series are all (at least jointly) exo-

---

13. I use Cochrane's notation, and also his data, kindly supplied.

genous, and the estimated VAR equations are interpreted as structural. I include the dc series, interpreted as indicating the exogenous evolution of "permanent income," because that process, along with the two series included in Cochrane's equation (37), is needed for a complete statistical model of the evolution of the primary budget surplus. On the other hand, I do not include the $\tilde{r}_t^a$ series, included in Cochrane's Table 5 VAR, because this series (the ex post real return on the public debt) should be *implied* by the evolution of the three elements of x. Note that log-linear approximation of the government budget accounting identity[14] yields

$$\tilde{r}_t^a = \rho(vc_t + sc_t) + dc_t - vc_{t-1}. \tag{5}$$

Thus a statistical model of the form (4), combined with the identity (5), represents a complete model of the evolution of these four series.

Note that the VAR (4) will imply, in general, a time-varying expected return process. Because I allow for this, there is no need to adjust the coefficients of the VAR to make them compatible with the present-value relation, as Cochrane does with the numbers reported in equation (37). These expected real returns, like "permanent income" expectations, are assumed to evolve exogenously with respect to the nominal variables, as would make sense under the assumption of perfectly flexible prices. Finally, I do not assume that the evolution of either "permanent income" or expected real returns is necessarily exogenous with respect to the fiscal disturbances. The same real disturbances that determine the path of the real primary budget surplus (e.g., variations in military spending needs) may well affect real activity and investment demand, and hence equilibrium consumption and real rates of return. So I simply assume jointly exogenous processes for the real primary surplus, consumption, and the expected real rate of return, the evolution of which can be described in terms of a state vector with three elements each period. The present-value relation then implies that vc_t will also be a linear combination of these three states, and so we can use vc_t, sc_t, and dc_t as proxies for the three states (given that expected returns are not directly observed). Under this interpretation, there are no *a priori* restrictions upon the elements of A.

The coefficients of the OLS regressions used to estimate the VAR are presented in Table 1. (Constants are neglected in the table, though included in the regressions.) These regressions are reasonably similar to the corresponding equations in Cochrane's Table 5. In particular, the coefficient of 0.067 on vc_{t-1} in the sc_t equation is consistent with the evidence that Bohn (1998) interprets as showing that surpluses are ad-

14. Compare Cochrane's equation (41).

Table 1   VAR COEFFICIENTS

Equation	Regressor			R^2
	vc_{t-1}	sc_{t-1}	dc_{t-1}	
vc_t	1.000	−0.634	−2.508	.95
(s.e.)	(.041)	(.198)	(.641)	
sc_t	0.067	0.455	1.662	.67
(s.e.)	(.022)	(.109)	(.352)	
dc_t	0.007	−0.041	0.355	.15
(s.e.)	(.011)	(.052)	(.169)	

justed in response to variations in the size of the public debt; and the pattern of positive and negative coefficients on sc_{t-1} in the sc_t and vc_t equations respectively is consistent with the evidence that Canzoneri, Cumby, and Diba (1998) interpret as showing that positive disturbances to government budget surpluses imply further high surpluses in the future, while reducing the size of the government debt. Nonetheless, one can interpret all of these coefficients as being consistent with an exogenous surplus process, as just discussed. Using the identity (5), the estimated coefficients imply a real-return equation of the form

$$E_{t-1}\tilde{r}_t^a = 0.064 \, vc_{t-1} - 0.219 \, sc_{t-1} - 0.483 \, dc_{t-1}, \tag{6}$$

which is also similar to the corresponding equation in Cochrane's Table 5.

I now adjoin to this model of the fiscal variables a monetary policy rule of the form

$$R_t = \phi_p \pi_t + z_t, \tag{7}$$

where z_t is an exogenous time-varying intercept, that may be thought of as reflecting a time-varying implicit inflation target. This would coincide with the Taylor specification (3) if one were to assume that z_t varies linearly with detrended log GDP. Instead I shall assume that z_t varies as some function of the same real state vector x_t as contains all available information about current and future expected real returns, permanent income growth, and real government budget surpluses, and write

$$z_t = \alpha' x_t, \tag{8}$$

where α is a vector of constant coefficients, and the constant term is omitted as in (4). (Note that this assumption implies that monetary pol-

Table 2   INFLATION FORECASTING REGRESSION

	Regressor				
	π_{t-1}	vc_{t-1}	sc_{t-1}	dc_{t-1}	R^2
π_t	0.677	−0.027	0.088	0.524	.66
(s.e.)	(.231)	(.026)	(.066)	(.275)	

icy does not introduce any additional source of randomness beyond those already reflected in the state vector x_t.) This equation is in turn connected to the rest of the equation system by the assumption that in equilibrium, expected holding returns on the public debt and on the riskless short-term nominal instrument whose return is controlled by the Fed must be equal (or at least equal up to a constant premium). Thus an additional equilibrium condition is

$$E_t \tilde{r}^a_{t+1} = R_t - E_t \pi_{t+1}. \tag{9}$$

Under this assumption about the form of the monetary policy rule, one may estimate the coefficients ϕ_p and α for Cochrane's sample period in the following way. Equations (6) through (9) imply that expected inflation at any point in time may be written

$$E_t \pi_{t+1} = \lambda \pi_t + \gamma' x_t, \tag{10}$$

where $\lambda = \phi_p$, $\gamma = \alpha - \xi$, and ξ is the vector of coefficients multiplying the vector x_{t-1} in (6). Given (10), we can construct a time series for expected inflation by regressing π_t on π_{t-1} and the vector x_{t-1}, and using the fitted values as our series for expected inflation. The coefficients of this regression are given in Table 2.[15] Combining the implied expected inflation series with the expected real return series implied by (6) allows us to construct a series for expected nominal returns on public debt. According to (9), this should coincide with the nominal interest rate R_t controlled by the Fed.

Since the constructed series is a linear combination of π_t and the elements of x_t, one immediately has a representation of monetary policy of the form (7)–(8). The coefficient values we thus obtain are $\phi_p = 0.677$ and

$$z_t = 0.037 \, vc_t - 0.131 \, sc_t + 0.041 \, dc_t. \tag{11}$$

15. Here the inflation variable π_t is the annualized first difference of the log of the GDP deflator, denoted dp_t by Cochrane.

Note that these values do not necessarily imply that the central bank responds to fiscal variables as such. Representation (11) of the time-varying intercept in the monetary policy rule is almost identical to a specification of the form

$$z_t = 0.588 E_t \tilde{r}^a_{t+1} + 0.325 \, dc_t.$$ (12)

This last specification involves no explicit dependence upon fiscal variables, and makes a certain degree of intuitive sense: the Fed raises interest rates, for any given level of inflation, when expected real returns are high, or when growth is strong. [Consumption growth is probably not the best proxy for this last concern, but a representation of the form (8) allows us to model the inflation dynamics implied by the monetary–fiscal policy regime without introducing laws of motion for any additional real variables.]

One further aspect of government policy remains to be specified, and that is the composition of the public debt, which matters for the response of inflation to shocks for reasons that are well explained by Cochrane. I shall simplify the analysis, as in Woodford (1998b), by assuming that the public debt is at all times made up of a single type of government bond, a claim to a perpetual stream of riskless nominal coupons that decay geometrically with time. In Cochrane's notation, this implies that at all times $B_t(t + j) = \theta^{j-1} B_t(t + 1)$ for all $j \geq 1$, where θ is a constant factor satisfying $0 \leq \theta < r\pi$, and π is the steady-state inflation rate. (In fact, this structure of the aggregate stream of coupons is all that matters for our analysis, and not the actual existence of any perpetuities with geometrically decaying coupons.)

Now let Q_t denote the price of such a perpetuity in period t, after payment of the period t coupon, where a unit of the perpetuity pays a coupon of one dollar the next period, and let $q_t \equiv \log(Q_t/Q)$ indicate percentage deviations in this price from its steady-state value. Then the return on government debt satisfies

$$r^a_t = \frac{1 + \theta Q_t}{Q_{t-1}} \frac{p_{t-1}}{p_t}.$$

Log-linearization of this yields

$$\tilde{r}^a_t = \omega q_t - q_{t-1} - \pi_t,$$ (13)

where the duration parameter $\omega \equiv \theta/r\pi$ is necessarily less than one. (The parameter ω indicates the steady-state fraction of the value of the public debt that may be attributed to coupon payments more than one year in the future.)

The expectations theory of the term structure [i.e., combining (6) with (13) and integrating forward] implies furthermore that

$$q_t = - \sum_{j=0}^{\infty} \omega^j E_t R_{t+j}. \tag{14}$$

Equations (13) and (14) then indicate how inflation and expected Fed policy must be related to the ex post real returns on government debt. However, these real returns must also satisfy the identity (5); under our assumed non-Ricardian fiscal regime, the evolution of $\tilde{r}_t^a$ is thus completely determined by the evolutions of the exogenous states x_t. In this case, the fiscal theory of the price level implies that *inflation* is endogenously determined each year to satisfy (13). Thus equations (5), (13), and (14) determine equilibrium inflation as a function of the exogenous real states and expected Fed policy. These equations, together with law of motion (4) for the exogenous real states and monetary policy rule (7)–(8), constitute a complete system to determine the rational expectations equilibrium paths of x_t, $\tilde{r}_t^a$, π_t, R_t, and q_t.

A first question about this equation system is whether monetary and fiscal policy rules of this kind imply a determinate rational expectations equilibrium. Here the answer, as in Leeper's (1991) analysis, is that there exists a unique stationary equilibrium inflation process if and only if $|\phi_p| < 1$, so that monetary policy is "passive" in Leeper's sense. Our estimated monetary policy rule need not have this property, but it happens that it does ($\phi_p = 0.677$). As I have argued above, this is an important check upon the coherence of the proposed structural interpretation of the VAR in terms of an exogenous surplus process.

In the case that $|\phi_p| < 1$, the unique stationary equilibrium involves inflation evolving according to a law of motion

$$\pi_t = \phi_p \pi_{t-1} + (\alpha' - \xi')x_t + f'\epsilon_t, \tag{15}$$

where

$$f' \equiv [\phi_p \omega(\delta_0' + \omega\delta_1') - \omega\alpha'] \cdot (I - \omega A)^{-1} - \delta_0'$$

and $\delta_0' \equiv (\rho \ \rho \ 1)$ and $\delta_1' \equiv (-1 \ 0 \ 0)$ are the vectors of coefficients on x_t and x_{t-1} respectively in (5), and where ϵ_t is again the vector of exogenous disturbances in (4). This equation, together with (4), completely describes the evolution of inflation and the real states, as a function of the history of disturbances ϵ_t. It will be apparent from (15) why the bound on

$|\phi_p|$ is required for existence of a stationary inflation process. It will also be obvious that this inflation process satisfies (10). Thus our method of estimation of the monetary policy rule necessarily delivers a rule that—if it is consistent with the existence of a stationary equilibrium at all—will imply an evolution of expected inflation that is consistent with our regression forecasts. What are *not* automatically granted are correct predictions about the *surprise* component of inflation, the part of each year's inflation that is not explained by the regression reported in Table 2. It is thus of particular interest to test these predictions.

Equation (15) implies that

$$\pi_t - E_{t-1}\pi_t = f'\epsilon_t,$$

and our estimated coefficients imply numerical values for the vector of coefficients f, for any given value of the duration parameter ω. The predicted values for the elements of f thus represent a testable cross-equation restriction implied by the theory. These three coefficients are each plotted, as a function of ω, in Figure 1. We can then compare these predictions with the coefficients of a regression of the residuals from our inflation regression [interpreted as an OLS estimate of equation (15)] upon the residuals from the VAR (4). These estimated coefficients $\hat{f}$ are also shown in Figure 1, by the dashed horizontal line in each panel. The dotted horizontal lines in each panel indicate a plus and minus two-standard-error confidence interval for each estimated coefficient.[16]

One observes that the signs of the point estimates are consistent with the fiscal theory of the price level in each case: positive innovations in any of the three series (*vc, sc,* or *dc*) are predicted to result in an unexpected *reduction* in inflation, and in the U.S. data that is what occurs.[17] The quantitative magnitudes of these effects are also roughly what the theory predicts, especially if one takes into account the fact that U.S. government debt is not of extremely short duration. Cochrane's Figure 15 shows that about 50% (on average) of the present value of coupons due on U.S. government liabilities has been due within a year; this suggests $\omega = 0.5$ as a reasonable calibration of the duration parameter.

16. These standard errors are computed treating the residuals from the inflation forecasting regression in Table 2 as data, and so do not take into account the uncertainty of our estimates of the residuals themselves. Hence they exaggerate the precision of these estimated effects.

17. According to the crude standard-error measure used in producing the figure, the estimated decline is significant at nearly the 5% level in the case of an *sc* innovation, and much more significant in the other two cases.

Figure 1 THEORETICAL AND ESTIMATED RESPONSES OF INFLATION
         TO VAR INNOVATIONS

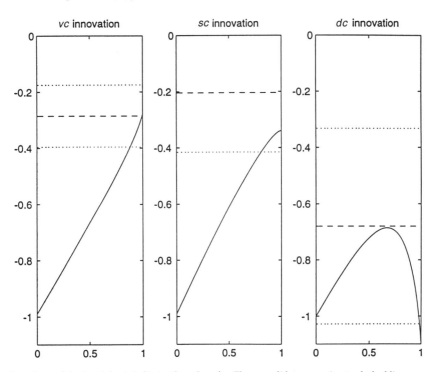

In each panel, horizontal axis indicates the value of ω. Theory: solid curve; estimate: dashed line.

Increasing ω to this extent decreases the predicted response of inflation
to each of the innovations, as more adjustment occurs through unexpected changes in bond prices rather than in inflation,[18] and in each case
this moves the prediction closer to the point estimate. Nonetheless, the
point estimates indicate smaller responses, especially to the *vc* and *sc*
innovations, than are predicted by the fiscal theory. In the case of the *vc*
and *sc* innovations, the predicted response lies outside the 95% confidence intervals plotted in the figure (though these are probably too
narrow). This problem could be solved by assuming a value of ω on the
order of 0.9, but this would seem to be inconsistent with the actual
average duration of U.S. government liabilities.

　　Another problem is that the theory predicts that unexpected inflation
should be *entirely* explained by the three VAR innovations, and it is not;

18. See Woodford (1998b) for further analysis of this effect.

Figure 2(a). ACTUAL AND THEORETICAL INFLATION SERIES,
          CASE $\omega = 0$.

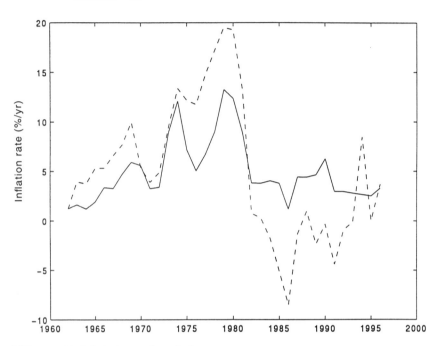

Solid curve: actual; dashed curve: theoretical.

in fact, these innovations explain only 57% of the variation in the inflation residuals. Of course, the prediction that unexpected inflation
should depend only upon the disturbances ϵ_t depends upon our assumption that the z_t-intercept in the monetary policy rule is a function of the
variables x_t; if we allow z_t to depend upon some other random state as
well (representing exogenous disturbances to monetary policy, or simply
another state variable to which the Fed responds), then unexpected
inflation should depend upon that state too. This generalization would,
however, complicate the previous discussion, especially our consideration of how the parameters of the monetary policy rule can be inferred
from the coefficients of the inflation forecasting regression (10), and so I
do not pursue it here.

I turn now to the extent to which this theory of inflation determination
can explain the U.S. inflation time series. Figures 2a–c compare the
actual inflation time series with the prediction of the model, obtained by
simulating (15) given the historical evolution of the state vector x_t, under

Figure 2(b). ACTUAL AND THEORETICAL INFLATION SERIES,
CASE ω = .5.

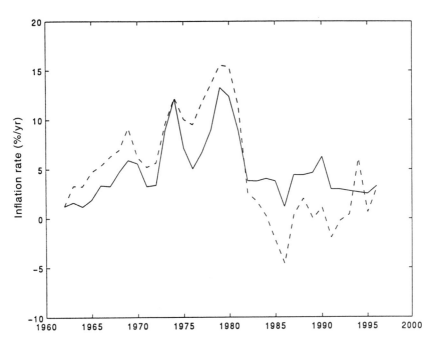

Solid curve: actual; dashed curve: theoretical.

three different assumed values for ω. The simulation assuming $\omega = 0$ (all
government debt matures within a year) correctly predicts the great
inflation of the 1970s and the sharp disinflation of the early 1980s; so
these gross facts are clearly not problematic for a fiscalist account, as
Cochrane emphasizes. But this simple model greatly overpredicts the
volatility of inflation variations. Its failure demonstrates that simply
choosing coefficients consistent with the inflation-forecasting regression
(10) is hardly a guarantee that the model will do well at explaining
overall inflation variations; it is clearly crucial to correctly predict the
unforecastable movements in inflation, which (at the annual frequency)
are no small part of the story.

Figures 2b and c show that allowing for longer-duration government
debt greatly improves the model's ability to account for the historical
inflation dynamics. In fact, the simulation assuming $\omega = 0.99$ (essentially, the entire government debt made up of consols) does quite a good
job of accounting for both the magnitude and timing of all the main

Figure 2(c). ACTUAL AND THEORETICAL INFLATION SERIES,
CASE ω = .99.

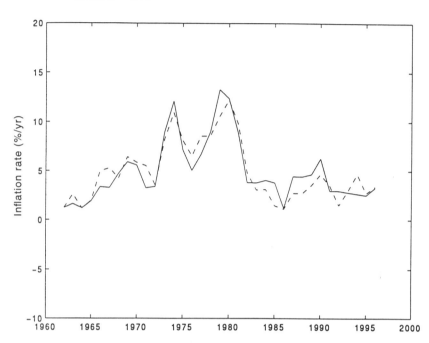

Solid curve: actual; dashed curve: theoretical.

variations in the U.S. inflation rate over this 35-year period. This indicates that even though more than 40% of the variation in unexpected inflation is uncorrelated with any of the disturbances ϵ_i, a model that neglects other sources of unexpected inflation variation can still do quite well at accounting for medium-frequency inflation variation. Thus this particular prediction of our simple model is not such an embarrassment as it might have seemed.[19]

However, the assumption that U.S. government liabilities consist entirely of consols is plainly incorrect. Under the more realistic assumption that ω = 0.5, the model's predictions are still quite inaccurate—for example, it implies that the fiscal consolidation of the mid-1980s should have led to actual deflation, at rates as high as 5% in a single year, something

19. A variance decomposition of the VAR obtained by adjoining an unrestricted inflation equation to the equations in (4) shows that while the inflation innovation orthogonal to the other three innovations accounts for 43% of the variance of unexpected inflation variation at a 1-year horizon, it accounts for only 23% of the variance at a 10-year horizon.

that was certainly not seen. The reason that the model does better under the assumption of a higher ω would seem to be that longer-duration debt implies that more of the adjustment should occur through unexpected changes in bond prices instead of unexpected variations in inflation, and that better matches what has happened, even though much of U.S. government liabilities are of relatively short duration.

The reason for this failure of the model may be its assumption of perfectly flexible prices, and hence exogenous expected real rates of return. This implies that inflation surprises affect bond prices only through their effect on expectations of future inflation, and not through any possible effect upon expected real rates of return; then, given evidence on the degree to which inflation surprises change forecasts of future inflation, inflation surprises can only be associated with larger bond-price movements by increasing the duration of the bonds. Consideration of whether a sticky-price model like the one used in Woodford (1996), in which fiscal shocks affect both inflation and real rates of return, can better account for the data is an obvious topic for further study.

This brief treatment should suffice to illustrate how assuming a particular form of monetary policy rule allows us to increase the number of testable restrictions implied by a proposed structural interpretation of fiscal-variable VARs such as Cochrane's. We have seen that in the case of the kind of monetary policy rule proposed above, the interpretation in terms of an exogenous process for the primary budget surplus passes some of these tests, though it is less consistent with others.

5. Ricardian and Non-Ricardian Interpretations Compared

A Ricardian interpretation of the VAR reported in Table 1 is also possible, but is less consistent with the monetary policy rule estimated above. It would be possible to treat the sc_t equation of the VAR,

$$sc_t = a_{21} \, vc_{t-1} + a_{22} \, sc_{t-1} + a_{23} \, dc_{t-1} + \epsilon_{2t}, \tag{16}$$

as an estimate of a feedback rule for the government budget surplus, as in Bohn's (1998) interpretation of his surplus regressions. Under this interpretation, the joint evolution of the primary surplus and of the real value of the government debt would be determined by the fiscal rule (16) and the accounting identity (5), given an exogenous process for "permanent income" growth dc_t, and the endogenous evolution of the ex post returns $\tilde{r}_t^a$ on government debt.

Substituting equation (13) for this last variable, these two equations can be written in matrix form as

$$\tilde{x}_t = B\tilde{x}_{t-1} + Ce_t + Dy_t, \tag{17}$$

where $\tilde{x}_t$ is the vector of fiscal variables $[vc_t \ sc_t]'$, e_t is a vector of exogenous variables including e_{2t}, dc_t, and dc_{t-1}, and y_t is a vector of nominal endogenous variables $[q_t \ q_{t-1} \ \pi_t]'$. Here the matrix B is given by

$$B = \begin{bmatrix} \rho^{-1} - a_{21} & -a_{22} \\ a_{21} & a_{22} \end{bmatrix}.$$

The estimates in Table 1 imply that the eigenvalues of B are 0.87 and 0.53, both inside the unit circle. It follows that (17) implies bounded fluctuations in $\tilde{x}_t$ in the case of *any* bounded fluctuations in the variables e_t and y_t. Thus avoidance of unbounded growth in the value of the public debt does not place any restriction at all upon the paths of inflation and bond prices, apart from requiring that those variables themselves fluctuate within bounds, and such a fiscal policy rule is (at least locally) Ricardian. Thus the VAR itself does not exclude a Ricardian interpretation.

But suppose that we again assume a monetary policy rule given by (7) and (12),[20] where ϕ_p is estimated in the way explained above, and also again assume that $r_t \equiv E_t \tilde{r}_{t+1}^a$ is an exogenous stochastic process, determined by factors unaffected by the evolution of the nominal variables y_t. Then substitution of (7) and (12) into (6) to eliminate R_t yields an expectational stochastic difference equation for π_t. Eliminating R_t in the same way from the quasidifferenced form of (14),

$$q_t = -R_t + \omega E_t q_{t+1},$$

similarly yields a stochastic expectational difference equation for q_t. These two difference equations, together with (17), then constitute a system that can be written in matrix form as

$$\begin{bmatrix} E_t y_{t+1} \\ \tilde{x}_t \end{bmatrix} = \begin{bmatrix} H & 0 \\ D & B \end{bmatrix} \begin{bmatrix} y_t \\ \tilde{x}_{t-1} \end{bmatrix} + \begin{bmatrix} G \\ C \end{bmatrix} e_t, \tag{18}$$

where the vector of exogenous state variables e_t is now augmented to also include r_t. The system of equations (18) then includes all of the restrictions upon the evolution of the endogenous variables imposed by

20. Note that under the present specification of the fiscal rule, (11) and (12) are no longer equivalent monetary policy specifications, as vc_t and sc_t are no longer exogenous with respect to the nominal variables. Hence it is necessary to specify that the assumed form of monetary policy rule is given by (7) and (12).

the model; any stationary solution of this system represents a stationary rational expectations equilibrium.

Given that the vector y_t includes two state variables (q_t and π_t) that are not predetermined, the system (18) has a unique stationary solution if and only if the square matrix has exactly three eigenvalues inside the unit circle and two outside.[21] The block-triangular form of the matrix implies that the eigenvalues are just the eigenvalues of B together with those of H. As just discussed, the VAR point estimates imply that both eigenvalues of B lie within the unit circle. The matrix H is given by

$$H = \begin{bmatrix} \omega^{-1} & 0 & \omega^{-1}\phi_p \\ 1 & 0 & 0 \\ 0 & 0 & \phi_p \end{bmatrix},$$

so that its eigenvalues are 0, ω^{-1}, and ϕ_p. Since we necessarily have $\omega^{-1} > 1$, there is a determinate equilibrium inflation process, under this policy regime, if and only if $|\phi_p| > 1$, as in Leeper's analysis.

Our point estimate for ϕ_p, however, is well below the critical value of one. If we take that estimate as correctly identifying U.S. monetary policy, it would imply that rational expectations equilibrium should have been indeterminate, under the Ricardian interpretation of the VAR. *One possible equilibrium would be exactly the equilibrium associated with the exogenous primary surplus process,*[22] but there would also be a vast set of additional stationary equilibria, involving alternative responses of inflation and bond prices to the real disturbances, and also involving responses of the nominal variables to "sunspot" shocks. This richness of possibilities might be regarded as a virtue—for some other member of the set might fit the U.S. time series better than does the unique equilibrium consistent with an exogenous surplus process. But we would be left with no explanation of why that particular equilibrium should have been realized rather than some very different one, and in this respect our understanding of U.S. inflation history would have to be judged less complete.

Of course, one might argue that the data do not clearly reject the hypothesis that $|\phi_p| > 1$; the standard error of the estimate of the coefficient on π_{t-1} in Table 2 is large enough to allow this. And perhaps more

21. Here I assume stationarity of the exogenous disturbances e_t, and ignore certain nongeneric cases that can be shown not to apply here.
22. Note that system (18) has three exogenous disturbance processes, dc_t, r_t, and the fiscal shocks ϵ_{2t}, just like our previous non-Ricardian model, and if the joint law of motion of these processes is as assumed in that model, the equilibrium under the non-Ricardian regime is also an equilibrium under the Ricardian regime.

to the point, our estimates depend upon an assumed specification of the monetary policy rule, (7)–(8), that may well be incorrect. Future work will surely need to consider alternative specifications. As noted above, much work does find support for specifications consistent with determinacy of equilibrium under a Ricardian fiscal regime, at least for post-1979 U.S. monetary policy. Future work will surely want to consider the possibility that the Ricardian or non-Ricardian character of U.S. fiscal policy may also have changed over time.

Narrative evidence about the nature of shocks can also help to distinguish among alternative possible interpretations of the time series; here, too, there are important reasons to prefer a Ricardian interpretation, at least of U.S. experience since 1980. The non-Ricardian interpretation of the U.S. data offered by Cochrane, and in the above account, attributes the disinflation of the early 1980s to a large increase in the equilibrium value of the public debt, resulting from fiscal developments that increased expected future budget surpluses. Cochrane shows that the increase in the value of the public debt occurred, and according to his VAR forecasts, the increase in expected budget surpluses occurred as well.

However, a Ricardian interpretation of these facts remains possible, which is that an exogenous change in monetary policy caused the disinflation, which resulted in a windfall to bondholders, which in turn required at least a prospective increase in the size of primary surpluses, in order to allow the increased real debt service to be paid. The two views of the causal connection between events are equally coherent, but the Ricardian story has the advantage that considerable narrative evidence also exists of a deliberate change in U.S. monetary policy in the period 1979–1982, intended to bring down inflation. Furthermore, the political efforts to reduce government budget deficits in the U.S., beginning in the mid-1980s, seem to have a great deal to do with concern about the size of the public debt and about the size of the associated debt service. It is less easy to identify the exogenous fiscal changes that might have increases expectations of future surpluses for independent reasons, as the non-Ricardian story would require.

On the other hand, the Ricardian interpretation is less clearly applicable to the inflation of the 1970s. There is little narrative evidence to indicate that the losses suffered by bondholders in that period resulted from a deliberate decision at the Fed to increase the U.S. inflation rate. And on the other hand, at least some of the exogenous fiscal shocks *can* be identified. For example, the large primary deficit in 1975 can be attributed to a one-time tax rebate, a deliberate change in fiscal policy intended to stimulate the economy.[23] Furthermore, there is little evidence in discussions of fiscal policy in the period 1965–1979 (by contrast with the 1980s and 1990s) to suggest a concern with budget balance as either a goal or a constraint. To the contrary, influential policy advisors celebrated the liberation of fiscal policy from the fetish of balanced budgets[24]; and while mainstream economists always supposed that deficits in times of recession would have to be offset by surpluses during booms, this advice was not formulated in a way that would ensure a Ricardian regime, and may in any event have had little effect upon the way fiscal policy was conducted in practice or understood by the public. Hence a non-Ricardian interpretation of this period may well prove fruitful.[25]

REFERENCES

Benhabib, J., S. Schmitt-Grohé, and M. Uribe. (1998). Monetary policy and multiple equilibria, Federal Reserve Board. FEDS Paper 1998-29. June.
Blinder, A. S. (1981). Temporary income taxes and consumer spending. *Journal of Political Economy* 89:26–53.
Bohn, H. (1998). The behavior of U.S. public debt and deficits. *Quarterly Journal of Economics* 113:949–964.
Canzoneri, M. B., R. E. Cumby, and B. T. Diba. (1998). Is the price level determined by the needs of fiscal solvency? CEPR Discussion Paper no. 1772. January.
Clarida, R., J. Galí, and M. Gertler. (1998). Monetary policy rules and macroeconomic stability: Evidence and some theory. Cambridge, MA: National Bureau of Economic Research. NBER Working Paper 6442. March.
Heller, W. (1966). *New Dimensions of Political Economy.* New York: W. W. Norton.
Kutter, M. (1998). Application of an optimization-based econometric framework for the evaluation of monetary policy: German monetary policy 1973–1989. Department of Economics, London School of Economics. Unpublished. May.
Leeper, E. (1989). Policy rules, information and fiscal effects in a "Ricardian" Model. Federal Reserve Board. International Finance Discussion Paper 360. August.
———. (1991). Equilibria under "active" and "passive" monetary and fiscal policies. *Journal of Monetary Economics* 27:129–147 (1991).
Loyo, E. (1997). The wealth effects of monetary policy and Brazilian inflation. Department of Economics, Princeton University. Unpublished. November.
Rotemberg, J. J., and M. Woodford (1997). An optimization-based econometric framework for the evaluation of monetary policy. *NBER Macroeconomics Annual*

23. For details, see, e.g., Blinder (1981).
24. See, e.g., Heller (1966) and Stein (1969).
25. The suggestion of Canzoneri, Cumby, and Diba (1998), that if U.S. fiscal policy had ever been non-Ricardian, it would surely have been in the period *since* 1980, is thus exactly the opposite of what I would propose. Note that Shim (1984) finds an important role for fiscal shocks in explaining U.S. inflation in the period prior to 1980. In private communication, Shim reports that his estimates proved unstable when he attempted to update his work, adding data from the early 1980s.

1997. (Expanded version: Cambridge, MA: National Bureau of Economic Research. NBER Technical Working Paper 233. May 1988.)

———. (1998). Interest-rate rules in an estimated sticky-price model. In *Monetary Policy Rules,* J. B. Taylor, (ed.). Chicago: University of Chicago Press.

Shim, S. D. (1984). Inflation and the government budget constraint: International evidence. Department of Economics, University of Minnesota. Unpublished Ph.D. Dissertation. August.

Sims, C. A. (1994). A simple model for the study of the determination of the price level and the interaction of monetary and fiscal policy. *Economic Theory* 4:381–399.

Stein, H. (1969). *The Fiscal Revolution in America: Policy in Pursuit of Reality.* Chicago: University of Chicago Press, 1969.

Taylor, J. B. (1993). Discretion versus policy rules in practice. *Carnegie-Rochester Conference Series on Public Policy* 39:195–214.

———. (1998). An historical analysis of monetary policy rules. In *Monetary Policy Rules,* J. B. Taylor (ed.). Chicago: University of Chicago Press.

Woodford, M. (1995). Price-level determinacy without control of a monetary aggregate. *Carnegie-Rochester Conference Series on Public Policy* 43:1–46 (1995).

———. (1996). Control of the public debt: A requirement for price stability? Cambridge, MA: National Bureau of Economic Research. NBER Working Paper 5684. July.

———. (1998a). Doing without money: Controlling inflation in a post-monetary world. *Review of Economic Dynamics* 1:173–219.

———. (1998b). Public debt and the price level. Department of Economics, Princeton University. Unpublished. July.

Discussion

Benjamin Friedman expressed puzzlement at Cochrane's claim that the fiscal theory of the price level is untestable. He argued that an empirical test is certainly possible if one is willing to make auxiliary assumptions. As this is the usual situation in macroeconomics, the fiscal theory isn't really unique in this regard. Cochrane agreed with the spirit of Friedman's remark, drawing the analogy to the quantity theory, which is an identity and hence similarly untestable unless one makes additional assumptions (for example about the behavior of velocity). While not denying that the theory was testable in principle, however, Cochrane cautioned against making inferences based on simple reduced-form methods, for example, by examining which variables lead others in estimated vector autoregressions.

Frederic Mishkin also agreed with Friedman, emphasizing that a legitimate test of the theory requires some exogenous change in the economic environment, like those that Milton Friedman and Anna Schwartz attempted to identify in their monetary history. Ben Bernanke suggested that a major fiscal reform, for example a restructuring of the social security system, might provide a useful test case for the fiscal theory.

Herschel Grossman questioned whether non-Ricardian fiscal regimes are possible. He used as an example the individual borrower who cannot mortgage the same house twice, and he argued that the government cannot sell more debt at a given point in time unless it credibly promises to increase future surpluses. Cochrane disagreed, noting that changes in the price level effectively allow the government to change the real value of its debt. By analogy, an individual could issue more nominal claims against his real assets, at the expense of earlier purchasers of those claims.

Mishkin suggested that in the United States, in practice, the monetary authority moves first and the fiscal authority follows. He doubted therefore that the fiscal theory could be a good model of postwar U.S. inflation, although it might well be relevant in other contexts. Michael Woodford disagreed, noting that the Federal Reserve cannot and does not ignore the fiscal side of the economy.

Marvin Goodfriend expressed the view that it will not be fruitful to try to find a purely fiscal explanation of U.S. inflation. As long as there is a transactions demand for money in the economy, monetary policy will have some role to play in the control of the price level.